China's Rise: Strength and Fragility

China's Rise: Strength and Fragility

AU LOONG YU

with contributions from
Bai Ruixue, Bruno Jetin
& Pierre Rousset

Resistance Books
IIRE
MERLIN PRESS

Published in 2012 by
Merlin Press Ltd
6 Crane Street Chambers
Crane Street
Pontypool
NP4 6ND
Wales
www.merlinpress.co.uk

in association with Resistance Books and IIRE
www.resistancebooks.org
www.iire.org

China's Rise is issue number 54
of the IIRE Notebooks for Study and Research

Edited by Au Loong Yu, Fred Leplat and Terry Conway

ISBN. 978-0-85036-637-2

Resistance Books and the International Institute for Research are grateful to New Politics (New York), the International Encyclopaedia of Revolution and Protest (Wiley Blackwell), WorkingUSA: The Journal of Labour and Society (Wiley Blackwell), and New Left Review (London), for their kind permission to reprint articles.

All the contributions by individuals and permissions from other publishers are indicated at the appropriate point in the footnotes.

Catalogue in Publication data is available from the British Library

Printed in the UK by Imprint Digital, Exeter

CONTENTS

PART 3 – Discussion

CONTRIBUTORS

Au Loong Yu is a labour researcher based in Hong Kong. He was one of the founding members of Globalization Monitor, an NGO which promotes public education on the impact of globalization in China. He was one of the leading spokespersons of the People's Alliance during the actions against the 6th Ministerial meeting in Hong Kong in 2006. He is currently a member of the editorial board of *China Labour Net* and *Working USA: The Journal of Labor and Society*. In recent years he has contributed essays to journals such as *New Politics* and *Working USA*.

Bai Ruixue is a member of the editorial board of China Labour Net.

Pierre Rousset is member of the Board of Editors of *The International Encyclopedia of Revolution and Protest* (2009) to which he contributed on China, Philippines and Thailand. He is a founding director and a fellow of the IIRE. He was an activist during the French May 68 and has been engaged since then in international solidarity. He has written extensively on Asian social and national liberation movements, on the global justice movement and ecology. He is editor of the bilingual website www.europe-solidaire.org.

Bruno Jetin is an Assistant Professor of Economics at Université of Paris Nord (France). His publications include *'Distribution of income, labour productivity and competitiveness: Is the Thai labour regime sustainable?'* Cambridge Journal of Economics, (2012) and *'Ten years after the crisis: A bright future for growth in Thailand?'* in *'After the crisis: Adjustment, Recovery and Fragility in East Asia'* (2009). Tulika Books, New Delhi.

INTRODUCTION

China's Rise – Strength and Fragility is a contribution from a Marxist perspective to the increasing literature on China; an analysis of the political, economic and social changes that have changed China from a poor developing country to the status of global power progressively contesting US hegemony, with a gross domestic product which made it the second most important economy of the world in 2010.

This dramatic change has occurred over the last 30 years, but in particular since the 1989 Tiananmen Square massacre – which occurred the same year as the fall of the Berlin Wall. These events marked a turn towards the restoration of capitalism in both the USSR and China.

The nature of the Chinese state, the economy and the ruling elite is examined at length by Au Loong Yu. In a sustained manner, he argues that the Chinese Communist Party in the mid-1980s under Deng Xiaoping consciously adopted a policy of privatisation. This was led by state and party officials who enriched themselves by accumulating capital through their management, and then private ownership of state-owned enterprises (SOEs). To accelerate this, over 40 million workers in SOEs were sacked in the mid-1990s and replaced with migrant workers from rural China who were employed on worse conditions in barracks-like factories. The *hukou* system, or household registration, a system dating back a two thousand years, is still used to regiment workers and introduce 'social apartheid'.

Bruno Jetin, in his chapter 'China: unavoidable rise or possible decline' argues that, since 1992, China has described itself as a 'socialist market economy with Chinese characteristics' when, in fact, it already has all the features of capitalism itself – but with Chinese characteristics. He looks at China's possible future developments and asks: what is the importance of China as a producer and consumer of goods and services in the world economy? Can China become a producer of technological innovations going beyond its present stage of importer and user of foreign technology? What are the main internal obstacles that can slow down or even reverse China's rise?

The authors of this book agree that 'the Chinese characteristics' of the 'socialist market economy' include the fact that there is little distinction between the private and public sectors in China today. The proprietors of both private and state sectors are party and state officials, sometimes belong to the same family and share the same interests:_a high rate of economic growth and political stability. The concept of 'bureaucratic capitalism' is developed to encapsulate the uniqueness of the Chinese brand of capitalism.

Au Loong Yu argues that it is the particular combination of the coercive powers of the state and the power of capital which are behind China's rise and which have enabled it to promote rapid industrialization and take anti-cyclical measures, such as investment in major infrastructure projects, to benefit capital in the midst of the current great recession.

A degree of nationalism has also been used to attempt to unite the country behind the project of the bureaucracy. Nationalism fills the ideological vacuum left by the discrediting of Maoism. This is particularly explored in 'China: globalisation and nationalist responses' but also in the chapter 'Tibet: voluntary union or forced assimilation' in which Au Loong Yu also examines critically the policies and role of the Dalai Lama

Pierre Rousset, in 'Maoism: contributions and limitations' looks at the origins of the Chinese Communist Party and the impact of the long struggle for national independence of this vast country. The victorious 1949 revolution, under the leadership of the CCP, resulted in the abolition of the capitalist mode of production. Maoism was a renewal of Marxism after the dark days of Stalinism and exerted a tremendous influence across the globe. Rousset argues that the Chinese revolution, a revolution which was personified by the Maoist leadership, has massively shaped the contemporary world. Furthermore, he argues that Maoism was not just a Chinese copy of Stalinism, but (among other characteristics) an attempt at a 'sinification' of Marxism which was a collective effort, carried out more or less consciously, by the Chinese revolutionary left which was pluralist at its birth.

The CCP proved able to lead the revolutionary process until the foundation of the People's Republic and the initial social transformations, but failed to develop a 'Chinese road' to socialism because pluralism in the party was obliterated during the revolutionary war. Two decades after the 1949 victory, the Maoist leadership disintegrated in the chaos of the 'Cultural Revolution', a failure which laid the ground for the completion of the bureaucratic counter-revolution and, later, for the bourgeois counter-revolution.

The rise of capitalist China has fundamentally changed the lives and conditions of the 1.3 billion inhabitants of that country. China has been modernized to the point that now half of the population lives in urban areas. A number of chapters by Au Loong Yu and Bai Ruixue examine recent struggles of workers and peasants which are becoming more and more audacious. Chinese state capitalism is beginning to exhaust its strength as it increasingly relies on rapidly expanding public debt, and recent successful struggles by workers suggest that they are not only beginning to overcome the demoralization inflicted by the crushing of the democracy movement in 1989, but that they are building up their confidence in fighting against this unjust system.

Fred Leplat, August 2012

PREFACE

Au Loong Yu

According to Justin Yifu Lin, the former World Bank Chief Economist and Senior Vice President, from 1979 to 2010, China maintained an annual GDP growth rate of 9.9 percent and increased its economic size over 20-fold.[1] Such a continuously high growth rate has not been matched by any country in the world in contemporary times. Some studies show that this growth rate has been exaggerated and that a more realistic appraisal would be around 7.5-8 per cent, meaning that China was, therefore, just repeating the performance of Japan and the four Asian dragons in the post war boom.[2] This opinion should be given serious consideration.

Yet, even if China were not completely unique in its performance, its high growth rate still enabled it to transform itself from a vast, largely peasant country into a significantly urbanised society; a transformation with repercussions that should not be underestimated. It is now the world's largest exporter and manufacturer and the second largest economy. In terms of GDP per capita, it has entered the rank of upper middle income countries, according to World Bank criteria.

China changes so fast as to quickly make theory about the country obsolete. When the 20th century drew to a close there was much talk about China's imminent collapse[3], however in just a few years this was replaced by the discourse of the Rise of China. More recently there has emerged a kind of 'Sinomania', which tries to depict China as offering an 'alternative modernity'.[4] In mainland China, certain pro-government supporters even speak of China under the Chinese Communist Party (CCP) as having restored the past glory of the Han and Tang dynasty or of the party finally having developed a 'Chinese model' which will promise prolonged prosperity for everyone.

China's rapid growth also brought with it a great concentration of wealth, at the expense of working people and the environment. Time and time again, many writers have predicted massive upsurges or even revolution as a response to this overtly unjust situation. In early 2011 when the Middle East revolutions were unfolding rapidly, there was hope that China would follow suit after some small demonstrations appeared on the streets in Beijing and Shanghai in February 2011.

It did not happen. The mystery of China finds expression in the contradictory results of surveys conducted by international agencies just months before the Middle East revolutions. In 2010, six months before the Middle East revolution, both the Pew Research Center and the Gallop Market Research Corp conducted opinion polls across many countries. It is interesting that, although both surveys had identical results concerning the Middle East's opinion poll – most of the respondents thought that their situation was struggling rather than thriving – the two surveys contradicted each other over China. The Pew survey found that 'China is clearly the most self-satisfied country. Nearly nine-in-ten (87 per cent) of Chinese are happy with the direction of their country, 91 per cent feel good about the current state of their economy and 87 per cent are optimistic about China's economic future.'[5] In contrast, the Gallup survey found that only 12 per cent of respondents thought they were thriving, while as many as 71 per cent thought that they were struggling.[6] In March 2011 the Pew Research released an article with the title *Upbeat Chinese May Not Be Primed for a Jasmine Revolution*, which can also be interpreted as the agency claiming credit for its survey's result being more accurate.[7] It is doubtful if the result can be interpreted as such, but the two contradictory surveys about China once again reflect the puzzle about China.

Why does China grow so quickly? Why did so few expect this? Will the growth continue? Where is China heading? Is it showing an alternative way to modernization? Is it going to challenge US hegemony in a serious way? Or is it facing the danger of implosion?

China's rise is one of the biggest riddles of the opening of the 21st century. It finds expression in the different names given to the state system in China. A Chinese scholar, currently teaching in Hong Kong, reported that a total of 18 different names have been used to describe China's system, from authoritarian capitalism, commercial Leninism to Confucian capitalism.[8] The list is surely not complete. He did not mention that the CCP still regards the state as 'socialist' with Chinese characteristics and that there are people outside of China who endorse this view.

The Economist categorized China as state capitalism in its special report in January 2012.[9] There is some rationale in arguing this, considering that China's spectacular growth itself has been to a great extent state led. Recently the World Bank released its report *China 2030*, once again recommending that the Chinese government promote more privatization and deregulation. It based its argument on the conventional wisdom that only the free market and the private sector can bring efficiency and growth. This, however, does not stand up to scrutiny.

The failure of the World Bank to give correct assessment on the role of the state in promoting economic growth is not because of the difficulty in gathering accurate information, although the vast size of the country and its great contradictions, the heavy censorship of the official media, the non-existence of privately run media and the very limited academic freedom etc. do make it extraordinarily difficult. The reason for the failure on the part of the World Bank is more because it is blinded by its entrenched interest in pushing a neo-liberal agenda in China and the rest of the world.

If China is a kind of state capitalism then it is so special that it deserves its own name. The name bureaucratic capitalism is more appropriate for China because it captures the most important feature of China's capitalism: the central role of the bureaucracy, not only in the transformation of a state which was once deeply hostile to capitalism to one which is thoroughly capitalist, but also in enriching itself through the fusion of the power of coercion and the power of money. This has given new impetus to the bureaucracy's drive towards industrialization and state-led investment in infrastructure and also to making China into one of the most business-friendly countries in the world by its harsh repression of labour. Its firm grip over the country also enables it to bail out the market swiftly and determinedly during business cycles, especially in 2008 when the biggest market failure in decades broke out.

It is striking that the bureaucracy, in the period of 'socialist construction', not only made the landlord class and the bourgeoisie disappear altogether, but also substituted itself for the working class as the leading force of modernization. Then in the period of capitalism, even with the rebirth of the private capitalists, the bureaucracy again, substituted itself for the private capitalists as the leading force in capital accumulation; in the course of which it banished the state workers to the ranks of the unemployed and created a whole new working class out of rural migrants. In sixty years, it has so overwhelmed all other classes that they seem to be entirely at the party's mercy. No wonder the leaders of the CCP have been increasingly confident in reclaiming the glory of the once-great Chinese empire.

How could the Chinese state bureaucracy attain such power? What is the social base of this power?

Max Weber's theory about charismatic innovation and bureaucratic rationalisation may shed some light on these questions. Yet, his ruler-centric approach, as Kieran Allen has remarked in his book on Weber[10], makes his theory rather ahistorical because he dismisses the masses as irrelevant in the unfolding of great historical events. In contrast, Marx and Engel's discussion about the autonomisation of the state and its bureaucracy, and later the Marxists' debate about the rise of the Soviet bureaucracy in the context of the isolation of the Russian revolution, enables us to have a glimpse of the intense class struggles involved in the process. It also enabled Marxists, or at least some of them, to predict that the phenomenon of the Soviet bureaucracy rising above all classes in a collectivized society would be temporary; it would either have to restore capitalism or be swept away by a workers' revolution before it could transform itself into a historically new ruling class. Either way the bureaucracy would see its power greatly challenged. The demise of the Soviet Union proved them right.

China however, apparently offers a very different case.

In Mao's China, although the workers were generally docile, they also had a role to play in bringing Mao's version of 'socialist construction' into crisis, from the latter stage of the Cultural Revolution to Mao's death, by staging wide spread passive resistance through a 'go slow' to Mao's super ambition of 'communism in one country' . There was what was termed 'planned chaos' in the whole economy at that time. While it was one of the factors which bred workers' lack of work discipline, their passive resistance further exacerbated the crisis. The uprising of workers again, in 1989, on a tremendous scale eventually led to the party-state entering into such a crisis that Deng Xiaoping decided that it was necessary to save the skin of the bureaucracy not only by crushing the democracy movement but also by decisively restoring capitalism from 1992 onward.

Up to this point, China's trajectory of capitalist restoration was basically the same as that of the Soviet Union. What followed, however, was very different. Unlike in the Soviet Union, China's capitalist restoration was accompanied by even more rapid industrialization. It is the success of this second wave of modernization, that brought even more wealth and power to the bureaucracy, which demands an explanation from all those who are concerned about the fate of the Chinese people.

What is paradoxical, however, is that the Chinese bureaucracy, in its course of modernization and self-enrichment, also fundamentally changed the extremely backward social conditions which brought it to such a powerful status in the first place. The strength of the Chinese bureaucracy was no more than the result of a certain set of class relations defined by the 1949 revolution. Today China has been modernized under the bureaucracy to the point that the set of class relations has also fundamentally changed from what it was in 1949. Today the working class comprises more than two fifths of the Chinese working population. Industrial workers account for one quarter of the world's total. Service workers account for one fifth. They are increasingly becoming impatient with the barracks capitalism imposed on them. By fulfilling the dual role of political repression and of capital accumulation, the bureaucracy is also increasingly making itself the main target of popular anger. From a Maoist revolutionary party it has now evolved into a curse for more and more people and for the environment. A prolonged contest between the haves and the have-nots has started.

But the tremendous increase in the numbers of workers does not automatically bring about the class consciousness which would enable them to struggle, not only against the unjust system, but also to set their own agendas. A serious study of the two sections of the working class – the state sector and the rural migrant workers – will find few encouraging signs. There have been spontaneous struggles but they are mostly confined to single plants and the workers involved usually do not go beyond immediate demands. What are the political, social and cultural forces at work inhibiting their struggles from taking more organized forms?

And how about the rebirth of private bourgeoisie? Will their growth in number and economic strength eventually bring them into conflict with the ruling bureaucracy?

This book does not attempt to answer all the questions raised. As acknowledged at the beginning of this preface, China has too many mysteries to solve and its observers must be prepared for more, not fewer, surprises in the coming years. The purpose of this book is rather more limited; apart from stimulating debate it also tries to fill in certain holes in China's jigsaw puzzle by bringing back the role of classes, the state and its bureaucracy and to show how their interaction with each other shapes China's recent past and future. This is not an academic topic but one which concerns the fate of many millions of Chinese people and because of this, it also concerns the fate of many millions more in the rest of the world.

On behalf of the other contributors of this book, I would like to thank Fred Leplat, Geoff Ryan, Terry Conway and Xiaobai for their hard work in editing and proofreading. I am also grateful to Juli and May for providing valuable information and experiences, hard earned from their work in China. Hung and Lam Chi Leung have helped in collecting useful materials for one of the chapters and for this I am grateful to them. Eva Tao has also helped in translating one of the chapters and for this I would like to thank her as well.

10 August 2012

Note

1 *China's Economic Development and Cultural Renaissance in the Multipolar Growth World of the 21st Century,* Justin Yifu Lin, 2011. The essay is accessible at World Bank website: http://siteresources.worldbank.org/DEC/rces/84797-1104785060319/598886-1104852366603/599473-1223731755312/Lin-China_Economic_Development_and_Cultural_Renaissance_in_the_Multipolar_Growth_World-Beijing_Forum.pdf

2 *How to Think about China,* Jonathan Anderson, Chinese edition, CITIC Press Corporation, 2006, Beijing, Chapter 5.

3 For a similar view one can refer to *China on the Brink – The Myths and Realities of the World's Largest Market,* Callum Henderson, 1999, McGraw-Hill. Although the author's prediction was more moderate than the title might have suggested, he still thought that China's economic success might not survive the economic crisis in the late 1990s. His error is precisely a result of his mistaken faith in the free market – as a 'fundamental believer in the market', he argues that only a free market can promote sustained economic growth. See the Conclusion'

4 See Perry Anderson's critique of Martin Jacques's book W*hen China Rules the World: The Rise of the Middle Kingdom and the End of the Western World* in the London Review of Books, titled *Sinomania.*

5 It can be downloaded at http://www2.lse.ac.uk/IDEAS/programmes/transatlanticProgramme/pdf/pewGlobal.pdf

6 http://www.gallup.com/poll/147167/High-Wellbeing-Eludes-Masses-Countries-Worldwide.aspx#1

7 http://pewresearch.org/pubs/1945/chinese-may-not-be-ready-for-revolution

8 *The Chinese Model, For and Against,* Ding Xueliang, Oxford, Hong Kong, 2011, p. 70.

9 January 21, 2012.

10 Max Weber, *A Critical Introduction,* Kieran Allen, Pluto Press, 2004.

ON THE RISE OF CHINA AND ITS INHERENT CONTRADICTIONS

Au Loong Yu

The rise of China is undoubtedly one of the most important issues and the biggest mysteries at the beginning of the 21st century. For the American elite, the biggest unknowns are the answers to the questions; 'is the rise of China a threat to US hegemony or is China a partner?' and 'will the so-called 'Beijing Consensus' replace the 'Washington Consensus' in the future?'[1] For those Chinese who are concerned to develop a vision of a democratic China, the biggest riddles for them are the questions; 'does the rise of China mean that the dictatorship by the Chinese Communist Party (CCP) can continue uninterrupted for many years to come?' and 'does this mean that China's democratic future is very bleak?' To answer these questions, one cannot avoid returning to a fundamental question: 'what is the nature of capitalism in China?'

China as bureaucratic capitalism

It is very common for today's writers to describe China as authoritarian capitalism. If the term means a society which combines economic freedom to accumulate capital and a despotic state, then China undoubtedly falls into this category. The problem is that the term is so broad that it does not have much analytical value to help an investigation on China. For instance, in his widely read book *The Beijing Consensus,* Stefan Halper characterizes China as a kind of 'authoritarian capitalism', alongside Russia, Iran, Venezuela and other countries, in contrast to liberal democracy.[2] This blurs the distinction between those countries which lived through socialist revolution, then experienced capitalist restoration (the former Soviet Union and China) and those countries which, while they have experienced social upheaval did not go through socialist revolution as such. Iran has not experienced the kind of high-speed economic development that China has. Although both countries are undoubtedly capitalist, putting Venezuela in the same bag as China and claiming they have the same type of authoritarian capitalism ignores the basic fact that Venezuela does have representative democracy, while China has none. This kind of arbitrary classification does not help to understand the rise of China.

This classification also blurs the difference between China and the former Soviet Union and disregards China's special features. Recognizing the differences, however, is the key to making sense of the rise of China and its impact on the world.

Another name tag applied to China is 'state capitalism'. *The Economist* published a special report on 'state capitalism' and included China in this category. It explained the rise of state capitalism as follows:

> The crisis of liberal capitalism has been rendered more serious by the rise of a potent alternative: state capitalism, which tries to meld the powers of the state with the powers of capitalism.[3]

The term state capitalism is used to mean very different things by different people. In one left-wing interpretation[4], it is defined as a state where private capital and market competition have largely been eliminated, and the state machinery acts as the sole representative of the bourgeois class in fulfilling the role of capital accumulation. The Soviet Union these theorists claim fitted this definition. The use of the term here does not refer to this form of state capitalism; I use the term state capitalism to mean the public sector and state intervention within a mixed capitalist economy, without any reference to what kind of political system is involved. In a narrower sense, I also refer to a kind of capitalism where the state sector has become dominant in relation to the private sector. In western Europe, the weight of the state sector has varied throughout the decades but, even in its heyday, it did not dominate the economy, although it might have dominated certain sectors in the commanding heights.[5] In contrast, in some developing countries like China the state sector can be very dominant.

It is tempting to describe China as a combination of authoritarian capitalism and state capitalism, given that it combines a despotic political system and a strong state sector with a capitalist economy. However, I prefer to characterize China's present system as a kind of bureaucratic capitalism, because apart from common features it shares with authoritarian state capitalism, it also carries its own particularity which has a bearing on the concrete relationship between classes and the state in China.

Maurice Meisner's book *The Deng Xiaoping Era – An Inquiry into the Fate of Chinese Socialism 1978-1994* has a chapter exclusively devoted to an analysis of Chinese bureaucratic capitalism. He argues that

> Perhaps it is logical that the marriage of the "market" to an entrenched bureaucratic apparatus would yield not a "socialist market economy," as official ideology labels the result, but rather a form of bureaucratic capitalism.
>
> Bureaucratic capitalism, 'a term that refers to the use of political power and official influence for private pecuniary gain through capitalistic or quasi-capitalist methods of economic activity', is hardly a novelty in world history. But nowhere has it been more prominent than in the history of China, in both traditional and modern times.[6]

Like all Communist Parties when they are or were in power, the CCP's exclusive right to 'lead' the country is written into the constitution. The Communist Party is nothing but the party of the bureaucracy, whose elite has been firmly in control of state power and all state-owned enterprises (SOEs) for more than six decades without any pretence of making the state neutral. The CCP controls all levels of administrative, legislative and judicial power as well as the armed forces. It also extends its control to include all media and publishing houses, and although now in a weaker sense, thought control continues to be imposed by the party. Within the economy, since the 1980s the party has allowed the resurrection of private capital and the planned economy has been dismantled. While in the Soviet Union, the restoration of capitalism also meant the demise of the Communist Party, China is one of the few countries whose process of restoration was led by a Communist Party. A pluralistic economy has not, as the liberals expected, brought with it a 'civil society'. Civil liberties are continually suppressed. All NGOs are compulsorily linked to respective government departments or public institutions. Even the 400 different national industry associations were founded by government officials.[7]

Party officials are not even content with their absolute control of the state. Its leaders are trying to make their control hereditary, hence the phenomenon of princelings being appointed to high posts and the appearance of the term *guanerdai*, which means children of mandarins recruited en masse to comfortable state posts. In both cases they achieve this not because of their merits but because of their parents. In other authoritarian countries, this phenomenon does exist but it is more likely to be limited to the upper ruling group. In China, however, this goes through all levels of the administration, except the rank of office workers.

A second feature of the current Chinese bureaucracy is that all levels of its leading officials are also a type of capitalist who have used their coercive power to own capital, directly or indirectly, and to profit from it. Minor officials are often able to have a share of the bonus as well. In most capitalist countries, the exercise of state power and capital accumulation are taken up by two distinctive social groups, namely the bureaucrats and the capitalists. Chinese bureaucrats combine these two functions and are simultaneously entitled to a salary (plus benefits) and a share of the surplus value. This transcends the general phenomenon of collusion between government officials and the capitalists. Bureaucratic capitalists monopolize the most profitable sectors of the national economy and become the core group of the new bourgeoisie. Those private capitalists who are not the cronies of bureaucratic capitalists must accept a marginalized position.

To portray the present Chinese state as autonomous from or even suspicious of the bourgeoisie, to contend that it has not subordinated itself to their class interests, and hence that China remains non-capitalist or even 'socialist,' is completely wrong. This however is the position Giovanni Arrighi takes in his book *Adam Smith in Beijing*.[8] His analysis treats the bureaucracy and the capitalist class as necessarily two entirely different or even opposing social groups. This is contradicted by what has happened in China since 1989, where the bureaucracy *is* the capitalist class. This metamorphosis was the conscious choice of the bureaucracy, not an unexpected result of having embarked on the 'slippery slope' of market reform. Deng Xiaoping was already feeling his way in this direction in 1984 when China promised Britain that Hong Kong's 'laissez faire' capitalism was to be maintained for fifty years after Hong Kong was handed back to China. Later, he was reported to say that capitalism in Hong Kong should be allowed to continue beyond that deadline. In 1987 he told an African delegation 'do not follow socialism. Do whatever you can to make the economy grow.'[9]

The Chinese state serves, above all else, the interests of the bureaucracy, both their collective and their individual interests – political and commercial. So do the SOEs, State Holding Enterprises (SHEs) and other public economic institutions. One may even say that the bureaucracy has privatized the state. Marx once remarked that the bureaucracy, far from being the universal class as claimed by Hegel, is just another 'particular' class. He also said that 'the aims of the state are transformed into aims of bureaus, or the aims of bureaus into the aims of the state...The bureaucracy has the essence of the state... in its possession; it is its private property'.[10] Where Marx considered this as an entrenched tendency within the bureaucracy, it is only in present day China that it has fully completed this evolution on such a scale.

The CCP monopolizes all political power now just as it did in Mao's era.

Yet in Mao's era even if the state served the interests of the bureaucracy in the first instance, both the legacy of the revolution and the kind of anti-capitalist regime following it put limits on the privileges of the bureaucracy; the bureaucrats could only appropriate social surplus in the form of use value, not exchange value, and this barred them from effectively accumulating capital. Moreover, they could not pass their privileges to their children. Their privileges were further limited as the state had the responsibility of guaranteeing job security to workers and basic survival to peasants. Hence Mao's state, while not socialist, was not capitalist, nor was it a state whose sole purpose was to serve the interests of the bureaucracy.

In contrast, in the Deng/post Deng period, the Chinese state and its SOEs/SHEs only serve the general interests of all capitalists, for example when police arrest strikers, or when the state sector invests in infrastructure. In this sense bureaucratic capitalism is still a type of state capitalism in the service of the bourgeoisie. However, considering the degree of the party's privatization of the state, the extent of the bourgeoisification of the bureaucracy, and the fact that it is this bureaucracy which constitutes the core of the bourgeoisie, Chinese authoritarian or state capitalism deserves a special name for itself. Even if bureaucratic capitalism, in terms of the law of capital accumulation, does not differ substantially from common authoritarian capitalism, it suggests a different kind of relation between the bureaucracy and all other social classes, which has a bearing on efforts to work for an alternative.

In a capitalist country where liberal democracy exists, the legislative and the executive power rests with the political parties which win elections, and which are supposed to embody the general will of the people. In reality these political parties, rather than serving the people, move in an orbit which is determined by the gravitational force of the propertied class. The politicians govern but do not rule. Within this separation of political and economic power there is a well-defined task for the bureaucracy, namely the task of implementing policies made by elected political leaders. Even if the top bureaucrats are more powerful than they appear to be, their power is checked by a combination of liberal democracy, political parties and the bourgeoisie, so much so that, in the end, the objectives of the bureaucracy correspond, broadly, with those of the bourgeoisie. This influence of the bourgeoisie over the bureaucracy extends to the state-owned sector as well. The former makes sure that the latter does not compete with the private sector by assigning them the mission of running those branches of the economy which are essential to the accumulation of capital but whose profit rates are too low to attract private capital. The bourgeoisie, through its political leverage, is able to bend both the bureaucracy and the state sector to its will. Since 1980, with the new agenda of neoliberalism, the bourgeoisie in the west was able to downsize the state sector by unleashing waves of privatization, so much so that today the state sector accounts for a very small share of the economy.[11]

In western Europe, it is only in rare situations that the state bureaucracy subjects all classes under its domination. As Engels describes: 'Periods occur in which the warring classes balance each other so nearly that the state power, as ostensible mediator, acquires for the moment a certain degree of independence of both. Such was the absolute monarchy of the 17th and 18th centuries, and also Bonapartism.' In the same article he added one more element which is reinforcing the autonomy of the state, namely the competition between nation states. 'The state power grows stronger… as adjacent states become larger and more populous.'[12]

In backward capitalist countries, where 'periods occur in which the warring classes balance each other so nearly', and where the need to strengthen and modernize one's country in order to resist imperialism or to compete with other states appears so urgent, it may give rise to a situation where the state bureaucracy is able to subject all classes to its domination for decades, as was the case in South Korea during the 1950s-1980s. This kind of authoritarian capitalism is also more likely to nurture a large state sector. The lack of democratic control implies that both the state and its enterprises are plagued with corruption. Although in a broad sense state capitalism serves the whole bourgeoisie, it first and foremost benefits the ruling clique and its cronies.

China has undergone both a socialist revolution and its eventual degeneration which has shaped a very different set of relationships between the state, the bureaucracy and social classes and which has allowed bureaucracy to "entrench" itself to the extent that it essentially privatized the state. Without understanding the revolution and its later development one will not be able to understand the dynamics of bureaucratic politics in China.

In the past 60 years, the CCP has treated classes as if they were its toys. Under Mao, it eliminated the landlord class and the bourgeoisie and created a new working class in the state-owned enterprises. Then in the subsequent thirty years, it resurrected the bourgeoisie, banished the state workers to the ranks of the unemployed and created a whole new working class from rural migrants. Throughout this process, only one thing has remained constant, which is the party's dictatorship and its goal of modernization, with itself as the main beneficiary.

Pyotr Struve's statement 'the farther east one goes in Europe, the more cowardly does the bourgeoisie appear'[13] is well known to Marxists. But what about the reborn bourgeoisie in China today? Surely Struve was referring to the original meaning of the bourgeoisie, and in China today this means the private capitalists. During the 1980s and 1990s, the liberals expected that with the growth of private capitalists they would eventually become the vanguard of Chinese democratic struggles. They were completely wrong. They forgot the basic fact that private capitalists owe their very existence to the party. Furthermore, they rely on the party to keep the workers and peasants in bondage; without this support it would be impossible for them to exploit the toiling masses so unscrupulously. Hence they dare not raise a single finger against the one-party dictatorship. The more ambitious among them are content to seek membership of the party or the title of representative to the People's Congress, or most importantly, a cosy relationship with leading mandarins. This is also the difference between a country which once underwent a social revolution and those authoritarian capitalist countries which did not.

Forms of bureaucratic capital

Since the mid-1990s, the CCP has promoted two waves of privatization. The first was aimed at privatizing small and medium-sized SOEs, while reforming larger ones into joint stock companies. The second wave was the privatization of urban and suburban land. These two waves of privatization established the dominant role of bureaucratic capital, although private capitalists did also benefit.

The term bureaucratic capital describes the kind of capital owned or controlled by bureaucrats through their monopoly and exercise of state power, from which they profit. The first type is capital individually owned by the bureaucrats. It is formed when officials, in their personal capacity or through family members, begin to set up private companies and are able to garner profit from them through the abuse of their power. Since the mid-1990s, the CCP privatized small and medium-sized SOEs, which opened up a second channel for the bureaucracy to enrich itself when many of these enterprises fell into the hands of local bureaucrats, former plant managers or their cronies. A third channel for bureaucrats to become part of the bourgeoisie has been through the receipt of shares from private capitalists as a bribe.

The second type of bureaucratic capital is the collective capital of the bureaucracy. Nominally, the SOEs/SHEs or assets controlled by government departments are all owned by the state. However since the Communist Party has a statutory right to rule the country, in practice this gives party officials the right to use the state-owned economy in any way they see fit.[14] The reform of large SOEs into joint-stock companies since the 1990s is a typical example. After the completion of this reform, these SOEs/SHEs no longer saw their mission as delivering public goods but rather as making money. The reform also allows parent companies to have their subsidiaries listed domestically or overseas, thus becoming mixed ownership companies. By learning financial skills and by controlling these parent companies, party officials along with all their business relations are able to control the appointment of the top personnel in these subsidiaries. Thanks to this arrangement, party officials make a fortune from these state properties without nominally owning them. This kind of corruption may not be unique to China, but the scale involved probably is. The Nationalists and some of the New Leftists who argue that a state-owned economy is necessarily more progressive than private capital ignore the fact that the former is no different from the latter in terms of their ultimate purpose; namely to make money for mandarins and private shareholders, although their critique of privatization is more grounded.[15]

Another type of bureaucratic collective capital involves companies created by government departments, mostly in relation to businesses or sectors which fall under their particular jurisdiction. For example, the labour department might set up a labour dispatch company, the fire department might set up companies selling fire-fighting supplies, the police might set up security companies, etc. The sole purpose of these companies is to make a profit. A recent example is the Chongqing Security Group, founded by the Chongqing police force – which was headed by Wang Lijun until his arrest after he defected to US embassy to escape from a plot by former head of Chongqing, Bo Xilai[16] – and run by its leading officials. This company recently applied for listing in China, disregarding the legal ban on police departments running security companies.[17] It is also common for government departments to make use of the assets they control to make money. For instance, in the 1980s this was more likely to involve holiday resorts owned by departments – even during Mao's era many of these resorts were built for the exclusive use of the state and party officials. Since the mid-1990s it has been more likely that municipal government officials made use of the land they occupied and in collusion with developers redeveloped them with new residential or commercial buildings. The profits garnered flow back to the *xiaojinku* – literally 'little treasuries' – of the departments, and are in general not accounted for in their budgets. Bonuses are paid to the officials by the department head through this *xiaojinku*. These departments' companies can also serve as a platform for receiving or paying bribes. In the recent widely reported downfall of Bo Xilai, his one-time crony and head of police, Wang Lijun, created a 'Research Institute of the Public Security Bureau' to make money and receive bribes.[18] Just how many of these kind of companies exist nationwide is a mystery.[19]

In addition, it is also quite common for local capitalists to give shares of their corporations to government departments in exchange for favours.

Another source of 'grey income' for officials comes from their role as executors of the coercive power of the state machine. It is an open and permitted practice for all levels of government officials to receive a commission when they impose levies or fines on people or companies.[20] With an internal security budget surpassing the defence budget in 2011, and reaching US$ 95 billion, one wonders how much of this goes into the pockets of government officials as extra income.[21] On top of this there is also extra income from general bribery. This income does not directly constitute bureaucratic capital but definitely becomes one of its sources. Since the bureaucracy directly profits from the coercive power of the state, no wonder it continues to pursue its own expansion, especially among those departments directly responsible for security. In one county alone there are 12,093 informants which is equivalent to 3 per cent of the population. A scholar commented that if this level of surveillance is extended to the whole country, it will far exceed the East Germany figure of 1.5 per cent.[22] Maurice Meisner pointed out that in the late Qing dynasty about 40,000 imperial officials managed the world's largest empire. The KMT (Guomindang) regime had 2 million officials. In 1958, the new republic had 8 million state cadres and it grew to 21 million in 1978.[23] Today the number has grown further to between 50 to 70 million, and if you take the latter figure then the proportion of civil servants to civilians reaches 1:18, much higher than the US figure of 1:94.[24] In this aspect, China is the best example of the so-called Parkinson's Law concerning the inherent tendency of the bureaucracy to expand its ranks. This inevitably diverts resources from the population in favour of government consumption. According to Ding Xueliang, Chinese government expenditure as a share of GDP increased from 16.48 per cent in 1952 to 26.76 per cent in 2004 and for decades has been higher than the world average and that of the entire former 'socialist bloc'.[25]

Bureaucratic capital cannot develop freely without the leverage of crony capital. The collusion between these two different kinds of capital is so intense that each intersects with the other, and they thrive or fall together. No one knows for sure the actual scale of bureaucratic and crony capital and the boundary between the two because these are carefully guarded secrets. Marx once talked about the universal spirit of the bureaucracy being secrecy.[26] This is especially the case among the Chinese bureaucracy which has thoroughly bourgeoisified itself.

The process of the bourgeoisification of the bureaucracy, although it may be supported by particular policies, more often than not is against other official policies or laws. For example government departments running their own companies and making money from these is explicitly banned by a 1984 directive.[27] Although the CCP repeatedly reminds leading cadres of this ban, the latter simply do not give a damn especially when such directives often do not carry any penalties for anyone who breaches them. Leading cadres are fully aware that it is just a formality and no one bothers about its implementation. While ordinary people must obey all laws, the party always stands above the law. Within the party another set of rules prevail; you can do whatever you want, as long as you have *houtai*, or the backing of a patron. This open contempt for the rule of law greatly facilitates the enrichment of the bureaucracy. But this will run into its limits and eventually even turn against the bureaucracy.

The economic incentives of bureaucratic capitalism

The bourgeoisification of the bureaucracy resulted in a tremendous level of corruption but at the same time ironically, also injected new incentives into the fast growing economy.

In Mao's period, China's average annual GDP growth was 6 per cent,[28] which is not at all low. The party's incentive in rapid industrialization did not come from profit-seeking. It flew from the need to *chaoyingganmei*, or to overtake the UK and US in the Cold War. This political task was embodied in the targets of the five-year plans, and the promotion or demotion of officials was linked to whether the targets were met. This mechanism proved to be effective in the pursuit of the quantitative expansion of the economy.

In the period of bureaucratic capitalism, the Communist Party, although no longer hostile to capitalism or imperialism, still sees the need to overtake the west and Japan as its duty. This time it is motivated less by the imperative of a defensive situation against the background of the Cold War, but more by the new ambition of pursuing the rise of China. Hence the party still links the promotion or demotion of officials to how successfully they increase GDP.

In addition to this old incentive, there is now a new incentive of pursuing state-led growth, namely the profit-making impulse from bureaucratic capital. Whether it is the development of SOEs/SHEs, or investment in infrastructure mega-projects, or government procurement, or the sale of state resources, party officials at all levels can always profit, directly or indirectly, through their companies or their cronies. No wonder officials so vigorously pursue economic growth.

On the surface, there seems to be a contradiction in the facts. Isn't it true that since the 1990s the two waves of privatization resulted in a great shrinkage of the state sector, from 80 per cent in 1979 it now drops to one third of the industrial output?[29] And is there not also a fall of state revenue in relation to Gross National Product (GNP)?[30] Therefore is it not correct to say that instead of an expanding state power there is a shrinking state? This is what the nationalists argue but it is a one-sided view. What matters is not just the falling share of the state-owned economy in relation to GDP, but also the fact that, despite this fall, gross state industrial production has continued to grow in absolute terms, except briefly between 1997 and 1999, against the background of rapid economic growth.[31] On top of this, the state consciously remains in control of the commanding heights of the economy[32] and most of the listed companies are SOEs/SHEs which, with government help, can always expand their market share through coercion.[33] To sum up, the monopoly of the state over key industries still enables it, despite privatization, to exercise strategic control over the national economy as a whole.

Moreover, when the two waves of privatization drew to a close, the share of state-owned economy had been stabilized, and fiscal revenue returned to its previous level.[34] This is also the case in privatized enterprises since they are more likely to be owned and run by former officials and their cronies and maintain good connections to local government, they are therefore still indirectly under the latter's influence.

This contradicts what the neoliberals predicted. They claimed that without a complete dismantling of the state-owned sector in favour of private capital, there would be no be real market reform or free development of the private sector. The truth is that the growth of the state sector in absolute terms and its monopoly over the commanding heights of the economy has not squeezed out market relations, but rather the opposite has occurred. When the party manages SOEs/SHEs just like any other commercial company, so that today they rely more on the stock market to raise money than private capital does, it presumes that there will be further expansion of market relations. In fact, the party goes even further down the road of neoliberalism when it extends commercialization and profit maximization to public utilities or social welfare, from the water supply to medical care, from education to public mass media.[35] This led David Harvey to remark that 'the outcome in China has been the construction of a particular kind of market economy that increasingly incorporates neoliberal elements interdigitated with authoritarian centralized control.'[36]

If the state sector has not squeezed the market as a whole, it has also not squeezed the private sector. Spokespeople for private capital have claimed, and have often been echoed by western media, that there has been a phenomenon of *guojinmintui*, or the advancement of the state sector at the expense of the private sector. Given that for the past twenty years the private sector has advanced from being close to nothing to today accounting for two thirds of industrial production , this is an exaggeration. It is in the interests of the bureaucracy to allow the development of the private sector. The situation with the state sector is not as clear cut as the neoliberals argue because the so-called SHEs have a minority of private shares and also because much of foreign capital is in joint ventures with SOEs/SHEs, for instance in the automobile industry. The private sector also provides the state with tax revenue, bribes and market opportunities. It goes without saying that the private sector is also a necessary prerequisite for the development of capital owned by the bureaucrats individually.

In short, there are sectors from which the state has withdrawn partially or totally, but there are also sectors like banking and insurance, communication, energy, transport etc which the state has always kept under its control or where it has expanded its share in recent years, for instance in the high-tech sector and new industries like new energy, high-tech machinery, new materials etc. During this process competition between the state and the private sector remains but the former has not squeezed the private sector. Mainstream views tend to believe that the state-owned economy and state intervention do more harm than good for economic development, hence in a 1997 World Bank report on China – repeated again in another report in 2012 – it argued that China should allow its state sector to shrink in favour of the private sector.[37] But the actual process has proved them wrong; China has continued to grow rapidly since 1997 precisely because of simultaneous growth in both sectors. Without the state sector this would have been impossible. And as long as the cake continues to grow bigger and bigger, there is enough room for both sectors. What the warning of *guojinmintui* reflects is less about the truth but more about the permanent fight between bureaucratic capital and private capital over bank loans and market share. Spokespeople of private capital became angry when it did not benefit from the 2008 government bailout, amounting to four trillion RMB. This added fuel to the continuous debate within the bureaucracy on the issue of the appropriate proportion between these two sectors. How far this debate may develop into a more crystallized political division remains to be seen, however, in the event of economic slowdown this is more likely.

For two decades, the liberals have been arguing for more market and the nationalists for more state control; with each seeing the other as reactionary. The truth is that under the party-state regime, both the state and the market are just tools for exploiting the labouring masses; neither carries any progressive element. The debate reflects the fight between these two sectors of capital.

The advantages of bureaucratic capitalism

The 1997 World Bank report *China 2020: China Development Challenges in the New Century* listed four main factors which supported China's extraordinary growth: a high saving rate, structural change (by which it means both the productivity leap which took place as workers moved from low-productivity agriculture to more productive employment in industry and services and the changes in ownership), pragmatic (market) reform, and:

> Economic conditions in 1978, which were especially receptive to reform; China's economy could be described as a dry prairie, parched by years of planning, awaiting the first sprinklings of market reform.[38]

The subsequent argument in the report shows that it sees market reform as the most important factor. The 2012 World Bank report *China 2030* basically follows the same line of argument.[39] The problem with this view is that it plays down the paramount role of the bureaucratic state as the "capitalist roader", in the course of which it also ignores the whole historical context of how this state was born through the 1949 revolution and how the latter's legacy helped the party state to achieve its mission. An investigation along this direction necessarily leads us to study the relation between classes and the party-state and how this enables the latter to rise above the former, although the success of Chinese bureaucratic capitalism also relies on the interaction between the party-state and a series of other factors, including the particularities of China, the advantages of its backwardness, and the neoliberal world order.

The state has always been the key player in making China into one of the most business friendly environments in the world, which explains why it can attract so much foreign investment in the first place. The most important aspect of this is the huge public investment in infrastructure, especially in coastal regions and in export processing zones, which in general private capital was reluctant to take on. However, the government does more than this. It also actively supports and invests in so-called 'pillar industries', chosen by the government. Under the encouragement of this fiercely pro-business government private capital, domestic and foreign, invested ambitiously to take advantage of the growing market. In just two decades, three major manufacturing bases emerged, each with its own specialized area of development.

The first of these is the Pearl River delta, initially based on labour-intensive export processing industries which has, in recent years, with support from the provincial government, gradually upgraded to more capital-intensive industries such as the car industry. The second base is the Yangtze River delta which has mainly capital-intensive industries such as automobiles, semiconductors, mobile phones and computers. The third base is Beijing's *Zhongguancun*, the so-called Chinese Silicon valley, which, with close cooperation between the government, business and academia has been able to take the lead in high-tech development in China.[40] The rapid upgrading of Chinese manufacturing can be illustrated by one fact: in the four years between 2004 and 2007, the amount of value added by Chinese employee per capita nearly doubled, rising from US$ 9, 726 to 17,913.[41] Meanwhile, with encouragement from the government, Chinese tertiary education has exploded to a point where every year it turns out a gigantic number of science and technology graduates, the scale of which other countries with a similar level of development would find hard to attain. In the ten years between 2000 and 2009, Chinese University graduates increased 4.6 fold.[42] In 2007 there were 360,780 college graduates majoring in science and technology,[43] whereas, according to a Japanese scholar, Thailand has around 14,000 graduates every year, although he added that in terms of quality of technicians China was rated behind ASEAN countries.[44] Although China still has to rely on imported high-tech products, its strong industrial base and technically skilled professionals make it more ready to assimilate foreign technology, and hence more likely to achieve their localization.

Another element of the favourable business environment, which the CCP has helped to create, is the repression of working people. This is not something unique to China, but in terms of degree not many countries can rival her. Not only do workers have no freedom to establish independent trade unions, but even NGOs have been suppressed. For the few NGOs which manage to survive, they continue to operate only in the shadow of spies.[45] Only when civil liberties have been suppressed to such a degree can capital succeed in suppressing wages to such a low level for so long. According to a World Bank report, wages in China as a share of GDP declined from 53 per cent in 1998 to 41.4% in 2005, as opposed to 57 per cent in the US.[46] But the benefits which the party-state has brought to capital are not confined to holding down wages – in fact the Chinese wages are not the lowest among Asian countries. The attractiveness of Chinese labour also lies in the fact that the party-state with its barracks-like factory regime, has helped to train a docile work force. This enables capital to extract the maximum labour from workers and achieve staggering labour productivity. Even if the number of young workers has started to dry up in recent years, the fiercely pro-business state is always ready to help capitalists by providing an adequate supply of labour. Although the planned economy was dismantled long ago, local governments still consider looking for an adequate supply of labour for capital as one of their main tasks, to the extent that they often set a target to make sure enough workers are sent into factories, this prompts local authorities to fulfil the target by making students at vocational middle schools work as interns.[47]

This ultra-favourable investment environment was possible only thanks to the 1989 crackdown on the democratic movement in Tiananmen Square. Only by smashing the students' and workers' struggle for democracy could the party make a final turn in its long metamorphosis from anti-capitalist to pro-capitalist. The fiercely pro-business societal structure, complete with privatization and the bourgeoisification of the bureaucracy could only be born out of the ruins of the 'iron bowl'.

However, it required much more than the crackdown of the workers to guarantee the safe leap forward to capitalism. Privatization prompted the management of SOEs and their government bosses to run down the enterprises and deliberately plunder their assets. This resulted in huge losses for these enterprises which then had a knock-on effect on the banks, which ended up with a huge number of non-performing loans. A big crisis, which was just seen as another price to be paid for the leap to capitalism, began to unfold in 1998. Then the 'benevolent' state came to the rescue by socializing the debt and laying off 40 million state workers in order to make the SOEs competitive again. The state has proved itself to be absolutely useful, not only in keeping its house in order but also by acting as the lender of the last resort when the economy is threatened by crisis or business cycles. The state did the same thing in 2008 when the global financial crisis spread to China. They pumped four trillion yuan of rescue money plus ten trillion yuan in loans borrowed by local governments into the economy so as to fill the hole left by a sharp decline in investment. The EU and the US took similar measures, but China stood out for its rapid response. A scenario such as in the US when Congress, for a while at least, resisted the Bush administration's bailout plan could never happen in the Chinese People's Congress.

China's powerful state intervention would not be so effective without the interaction of other factors. One of these is China's unique situation as the most populous country in the world. Even with a per capita income of US$4,382 in 2010 China is able to rank second in the world in terms of GDP, which implies a huge domestic market. This also explains why bureaucratic capital and private capital can thrive together. Similarly, even if the party has allowed the influx of FDI, with so many branches of industry opened up for them, foreign investors have not been able to control these industries. Here again the depth of the domestic market provides enough room for domestic capital to grow and compete with foreign capital. Surely in this respect, the visible hand of the state supporting domestic firms in crucial industries helps a great deal.

China's huge rural population feeds the rapid industrialization with a 250 million strong, cheap and educated supply of labour. On top of the existing urban labour force, this is another important factor which must be taken into account. The scale and pace of the proletarianization of peasants is not to be found in any other developing country today or in history. The aforementioned World Bank report regards China's abundant supply of poor rural migrants as an advantage of its backwardness. This concept may be useful in explaining the rise of China but I would like to place it in the context of the 1949 revolution and how this shapes the relations between classes and the party.

When the CCP peasant army took power in 1949, the peasantry was largely the same as had existed for two thousand years, but the CCP was no longer an exclusively peasant-based organisation in the traditional sense of the word. It was, and still is, a weird combination of despotic traditions and of a modernization programme (the question of under the label of which kind of 'ism' the CCP chose to achieve modernization was obviously an entirely secondary matter). Hence, it used the peasants as a steady supply of soldiers for its standing army and expropriated their agricultural surplus, as many exploitative classes and absolutist states have done in the past. Yet its exploitation of the peasants served a somewhat different purpose; it was not just for its own consumption, nor just for national defence, but first and foremost to provide funds for 'socialist industrialization'. Although not really 'socialist', China's industry did achieve the first stage of modernization when Mao's era drew to an end.

In the next period when the Great Leap Forward to Capitalism was kick-started, the state turned to the peasants again, this time to use them for cheap labour to serve the burgeoning industries. The CCP's success in this effort rests on the fact that it took advantage of the backwardness of the peasants and of all the traditional tools in order to tame them. One of these tools was the *hukou* system, or household registration system, which has been in place for two millennia. The party not only fully revived the tradition in 1958, went further by making it even more stringent so as to prevent the farmers entering the city. The party, in combining the household registration system with capitalism, transforms it into a form of social apartheid with Chinese characteristics. Whereas in white-dominated South Africa, apartheid targeted black people, Chinese social apartheid targets a particular class, namely the peasants. Under this social apartheid, peasants are dismissed as second-class citizens and this identity is hereditary. Although since the 1990s the system has been relaxed so as to allow rural migrant workers to work in cities, institutionalized discrimination against peasants is still largely intact; to the extent that it legitimizes the deprivation of peasants' rights to basic education and welfare in the city by the state, as well as the capitalists' excuse for driving down their wages. On top of these benefits for the bourgeoisie, this institutionalized discrimination also has a spill-over effect: since migrant workers cannot take root in the city, their identity as workers is temporary while their identity as peasants is permanent. Hence they are never able to plan for the long term while they are working in the cities. This explains why, even if they are willing to strike for wages, it is difficult for them to commit to long term organization. And without any commitment to organizing collectively, there cannot be any step forward in developing class consciousness.[48]

To sum up, the household registration system has proved to be a powerful tool to develop a flourishing capitalism in China. This is China's advantage in being backward because this tool is based on tradition.

Again, it is the Leviathan state which is paramount in making all these elements work in favour of the modernization project. Thanks to the legacy of decades of wars and revolution, the CCP was able to rebuild a super-strong state in 1949 and was able first to do away with the landlords and the bourgeoisie, and then to implement the planned economy and radical industrialization through the imposition of military-style discipline. Although with terrible and often unnecessary social and economic costs, the state was always able to over-fulfil the targets in the plan. In contrast, although many other developing countries, such as India, launched five-year plans in the post-war period, they were unable to achieve their targets because the bourgeoisie intensively resisted these plans and the relevant states lacked the institutional muscle to force these through.[49]

In the period from 1950 to 1980, when China grew 6 per cent annually, India grew only 3.5 per cent each year.[50] In 1980, China's GDP per capita was just 21 per cent higher than that of India, but at that time China already enjoyed a bigger advantage, namely a more powerful manufacturing sector and a more educated work force under a super strong state. The Mao era of industrialization also brought a substantial increase in the size of the working class, from eight million in 1949 to 100 million in 1979, more than a tenfold increase.[51] By contrast, in the thirty years between 1919 and 1949 the number of workers had little more than doubled.[52] The state, although draining too many resources away from the rural regions, nevertheless also promoted education and health, raising the cultural level of the new generation of farmers to a new historical level, so much so that in the 1980s, in terms of literacy rates, enrolment rates at primary and secondary schools and average life expectancy, China significantly surpassed India.[53] These achievements provided a better educated work force for the industrialization in the next period. It is not surprising that in the ensuing decades China grew faster than India, so much so that in 1998 in terms of GNP per capita China was 74 per cent higher than India.[54] The Indian economist Pranab Bardhan remarked that "compared to India, Chinese were better 'socialists' during the planning era and better 'capitalists 'during the reform era"[55] Once again, this confirms that China's rise is very much related to developments which come from the revolution and its elimination of the unproductive nature of the semi-feudal land ownership, although most mainstream opinions are more likely to disagree or simply ignore this fact.

Ironically, the unfulfilled mission of this revolution also eventually proved to be beneficial to the rise of capitalist China. The 1949 revolution failed to liberate Hong Kong, Macau and Taiwan from capitalism. Thirty years later, when China badly needed capital, technology and management professionals for the burgeoning industries, it was these three places which provided the party-state with enough resources. From the early 1980s until 1989, capital from Hong Kong was the first batch of foreign investment pouring into China. It was, however, not just about money. It was the success story of Hong Kong (and the other three 'dragons') which gave confidence to the top party leaders that, judging from Hong Kong's experience, capitalism could really work.[56] In the second stage, from Deng Xiaoping's southern tour in 1992 onwards, Taiwan's capitalists rushed to China and invested even more heavily in capital and technologically intensive industries, such as petro chemicals, information technology and precision instruments. (In recent years the South Korean media described the combination of mainland China and Taiwan in terms of capital and technology in electronics and related industries as 'Chiwan', and were deeply worried about being out-competed.)

During the same period, Hong Kong evolved into the financial centre for the listing of mainland SOEs/SHEs and private firms. Without Hong Kong, the Chinese companies would not be so rich in capital. Macau satisfies a very different kind of need for the bureaucratic capitalists: it serves not only as a casino city, but it is first and foremost a perfect platform for money-laundering and a springboard for capital flight.[57] Without Hong Kong, Macau and Taiwan, the story of the rise of China would be very different.

However, without the major change in the world situation which happened from the 1980s, China's story would also be very different. It was the neoliberal turn in the advanced countries which made possible the removal of capital controls and the hollowing out of industries in the west and then Japan. It is this change on the world stage which eventually made China into one of the highest recipients of foreign investment for many years.[58] The global shift of manufacturing from the rest of the world to China has been one of the factors which enabled Chinese manufacturing to grow tremendously, so much so that in 2010 China overtook the US to become the top manufacturing country in terms of its share of world output, standing at 19.8 per cent, up from 3 per cent in 1990.[59]

China's ability to attract a great amount of foreign investment cannot be explained by China's superior investment environment alone. There was a fundamental change in class policy in China, which quickly brought about changes in foreign policy. Deng's decision to attack Vietnam in 1979, after his return from visiting the USA, revoking the material support it had given to those Asian Communist Parties which involved in armed struggle against their capitalist state, was in practice sending a message to the USA: we are no longer interested in fighting capitalism and we are rather more interested in a joint venture for making a fortune together!

But China's growing dependence on foreign investment throughout the 1990s aroused fears among leftists and nationalists that China might sink back to semi-colonial status, dominated by western and Japanese imperialism. Indeed, until 2003 when a change of leadership occurred, China's economic development increasingly exhibited characteristics of dependent capital accumulation. Foreign investment became more dominant in some industries, with half of the output value of exports coming from foreign companies. Chinese companies, being at the bottom tier of the global chain of value added, gained very little from playing the role of the sweatshop of the world. The terms of China's accession to the WTO were a huge concession to foreign capital, if one compares this to the terms on which India was admitted.[60] This economic trend of an overly-accommodating attitude towards foreign capital was also increasingly manifested in the political arena. Among economists, those who were considered close to certain sections of party officials called for more accommodating policies for foreign investment and more privatization. These people were attacked as representatives of the new comprador class by Chinese New Leftists.[61] However, the fear that China might sink into semi-colonial status has not been realized. Although foreign investment has developed by leaps and bounds, so has domestic investment, hence in 2009 the share of foreign investment in manufacturing was 28 per cent, not much higher than the 2002 figure of 27.7 per cent,[62] albeit in certain areas such as electronics and information technology it enjoys a more dominant position.[63] Foreign capital is also dominant in the export sector. In the domestic market the picture is even more different. A study shows that among the 39 main branches of industry, foreign capital is able to enjoy a market share greater than 30 per cent in only one of them. The study also shows that in sectors in which economic sovereignty or 'national security' may be a concern, from scarce minerals, natural monopolistic sectors, equipment industry to defence industry, banking and insurance, mass media and publishing industry etc., domestic firms, especially SOEs/SHEs, remain dominant.[64]

There are two main reasons for China's resistance to domination by foreign investment. One reason is political: the CCP has very strong nationalist sentiments. Its very mission has been to secure China's independence through a revolution and it has been true to its programme, first by resisting the Japanese occupation and then by making a revolutionary war against the Guomindang, which the CCP considered represented the comprador class. At the height of the Cold War, Mao dared to confront the Soviet Union and the United States simultaneously. This is a party which has so much national pride that it would not tolerate China sliding back to semi-colonial status. This also explains why, against the expectations of some, Deng told Thatcher in 1982 that China would take back Hong Kong in 1997 when the unequal treaty of 1842 expired. With the US bombing of the Chinese Embassy in Yugoslavia in 1999, against a background where foreign investment occupied a growing share of the Chinese market, the call for protecting China's sovereignty and its market became stronger. As far as foreign investment is concerned, the party-state imposed controls over the sectors in which FDI can invest from the very beginning. In 1995 the State Council issued the *Catalogue for the Guidance of Foreign Investment Industries*, which laid out the sectors in which FDI is encouraged, permitted, restricted, or banned altogether. It has been repeatedly revised to put forward what is considered to be the best of China's 'national interest'. Since the change of leadership in 2003, the party has put greater emphasis on autonomous development and innovation. In 2007 the *Catalogue* was again revised, and while it relaxed some of the previously restricted sectors, it also imposed new restrictions on FDI in sectors in which China could already produce or where there were scarce resources.[65] To sum up, the party-state is always in the position to dictate the space in which FDI can operate freely in order to meet its own interests. Meanwhile the government has spent a huge amount of state funds to achieve the goal of more autonomous development. Indeed, with the rise of China, the party has begun to put the restoration of past glory, of being a major empire, back on the agenda.

The other reason for China's resistance to domination by foreign investment is an economic drive to support more autonomous development, described as economic nationalism by the western media. As previously said, the bureaucracy's interest is tied directly to the expansion of state machinery and state capitalism; hence it is highly motivated to see an expansion of domestic firms. Moreover, the bureaucracy increasingly finds being at the lowest end in the global chain of value added humiliating or even unbearable and is determined to move upwards to satisfy its ever-growing appetite for a larger share. With a super-strong state and a huge market at its disposal, the party-state, once determined to fight for its fair share, has much more bargaining power than many developing countries in dealing with western powers and Japan. For instance even though the Chinese government made too many concessions to western powers in its accession to the WTO in 2001, in agreeing that technological transfers to Chinese companies should rest entirely with foreign investors and that they will make no attempt to intervene, this does not stop the Chinese government from successfully making TNCs transfer technology in exchange for market accession to China. One example is the so-called war over standards. The Chinese government was successful in making TNCs transfer technology so that it could establish its own standard for video CDs, mobile phones and WLAN (Wireless Local Area Networks). The state wanted a national standard for all these new fields of technology because it wanted state companies to be assured of a market share, while the state was assured of 'national security'. On each occasion, the TNCs initially resisted the Chinese government but eventually they were forced to agree to the deal in exchange for market access.[66] Again, the huge Chinese market gives enough room for both western standards and Chinese standards to exist side by side, as is illustrated in the Chinese mobile phone market where three standards (European, US and Chinese) co-exist.

To sum up, China's economic development is characterized by its inherent contradictions. Features of dependent accumulation and of relatively autonomous development co-exist, although the latter, with the help of the party-state, has been gathering more momentum in recent years. The advantages of the so-called Chinese model are shaped by a combination of various factors such as the general law of capital accumulation and China's specificities and in particular the legacy of its specific social upheavals and revolutions which cannot be simply copied in other parts of the world.

Bureaucratic capitalism and its potential opponents

Isaac Deutscher once said that Stalin 'drives barbarism out of Russia by barbarous means'.[67] Mao and Deng have done pretty much the same thing to China and while they have accomplished this, they have also nurtured their own potential opponents. In Mao's era the working class reached 100 million. In 2008, urban employment increased to 302 million, while rural employment was reduced to 472 million.[68] In today's China, half of the population live in urban areas. There is more to this than just numbers. Most of those who have stayed in rural areas are women, children or the elderly. The most productive population lives and works in the cities and towns, hence the average urban population carries more social and economic weight than the average rural one. The changes in class structure and the economy will, from a historical perspective, fundamentally change the power base of the Chinese Communist Party.

Although the modern working class has rapidly grown in size, its structure has been transformed fundamentally following the great wave of privatization and even more rapid industrialization. The state and collective sector has nearly halved from 110 million to 61 million workers[69], meaning that the majority of the present day working class is composed of rural migrant workers who have no collective memory as a class prior to coming to the cities. Each for their own reasons, neither section of the working class has been able to develop a movement to defend themselves from the barbaric capitalist assault since the mid-1990s.

In a recent article Mingqi Li argued that the older generation of SOE workers are a class which developed a 'relatively complete class consciousness.'.[70] This is disputable as one cannot say workers have developed 'complete class consciousness', even if 'relatively', until they have some idea of socialist democracy and are aware that the one party dictatorship goes against the very principle of socialism. Yet throughout Mao's period, the appeal of socialist democracy remained very weak among workers. Not only did very few of them question the party's social apartheid against the peasants, many of them felt privileged to the extent that they might not treat their workmates who came from rural areas, or those from collectively owned enterprises, on an equal footing. Therefore, one may say that the consciousness of the SOE workers during Mao's period was more that of social layer with a privileged status, than that of a modern working class with a mission to break down all the barriers between workers and forging a lasting union among them. If the SOE workers in that period did display some traits of a modern working class consciousness, these were mixed with the exclusiveness associated with their privileged status and also their servility towards the party, which continued to act as a brake on the development of a full working class consciousness.

In Mao's China there was not a total absence of resistance by workers, however. In 1957 during the period of the Cultural Revolution, as well as during the 1976 Tiananmen Incident[71] and the Beijing Spring of 1979, the most independent section of the workers did, to varying degrees, rise up against this despotism, often with a distinct socialist element. But these struggles were not on a national scale. It was another ten years, until 1989, before there was a nationwide revolt, first initiated by students but then joined by tens of thousands of workers, which sprang up in defiance of the party's martial law, to protect the students who were occupying Tiananmen Square. The CCP reacted by brutally suppressing the movement. During the next twenty years, the working class was completely restructured. More than 40 million state workers were laid off in the wave of privatization and those who kept their jobs experienced downward mobility. SOE workers experienced the most depressing period in contemporary China. Meanwhile, even for laid-off SOE workers, most of them were not pauperized to a point where they became homeless – the legacy of the 'socialist' past still entitled them to buy, at a price lower than market price, the apartment in which they had been staying for years.

Meanwhile, since the mid-1990s, a new working class, composed of 250 million rural migrants, was formed. At the beginning, this was a large army of migrant workers with no knowledge of their rights. Local government officials deliberately kept them in the dark and shamelessly sided with the capitalists in denying their rights. Coming from rural areas, they could only passively adapt to the barracks-like factory regime, and since they did not have a high self-esteem or high expectations, the absolute majority of them adapted well to the system. Only when the management occasionally went too far, for instance by beating up workers, would some respond with spontaneous strikes, though these were confined to a single plant. This was not just because of government repression but also because the rural migrant workers had not developed any idea of long-term organization. An additional factor was that although their wages are very low, their income is high relative to that of peasants . Those migrant workers who have had the opportunity to upgrade to skilled workers have moved up the social ladder. In recent years, the regular increase in the minimum wage further improved their livelihood compared to the first generation of migrant workers. Therefore, despite widespread spontaneous strikes, the discontent of these rural migrant workers has not reached boiling point. This has been one of the reasons why the party-state has experienced more than twenty years of stability.

However, the working class continues to grow in number, along with its cultural and educational level, which irresistibly raises workers' self-esteem and expectations, injecting into them new strength of resolve.

State sector workers on the other hand have not yet overcome the demoralization inflicted by the defeat of 1989 and of the massive privatization. However, the 2009 struggle by workers at Tonghua Steel which successfully resisted privatization is noteworthy. Violent actions against managers by workers are not uncommon since the onset of the enterprise reform but they have usually been individual actions. When workers have conducted collective protests they have tended to be moderate for fear of reprisals. The Tonghua Steel workers' struggle was both collective and violent; the workers collectively killed a manager, something that has never happened before.[72] Whether this signifies the end of their demoralization is still hard to say. Yet, it is also obvious that the demoralizing effect of the June 4 1989 Tiananmen Square massacre will draw to an end sooner or later, along with the old illusion that the party-state is benevolent.

Not only has the number of workers in the state sector significantly reduced, but the composition of this section of the working class has dramatically changed as well. In the labour intensive industries such as manufacturing, even rural migrant workers form a part of the workforce of the SOEs. It is no longer the case that SOE workers are necessarily urban residents with a higher income than workers from other sectors. This implies downward mobility for SOE workers, but at the same time, with the continuous increase in wages among rural migrant workers, it also means that the gap between workers from the two different kinds of household registration is narrowing. This, in the long term, will facilitate mutual understanding between the two sections of the working class. Meanwhile, the new generation of SOE workers are not burdened by the 1989 defeat; in fact most of them do not even know about it.

Rural migrant workers today are more aware of their legal rights, especially in the coastal areas, and are more likely to strike when they feel that they have suffered an injustice. For decades the CCP's policy was to prohibit strikes.[73] However for the past ten years there have been so many wildcat strikes that today local governments have in practice acknowledged that they have to tolerate these strikes, as long as strikers do not try to block roads or the employers concerned have no connection with government officials. It is very common for these spontaneous strikes to win partial victories, which has also prompted the party's decision to raise the minimum wage in recent years. This proves that rural migrant workers, even if they have not yet developed any class consciousness or any organization, are still able to fight to increase their share of income in relation to profit. Although there are no sustainable labour organizations, a network of labour activists and 'barefoot lawyers' has been formed. Even if some of them only work to earn money, their overall effect helps to promote workers' awareness of their rights.

Today most of the young rural residents hardly plough the land and an increasing number of them are either born or raised in urban areas and are much less attached to their home villages than their parents. They also have higher education than them. All this contributes to the development of a higher self-esteem and expectations among these young rural migrants. The struggle in 2010 by the Honda Foshan workers was a new sign of hope. The young migrant workers not only demanded a pay rise, but they were also bold enough to break a taboo and demand the re-election of the workplace trade union representatives. Their struggle reflected their democratic aspirations and also their ability to carry these through. Their partial success also shows that, at least in the Pearl River delta, local governments have understood that repression alone is no longer effective.[74]

Migrant workers, with their hard earned money, are also improving the lives of their families left behind in their home villages and are raising their children's educational level by paying their school fees. Rural migrant workers actually act as a bridge between urban and rural areas. They bring back to the village knowledge gained in the city, including their experiences of economic struggles. Today's rural population, especially the new generation, are no longer the peasants of thirty years ago who lacked modern culture. Some of them have thrown off their mentality of subordination and the fatalistic outlook which had endured in these communities for centuries. These people are likely to have an awareness of themselves as citizens and a view that things can change for the better if they try, although for most of them it is still confined to individual endeavours such as learning new skills and/or frequently changing jobs. The changes in outlook and expectations among the peasant population are also slowly forcing officials to adjust their decades long polices of harsh repression.

The struggle in Wukan village against land grabbing at the end of 2011[75] was a new sign of hope for farmers. The villagers were able to break taboos and establish their own organization to coordinate the fight. What was even more significant was that the Guangdong provincial government recognized this organization, negotiated with it, and concluded the talks by allowing the organization subsequently to hold formal and democratic elections of the village committee. This broke with the past policy of the party-state never to permit autonomous organizations of people or to allow free elections.

The party-state has remained very stable for the past two decades. An important reason is the fact that high growth rates contribute to the emergence of a growing 'middle-class', composed of relatively high paid white-collar workers, professionals, and small capitalists. Most of them have fared much better than their parents. It is not surprising that over the past decades they have focused on climbing up the social ladder. However, with the growth of the monopoly of bureaucratic capital, the horrifying scale of corruption and environmental pollution, this middle class is increasingly concerned about its further opportunities for upward mobility, or about its own interests being infringed upon by corrupt officials. In recent years there have been many local protests against environmental pollution, where both working people and middle class residents joined together.[76]

To summarise, the three decades of accelerated industrialization have dramatically modernized China's class structure as well as changing people's thinking on a more gradual basis. Amongst workers and peasants and the middle class, more and more people have developed a civic awareness and an aspiration for democracy. Though rising mass struggle is still not evident, fear is receding. In the previous period, workers or farmers were only seen as 'vulnerable groups' by the media and intellectuals who saw them as people who should be pitied but not really respected, let alone feared. In recent years however, one hears more complaints by bureaucrats who say that 'now it is more difficult for the government to control the masses'. The deputy secretary of the Guangdong Province, Zhu Mingguo, warned party cadres following the events at Wukan that 'when the masses get angry, you will know what the meaning of power is.'[77] This is why in recent years some local governments have become more tolerant of mass protests and sometimes prefer to make concessions. The power of the masses is slowly expanding the space for further struggles.

However, a numerical growth of the working class does not automatically lead to a growth of class consciousness. The current authoritarian social and cultural context, and the legacy of China's two millennia of absolutism and the corporatism which the Communist Party revived, continues to hamper working people from developing a democratic practice. It is common that when workers take collective action they spontaneously make decisions democratically, as the Honda case and others show. Yet long term organization requires more sophisticated procedures and here both the Chinese tradition and the party's practices have very little to offer.

It was not accidental that when Sun Yat Sen, founder of the Republic of China, first agitated for democratic revolution during the late Qing dynasty he found it necessary to first introduce procedures for running meetings. He was not successful in promoting these kinds of democratic practices, however, as all subsequent Chinese governments had hardly any interest in functioning democratically. Hence democratic conduct, such as basic procedures for meetings, has to be learned afresh. (Even in Taiwan and Hong Kong today, many trade unionists do not like voting as they consider it 'divisive'.) The positive side is that it is always possible to learn these things, especially when independent-minded activists find out that democracy really does enable the working class to realize its collective power and is therefore inherently beneficial to its cause. In the final analysis, even if the cultural legacy must be taken into account, one must also bear in mind that in a broader sense this legacy also allows humans to learn to change through conscious actions, especially when the material conditions of their lives have greatly improved their ability to act.

Ironically, although Hong Kong has played a huge role in helping the party-state to promote capitalism, it has also contributed partially to the development of a democratic awareness on the mainland, or in recent years at least in South China. NGOs of Hong Kong origin which work on the mainland, or Hong Kong solidarity movements with mainland dissidents and labour activists, and last but not least, its own political liberalization are all indirectly influencing people on the mainland. Retired and dissident high ranking party officials often publish their memoirs in Hong Kong and every year some mainland Chinese will come to Hong Kong to join the 4 June 1989 Tiananmen Square memorial events. More and more mainland expectant mothers come to Hong Kong to give birth to so that their children will obtain the right of abode and be raised in a freer environment. Neither is it one-way traffic between Hong Kong and China as far as democratic aspirations are concerned. One must not forget that it was the great 1989 democratic movement in mainland which gave the first great impetus to Hong Kong's democratic movement.

All these forces are slowly working to make the party-state tone down its habitual contempt for the legitimate rights of the people. Today, to try to force the authorities to respect the political rights of its citizens is still a futile or even risky undertaking. But in matters concerning economic rights, it is now less risky and it is not rare to see people successfully fighting for these rights. The CCP is reacting by improving labour legislation so as to channel struggles into a long judicial process. Some argue that the CCP is now beginning to evolve into a more law-abiding regime.[78] If this becomes the case it will only be because the workers are beginning to take matters into their own hands. More workers are now fully aware of the fact that since government officials rarely prosecute unscrupulous employers, it is better to take direct action – which more often than not is illegal – rather than just relying on the legal process. For a long time, the arbitrary rule of the party-state worked in its favour as it was free to do whatever it wanted. Yet now it is increasingly undermining itself by pushing bigger and bigger groups of people to rebel.

However, an alternative is still lacking. The sharp turn to the right in both the political and economic arena over the last twenty years is also reflected in a similar turn in social thinking. Marxism and socialism are both deeply discredited. The experiences of the intellectuals have led to most of them abandoning any faith they had in left-wing ideas. Under Mao's version of socialism, intellectuals were discriminated against as *choulaojiu* (literally 'Stinking Number Nine', because they were the group given the lowest social status)[79]. Under Deng and his successors, for the first time since the 1949 revolution, not only has the discrimination stopped but the intellectuals are also now able to quickly move up the social and political ladder because of fast economic growth. Hence most of them draw the conclusion that socialism is bad and capitalism is a comparatively better choice. For the minority of intellectuals who still aspire to some kind of socialism, their references are likely to be more Stalinist in essence than genuinely socialist, as they still defend the one party dictatorship. Both liberals and certain New Leftists, on the other hand, share the same hostility towards a democratic labour movement organised from below. Although a turn to the left has not yet occurred, a new generation of intellectuals is now beginning to occupy the social scene which does not have the ideological burden of the past and is beginning to think differently. Their sensitivity to human rights and civil liberties helps raise the awareness of these rights among the public, although this is still more likely to be wedded to liberal discourses. For the first time in many years, there are university students who are beginning to develop sympathy with workers and peasants and to try to improve their lives, although the scale of this remains very small. In contrast, the students in 1989 were very suspicious of the Beijing Autonomous Workers' Association.[80] If Chinese socialists want to revive the credibility of socialism they need to show active support for any extension of civil liberties and political freedom without, at the same time, succumbing to the liberal discourse about the free market.

China's rise reaches bottleneck

The Great Leap Forward to Capitalism, although successful, resulted in the Chinese people paying a terrible social, economic and environmental price. At the same time, it has created new contradictions which may begin to create a ceiling on continual high economic growth.

With poor energy efficiency, fast economic growth has drained so many resources that today half of China's oil consumption comes from imports, whereas in 1992 China was still self-sufficient.[81] The growth of industry also overuses and pollutes water resources to the extent that today 400 out of 660 cities in China do not have sufficient fresh water, and among these cities, 136 of them are experiencing severe water shortages.[82] China's rise has taken such a toll on the environment that most well informed scholars know that the current growth rate is unsustainable.

'Human resources' are beginning to dry up as well. Ten years ago, the business sector was still celebrating the unlimited supply of labour. China has been so successful in attracting FDI from all over the world that today the supply of labour is beginning to fall. Strictly speaking, Chinese labour resource is still abundant. But the numbers of those who are young or strong enough, have basic education and are willing to work very hard in very bad conditions in exchange for very low wages is getting smaller. This sector of the labour force is precisely what sustains the so-called 'China's price'. The drying up of this kind of labour means that China's low wage advantage is diminishing, which will again affect China's ability to attract foreign direct investment and to export.

Another bottleneck that China is running into is exports. Firstly, China is unlikely to maintain a 23 per cent average annual growth rate for its exports indefinitely, as it did in the past ten years, without creating trade wars with other countries. Secondly, shrinking European and American markets, due to the financial crisis of 2008 and its aftermath, is beginning to impact on China's economy. This could be particularly serious for China as it is heavily dependent on foreign investment and exports. In 2004 China's imports and exports account for 70 per cent of GDP, an unusually high proportion for a large country like China.[83] This means that China's integration into global capitalism goes so deep that the latter's great downturn will mean that China's exports will soon lose momentum. Rising wages and the appreciation of the yuan have already led to many export factories closing down or losing money.

China's second engine of growth comes from its high investment rate, which is increasingly led by the government. For decades it has stood at more than 40 per cent,[84] which is even higher than that of South Korea during its high growth period. This has been achieved by suppressing wages and the prices of agricultural produce, however, this results in a lack of consumer demand. Central government has been advocating a redistribution of income in favour of workers and peasants to stimulate domestic demand, but this has not been very successful. Between 1978 and 2009, private consumption went down from 49 per cent to 37 per cent. In contrast, in 2008-9 the figures for South Korea, Malaysia, Indonesia and India are 55 per cent, 50 per cent, 61 per cent and 59 per cent respectively.[85] One result is persistent overproduction, with the first round of severe overproduction occurring in the period 1997-2000. In 1998, official statistics showed that China had nearly 500 kinds of products with a capacity utilization rate of below 60 per cent. This problem was solved only by plant closures, massive layoffs, and enormous bailouts. Once the trouble was over, another round of crazily rushed investment kick-started again, paving the way for the next round of overproduction, this time in the real estate market.

The second wave of privatization, where bureaucratic capital has colluded with private capital to grab urban land and develop it into new projects, underpinned the recent housing boom. Prices are now so high that they are entirely beyond the means of the lower middle class. With the support of public credit, the market is creating a huge bubble. The crisis in 2008 actually made it worse. In that year real estate loans stood at 600 billion yuan, which then surged to 2.46 trillion yuan in 2009 and rose again in 2010 to 2.9 trillion yuan, a fourfold increase in two years.[86] When such investments failed to create enough returns, they turned into unperforming loans for the bank. The state may again soon have to play the role of lender of last resort, as it did at the turn of the century, only this time the bailout will have to be even larger.

The great recession in the US and EU in 2008 prompted the Chinese government to launch the great rescue package of 4 trillion yuan, on top of a 10 trillion investment plan by local governments. The result was that total local government debt rose from 1.5 trillion yuan in 2002 to 10.7 trillion yuan in 2010, which is equal to 27 per cent of the GDP, causing concern among bankers in the west.[87] This is because if one adds domestic and external debt owed by central government, which now stands at 17.4 per cent of GDP, to these local debts, then total public debt reaches 44.3 per cent of GDP.[88]

Pro-government scholars have tried to comfort foreign investors by saying that this is still far from the warning level of 60 per cent. The problem is that these are only official figures. It is well known that there are hidden debts, but the amounts remain a mystery. Furthermore, even if the current debt level does not cause an immediate crisis, if local public debt can increase sevenfold in eight years, this reveals the imperative of bureaucratic capital to borrow money without ever thinking about how to repay it. This indicates that bureaucratic capital is taking central government hostage by forcing it to bail it out. Therefore, it may not take very long for total debt to increase to 60 per cent from its current level.

Local officials have been crazily borrowing money to invest in suspicious projects, despite the initial ban on local governments issuing bonds. These local governments simply get around the ban by creating companies to borrow on their behalf. In 2011, central government responded to these illegal acts, not by prosecuting local officials, but instead by permitting a number of localities ie Shanghai, Zhejiang, Guangdong and Shenzhen to issue local public bonds.[89] The party-state, while it is able to stamp out all out-spoken dissidents with ease, is entirely impotent in checking the greed of its officials. This has laid the ground for a future debt crisis.

As long as the economy continues to grow, guaranteeing government revenue, then it is not difficult for the central government to play again the role of lender of last resort. The problem is that it is difficult to maintain an annual growth rate of 8-9 per cent by flooding the market with more credit, without first causing higher inflation and promoting an even bigger bubble. One may say that today, China has reached a point where it cannot guarantee stable and rapid economic growth without first rebalancing its economic structure.

As mentioned previously, central government has decided to raise the income of the poor as one of the measures to rebalance the economy. Depicted by some as a Chinese New Deal, the current leadership has, in recent years, increased the minimum wage, rescinded the agricultural tax and levies at the village and township level, granted agricultural subsidies to peasants, embarked on a massive housing project for the poor etc. Some of these policies have been implemented. As a rule, however, the greater the amount of money involved, the more likely it is that a large portion of it will eventually end up in the pockets of the bureaucrats.

As a result, the buying power of working people remains very low, while the gap between the rich and the poor grows even larger as the bureaucracy takes advantage of the financial crisis of 2008 to make a fortune. Again, this proves that the biggest obstacle for the implementation of a New Deal is the CCP itself. The only way to fight corruption is to put the bureaucracy under democratic control. Such an idea, however, is something which the CCP hates. It can deliver minor economic benefits to the people if hard pressed either by protests or by imbalances of the economy, but it can never allow itself to be placed under democratic scrutiny.

Most of the bureaucrats are only interested in solutions to solve economic imbalances that will directly benefit them. One of these solutions is to export surplus capital. This has been energetically led by the state; hence it is no surprise that it is chiefly the SOEs/SHEs which benefit. As early as 1998 when an economic crisis set in, the State Economic and Trade Commission released a policy document *Index of Over-Invested Production lines for Moving Abroad* to encourage enterprises to export surplus capacity.[90]

At the 2001 National People's Congress, Premier Zhu Rongji officially announced the 'go global' policy, and included this strategy in the Fifteen Yearly Plan. Since then China's foreign direct investment has grown by leaps and bounds, from US$ 29.9 billion in foreign investment and by stock in 2002, to US$ 184 billion in 2008. In 2009, China's foreign direct investment ranked sixth in the world.[91] This is just the official figures, without taking into account the huge amount of capital flight and the FDI owned by Hong Kong subsidiaries of SOEs/SHEs. An increasingly large amount of foreign investment necessarily requires the Chinese government to pursue an expansion of its influence in international affairs and in the internal affairs of the host countries. Therefore, despite the Chinese government's insistence on a 'peaceful rise' and non-interference in the internal affairs of foreign countries, the global expansion of its economic power necessarily ties it to a policy of political and military expansion.

In the short to medium term, if China ever starts a war, it will most likely be a war with a small country rather than with a hegemonic power like the USA. Today China is too strong for any hegemonic power to conceive of a winning war against it, and for its part the CCP does not consider such a war as beneficial. Its economic interests are now so fully integrated with the USA and the EU that war is excluded in the medium term. Moreover, as long as Taiwan remains under the protection of the United States, the Chinese government has to maintain a prudent policy in its expansion of international influence. If war with the USA is unlikely, it does not mean that the two countries have no conflicts. China and the USA have common interests in maintaining the global production chain, but Chinese bureaucratic capital is determined to fight for a greater share, while US monopoly capital is trying to keep its portion. Therefore, the two countries will continue to compete in the economic, political and even military arena. China will do the same with other countries, if to a lesser extent. Therefore, China's rise necessarily accelerates economic competition and the arms race between all the big powers.

The past success of the party-state has been heavily reliant on imitating foreign technology. This will reach its limit when a higher level of development demands genuine innovation, in which China is still falling behind the west and Japan. The party knows this but it does not understand that it is itself precisely the obstacle in the way of a breakthrough of indigenous innovation, because for this to happen would require a free academic environment, the rule of law and a more open culture and education; all of which are incompatible with the one party rule.

Many forces are now at work to place a limit on China's rapid economic growth. In the near future, a sharp drop in exports, an even weaker domestic demand or the bursting of the real estate bubble may trigger an economic crisis. However, Chinese bureaucratic capitalism determines that the state is always on the alert to bail out itself and the private capitalists. This implies that China, like many countries today, is going down the road of accumulating an unsustainable debt.

What characterizes today's situation is the way in which the party-state is beginning to exhaust its capacity to keep the economy going at this high speed. Some of the advantages of China's state capitalism are increasingly turning into hindrances. State-led investment is so corrupt that increasing amounts end up in failed projects and then in nonperforming loans. The bureaucracy, having devoured an ever bigger portion of the national income, makes itself the common target of all classes. Society is increasingly unable to bear the burden of the predatory bureaucrats.

When the economy is still growing, all of these contradictions remain manageable for the bureaucracy; even if the private capitalists and foreign capital are discontented with the monopoly imposed by bureaucratic capital, or if within the bureaucracy there is disagreement over pro-state versus pro-market actions. However, in a serious economic downturn these conflicts may become so serious that the risk of spinning out of control becomes higher. This time they will develop within a context different from the last crisis at the turn of the century: the borrowing ability of the state rapidly declining, a bureaucracy plagued with centrifugal forces, corruption and the growth of internal divisions, an awakening working class gradually recovering from the defeat of 1989, and a peasant population keen to defend its land. Therefore, the coming economic crisis may have more chance to develop into a political crisis than was the case at the turn of the century.

In most capitalist countries, the political and economic spheres are separate from each other; hence the economic struggle of labour tends to be sectoral and usually non-political. Hence it is possible for the development of a non-political trade union movement, although the value of this to labour has been much debated. In China the two spheres are to a great extent merged, so that the invisible hand of the market is always underpinned by the visible boot of the state, therefore even a non-political independent trade union is not tolerated. Strangely, a strategy of 'depoliticization' of the labour movement is precisely what is advocated by Han Dongfang and his *China Labour Bulletin* after they dropped their previous position of fighting for an independent trade union movement. It is not realistic, however, because the despotic state and the repressive factory regime stand and fall together. To argue that Chinese labour disputes 'do not represent a threat to the state and can in most cases be resolved within the enterprise without recourse to government intervention' is to forget that the very interest of bureaucratic capital determines that the latter necessarily sees labour struggles for economic betterment as a threat to its state.[92] It is improbable that a trade union movement from below can fully develop without at the same time winning basic civil liberties and eventually democratizing the state. Either economic strikes remain isolated and are heavily repressed, or when they occur in the midst of a political crisis, they have the chance to broaden out as they necessarily clash with the party-state and become politicized through the raising of demands for civil rights and political freedoms.

The faction fight within the Chinese Communist Party

When the Soviet bloc disintegrated in the early 1990s, many people expected that the CCP would follow suit soon. Today, many more think that the party-state will remain stable for years to come. There is increasing pessimism about the future of democracy in China.[93] This argument is often posed in the same way as other theories which see China as a 'super-stable structure' which is incapable of developing democracy on its own.[94]

We are not that pessimistic about future of democracy in China. The phenomenon of a bureaucracy rising above all classes for more than sixty years is the product of specific historical conditions and a special set of class relations, not ordained by any mysterious and ahistorical 'cultural structure'. When the historical conditions and the set of class relations change, they also necessarily change the power of the bureaucracy.

In the last analysis, the fact that the bureaucracy was and still is able to promote itself as the supreme ruler in the former Soviet Union and today in China, originates from a workers' and farmers' revolution which eventually degenerated because of social backwardness and its international isolation. Socialism can only be built in affluent societies, where the material conditions for workers self-management, such as the shortening of work hours and free education for all, at least are possible. In backward countries like Russia, although the working class did have the ability to establish their revolutionary government, poverty also made it difficult for them to move forward to socialism, without the revolution being extended to the advanced countries. It was inevitable that the Russian Revolution could not go forward when it was isolated, and very soon the workers' government evaporated into thin air while the bureaucracy usurped all the power. This was just the first step towards capitalist restoration. As Trotsky said, 'The Soviet bureaucracy has gone far toward preparing a bourgeoisie restoration ...Privileges have only half their worth, if they cannot be transmitted to one's children....The victory of the bureaucracy in this decisive sphere would mean its conversion into a new possessing class.'[95]

The process proved to be much longer one than Trotsky expected, however, and allowed the Soviet Union to attain such a high level of industrialization that in the 1980s it was predominantly urban. A new generation with higher education and expectations gave rise to a movement from below, in the midst of a growing economic and social crisis. Gorbachev responded with Perestroika, which only exacerbated the contradictions. The bureaucracy, under pressure from below, found it necessary to act quickly to restore capitalist property relations. Yeltsin succeeded, but there was a price to pay. He had to dismantle both the party and the Soviet Union itself before he could decisively defeat the Stalinist wing of the party. The side effect of his victory was a considerably weakened bureaucracy.

A severe economic recession hit the working class very hard and it was deeply demoralized. Yet they and other social classes, for the first time in many years, gained some basic political freedoms. Representative democracy was installed, although more in form than in substance, and this at least allowed for some political pluralism: bourgeois and workers' based opposition parties do exist. Later Putin's government was able to regain some lost ground, but he is unable to eliminate political pluralism altogether. All classes of society continue to struggle with the bureaucratic regime and make any attempt to reinstall a totalitarian regime almost impossible. Therefore, even if Russia exhibits some features of bureaucratic capitalism, it is only a weak version of it, and hence not so different from common authoritarian capitalism.

China's trajectory of capitalist restoration was basically similar to that of the Soviet Union, but in China's case it was more drawn out and consisted of two stages spanning twenty years. In 1982 the CCP had already abolished the constitutional right to strike, which signalled the first change in the class role of the state. A transformation of the class character from anti-capitalist to pro-capitalist took place within the state in 1988 when the CCP amended the constitution, legalising private enterprises and the sale of land-use rights.

If the 1988 event only revealed the party leaders' intention, then the 1989 crackdown on the democracy movement was an unmistakable sign that the party now wanted to implement its plan even if it meant a bloodbath. In 1992 the southern tour by Deng Xiaoping marked the Great Leap Forward to Capitalism in the social and economic arena. Martin Hart-Landsberg argues convincingly that China's economy had become capitalist since the turn of the century.[96]

If China diverged from Russia after the period of 1989-1991, with China emerging as a strong capitalist state with spectacular economic growth, the fact that the CCP was able to stay unified, while the Soviet Communist Party was split, was crucial.

Deng Xiaoping could keep his party unified because the Chinese revolution was more recent than that in Soviet Union. In China in 1989, the leaders of the revolution were still alive and in command, even if Deng Xiaoping (and to a lesser extent, Chen Yun) were considered as the second generation of leaders within the party.

Although Deng was far less charismatic than Mao Zedong, he was still recognized as the unchallenged leader. His charisma (and also that of Mao to an even greater degree) could be explained by the fact that he embodied the leadership of a great revolution which had substantially improved the lives of workers and peasants, even if more recently that leadership had transformed itself into a conservative bureaucracy. But this was also a revolution which had always exhibited bureaucratic substitutionism and personal dictatorship. This explains why Deng with relative ease could place his opponent Zhao Ziyang under house arrest in 1989, thus ensuring the unity of the party, and then suppress the democracy movement. Gorbachev, by contrast, was no more than a latter-day bureaucrat. Even if he exhibited skills as a politician, he lacked the necessary authority as a charismatic leader to keep the party united behind him.

The moment when Deng repressed the movement signified that the CCP had completely betrayed the revolution and had transformed itself into a political party of capital and of bureaucratic capitalists. However, the combination of the exercise of coercive power with the accumulation of capital has now made the party-state too visible a target for the people, who are increasingly disgruntled. In Mao's era, even though the party-state was very repressive, it nevertheless did deliver job security to the workers. Today it is very obvious that while it continues to repress and exploit the people, the party-state has very little to give to them. It has increasingly lost its legitimacy due to the tremendous number of corruption cases involving the leading circles of the party. This is also why the party has been more and more interested in promoting nationalism, or even xenophobia, in recent years – it is the last political resort it has to divert domestic problems into external ones.

Yet even if this is a very convenient political leverage for the party, it is limited by a situation for which the CCP itself is responsible. Not only is the Cold War long over, but today China, through the choices of its government, is totally integrated into global capitalism as a close economic partner of the USA and the EU, something from which its capitalists have benefited heavily. This allows a relatively narrow space for the CCP to play the card of nationalism and makes a nationalist appeal not at all convincing. Ordinary working people today, are more concerned about their job security, their pension and a future for their children, than the imaginary foreign enemies who are apparently always ready to attack China.

While people should not underestimate the potential rise of nationalism, for the immediate period ahead the party-state and its bureaucratic capitalists will find themselves the main target of all classes. This will increase the chances for a faction fight within the party.

Leading party cadres have always been divided into cliques whose main purpose was to fight for power and influence. Market reform has introduced additional centrifugal forces into the bureaucracy. There has been fierce competition between different regions to attract investment and vie for market share. Since economic benefits are proportional to the coercive power of cadres' position, this fuels even greater power struggle between the cliques. More often it is a zero sum game, and those who lose may end up in jail. Nevertheless, there has been no serious disagreement over the principle of restoring capitalism, or over the strategy of striking an economic alliance with the west. This is because the economy has been growing for the last twenty years, and therefore faction fights within the party have been kept under control and have not developed into serious political divisions. Although there may have been party cadres who are more inclined towards the liberals and others who are closer to the nationalists, there seem to be, as yet, no crystallized political factions within the party.[97]. What can be sure is that Chinese bureaucratic capitalism has begun to enter a bottleneck. With a possible economic crisis and protests becoming more widespread, political divisions may develop over whether, for example, concessions should be made to private capital and/or foreign investors? Should more privatization be promoted? Should China consider maintaining good relations with the west rather than fighting with it for a bigger share of the pie? Should mass protests be heavily repressed, or not? Confronted with different choices, this fifth or sixth generation of leaders will find itself lacking the authority to settle the deep divisions among them; hence the possibility of a split will be greater than was the case in 1989.

With charismatic figures receding into history, their successors have tried to modernize the party by introducing rules within the leadership to avoid never-ending power struggles over succession, something which the People's Republic has not lacked in its history, and which in the end could be detrimental to the bureaucracy as a whole. While Deng was still alive, the party had already dropped the previous practice of allowing top leaders to remain in office until they died, and had imposed an age ceiling and a maximum period of two terms for top office holders. Since Hu Jintao became president, the top leadership has introduced consultative voting among central committee members for the selection of successors to the political bureau.

This kind of reform may enable the party to avoid the worst kind of struggle for succession, but it is still a far cry from democratic elections throughout society that can be seen as fair and legitimate. Hence the present reform to choose the top leaders will not satisfy the powerful princelings who find themselves in a minority, and will not stop those with ambition from challenging the results of this kind of 'restricted consultative democracy'. The struggle over succession will largely be settled by strength, manoeuvring and plotting. Although at the time of writing it is still far from clear, it is widely believed that the fall from power of the former head of Chongqing, Bo Xilai, might be a result of one of these power struggles over succession. This was implicitly confirmed by an article, published on the official website Guangming Wang, attacking Bo for being too ambitious in trying to build up his personal influence and linking this alleged mistake of his to the excesses of personality cult during the cultural revolution. He was however expelled from the party for criminal charges instead – corruption, abusing his power over the murder of British businessman Neil Heywood and having so-called 'improper[98]' sexual relations with several women.[99] With a background of increasing economic problems and a population increasingly more angry over widespread corruption, the inability of the party to introduce a fair way to choose successors acceptable to all, increases the risk of a political crisis at least once every ten years, when the term of politbureau standing committee members expires.

The party has been very successful in modernizing China and through this has enriched its cadres, but precisely because of this it has changed the conditions which brought it to power. Today, China has been modernized to the point where the working class comprises more than two-fifths of the working population, and it is a more and more disgruntled class. The bureaucracy has been so successful in satisfying its greed that it has depleted natural resources and the ecological balance is at breaking point. From a Maoist revolutionary party it has evolved into an entity which is a curse for the environment and for the people. By fulfilling the dual role of political repression and capital accumulation, it will make itself the main target of popular anger.

The struggle from below will inevitably grow in the next period, and this fact pressurizes the party-state to shed the worst features of bureaucratic capitalism. The degree to which bureaucratic capitalism evolves into common authoritarian capitalism or even into liberal democracy will be decided by the revolt from below. The renaissance of a socialist labour movement may be able to reap even bigger fruit, although for the moment I have no clue as to how close this is. There is nevertheless one thing that is certain: a new period of crisis of bureaucratic capitalism has opened up, and the party-state will find itself more and more challenged by all the other classes, with the working class posing the biggest potential threat. Eventually history may prove that the vision of certain pro-government writers, who think that the CCP's absolutist regime is comparable to the great Han and Tang dynasties which lasted two or three hundred years, is too much of a fantasy.

For twenty years since the defeat of the 1989 movement and the onset of full scale restoration, the Chinese toiling masses and intellectuals have experienced deep demoralization and de-politicization rarely seen in contemporary Chinese history. This period may come to an end in a not too distant future, given all the contradictions accumulated and what the people have learned. It is time to remind ourselves of the remark made by Marx in days of the great political downturn in 1863, that 'these may be again succeeded by days into which 20 years are compressed.'[100] You should not exclude the possibility that in an economic and political crisis, the party-state may find itself split or that events spin out of its control, triggering a revolutionary situation as almost happened in 1989.

With a despotic state in its hands, the Chinese bureaucracy is more than capable of containing the economic cycle, but its largely medieval social and political thinking means that it lacks the flexibility to deal with a political crisis and a people in revolt, and this means it may exacerbate the crisis rather than contain it. But even if in the future a revolutionary situation begins to emerge it does not necessarily imply a revolution will actually take place, let alone its succeed. This requires long-term education and organizing among the masses, but in a situation such as in China where civil liberties do not exist, this is particularly hard. However, a political crisis is inevitable in the medium term, and this will give the people an opportunity to find ways to organise against the despotic state. How far they can go is still unknown, given the effect of decades of atomization. Yet the struggle now is in front of us, not behind us.

In the final analysis, the historic role of the bureaucracy acting as a substitute for a bourgeois class in modernizing the country is a contradiction in itself: it was both the result of backwardness and also its embodiment. Hence with every two steps forward it made towards modernization, it was also pulling the country back one step. It pretended to be omnipotent but in fact it was so backward in culture that it necessarily made a plethora of mistakes. The Chinese bureaucracy was particularly backward: in 1978 only 6 per cent of those who occupied positions of responsibility in the party and state organs had college-level training.[101] Today, although many leading cadres may have masters or even doctorates degree, very often these qualifications are bought with cash. The omnipotent bureaucracy has, once again, proved to be impotent in modernizing the country without making the people and the environment suffer. If it ever had any historic usefulness, it has long exhausted this. From a socialist point of view, it is time to reassert the idea of socialism as a fully developed democracy, which does away with the bureaucracy by creating the conditions for the state to wither away altogether.

This date of reckoning may not be close. The new generation of workers and peasants still has much to learn in its fight for justice. Moreover, with socialism discredited, today few intellectuals are willing to fight for it. Those that still adhere to these principles may have to be patient in preparing for a renaissance of socialist ideas and the rebirth of mass movements.

October 2012.

Notes

1 *The Beijing Consensus, How China's Authoritarian Model will Dominate the Twenty First Century?* Stefan Halper, Chapter two, Chinese translation, Basic Books, Taiwan, 2010. The original idea of the 'Beijing Consensus' was raised by Joshua Cooper Ramo, but when he wrote his book in 2004, *The Beijing Consensus,* he did not mean to present it as a challenge to the Washington Consensus. His idea of 'Beijing Consensus' continues to be disputed by other scholars. See, for instance, Ding Xueliang's *The Chinese Model, For and Against,* Chinese edition, Oxford, Hong Kong, 2011.

2 Ibid.

3 *The Economist,* January 21, 2012.

4 Most notably by Tony Cliff of the British Socialist Workers' Party. *State Capitalism in Russia* was first written in 1947.

5 In 1976 state-owned enterprises accounted for 12 or 13 per cent for Britain, France and Germany respectively; Italy has a much higher proportion, reaching 24 per cent the same year. *Guoyou jingji buju,* State-owned Economy, by Chen Hong, China Economic Publishing House, 2012, Beijing, p. 85.

6 *The Deng Xiaoping Era – An Inquiry into the Fate of Chinese Socialism 1978-1994,* Maurice Meisner, Hill and Wang, 1996, chapter eleven, p. 300.

7 'Most have been staffed by government officials, have had their offices in government buildings, and have been financed out of the government coffers.' *Transnational Political Alliances: An Exploration With Evidence from China,* Scott Kennedy, p.184, http://bas.sagepub.com/cgi/content/abstract/46/2/174

8 *Adam Smith in Beijing* Giovanni Arrighi Verso, 2007, p. 332 and 369.

9 The speech was suppressed but was eventually reported in Hong Kong by the former chief of General Administration of Press and Publication, Dao Daozheng. See *Ming Pao Daily,* October 14, 2008.

10 *Critique of Hegel's Philosophy of Right,* quoted from Hal Draper, p. 81. See also http://www.marxists.org/archive/marx/works/1843/critique-hpr/

11 In 2002 the state sector as a share of GDP dropped to 2.5, 9 and 8.3 per cent in Britain, Italy and Germany respectively. France's figure stood at 12.8 percent, more or less the same as the 1970's figure. *Guoyou jingji buju* (State-owned Economy), by Chen Hong, China Economic Publishing House, 2012, Beijing, p. 85.

12 Friedrich Engels Origin of the Family, Private Property and the State , http://www.marxists.org/archive/marx/works/1884/origin-family/ch09.htm

13 Pytor Struve January 26, 1870, – February 22, 1944. Struve was initially a legal Marxist but after the Russian revolution became a White.

14 In 1991, under the initiative of various princelings, a meeting was held to discuss a document called *Sulian jubian zhihou zhongguo de xianshi yingdui yu zhanlue xuanze* (The Aftermath of the Dramatic Changes of the Soviet Union and the Realistic Response of China and its Strategic Choice). The main idea was to call for state property to be handed over to the Communist Party to fend off challenges to the party-state. It was not accepted by Deng Xiaoping, who probably saw it as too risky. Keeping SOEs in the hands of the state in name only, while continuing to allow the party to have full control of them, is obviously a better choice for the bureaucracy. See: *The Party: The Secret World of China's Communist Rulers,* by Richard McGregor, Penguin, 2010, Chapter one.

15 There is a small circle of nationalist or "new leftist" economists including Han Deqiang, Yangfan, Zuo Dapei, He Xin etc who have vigorously opposed privatization and defended both the state-owned economy and the one party dictatorship. See, for instance, *Buxu Zaimai* (No More Privatization) by Zuo Dapei, China Financial and Economic Publishing House, Beijing, 2006.

16 The son of Bo Yibo, one of the Eight Elders of the CCP, Bo Xilai was considered as a 'princeling' in China. Between 2007 and 2012 he served as a member of the Politiburo and secretary of the Chongqing branch of the CCP. He was once considered as a possible candidate for the highest governing body of the party, the Politburo Standing Committee, in the coming CCP's 18th Congress in 2012.

His political life ended when his former close ally Wang Lijun sought asylum at the American consulate when the latter felt his life threatened because of his knowledge about a homicide apparently committed by Bo's wife, Gu Kailai. Gu was convicted and sentenced to a suspended death sentence in August 2012. On 28 September 2012, Bo Xilai was expelled from party positions and handed over to the authorities for criminal investigations

17 *Meiti pinglun cheng Chongqing Baoan Jituan shi haogongsi, shangshihou jiangcheng zuiniu gupiao* (Media Comments that the Chongqing Security Group is a Good Company and will become the most popular stock upon listing), http://big5.xinhuanet.com/gate/big5/news.xinhuanet.com/fortune/2012-05/15/c_123129977.htm

18 *Ming Pao Daily*, 20 April , 2012.

19 For more details about the bureaucrats enrich themselves through setting up companies, please refer to *Zhongguo de xianjing* (The Pitfalls of Modernization), He Qinglian, Mirror Books, 1997.

20 For instance, there have been concerns about the whereabouts of the 20 billion Yuan of fines levied every year on expectant mothers for so-called 'illegal' pregnancies. It is widely assumed that the monies are simply being distributed to the officials. *Ming Pao Daily*, 14 June , 2012.

21 *China internal security spending jumps past army budget*, http://www.reuters.com/article/2011/03/05/us-china-unrest-idUSTRE7222RA20110305. The recent case of Chen Guangcheng may be telling. He is a civil rights activist and made his name in April 2012 when he escaped from his heavily guarded home and fled to the US embassy in Beijing. It was reported that local government spent 60 million yuan a year to monitor him. He was under round the clock surveillance by more than one hundred guards. These guards were officially paid 100 Yuan daily, yet they actually only got 90 yuan, with the 10 yuan being pocketed by their superiors. *Weiwen Chen Guangcheng, Shandong nianhua 6000 wan renbi* (To Put Chen Guangcheng Under Surveillance Shandong Provincial Government Spent 60 Million Yuan Annually) http://news.singtao.ca/toronto/2012-05-01/headline1335861094d3839957.html

22 *The Chinese model, for and against*, by Ding Xueliang, Chinese edition, Oxford University, Hong Kong, 2011, p. 86-7.

23 *The Deng Xiaoping Era: An Inquiry into the Fate of Chinese Socialism 1978-1994*, Hill and Wang, New York, 1996, p. 173-4.

24 The real number of civil servants remains a mystery. The official figure puts it at 10 million but this is widely considered a serious under-estimate. One must also take into account those informal public employees like public order team members and who are not accounted for in official statistics of civil servants. For the source of the figure of 50 million seehttp://big5.xinhuanet.com/gate/big5/news.xinhuanet.com/employment/2006-02/21/content_4206038.htm For the 70 million figure and a comparison with the US please refer to the following article: *Zhuanjia huyu yanking gongwuyuan enshu, lifa yazhi pengzhang* (Scholar Appeal to Strictly Control the Numbers of Civil Servants and to Legislate to Stop its Ballooning), http://news.xinhuanet.com/employment/2005-06/14/content_3082359.htm

25 *The Chinese model, for and against*, by Ding Xueliang, Chinese edition, Oxford University, Hong Kong, 2011, p. 89.

26 Marx, 'Critique of Hegel's Doctrine of State' http://www.marxists.org/archive/marx/works/1843/critique-hpr/

27 *Guanyu yanjin dangzheng jiguan he dangzheng ganbu jingshang banqiye de jueding* (The Decision on Strictly Banning Party/ Government Apparatus and Party/ Government Cadres to Conduct Commercial Activities and Founding Companies). http://news.xinhuanet.com/ziliao/2003-01/18/content_695462.htm

28 *Zhongguo de qiji: fazhan zhanlue yu jingji gaige* (The China Miracle: Developmental Strategy and Economic Reform), Lin Yifu, Caifang, Li zhou, Chinese University Press, 1995, Hong Kong, P. 53.

29 *The Chinese model, for and against*, by Ding Xueliang, Chinese edition, Oxford University, Hong Kong, 2011, p. 89. Since official statistics are not reliable, there has been debate about the actual share of state-owned enterprises in gross industrial production. Pro-government scholars like Chen Hong put the figure as low as 26.6 per cent, (see *Guoyou jingji buju*, or *The Distribution of State Run Economy*, China Economic Press, 2010, p. 5.) On the other hand, the report by Szamosszegi and Kyle in 2011 and presented to the US – China Economic and Security Review Commission considers that the state sector may be as much as 40-50 per cent .

30 Hu Angang, one of the Chinese economists who in mid-1990s sounded the alarm of a drastic decline in fiscal income in relation to GNP, seeing this as one of the dangers which might make China disintegrate. According to him, China's fiscal income (excluding income from loans) as a share of GNP dropped from 31.2 per cent in 1978 to 14.7 percent in 1992. *Tiaozhan Zhongguo* (The Challenges of China), Hu Angang, Xin xinwen Cultural Holding Limited Company, 1995, Taiwan. P. 71.

31 This does not include the collectively owned enterprises, which witnessed drastic drop in absolute terms until it become negligible. *Guoyou jingji buju* (State-owned Economy), by Chen Hong, China Economic Publishing House, 2012, Beijing, p. 146.

32 In 2006 the State Council forwarded a document by the State-owned Assets Supervision and Administration Commission, *The guiding opinion on promoting the adjustment of the state-owned capital and the reorganization of state-owned enterprises.* The document emphasized the need to maintain control over important branches of industries. http://www.gov.cn/gongbao/content/2007/content_503385.htm

33 A recent example was the agreement between Wuyi University in Guangdong and China Unicom, which stipulated that the latter enjoys the exclusive right to provide internet services, and that students are required to pay 100 yuan of installation fee. This resulted in students' protests in May 2012. *Ming Pao*, 8 May , 2012.

34 'The national fiscal revenue, including central and local government, has now reached 23 per cent of GDP. If one includes all other revenues outside of the budget or the system, China's macro government's tax revenue can reach 35

per cent, which is close to that of developed countries while much higher than many developing countries.' Liao Qun, *Hong Kong Economic Journal*, 4 April, 2012.

35 A WHO report says that 25.7 per cent of all deliveries worldwide were done by caesarean section, ranging from 2.3 per cent in Angolan facilities and 46.2 per cent in Chinese facilities. *Caesarean section without medical indication increases risk of short term adverse outcomes for mothers*, http://whqlibdoc.who.int/hq/2010/WHO_RHR_HRP_10.20_eng.pdf .China's unusually high caesarean section rate is chiefly because it is profitable for hospitals, hence doctors are more inclined to pursue patients to deliver their children by caesarean section. See *Wucheng yunfu poufuchan guanjue quanqiu* (Half of all Pregnant Women Deliver Their Children by Caesarean Section Which Rank Top Globally) *Ming Pao Daily*, May 19, 2012.

36 *A Brief History of Neoliberalism*, David Harvey, Oxford University Press, 2007 chapter five, p. 120.

37 In 1996 the World Bank released two reports, *Bureaucrats in Business* and *From Plan to Market*, which argues that the Chinese economy depends on the private sector rather than the state sector as the latter is low in efficiency .Quoted from *Transforming China, Globalization, Transformation and Development*, Peter Nolan, Anthem Press, London, 2004, P. 132.

38 *China 2020: China Development Challenges in the New Century*, World Bank, Washington, 1997, http://www-wds.worldbank.org/external/default/WDSContentServer/WDSP/IB/1997/09/01/000009265_3980625172933/Rendered/PDF/multi0page.pdf

39 *China 2030:Building a Modern, Harmonious, and Creative High-Income Society*, World Bank, Washington, 2012. http://www-wds.worldbank.org/external/default/WDSContentServer/WDSP/IB/2012/02/28/000356161_20120228001303/Rendered/PDF/671790WP0P127500China020300complete.pdf

40 *Made in China*, by Kuroda Atsuo, Toyo Keizai Inc, Tokyo, 2001. Chinese edition, chapter three to six, 2002, Taiwan.

41 *Zhongguo zhizaoye fazhan yanjiu baogao 2011* (Research Report on the Development of China's Manufacturing Industry 2011), edited by Li Lianshui, Science Press, p. 210.

42 *China Statistical Yearbook 2010*, China Statistical Press, Beijing, 2010, p. 757.

43 *China Statistical Yearbook* 2008, China Statistical Press, Beijing, 2008, p. 783.

44 *Higashi Asia Kokusai Bungyo To Chugoku* (The Competition and Cooperation between Chinese Manufacturing and its Asian Counterparts), edited by Kimura Fukunari, Maruya Toyojiro and Ishhikawa Koichi, 2002, Tokyo. Chinese edition, 2004, Taipei, p.121.

45 In 2010 Oxfam in Hong Kong was attacked by the Ministry of Education as 'an organisation that has been trying hard to infiltrate mainland China', *Oxfam Hong Kong Halts Mainland Training after 'Warning' from Authority,* South China Morning Post, 24 Feb , 2010. Ten years ago western companies investigating their suppliers in China was seen by the authorities as potentially dangerous and had to be put under close surveillance. Personal interviews.

46 *China Economy Quarterly Update*, Feb 2007, World Bank Beijing Office, p.6.

47 According to a report on internships in the electronics industry by the Research Group on the New Generation of Rural Migrant Workers, these vocational schools collude with local governments to force the students to work in factories like Foxconn. For the full report (in Chinese) see http://www.donews.com/it/201205/1216232.html See also the news report concerning the Chengdu municipal government which promised to guarantee Foxconn a supply of 10,000 workers if the latter agreed to invest there. The government then forced low ranking civil servants work in Foxconn factories whenever it was short of hands. See *Ming Pao Daily*, 29 April , 2012.

48 For more about the household registration system, please refer to chapter seven, *Disposable Labour under Social Apartheid.*

49 *Reviving the developmental state? The myth of the 'national bourgeoisie'*, Vivek Chibber, *Socialist Register* 2005, Merlin Press.

50 *The Dragon and the Elephant*, David Smith, Chinese edition, Contemporary China Press, Beijing, 2007, p. 59.

51 *China Statistical Yearbook* 1981, Economic and Information Agency, Hong Kong, p. 89. Despite the spectacular growth of industrialization, this has only resulted in a small decline in the rural population: from 89.4 per cent of the population it dropped to 87.5 per cent, a mere 2 per cent decline in 30 years. This is because China's starting point in its modernization was far too low in the first place.

52 In 1919 there were around 3 million industrial workers . *Zhongguo jindaishi* (Modern History of China), Lin Zengping, Hunan People's Press, Hunan, 1979, p. 813.

53 For a comparison of social achievement in Mao's era with other countries, see Mingqi Li's book *The rise of China and the demise of the capitalist world economy*, Chapter two, Pluto Press, 2008.

54 In 1980, the GNP per capita was US$290 and 240 for China and India respectively; in 1998 it was 750 and 430 respectively. *Zhongguo xiandaihua baogao 2001*(Report on the Modernization of China 2001), Beijing University Press, 2001, p. 99.

55 Quoted from *Industrial Growth in China and India, A Preliminary Comparison,* by R Nagaraj, *Economic and Political Weekly,* May 21, 2005, Mumbai, India

56 In addition to this is the fact that during the 1980s many Hong Kong Chinese businessmen, especially those who were either from the pro-Beijing camp or were opportunists, or both, enthusiastically acted as 'teachers' in helping Chinese government officials to learn commercial skills. Among the ranks there was the 2012 newly elected Chief Executive of Hong Kong, Leung Chun Ying, who taught party cadres all the tricks of the property market.

57 A well known capital flight case recently was Gu Kailai, wife of Chongqing former chief Bo Xilai, who was reported to have moved 6 billion US dollars out of China. *Ming Pao Daily*, June 23, 2012.

58 This makes the Chinese model very different from South Korea; because during its take off period South Korea hardly relied on FDI.

59 *China became world's top manufacturing nation, ending 110-year US leadership*, http://en.mercopress.com/2011/03/15/china-became-world-s-top-

manufacturing-nation-ending-110-year-us-leadership

60 See, for instance, *The The Post MFA era and the rise of China*, Au Loong Yu, 2005, http://www.asienhaus.de/public/archiv/post-mfa-era-china.pdf

61 see footnote 16.

62 For 2002 figure, see *Waishang zhijie touzi yu zhongguo waimao xiaoyi yanjiu* (Research on Foreign Direct Investment and the Efficiency of China's Foreign Trade), edited by Zhou Zehong, Shanghai Jiaotong University Press, 2008, p. 137. 2009 figure is calculated from China Statistical Yearbook 2010, China Statistical Press, Beijing, 2010, p. 507.

63 *Guoyou jingji buju* (State-owned Economy), Chen Hong, China Economic Publishing House, 2012, p. 7.

64 *Dui waizi zai zhongguo gongye hangye fenbu xianzhuang de chubu kaocha* (A Preliminary Study on the Situation of Foreign Capital among Chinese Industries), Xu Zhaoyuan and Chen Xiaohong, Development Study, Issue 2, 2010. This paper can be download from: http://wenku.baidu.com/view/a9424a573c1ec5da50e2704c.html?rl=regok

65 http://www.fdi.gov.cn/pub/FDI_EN/Laws/law_en_info.jsp?docid=87372

66 *Complicity, Campaigns, Collaboration, and Corruption: Strategies and Responses to European Corporations and Lobbyists in China*, Globalization Monitor, Section IV, 2010, Hong Kong.

67 He then added that "because of the nature of the means he employed, much of the barbarism thrown out of Russian life has crept back into it.", *Stalin*, Isaac Deustcher, Second Edition, Oxford, 1966, p.568.

68 *China Labour Statistical Yearbook 2009*, China Statistics Press, Beijing, 2009, p. 2.

69 *Chinese Statistical Yearbook*, China Statistics Press, Beijing, 1998 and 2009.

70 'The Rise of the Working Class and the Future of the Chinese Revolution', Mingqi Li, *Monthly Review*, June 2011, p.42.

71 The Tiananmen Incident took place on April 5, 1976 at Tiananmen Square in Beijing, China. The incident occurred on the traditional day of mourning, and was triggered by the death of Premier Zhou Enlai earlier that year. Some people strongly disapproved of the removal of the displays of mourning, and began gathering in the square to protest against the central authorities, then largely under the auspices of the Gang of Four, who ordered the square to be cleared.

The event was labeled as counterrevolutionary immediately after its occurrence by the Communist Party's Central Committee and served as a gateway to the dismissal and house arrest of then-Vice Premier Deng Xiaoping who was accused of planning the event. The Central Committee's decision on the event was reversed after Deng came to power in 1978, as it would later be officially hailed as a display of patriotism.

72 For more about the Tonghua Steel workers' struggle, see chapter nine, *New Signs of Hope: Resistance in China Today.*

73 There is no law in China which prohibits strikes, although the government can always prosecute strikers using other laws.

74 For more about the Honda Foshan workers' struggle, see chapter nine, *New*

Signs of Hope: Resistance in China Today.

75 Ibid.

76 Ibid, the section on environmental struggles.

77 *Zhu Mingguo tan Wukan* (Zhu Mingguo Spoke about Wukan Case), http://china.huanqiu.com/roll/2011-12/2302922.html

78 'The communist regime, for its own legitimacy and survival, may be compelled to crack down on corruption and impose serious judicial and legal reform. We cannot underestimate the determination and effectiveness of the Chinese regime's self-reform to establish a law based government'. *Against the Law – Labor Protests in China's Rustbelt and Sunbelt,* Ching Kwan Lee, University of California Press, 2007, p. 242.

79 In contrast, under Mao the working class was complimented as *laodage*, or the Eldest Brother, implying their so called 'leading class' status.

80 For more please refer to chapter nine, *New signs of hope: resistance in China today*.

81 'Today China needs US$5.40 of extra investment to produce an extra $1 of output, a proportion vastly higher than that in developed economies.' *The Writing on the Wall*, Will Hutton, Free Press, P. 153.

82 China Institute of Water Resources and Hydropower Research (IWHR), 2004. *Research on the Coordinated Development of Hydropower and National Economy.* Quoted from *China's Water Crisis and the Privatization of Urban Water in Kunming*, Globalization Monitor, 2011, p. 7.

83 *Waishang zhijie touzi yu zhongguo waimao xiaoyi yanjiu* (Research on Foreign Direct Investment and the Efficiency of China's Foreign Trade), edited by Zhou Zehong, Shanghai Jiaotong University Press, 2008, p. 48

84 *The Rise of China and the Demise of the Capitalist World Economy*, Mingqi Li, Pluto Press, p. 87-8.

85 *The Chinese model, for and against*, by Ding Xueliang, Chinese edition, Oxford University, Hong Kong, 2011, p. 197.

86 Editorial of *Hong Kong Economic Journal*, 16 June, 2011.

87 *Lenders face NPL spike*, E J Insight, Hong Kong Economic Journal, 29 June, 2011.

88 *Neidi defang zhengfu zhaiwu sige banben nage kekao?* (Four Different Statistics for Mainland's Local Governments' Debt, Which One is More Reliable?), Liao Qun, *Hong Kong Economic Journal*, 21 July , 2011.

89 In 2011 when the first draft of an amendment bill to the Law on Budget was first tabled it contained a clause which allowed all local governments to issue their own bonds. In the second draft tabled in June 2012, the clause was deleted. This has no bearing on the previous decision allowing the four provinces/cities to issue bonds however. *Zhongyang jinzhi difangzhengfu zixing juzhai* (Central Government Ban Local Governments Issuing Their Own Bonds), *Hong Kong Economic Journal*, 27 June, 2012.

90 http://www.chinavista.com/business/ciec/ch/chciec19981013.html#cn00006

91 For the source of these figures please refer to chapter two,

China going global.

92 *Protecting Workers' Rights or Serving the Party: The way forward for China's trade unions,* China Labour Bulletin, http://www.clb.org.hk/en/files/share/File/research_reports/acftu_report.pdf

93 A well-known Hong Kong commentator and a former supporter of the Chinese democracy movement, Chen Yun, recently published a book *Chengbang lun* (On City State, Enrich Publishing Ltd, Hong Kong. 2011) claiming that mainland people necessarily 'believe in totalitarian government', and concluded that Hong Kong people should forget about Chinese democracy altogether.

94 This is argued by Sun Long Gang in his well known book *Zhongguo wenhua de shenceng jiegou* (The Inner Structure of Chinese Culture), Tangshan Press, Taipei, new edition, 1993.

95 *Revolution Betrayed* Pathfinder Press, 1974, Chapter 9, pp. 253-4.

96 'China and Socialism, Market Reforms and Class Struggle'. *Monthly Review,* July – August, 2004.

97 It was said that the 'Chongqing model' under Bo Xilai and the 'Guangdong model' under Wang Yang represented, respectively, a nationalist / 'leftist' wing and the liberal wing of the party. For the moment it is very hard to judge whether the Chongqing model was invented only for the sake of advancing Bo's personal ambition, or that the division between the two "models" has been fully developed to the extent that they have real bases among the party.

98 Any sexual relationships outside marriage are deemed 'improper' in Chinese law.

99 *Bo Xilai xiachang zaizheng wenge moshi shi yitiao silu* (The Downfall of Bo Xilai once again Proves that the Model of Cultural Revolution is a Dead End), http://view.gmw.cn/2012-09/29/content_5243033.htm

100 Marx's letter to Engels 9April , 1863. http://www.marxists.org/archive/marx/works/1863/letters/63_04_09.htm

101 Meisner, p. 177.

CHINA GOING GLOBAL[1]

Au Loong Yu

Since the turn of the century China had already become a significant player of out-flowing Foreign Direct Investment (FDI), Foreign Portfolio Investment (FPI), and an international world lender. This is against the background of China's proclamation of seeking a 'peaceful rise'. It follows more than 20 years of huge FDI inflows, which for many years was second only to the USA and then for three consecutive years, from the beginning of 2002, surpassed it.

For some years the thinktanks of the Chinese government saw the relationship between *Yinjinlai*, literally meaning 'inviting in' (inflowing FDI), and *Zouchuqu*, or 'going global' (out-flowing FDI), as supplementary to its programme of modernization.[2] Another professor from the thinktank further elaborates the relations between going global and the WTO:

> Now that China has become a WTO member state, we on the one hand need to fulfil our domestic obligations while on the other we can also enjoy the privilege of national treatment (under WTO terms) afforded to Chinese enterprises when they enter the markets of WTO member states.[3]

I: The scale of China's outflowing FDI

According to official figures, throughout the 1980s, the average annual FDI outflow was only US$1 billion.[4] In the 1990s growth was relatively stable. In 2002, China's out-flowing FDI only amounted to US$ 2.85 billion, ranking 22nd in the world. This is much smaller than Hong Kong, whose out-flowing FDI amounted to US$17.69 billion. China's figure has experienced leaps and bounds since then; reaching US$56 billion in 2008 and ranking sixth, up from thirteen in 2006, according to the Chinese official figures.[5] (See Figure 1) It lags behind several developed countries but is top amongst developing nations. (See Figure 2)

Figure 1: China Outward FDI, 1990-2008

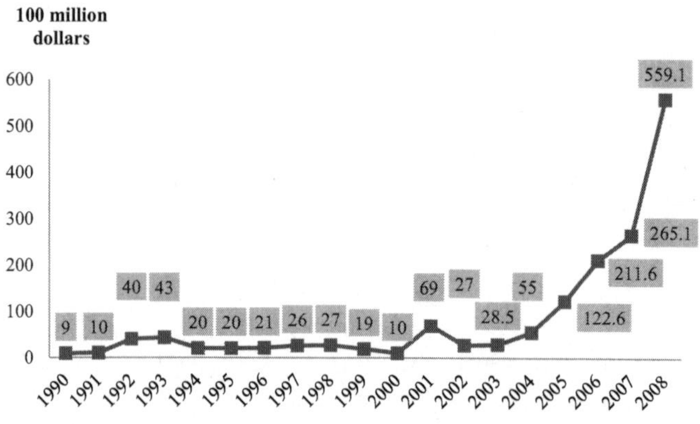

Source: 2008 Statistical Bulletin of China's Outward FDI.

In terms of stock, China's outward FDI was negligible in 1990. It then began to escalate and reached US $46.3 billion by 2005 according to the World Investment Report 2006. This is higher than the outward FDI of South Africa (US $38.5 billion) and Korea (US $36.4 billion), and significantly surpasses India, although it still remains behind Brazil.[6] Since then China's outward FDI by stock has risen rapidly (Figure 3 – note that the Chinese official figure for 2006 is higher than that reported in the World Investment Report).

In per capita terms, however, China's outward FDI is still very low. In 2005 it was only US $35 in contrast to the much higher South African figure of US $812 and the South Korean figure of US $763. This mirrors the same discrepancy in GDP terms. China's GDP is ranked fourth in the world in 2006, but in per capita terms it is ranked beyond 100, reflecting both its strength and weakness – one of the deep contradictions of China.[7]

The policy of going global resulted in the rapid growth of Chinese transnational corporations (TNCs). In 1995 there were only two Chinese TNCs listed in the Fortune 500. In 2007 this rose to 22.

Meanwhile, in 2006-8 China became the second most important foreign investor in developing countries of Africa (see figure 4 below). China's investment in Africa has been quite controversial both among governments and social movements.

Are the statistics reliable?

It is difficult, however, to make a precise evaluation of China's out-flowing FDI because of discrepancies in statistics. In the past, statistics on outward

Figure 2: Global FDI outflows, top 20 home economies, 2008–2009a

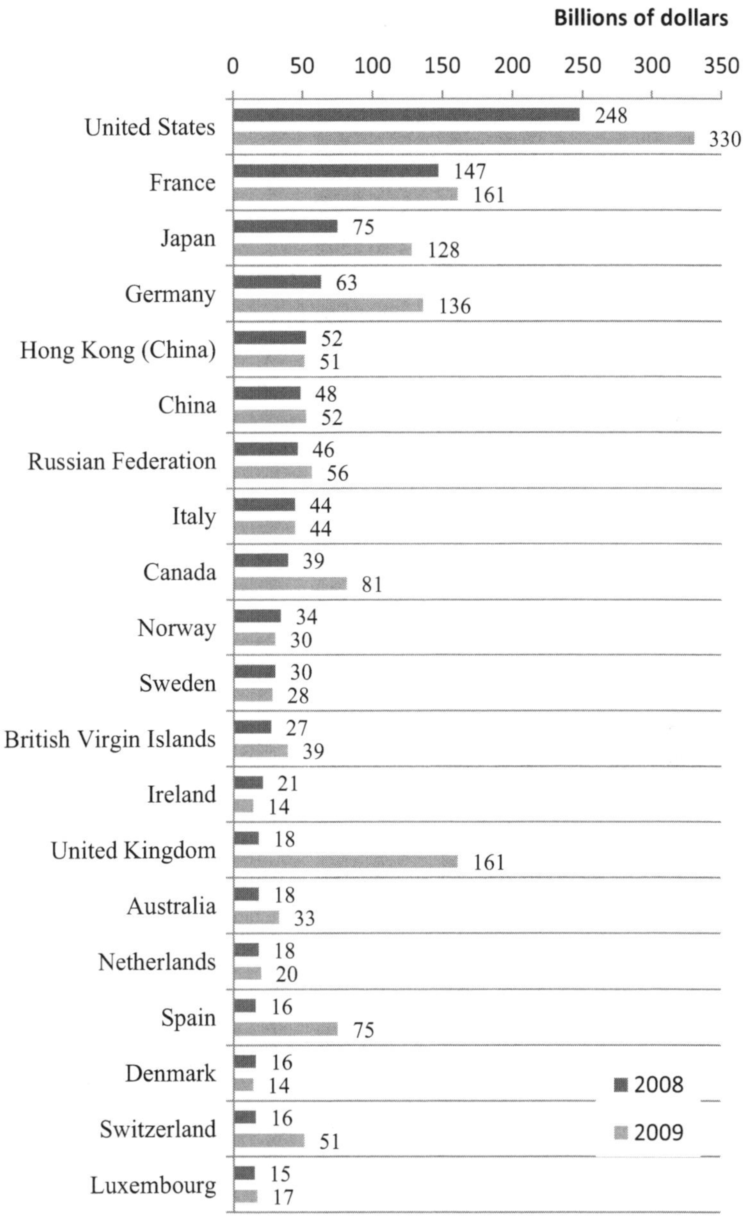

Source: World Investment Report, UNCTAD, 2010

Figure 3: China Outward FDI by Stock, 2002-2008

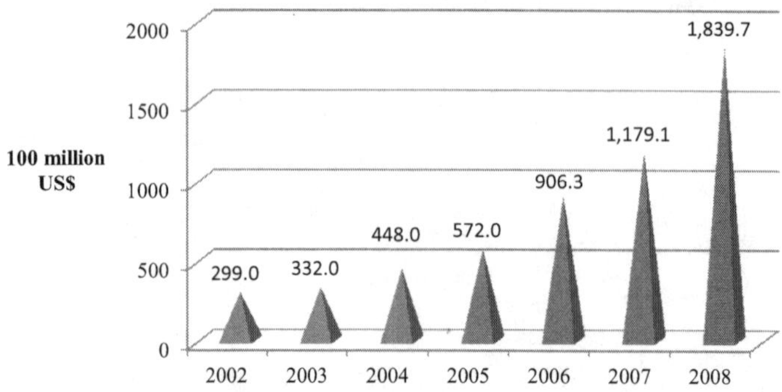

Source: 2008 Statistical Bulletin of China's Outward Foreign Direct Investment, p. 9. (note that the figures given here for the year 2004 and 2005 is slightly different from the World Investment Report by UNCTAD)

Figure 4: Major Developing Economy Investors in Africa 2006-8

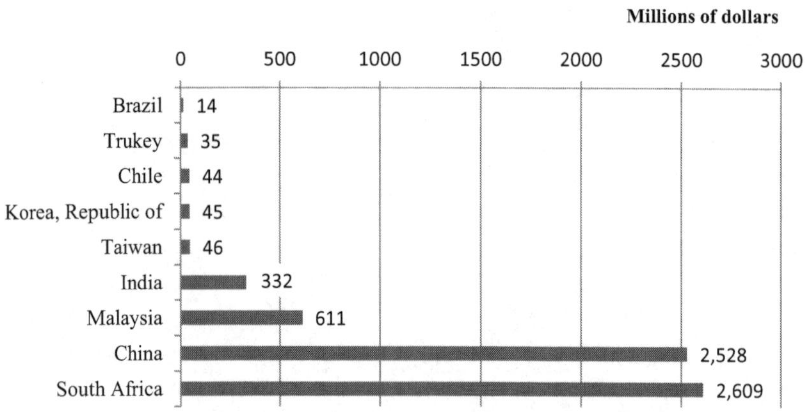

Source: World Investment Report 2010, UNCTAD

FDI were more or less considered to be a state secret. One could only make rough estimates by referring to the balance of payments statistics. Things only began to change in recent years when some of the statistics were released, although they were still incomplete.

The Singapore scholar Friedrich Wu remarked that 'China's Ministry of Commerce has consistently reported significantly lower outward FDI value figures in comparison to UN Conference on Trade and Development (UNCTAD) statistics, which adopt the more inclusive data based on the balance of payments statistics from the People's Bank of China. By failing to include the amounts invested abroad by firms using earnings from exports or loans raised in international capital markets for instance, the Ministry of Commerce has grossly underestimated the total value of China's outward FDI.'[8] The Chinese official figures for outward FDI were quite different from UNCTAD's figures, as table 1 below shows.

In December 2006, the Ministry of Commerce, the Administration of Foreign Exchange, and the National Bureau of Statistics, jointly published the first report on China's out-flowing FDI, taking collective responsibility for the issue.[9]

Table 1: China's Outward FDI according to two Different Sources

	2002	2003	2004	2005
UNCTAD figures	2,518	-152	1,805	11,306
China official's figure	2,700	2,850	5,500	12,260

Instead of clarifying the ambiguity around China's outward FDI, however, the report raises further questions. Figure 5 below compares China's official figures for out-flowing FDI to the world with the Hong Kong official figure for China's out-flowing FDI to Hong Kong alone. It is common sense that the former figure must be bigger than the latter, or, in the extreme case, equal to the latter – which would mean that China had

Figure 5: China's outflow FDI to the world and to HK (million of dollars)

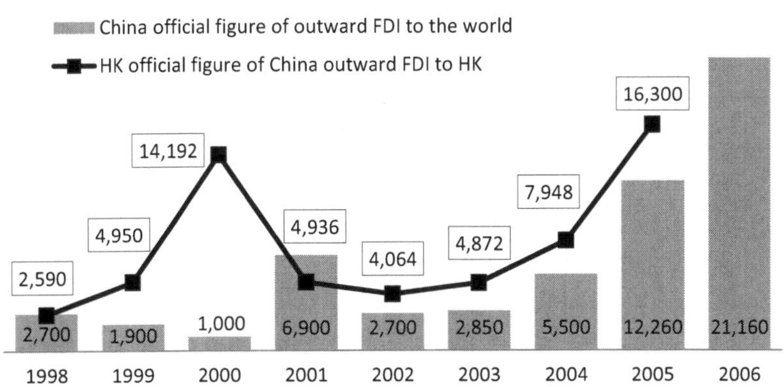

Source: 2006 Statistical Bulletin of China's Outward FDI and HK Annual Digest of Statistics, 2005 & 2006.

only invested in Hong Kong and nowhere else in the world. However, in the seven year period of 1998-2004, there were five years when Hong Kong recorded much more FDI outflow to Hong Kong than China did to the whole world. Then in 2000 Hong Kong experienced an inflowing FDI from China amounting to 14 times the amount of China's out-flowing FDI to the world. This is nonsensical. Could the Hong Kong figures all be wrong? In fact I am more confident in Hong Kong's figures as there is no known record of that government forging figures.

The obvious reason for the underestimation of China's overseas investment is that there has been serious capital flight. Yang Haizhen, the assistant professor at the Graduate University of the Chinese Academy of Science in China, wrote a book on the subject of capital flight, in which he stated that:

> In the transition from a planned economy to a socialist market economy, China has encountered the typical problem of corruption among transitional economies, which result in huge state assets being drained. Money ends up in the hands of the privileged (management of SOEs, or State-Owned Enterprises, and government officials etc.), and when they have accumulated great amounts of illegal assets they see moving it abroad as a way to legalize it.
>
> In 1982-85, there was almost no capital flight. In the period 1985-88, there was some capital flight, which was quite stable and not significant. It was around US$ 3-4 billion annually. In 1989-91 there began a big increase in both the amount and growth rate of capital flight, with an annual growth rate of 65 per cent. In 1991 the amount of capital flight reached US$ 22.6 billion. Between 1992 and 1994, the growth rate of capital flight slowed down, to an annual amount of US $27 billion. Beginning in 1995, capital flight entered a new period of rapid growth, and in 2000 it reached its peak, namely US$ 106 billion, which is equal to 518 per cent of the inflowing foreign capital from the same year, or 646 per cent of foreign debt. We can say that much of the capital inflow in 2000 was turned into outflow by means of capital flight.[10]

Yang tells us that capital flight may be carried out through 'trade mis-invoicing', which means either the under-invoicing of exports or the over-invoicing of imports. These techniques enable firms to keep overseas revenue which is supposed to flow back to the home country abroad.[11]

Another reason for the huge import discrepancy, which Yang did not cover, is smuggling. It is common knowledge in Hong Kong that there has always been serious smuggling between Hong Kong and mainland China, hence the imports to China, as recorded by its trading partners, tend to be dramatically greater than those recorded by China.[12] The revenues from smuggling often end up in money laundering operations in Hong Kong and Macau and then become clean money for overseas investment.

What makes China's figures on inflowing and out-flowing FDI problematic is also the phenomenon of round-tripping of investments. This refers to Chinese capital that first goes to Hong Kong and then re-enters China in the form of FDI so as to enjoy preferential treatment provided to foreign capital in China. According to UNCTAD's World Investment Report in 2006, in the case of inward FDI in China, round-tripped inflowing FDI is estimated from 25 per cent to about 50 per cent.[13] This has a significant meaning for out-flowing FDI, because this fake 'foreign' capital, after making a profit in China, can officially, or unofficially, be repatriated to overseas 'mother' companies. It also makes the official figures for both inward and outward FDI look incredible.

II: The three phases of China going global

There are mainly five types of Chinese TNCs (Transnational Companies):

1. Trading companies.
2. Manufacturing enterprises.
3. Oil and mining companies.
4. Financial institutions.
5. Construction companies.

Generally the development of these five types of company is related to the different phases of the going global strategy. In the earlier period overseas investment was chiefly trade. One source reported that trade made up as much as 60 per cent of all overseas investment.[14] A typical Chinese trading company, for example, was the China National Textiles Import and Export Corporation. In the later period China's overseas investment began to move to manufacturing and natural resources (for instance, Petro China), and even to high end products (Lenovo, ZTE etc).This was a response to the increasing short supply of domestic energy and also to intensified competition at home and abroad. It was only when China had accumulated huge foreign reserves and when the domestic financial markets had experienced both further liberalization and a boom since 2000; the rapid growth of overseas investment by financial companies took place. In 2001 the four Chinese commercial banks ranked between 7 and 29 in the top 1000 banks in the world. It was also in this period that Chinese FPI becomes significant.[15]

The first phase of going global and Hong Kong

According to China's official statistics, China's out-flowing FDI mainly goes to Asia. In 2003 it accounted for 80 per cent, and then 55 per cent in 2004 and 71 per cent in 2005.[16] Hong Kong was the top recipient of China's FDI by stock, and far out striped all other countries and regions. In fact back in 2003 Hong Kong already received 40 per cent of China's total outward FDI. According to Chinese official figures, the net outward FDI (non-financial sector) to Hong Kong up until 2005 accounted for 90 per cent of her FDI stock in Asia.[17] Hong Kong is the most important host region for China's FDI.

Hong Kong has always acted as a platform for China's going global strategy. This began in 1979 when China first promulgated her market reform. In the first half of the 1980s, China began to export small amounts of capital, the purpose of which was first and foremost political. Xu Jiatuan, the head of the Hong Kong New China News Agency who was also a *de facto* top diplomat representing China and then defected to the US in 1989 after the Tiananmen crackdown[18], revealed China's capital export plans against the background of the transition of the return of Hong Kong sovereignty to China. During this period China's top priority was to win over Hong Kong Chinese capitalists and gain their support for the sovereignty return. Xu Jiatuan said:

> We instructed the Hong Kong branch of the Bank of China and all of China's firms to work to stabilize the Chinese capitalists, to cooperate with them, to do business with them. It means to give them help both in terms of trade and the raising of capital.[19]

Another motive for capital exports to Hong Kong was to make use of Hong Kong's experiences to help Chinese firms to learn western skills in management, trade, and technology. It was a strategy of supposedly making Hong Kong a window for China's reform. For instance, the giant company CITIC (China International Trust and Investment Corporation) was founded in the early 1980s for this purpose.

Tan Xiao in his book *China: Strategy of 'going global'*, gives the aggregate figure of China's outward FDI between 1979 and 1983 as US$ 45.7 million, and then between 1984 and 1988 it is 665 million.[20] However, various sources indicated that China's capital exports to Hong Kong alone in these periods far exceed the aggregate figures provided by Tan. Xu Jiatuan estimated that in this period (the first half of 1980s) China's aggregate investment in Hong Kong was US$2-3 billion, and if reinvested earning from China's firms and their loans were included, then it might reach 10 billion. No one knows the exact figure because it was considered a state secret.

According to Xu, until 1983 the central government was still unfriendly towards the idea of investing abroad. This, however, could not stop provincial governments investing in Hong Kong. Guo Guochan, a Chinese scholar, wrote:

> In 1985, basically all the ministries and all the provinces and all the cities had already set up 'window companies' in Hong Kong. Then in 1986 and after, the government officials from the County, the Rural Township, and then even Village and Township Enterprises followed in their footsteps. In 1989 the number of Chinese firms was more than 2,500, and irregularities became a problem. The State Department spent the subsequent three years (1989-91) trying to clean the house. In 1991 it only kept 1,500 firms.[21]

Xu Jiatuan reported that

In 1987 and 1988 ... some Chinese firms set up parent companies, subsidiaries and sub-subsidiaries, which made them greatly over-sized. Some of the management was corrupt, accepting bribes, and involved in irregularities. It became out of control ... It was reported that the CITIC was involved in the illegal trading of foreign currency and there were lots of complaints about this.[22]

Phase II 1992-98: the birth of Chinese TNCs

After defeating the 1989 democracy movement, the party under Deng Xiaoping then felt secure to make a great leap forward to harmonize with global capitalism. In 1992, the 14th Congress of the Chinese Communist Party inaugurated the construction of a 'socialist market economy', which amounts to giving the green light to privatization or the commercialization of SOEs. The next year, when the 14th Party Convention of the Central Committee was convened, it passed a resolution endorsing 'Modern Enterprises' as a model for SOE reform. By 'Modern Enterprises' it meant transforming big SOEs into joint stock companies which would draw in private shareholders and see maximization of profit as their top priority.

By 1991 the State Council had already decided to start the experiment of building 100 giant SOEs through mergers.[23] For instance, six big power companies were founded through mergers, and they accounted for nearly half of the national electricity generated. In the car industry, six giants were created which accounted for 70 per cent of national car production. An oligopoly was formed quickly in many key industries. A wave of restructuring swept through the state sector.

The going global strategy is closely related to SOE reform:

1. If China has to open up her market to foreign capital, then only after immense downsizing would the big Chinese SOEs be able to compete domestically and then, later, internationally, with foreign capital.
2. Transforming SOEs into joint stock companies provides them with the necessary legal and economic conditions to float, first in the domestic market and then in Hong Kong and New York. It is their floatation in Hong Kong first which provides them with huge amounts of capital for further expansion both domestically and globally.
3. The creation of giant SOEs, and hence the oligopoly of key industries, not only enables them to enjoy economies of scale, but also allows them to a considerable extent to acquire monopoly rent, which enhances their ability to invest overseas.
4. The growing oligopoly in key industries means that medium size firms rapidly lose their market share and have to look to overseas markets as compensation. For example, in the oil industry, because of the three giants' dominant position, medium size firms like the Sinochem, have been forced to invest overseas.[24]
5. The immense privatization of medium and small SOEs resulted in a concentration of state assets going to cronies of the officials, and this is one of the main sources of capital flight and overseas investment.

Over -investment and export of capital

Beginning from the mid-1980s China began to experience an investment boom. Deng's tour to the south in 1992 encouraged all levels of government to engage in an even more crazy competition in investment, as provincial governments saw this as a chance to develop their regions. A rapid rise of investment inevitably squeezes consumption. Figure 6 below shows that final consumption fell from the highest level of 66.4 per cent in 1980s to 51.9 per cent in 2005. In contrast, capital formation has never been lower than 35 per cent since 1985, and in the periods of 1993-96 and 2003-05, periods of mad investment booms, the average reached 40.4 per cent and 42.3 per cent respectively. If one breaks down total consumption into government expenditure and household consumption, then the picture is even bleaker for the people: the former continues to rise at the expense of the latter. Over-investment and under-consumption for ordinary people resulted in inadequate domestic demand. It exacerbated the problem of over-capacity of the rapidly growing industries.

The decentralization of economic decision making, unleashed by the market reforms, resulted in fierce competition between provinces. In 1995,

Figure 6: Weight of Final Consumption and Capital Formation among GDP

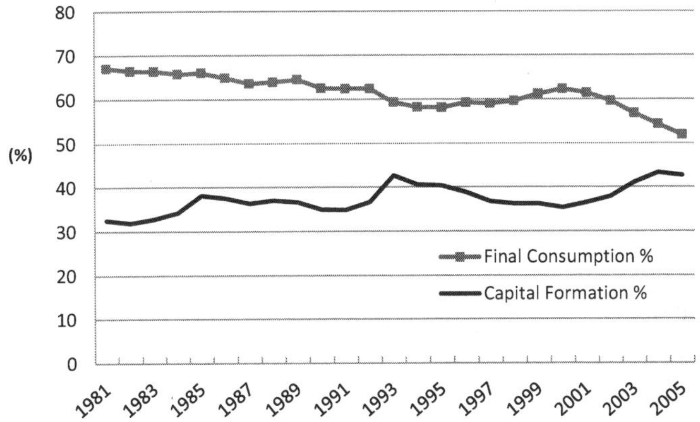

Source: http://www.stats.gov.cn/tjsj/ndsj/2006/indexch.htm

14 provinces planned to prioritize the development of metallurgy and machinery. Sixteen planned to prioritize the petro-chemical industry; 22 the car industry; 23 bicycles and washing machines. Twenty seven chose TV production as a key supporting industry; 28 synthetic fibres; 29 steel and fertilizer and plastic, and so on and so forth. Another consequence of this competition to invest was the fragmentation of investment funds, which often ended up leading to small scale production in industries where only large scale production is efficient. Hence there were 751 car plants all over the country, but they were only able to manufacture 1.5 million cars, which was only a fraction of the annual car production of General Motors. In 1997 the number of car plants dropped to 115 after restructuring but the numbers were still considered to be too big and inefficient.[25]

> Since the 1990s, the Chinese economy has shifted from a seller's market to a buyer's market … According to a survey on industry in 1998, with the exception of energy and raw materials, all other industry experienced general overcapacity. The utilization rate of productive capacity for TVs was 46.1 per cent, washing machines 43.3 per cent, refrigerators 50.5 per cent, air conditioners 33.5 per cent, bicycles 54.5 per cent, textiles 70 per cent.'[26]

In 1998 the now-dissolved State Economic and Trade Committee released a policy document: Index of Over-Invested Products for Moving Abroad. The title of the document is self-explanatory. It wants to export China's excessive capacity to solve domestic problems. It targets the first batch of industries and products that need to move abroad: light industry, machineries and electronics, motor cycles, refrigerators and TVs etc.[27]

The destinations of the exports of China's excessive capacity are chiefly developing countries.

Tan Xiao said:

> Our country possesses a whole range of relatively mature industry technology. To move these industries abroad in general and to developing countries in particular will, apart from solving the problem of overcapacity, enable us to improve our national industrial structure. We now encourage the export of our overcapacity industries to developing countries, especially to emerging markets like the Middle East, Southern region of Africa, Latin America, Far East Asia etc.[28]

While TNCs in the China's eastern region are increasingly interested in investing in developed countries, those in the western region, which are less advanced in technology than the east, see South East Asia and other poor developing countries as their natural destination for capital export.

He continued:

> As the firms in the Western Region with overseas investment chiefly invest in the former USSR, Vietnam, Laos, Burma, and those countries in Central Asia and South East Asia ...They chiefly export capital to relatively backward developing countries.[29]

The rush of investment to Hong Kong and the Asian Crisis

When Deng Xiaoping toured the south in 1992, it was a time when China was still being sanctioned by the west for her crackdown on the democracy movement. Hence Hong Kong became even more important as the most accessible place for China's investment. Setting up window companies on their own by the provincial governments was no longer enough. Buying shell companies and then floating them on the Hong Kong stock market was becoming more common. The CITIC group is famous for this practice. According to the Chinese scholar Yasheng Huang:

The number of Chinese firms investing in Hong Kong rose from 400 in 1991 to 2,000 in 1994 and their cumulative investments reached US$20 billion by 1993. By 1993, China had surpassed Japan as the number one investor in Hong Kong. Most of the Chinese firms in Hong Kong are unlisted.[30]

The rush to invest in Hong Kong peaked again in 1996 and 1997, because many provincial governments and their window companies were eager to set foot on the Hong Kong stock market before, or at least immediately after, the handover in July 1997. In 1993 Chinese companies' stocks only accounted for 4.78 per cent of the total value of the stock market. It rose to 8.48 per cent in 1996 and jumped again to 16.29 per cent in 1997. Since then it grew in leaps and bounds, reaching 47.67 per cent in 2006.[31]

In this period there was still tight mainland capital control over outflowing capital, therefore much of the Chinese money did not arrive in Hong Kong via the official channels. It came to Hong Kong via a growing network of 'underground banking'. According to the book *Investigation on China's Underground Banking*, written by a Chinese scholar, in 2004 alone, the amount of money which went through the underground banking network between mainland China and Hong Kong reached 100 billion yuan, or US$13.4 billion.[32]

The stock market boom was suddenly halted by the Asian Crisis. In October 1997 it hit Hong Kong and the stock market crashed. Many Chinese companies found themselves in trouble. Then the bankruptcy of Guangdong International Trust and Investment Corporation (GITIC), the window company of the Guangdong Provincial Government followed. It was only then that the public became aware of the hidden debt and all the secret borrowing practices of this company. Many local and foreign investors and lenders were furious over GITIC's bankruptcy. They were angry because these window companies had always used their government background as their proof of credibility in luring for loans, leading many investors to believe that they could not go bankrupt. The investors were wrong. What made things more unacceptable was that the scandal exposed the irregularities and even corruption of these window companies. Very soon the Guangdong Investment Ltd, another Guangdong window company, was in big trouble. This time it was saved by the public money of the Guangdong government, which simply gave the asset of Dongjiang's fresh water supply for Hong Kong to the company,[33] fearing that if it were to go bankrupt it might trigger off a meltdown for mainland Chinese firms. Eventually the crisis was contained. It was followed by wave after wave of arrests and trials of Chief Executive Officers (CEOs) and high-up officials in the Chinese companies, both in Hong Kong and in mainland China, reflecting the terrible scale of corruption.

Phase III 1999-present: the global offensive

The Asian Crisis sent those Chinese companies which heavily invested and borrowed in Hong Kong, into crisis. It did not spread to China, thanks to her capital control regime which was eroding gradually, but was nevertheless still in place. China's export-oriented economy continued to enjoy a high growth rate in the post-Asian Crisis period, and this created new 'push' factors for overseas investment.

Looking for overseas investment in energy and raw materials

To sustain rapid growth it is necessary for China to import more energy and raw materials. For example, China has been a net oil importing country since 1993 and today half of her consumption relies on imports. Sourcing from overseas pushes up the price of primary products and so they become increasingly costly to Chinese firms, which mostly have a low profit margin, especially in the export sectors. To get around this problem, China increasingly relies on acquiring overseas energy and raw material resources.

Figure 7 shows that trade has become less important in China's outward FDI, while mining (with oil as the most important element) accounts for a much higher proportion. China has become the world's second largest oil consuming country after the USA.[34]

The oil industry is also one of the model industries which have undergone the 'inviting in' and going global transformation. At the turn of the century the oil industry was restructured and made into three giant companies: Sinopec, Petro China and CNOOC. This was to prepare the industry to face direct competition from the world's three main oil giants (Exxon Mobil, BP Amoco, Shell) when the domestic market opened up under the conditionality of China's accession to WTO. In order to raise the competitiveness of the Chinese oil giants, 600,000 oil workers were sacked with miserable compensation. Their legitimate rights were also denied. The oil workers staged a 50,000 strong one month long demonstration in the Daqing Oilfield in March 2002, but they were subsequently repressed. Meanwhile, the three Chinese giants, on one hand compete with the three world giants; while on the other hand they closely collaborate with them in joint projects all over China – from oil stations to oil pipe construction to oil and gas extraction. It is not astonishing to see that when CNPC, the mother company of Petro China, encountered opposition to its attempt to float in New York in 2000 because of its involvement in Sudan's operation, it was saved by BP Amoco when the latter bought 20per cent of CNPC's shares. All three world oil giants have bought a significant number of shares in the three Chinese oil giants. Both sides share the same interests, while also competing with each other.

The three Chinese oil giants raised billions of dollars after listing in Hong Kong and New York, and are now able to acquire more overseas assets than in previously. After the failure to acquire the US oil company UNACO, China's oil giants seem to be more interested in looking for oil and gas assets in developing or smaller countries. In March 2007, China announced that she has targeted nine countries as suitable for investment by the nation's oil companies. The nine countries are: Bolivia, Ecuador, Kuwait, Libya, Morocco, Niger, Norway, Oman and Qatar.[35]

Figure 7: Composition of China out-flowing FDI in terms of industry

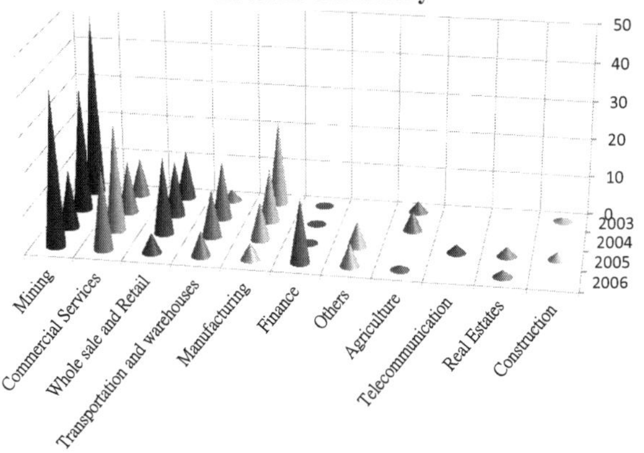

Source: for 2003-5 figures, see Chinese TNCs going out for the world, China Commerce Press, 2007, p. 4. For 2006 figures, see 2006 Statistical Bulletin of China's Outward FDI, p. 7.

Accumulating huge amounts of foreign reserves

The export drive has enabled China to accumulate huge foreign reserves, reaching US$1.43 trillion dollars in October 2007. It is estimated that two-thirds of the reserves are US bonds and securities. China has now become a major player in the global financial market. Her out-flowing Foreign Portfolio Investment (FPI) and foreign aid, which in the former period was negligible, now becomes ever more prominent.

China's huge foreign reserves also enable her state banks to become significant international lenders and a considerable portion of these loans act as aid to developing countries. Comprehensive statistics are lacking, though. One report quoted Professor Deborah Brautigam who used data from the China Statistical Yearbook and estimated that Chinese aid worldwide in 2005 was US $970 million, rising from US $650 million in 2002. World Bank officials suggest that Chinese aid to Africa alone might amount to US$2 billion, implying that the Chinese figures may be underestimations. The author of the report estimated that Chinese aid worldwide totals somewhere between US$1.5 and 2 billion.[36]

The China Export and Import Bank quickly evolved, after it was established in 1994, into China's main lending agency. Its accumulated loans in 2005 amounted to US $20 billion.[37] According to a Chinese report, its accumulated loans to Africa reached 50 billion yuan (about US$6.6 billion) in the first half of 2006.[38] Peter Bosshard quoted a Chinese researcher who gives a slightly lower figure of 44.4 billion yuan. He then quoted a World Bank report which reported US$12.5 billion in mid-2006 in African infrastructure investment alone, which may suggest that the Chinese figure is an underestimate.[39]

The UNCTAD's World Investment Report 2006 expected that China's outward FDI would surge because of the ever-increasing amount of 'China dollars'. It has made 'the promotion of outward FDI an imperative for the Chinese Government, leading it to adopt a going global strategy and take concrete measures to promote the internationalization of Chinese companies.'[40]

In the late 1990s, Chinese banks were technically bankrupt because of bad debt and non-performing loans as a result of the investment boom which turned sour. Nevertheless the government came to the banks' rescue. This was not enough, however, to make them competitive without sacking hundreds of thousands of bank workers. After these reforms the Chinese banks became attractive to investors. Under the conditions of China's accession to WTO, China had to open up her financial sector, including banking, to foreign capital in 2007. For the last few years foreign banks have been in a rush to become strategic shareholders of the Chinese banks. As of October 2005, 17 Chinese banks had accepted foreign strategic partners.[41]

After 'inviting in' foreign partners, Chinese banks then went vigorously global. According to the China Finance Net, in the first half of 2007, China's commercial banks had up to 110 branches in thirty countries, with a total asset base of 2000 billion yuan, or US$133.6 billion.[42] Today all four commercial banks have already been floated in Hong Kong and New York. The second aspect of going global is overseas investment. Previously the Industrial and Commercial Bank, the Construction Bank and the CITIC group bought several small and medium banks in Hong Kong. From then on the Chinese banks increasingly rely on acquisition and mergers as a way to expand. In little more than a year (August 2006 to October 2007) there were six acquisitions of foreign banks.[43] The recent acquisition of the Standard Bank of South Africa by the Industrial and Commercial Bank of China is quite significant because the former is the biggest African bank.

In terms of ownership, 81 per cent of Chinese outward stock FDI belongs to SOEs, while private enterprises only accounted for 1 per cent in 2006.[44] It has been government policy since 1998 to encourage private overseas investment. In October that year the Ministry of Foreign Trade and Cooperation released a document granting private enterprises and research institutes the privilege of export.[45]

The lack of investment opportunities in the real economy

Today China's savings amount to 15,000 billion yuan, and private funds have a total net asset of 3,000 billion yuan. The narrowing of domestic markets means that there is a lack of profitable investment opportunity, hence the fierce speculation in both the stock market and real estate market. There are lots of investors who are also looking overseas. In 2006 the government implemented the QDII (Qualified Domestic Institutional Investors) regime to allow banks and private funds to invest overseas. Again, it is Hong Kong which is the most active platform for China's outward hot money. In the second half of 2007, 15.6 billion Hong Kong dollars flowed into Hong Kong from mainland China under the QDII regime to take advantage of the booming stock market there. The market expects that in the foreseeable future the amount of outward portfolio investment from mainland China may reach 140 billion Hong Kong dollars.[46] The *Wall Street Journal* reported that 'by encouraging the movement of funds out of the country, Beijing is seeking to tackle those inflationary forces and alleviate pressure on the yuan to appreciate'. 'Steadily pushing forward the yuan's convertibility on the capital account is the longer term goal of changes in the system of foreign-exchange management,' the People's Bank said.'[47]

Going global officially proclaimed

At the turn of the century the Chinese government found itself at a crossroads. The model of export oriented growth and low added value had attracted criticism from various quarters, including from the nationalists, who saw this as a net outflow of revenues to the advantage of foreign capital. This outcry against foreign capital is in fact part of a new trend since the turn of the century. It is a period when the concern over the threat of 'recolonization' becomes more intense, as foreign capital begins to increase its market share rapidly. In 2000 foreign capital accounted for 24 per cent of gross industrial output, and for half export value.

The response of the party to these problems was not to roll back the neoliberal reforms, nor to impose any administrative restrictions on the inflow of foreign capital, but rather to embrace corporate-led globalization more enthusiastically in order to become the winner at the same old game. This approach was justified in the remarks of Zhang Ruimin, the CEO of Haier who said: 'western TNCs are all wolves. If we are to compete with them we must also turn ourselves into wolves'.[48] Who will be the sheep then? It looks like a game of using the devil to hit the devil.

When the CCP convened their 15th Congress in 1997, General Secretary Jiang Zemin had already spoken about the strategy of 'encouraging those overseas investments where our nation enjoys comparative advantages'. It was not until 2001, when Premier Zhu, in his policy address to the People's Congress, officially used the term going global strategy for Chinese firms. The following year the Central Committee report to the 16th Party Congress stressed the need to 'build our own strong TNCs and our own brand'.

In 2001 the government released its Tenth Five Year Plan. Regarding overseas investment it said:

1. Strive to raise the ratio between inflow and outflow FDI to 10:1.
2. The National Development and Reform Commission shall compile a list of the overseas investment of those resources of which China is in short supply, for instance, oil, gas, wood, ferrous and nonferrous metal etc. The objective of which is to ensure the sustainability of our country's economic development and our economic security as well.
3. Support the growth of overseas processing manufacturing.
4. Encourage overseas investments which aim at expanding global market share and high tech.
5. Strive to develop a batch of competitive TNCs in five years, and 50 Chinese TNCs big enough to enter into the 500 global giants in 2015.
6. Set up overseas research and development centres.
7. Expand overseas construction projects and the export of labour.[49]

In his speech to the recent 17th Party Congress in Oct 2007, General Secretary Hu Jintao reiterated the need to:

1. Support the growth of Chinese TNCs and the building of Chinese brands.
2. Develop international cooperation over energy resources.
3. Implement the strategy of Regional Free Trade Agreement (FTA).[50]

In terms of Hu's point on building Regional FTA, China is already committed to the building of ASEAN + China FTA in 2010, as well as dozens of FTA agreements with many other countries. It is again a reflection of the Chinese government's overall strategy in its response to the neoliberal agenda of the US Empire and the EU – endorse the agenda and try to make itself the winner of the same old game. This is the essence of 'inviting in' and going global.

III: China's current overseas investments

Acquisitions and mergers as a form of overseas investment

There are reports that Acquisitions and Mergers (A & M) accounted for an average of 20 per cent of all Chinese overseas investment before 2002.[51] Table 2 shows that Chinese outward FDI increasingly takes the form of A & M. As a late comer, A & M is the quickest way to expand globally. For instance, the CITIC group chiefly takes the form of A & M to transform itself into a global player, by buying up several dozen companies across Hong Kong, USA, Canada, Australia and Thailand etc. Many other big Chinese TNCs, especially those with government backing, like the three oil giants, follow the path of CITIC.

It is worth noting that 70 per cent of China's overseas investment consists of joint ventures or foreign-China collaboration projects, while solely owned companies account for 20 per cent. Most productive projects and oil projects are joint ventures; trading firms are mostly solely owned.[52]

Table 2: Breakdown of China's outward FDI in terms of new investment and A & M

Year	**New Investment**	**A & M**
2003	82.0%	18.0%
2004	68.2%	31.8%
2005	47.0%	53.0%
2006	63.3%	36.7%

Source: Wang Zhile, 2007, p. 100. For 2006 figures, see http://news.xinhuanet.com/fortune/2007-09/11/content_6700685.htm

Undertaking of overseas contracts

Another aspect of the going global strategy is the undertaking of overseas infrastructure contracts from roads and dams to telecommunications. Table

3 shows that in recent years the value of overseas contracts has increased significantly. According to the same source, the accumulated sales value of China's undertaking of overseas contracts reached 135.8 billion dollars, in 2005, which is more than the US $57.2 billion worth of FDI (non-financial parts), and accounts for 59 per cent of all overseas investment (excluding portfolio investment).[53] Accompanying this trend is a growth in the exportation of workers, which in 2005 reached 565,000. This figure rises if undocumented Chinese workers are included.

China considers this aspect of overseas undertaking as an important component of its going global strategy. A Chinese scholar noted that:

> Beginning from 11 December 2006, the transition period of our construction industry under the conditions of China's accession to WTO will have ended. Our construction industry will face direct competition at the same level on both the domestic and international playing field. Shall we simply remain on the defensive, or shall we go over to the offensive? That is the problem ... Our construction industry ... is more urgent than ever to the implementation of the 'going global' strategy.'[54]
>
> For a long period ahead of us, we will face very serious employment problems. We must not forget the fact that our huge quantity of cheap labour is one of our comparative advantages which enable us to compete in the international market.[55]

Table 3: Sales value of China's undertaking of overseas construction projects

Year	Sales value (in billions of dollars)	Annual growth rate (per cent)
2001	8.9	--
2002	11.19	25.8
2003	13.84	23.6
2004	17.50	26.0
2005	21.76	24.6

Source: Wang Zhile, 2007, p. 75

Giant Chinese companies

Market reforms successfully transformed big SOEs into profit-seeking corporations and then into TNCs in a very short time. Whereas in 1995 there were only 2 Chinese firms listed in the Fortune 500, in 2007 there were 22.

IV: The problems of going global

The weakness of Chinese TNCs

Although more Chinese TNCs are now large enough to be listed in the Fortune 500, they are chiefly monopolistic companies or primary productive companies like the power industry, oil, banks, telecommunications and foreign trade etc. Their present position owes more to strong government support than effective management or innovations. In fact, most of them are government owned.

Peter Nolan, an expert on China at Cambridge University, remarked in one of his books that:

> A closer look at these (Chinese) firms reveals that they typically benefited from a protected domestic market, and from state support through soft loans, state procurement and protected marketing channels. Despite their enormous achievements, these firms were without exception far behind the global leaders in terms of revenue, R & D expenditure, marketing expenditure and global market share. Without continued state support, they were most unlikely to be able to build on their considerable entrepreneurial achievements, and mount a serious challenge to the global giants in the respective sectors.[56]

Chinese firms are eager to invest overseas but many of them fail to conduct prior feasibility studies, or investigate the laws and market situation of host countries, resulting in losses. A study shows that only 55 per cent of overseas branches of Chinese firms are profitable – mostly non-manufacturing firms. Firms which are neither profitable nor loss-making account for 28 per cent. 17 per cent are losing money; most of these are manufacturing firms.[57] Another survey shows that only 30 per cent of overseas investment is profitable, 30 per cent experience losses, and 40 per cent barely make ends meet.[58]

In April 2000, the Hangzhou city government conducted a survey and found that there were a total of 53 non-trading firms which conducted overseas investment in 20 countries: 14 of the firms, (26.4 per cent) never really started overseas production at all; 15 of them (28.3 per cent) terminated their operations. The two figures imply a failure rate of 54.7 per cent for these firms from Hangzhou. According to one official, successful firms only account for 10 per cent.[59]

With regards to Chinese overseas portfolio investment, the case of the Singapore branch of China Aviation Oil Corp Ltd is revealing. In 2004 the company raised 180 million dollars on the Singapore stock market and announced that the money was for acquiring new assets. It turned out that the company used the money for portfolio speculation, resulting in the loss of US $550 million. The company was simultaneously under investigation by the Singapore government for irregularities, and compensation demands from investors as well.

It is reported that 60-70 per cent of A & M have failed. A study shows that after merging, one quarter of companies have experienced more than a 20 per cent drop in their share prices; only 36 per cent maintain income growth. In order to compete for oil resources, for instance, the Chinese oil companies tend to pay a high price, resulting in unbearably high project costs.[60]

Exporting scarce resources

Unlike in the west, China's huge capital exports are not the result of a fully developed domestic economy – where the market is relatively saturated, producing increasing amounts of surplus capital which is unable to find profitable investment at home. In contrast, China is still very poor in terms of GDP per capita and capital is a scarce resource. In the western region, a vast rural area remains underdeveloped and is capital-hungry. In the rural areas there are 360 million peasants who do not even have a piped water supply. Millions of children have no access to secondary education. Any government which claims to work for the benefit of common people should first and foremost use available capital to develop infrastructure and basic social services in the western and rural regions, rather than massively exporting this scarce resource. It is especially troubling that China has to acquire overseas oil and mineral resources, much of which are used to produce for export, and then the foreign currency earned is invested abroad again.

More volatility in the Hong Kong markets

The continuous flow of Chinese money into Hong Kong fed the bubbles in real estate and the stock market. The Hong Kong scholar Feng Guochao reported that:

> China's investment in Hong Kong is chiefly in the non-manufacturing sector, especially in real estate. China's huge investment in this sector brings about its high speed development. In 1992 and 1993, Hong Kong real estate prices went up by more than 100 per cent. The prices have already surpassed those in Tokyo.
>
> Certain kinds of Chinese investments are worrying. First and foremost, the SOEs use government funds for investment, and they face the issue of moral hazard. The investors may get involved in high risk speculation because they believe that even if the investment turns sour the state will come to their rescue; and if it reaps profit then they again will be benefited as individuals. This makes the market exceedingly volatile.'[61]

The stock market and real estate market bubbles finally burst when the Asian crisis hit Hong Kong in 1997. It took nearly a decade for Hong Kong to recover fully. We are probably now going through the same bubble economy and volatility as we had in the 1990s. This time it is even more obviously driven by Chinese policy – policy which is itself chopping and changing – and by hot money rather than economic fundamentals. In August 2007, the Administration of Foreign Exchange announced a Pilot Program for Domestic Individual Investment in Overseas Markets, without limitations on amounts invested. This sent the Hong Kong stock market into crazy speculation, especially as those mainland investors who received inside information had already put a lot of money into the Hong Kong stock market via unofficial channels. Then when the Chinese authorities took a sudden turn in November, announcing that the policy would be shelved, the market dropped violently.

While it is true that, with or without Chinese hot money, the boom and bust cycle in a money economy is inevitable, it is no less true that this hot money from China and elsewhere magnifies the scale of the cycle, increasing its volatility, and making it much more difficult to contain when a crisis breaks out. On top of this, the benefits and pain during a commercial cycle is not evenly spread. Even in boom periods the poor do not necessarily get proportional benefit. In Hong Kong whenever there is boom it also implies high rents which the poor cannot afford. It goes without saying that the poor are also the hardest hit in a crisis.

Corruption within Chinese overseas investment

As said, there are no reliable statistics as to the real scale of China's overseas investment due to lack of transparency. This necessarily breeds corruption. In the 2007 Corruption Perception Index issued by Transparency

International, Hong Kong's index is 8.3 and ranks 14th, while China's index is 3.5 and ranks 72nd. We are concerned that, in exporting her capital, China may export her corruption as well. We have already witnessed this in Hong Kong. Now there are overseas reports which suggest that China's companies are involved in corruption. Lately the Chinese TNC the ZTE Corp allegedly bribed close associates of President Arroyo of the Philippines in order to bid for a telecommunications project. I am not able to verify the allegation, or any other related reports. One thing is for sure though: without democracy, rule of law, freedom of speech and of association, it will not be possible to keep corruption among Chinese companies, inside or outside China, in check.

Is China's overseas investment helping developing countries?

As Chinese TNCs are becoming more ambitious, they may face more obstacles in investing in developed countries. For the moment China's outward FDI still mainly goes to these countries. The initial obstacles which CNPC faced in its first trial of IPO in the USA, and the unsuccessful acquiring of UNACO by CNOOC, however, means that Chinese TNCs find it necessary to diversify overseas investment. The probable alternative is poorer developing countries. Chinese scholar Tan Xiao advised the authorities that 'China is not able to directly compete with developed countries, but she can dominate small or medium size developing countries'. He then gave the example of Guangzhou's First Cigarette Factory, the three main brands which now have a market coverage of 90 per cent in Cambodia.[62]

Chinese projects in various authoritarian countries are always controversial. The most well-known examples are of course oil exploration in Sudan, and dam building and gas exploration in Myanmar, which draw international attention and criticism from human rights and environmental activists. Most recently, as the humanitarian crisis in the Democratic Republic of Congo broke out due to the civil war, the interests of the foreign mining companies behind it are again mentioned. When the host countries have no democracy or rule of law, it means that ordinary people cannot raise opposition to overseas investment when it harms rather than benefits them. Chinese companies moving to these countries make the threat quite real.

In Africa there is serious concern among civil society over China's economic activities. Dot Keet wrote that:

> Chinese imports and Chinese traders on the ground are ousting small local traders; and this, in turn, is resulting in pronounced anti-Chinese

xenophobia. Construction – many of which rely on imported Chinese workers, skilled and unskilled, and therefore do not create much local employment and do not transfer production/management skills ... Manufactured goods which are flooding into African countries are wiping out small, and even relatively larger producers which do not enjoy the direct and indirect subsidies that industries receive from Chinese authorities.'[63]

The Chinese government is well known for its hostility towards the labour rights; free association and the right to strike. There is growing concern that China's overseas investments – most of which are funded by state enterprises – are exporting China's anti-labour regime, particularly so when the host countries are keen to provide an excessively pro-business environment to foreign investors at the expense of the interests of their own workers. Three researchers from the Ghana Trade Unions Congress wrote that:

> There is popular perception [that] Chinese investors/employers are notorious for their disrespect for labour rights ... For the construction union (CBMWU), it believes that the gains it has made over the years in the areas of collective bargaining and social dialogue are being threatened by the Chinese and that if it does not act quickly both foreign and local construction firms may follow the bad example of the Chinese in a 'race to the bottom'. The General Secretary describes the entry of the Chinese in the construction industry as a 'direct threat to social protection' in Ghana. According to the General Secretary, the Chinese do not hesitate to sack workers who show any inclination towards unionism even though they (the Chinese management) claim that they are not against unionisation.
>
> The Chinese do not want to accept the five working days that prevails in Ghana. They indirectly force workers to work every day of the week. They also prefer to hire workers on temporary basis even for permanent jobs[64].

There are areas where China's investment in developing countries may have a positive side. For instance, China is more willing than western investors to invest in infrastructure, in addition to bringing in a lot of cheap consumer goods and capital goods. It is difficult to make a correct and objective balance sheet, however, first and foremost because of the fact that much of China's operation is not transparent.

The Chinese government, as usual, reiterates its policy of 'non-interference' and that its loans do not have strings as in the case of Western lenders. Yuza Maw Htoon and Khin Zaw Win responded that:

> Its loans do have strings, in the form of ties to the use of Chinese companies, guarantees of access to future oil production and, internationally, to African states toeing the Chinese line not only on Taiwan, but also in the forums of global governance institutions.[65]

Another researcher Ali Askouri wrote that:

> African states are still dominated by tribalism, elitism, and regionalism. To these characteristics one can add the weak institutions and administrative structures of African states, which limit their ability to solve internal disputes and conflicts … China's open-door lending policy does not appear to take these complexities into account. It is not surprising then if China's financial aid to African countries ends up fuelling on-going internal conflicts or nurturing new ones. Indeed, the open-door lending policy has brought China nothing but defamation, particularly among ordinary African people … China's recent experiences of pursuing its 'no conditions policy' have shown that many African governments who turned up at China's door were not qualified for any assistance by moral, ethical, humanitarian or any other acceptable standards.[66]

Aid for who and what?

Chinese overseas loans in Africa have been criticized in the west for supporting military regimes and environmentally destructive projects. For instance, in 2007 the then British International Development secretary, Hilary Benn, warned that the billions of dollars China was offering in unconditional aid and cheap loans to African governments risked driving countries that have only just benefited from debt relief back into debt, and undermined efforts to create democratic and accountable administrations.[67] This is hypocritical since it has been the British government's neocolonial policy towards Africa which has been responsible for the latter's indebtedness.

There are attempts to defend China, for instance by Sautman and Yan Hairong:

> China seems a lesser evil than the West on key issues in Africa's development and African dignity … A Nigerian official has also noted that 'the Western world is never prepared to transfer technology – but the

> Chinese do [and] while China's technology may not be as sophisticated as some Western governments', it is better to have Chinese technology than to have none at all ... For many Africans then, there is a 'Chinese model' ... an image of a developing state that does not fully implement Washington consensus prescriptions, does not impose onerous conditions on African states' policies and is more willing than the West to help develop predicates of industrialism in the global South, including by opening many factories in Africa ... This perception is now part of an image often labeled 'the Beijing consensus'.[68]

Before commenting on the lesser evil argument, let us first put the whole debate within a context of the qualitative changes of China's policy in foreign aid and investment since the reform. In February 2007 the *Beijing Review* carried an article to come to the defence of China's role in Africa. In responding to the accusation that China's role in Africa is colonialist, the author has this to say:

> Though China is not a colonialist, it is a successful capitalist in Africa. The path it has taken on that continent is consistent with the logic of market capitalism-liberal trade based on fair contracts ... Although capitalism implies exploitation to many, China's capitalists have to limit their exploitation within the framework of the WTO and abide by local laws ... To some extent, Chinese people's influence on African society may include environmental pollution, excessive development of resources and collusion between them and local officials. But these phenomena can be removed by the rule of law.[69]

The interesting point here is the honest recognition that Chinese overseas investments and lending are nothing but 'successful capitalist' practices, rather than 'socialist' which until today is the state religion that every Chinese citizen has to adhere to. These lines would not have been published if they were written in Chinese. Anyway, the essence of the comment here is absolutely in line with a 2000 State Council document on foreign aid, which includes the following:

> Through foreign aid policy and our funds, we shall be able to make the most of our overseas manufacturing and extraction projects. We shall look into the common needs of both the aid recipient countries and our country, and conduct accordingly a whole range of big projects which can bring high investment returns and also a big political impact. This

> will in turn give an impetus to the launching of more medium and small projects. Foreign aid has to be linked to the export of our machinery and high tech products.[70]

These practices are no doubt in alignment with 'capitalist' practices and have been quite common in many aid giving countries. China's present practices, however, are quite different from what she proclaimed in 1964.

In 1964 the Chinese government announced its Eight Principles Concerning Foreign Aid:

1. The PRC (People's Republic of China) considers that her foreign aid is granted in accordance to equal and mutual benefit, and never regards it as a unilateral favour.
2. The PRC grants aid with the utmost respect to the sovereignty of the aid recipient countries and never seeks any privileges for herself.
3. Aid recipient countries can request deferred payment of loans when necessary.
4. The objective of the PRC's aid is to make sure that no aid recipient country ends up relying upon more aid and is instead enabled to become self reliant, and independent with regards to development.
5. The projects which the PRC gives priority to are those which can quickly increase the revenues of the aid recipient countries.
6. The PRC provides the aid recipient countries the best of her own machinery and products, and the prices are negotiated in accordance to international prices. If the machinery and products delivered are defective, the PRC guarantees a return of the goods.
7. When the PRC provides aid recipient countries with a certain kind of technology, she guarantees the latter are trained until they can handle it.
8. Experts sent by the PRC shall enjoy the same level of benefits as those experts from the aid recipient countries. They shall not be privileged.[71]

The 1964 policy guidelines were in line with the overall foreign policy of China at that time, which was supportive of national liberation movements and more self-reliant growth models in developing countries; she was also fiercely against the US empire. On the other hand, the guidelines mentioned nothing about 'high investment return', and the spirit of the guidelines showed no evidence of following China's commercial interest. The going global strategy, hence, represents a regression of the Chinese foreign aid policy from relative progressive third-worldism to one which prioritizes

Chinese companies' commercial interests, within the broader context of a neoliberal strategy of seeking free trade agreements with other countries. Even if China's performance in developing countries is not as bad as that of western countries, this qualitative change from anti-capitalist to pro-capitalist implies that China now practically endorses all the barbaric logic of capitalism and the 'free trade' regime. China's entrance into competition with the west for markets and resources necessarily results in a further race to the bottom in relation to labour rights and environmental protection.

There may be a grain of truth to the 'China as lesser evil' discourse, especially for any particular African country hard pressed by the IMF or World Bank or any other western commercial banks, which now can turn to China for loans or investment. While it is always possible for progressive movements to render tactical support to China's aid or investment in well-defined circumstances, this has to be judged on a case-by-case basis, always bearing in mind that a tactical support should never imply giving up general criticism of the Chinese government, or any government, for their uncritical acceptance of 'the logic of market capitalism-liberal trade' and the WTO regime. Therefore my criticism of the Chinese government is not singling out China; rather, I am just extending my criticism of the unjust international trade and investment regime – a regime which western governments and their corporations have been trying hard to underpin – to the Chinese government. Failing to uphold a principled criticism of this regime and to extend it to the Chinese government may risk turning a blind eye to the negative impacts that China's foreign projects have on labour and the environment of host countries, or their long term interest in autonomous development. This also implies possible failure to give support to the labour and environmental movements in the host countries which are resisting exploitation by unscrupulous foreign investors, including Chinese companies.

There are discourses which expect China to act as a counter-force to the US empire. Being a huge country and one with a strong manufacturing base, China, to a limited extent, can take this role if it wants. But the problem is, does it want to? And how far will it go? More importantly, for whose sake? Though there is political disagreement or even competition between the two countries, one must not lose sight of the fact that both share the same socio-economic agenda of neoliberalism, and the same agenda of making profits through the close collaboration between TNCs from both countries. Even If China clashes with the USA in its rise to hegemony, it is just a struggle between two great powers to dominate weaker countries within a neoliberal framework; therefore it hardly benefits the working people in the latter countries in any substantial way.

The debate can be narrowed to a more concrete issue: does China's rise to the status of an important international lender to a certain extent challenge the hegemony of the international financial institutions and thus give some space for developing countries? Our response is that it is possible. It is also possible, however, that things work in the opposite direction. One must not forget that in this scenario China is only acting in accordance with her own commercial or political interests, which may or may not intersect with the interests of the developing countries. Even if the answer is 100 per cent beneficial to the developing countries, the question remains as to whether these benefits can trickle down to working people and the environment. Governments always claim that they do, but when there is no transparency regarding aid, no democratic mechanism to allow both the Chinese people and the people of the aid recipient countries to assert control over the aid, how on earth are we able to verify these claims?

Notes

1 This essay is adapted from *Preliminary Report on China's Going Global Strategy: A Labour, Environment, and Hong Kong Perspective*, published by Globalization Monitor, September 2010, Second Edition.
2 *Zouxiang Shijie de Zhongguo Kuaguo Gongsi*, Chinese TNCs going out for the world, edited by Wang Zhile, China Commerce Press, 2004, p. 20.
3 Ibid, p. 70.
4 Ibid, p. 31 - 32.
5 *2006 and 2008 Statistical Bulletin of China's Outward FDI*, jointly published by the Ministry of Commerce, the Administration of Foreign Exchange, and the National Bureau of Statistics.
6 World Investment Report 2006, UNCTAD
7 World Investment Report 2007, UNCTAD, p.115.
8 *The globalization of Corporate China*, Friedrich Wu, NBR Analysis, Vol 16, No 3, Dec 2005.
9 http://hzs.mofcom.gov.cn/accessory/200709/1190343657984.pdf. Posted on 21 September 2007.
10 *Ziben Waitao: Guoji Qushi yu Zhongguo Wenti,* Capital Flight: International Trend and China's Problem, Yang Haizhen, China Finance Press, 2005, p.144 & 156.
11 Ibid p. 27 and 152.
12 'Between January and April 1991, Korea exported 26,688 cars to China, yet on the Chinese side only 166 cars imported from Korea were recorded in the same period. It is commonly understood that the cars which went astray were in fact smuggled into mainland China.' *Maoyi yu touzi – Zhongguo dalu, Xianggang, Taiwan,* Trade and Investment, Mainland China, Hong Kong, Taiwan, Feng guochao, Commercial Press, 1997, Hong Kong, p. 72-3.

13 *Huigui Shinian de Xianggang* (Hong Kong economy 10 years after the handover), GuoGuocan, Joint Publishing (HK) Co. Ltd, p. 12.
14 *Zhongguo zouchuqu de fazhan celue*, The China Strategy of 'going global', by Tan Xiao, China Social Science Press, 2003, Beijing, p. 527.
15 Ibid p 525, 40-41.
16 Wang Zhile, p 8.
17 2006 yearly statistics, 18-20.
18 The British Colony refused China's request in setting up an office in Hong Kong which enjoyed the status of consulate.
19 *XuJiatun huiyi lu* ,Memoirs of Xu Jiatun, Hong Kong United Daily News Co. Ltd, 1984, P. 235
20 Tan Xiao, p. 40.
21 Guo Guocan , p. 172.
22 Xu Jiatun p. 257-9.
23 *Zhongguo guoyou qiye gaige ershi zhounian* (Twenty Years of Reform of Chinese state owned enterprises), edited by Wang Dongjiang, Zhongzhou Classic Press, Zhengzhou City, 1998, p. 184 & 191.
24 Wang Zhile, 2007, p. 12.
25 Tan Xiao p. 540.
26 Tan Xiao, p. 129.
27 China International Economic Consultants Co. Ltd, http://www.chinavista.com/business/ciec/ch/chciec19981013.html#cn00006
28 Tan Xiao p. 541-3.
29 Tan Xiao, 545-6.
30 *FDI in China, An Asian Perspective*, Yasheng Huang, Chinese University Press, HK, 1998, p. 57.
31 Guo Guocan, p. 208.
32 *Zhongguo dixia jinrong diaocha*, Investigation on China Underground Banking, edited by Li Jianjun, Shanghai People Press, 2006, p. 260. There is also the same underground banking between Taiwan and mainland China. On 31 Oct 2007 it reported that Taiwan authority uncovered an underground bank which undertook money laundering between the mainland and Taiwan, amounting to 5 billion yuan in just 2 years.
33 Hong Kong's fresh water relies on the Dongjiang river of the Guangdong province, and Hong Kong pays millions of dollars annually to Guangdong government for the supply.
34 It is projected that in 2015 China oil consumption will reach 3600 million tons, which is twice of her domestic production. SeeTan Xiao p. 255.
35 http://www.uofaweb.ualberta.ca/chinainstitute/nav03.cfm?nav03=57486&nav02=57275&nav01=57272
36 *The Chinese Aid system*, by Carol Lancaster, Center for Global Development, http://www.cgdev.org
37 *Export Credit Agency and Environmental Standard*, by Peter Bosshard.
38 Wang Zhile, 2007, p. 44.
39 *China's Role in Financing African Infrastructure*, by Peter Bosshard.
40 Chapter II, p.55.

41 *2005 Yinhangye fazhan gaikuang ji shiwu zongjie* ,An Overview of the Development of the Banking Industry in 2005 and the Balance Sheet for the Fifteen National Plan, Invest in China Web, http://www.fdi.gov.cn/pub/FDI/zgjj/hyzk/fwy/yh/t20060419_24224.htm
42 China Finance Net, http://bank.zgjrw.com/News/20071025/Bank/053137176500.html
43 *Ming Pao Daily*, 26 Oct 2007.
44 2006 statistics bulletin, 13 &14.
45 Tan Xiao p. 154.
46 *Ming Pao Daily*, 9 Oct 2007.
47 *China takes steps to ease transfer of funds overseas*, Wall Street Journal, 20-24 March 2008.
48 *Zhang Ruimin Haier de shouxi zhixingguan* (Zhang Haimin the CEO of Haier), http://www.cec-ceda.org.cn/jjh/view.php?id=75
49 Tan Xiao, p.5 & 148.
50 *Hong Kong Economic Journal*, 16 Oct 2007.
51 Wang Zhile, 2007, p. 45.
52 Tan Xiao p. 536.
53 Wang Zhile, 2007, p.77.
54 China Report.http://www.reportchina.com.cn/news_detail.php?id=298&nowmenuid=41&cpath=0050:&catid=5
55 Tan Xiao p 542.
56 *Transforming China – Globalization, Transition and Development*, Anthem Press, 2004, p. 221.
57 Tan Xiao 535.
58 Wang Zhile, 2007, p. 78.
59 Tan Xiao, p.172.
60 Wang Zhile, 2007, p. 78 and 119.
61 Feng, p. 131.
62 Tan Xiao, p. 241.
63 *China as 'Partner' or Neo-Colonial Operator in Africa.* http://www.tni.org/detail_page.phtml?act_id=16959&username=guest@tni.org&password=9999&publish=Y
64 *Chinese Investments in Africa, A Labour Perspective*, Edited by Anthony Yaw Baah and Herbert Jauch, African Labour Research Network, May 2009, p. 113 and 116.
65 *China's New Role in Africa and the South*, edited by Dorothy-Grace Guerrero and Firoze Manji, jointly published by Fahamu and Focus on the Global South, P. 205.
66 Dorothy-Grace Guerrero and Firoze Manji, p.152-3.
67 'Chinese aid to Africa may do more harm than good', *The Guardian*, 8 February , 2007, http://www.guardian.co.uk/world/2007/feb/08/development.topstories3
68 *Friends and Interests: China's Distinctive Links with Africa*, by Barry Sautman and Yan Hairong, in *China's New Role in Africa and the South*, edited by Dorothy-Grace Guerrero and Firoze Manji, jointly published by Fahamu and

Focus on the Global South, P 87, 95-6.

69 http://www.bjreview.com/print/txt/2007-02/05/content_54851.htm

70 http://wjm.tengzhou.gov.cn/zcfg/20061582939.asp

71 *Guoji xindai* (International Credit), published by the China Financial Press, 2003, Beijing, p. 251.

CHINA: UNAVOIDABLE RISE OR POSSIBLE DECLINE

Bruno Jetin

China's rise in the present global economy has been very fast by historical records. In three decades, China has shifted from a poor developing country to the status of global power progressively contesting US hegemony. Some commentators forecast that China could overtake the USA in the coming 20 to 30 years as the main centre of global economy before turning, at a later stage, into a military superpower. As always when one tries to forecast such complex events, there is high uncertainty regarding what could actually turn out. The present international crisis in the USA and Europe and its dampening effects on global demand is of course one important element of doubt. But the uncertainty concerning China's attempt to leap frog in technological innovations is another critical question. Finally, the social and political issues stemming from growing inequalities and the impossibility to express discontent, disagreement and proposals in a democratic political space creates another serious doubt about the possibility for the Chinese government to pilot China's rise without a profound political reform. Having in mind this radical uncertainty regarding the future, the objective of this chapter is to assess the present role and weight of China in the global capitalist economy and to present possible scenarios for its future evolution. I will address more specifically the following questions: what is the importance of China as a producer and consumer of goods and services in the world economy? Can China become a producer of technological innovations going past its present stage of importer and user of foreign technology? What are the main internal obstacles able to slow down or even impair China's rise?

China's paradox: the second biggest economy but still a developing country?

China is the country of paradoxes or one could say contradictions. Since 1992, China has described itself as a 'socialist market economy with Chinese characteristics' –when in fact it already has all the features of plain capitalism but yes, with Chinese characteristics. This 'capitalism with Chinese characteristics' is a special brand of capitalism where private ownership of the means of production is officially recognised and plays a growing role, where a new bourgeoisie can openly join the Communist Party as the 'nouveaux riches'. Yet the State and the leadership of the Chinese Communist Party still plays a dominant role in the economic and political sphere and captures a fair chunk of profit for its own sake through the State Owned Enterprises (SOEs).

One salient feature of capitalism is the capacity of the owners of the means of production to reproduce themselves from one generation to another as proprietors. The Chinese characteristic is that there is a fuzzy distinction between the private and public sector. Proprietors, either of private or state sectors, are members of the communist party-state and sometimes belong to the same family and share the same interests: a high rate of economic growth and political stability. In this sense, the concept of 'bureaucratic capitalism' developed in this book encompasses perfectly the Chinese brand of capitalism.

According to the second national economic census held in 2008, SOEs owned 30 per cent of the assets of the industrial and service sectors. They account for around 50 per cent of gross fixed capital formation (investment), and employ 13 per cent of non-agricultural sectors (Brandt and Zhu 2010). Apparently, SOEs seem to play a minor role in the economy. Yet, SOEs are among the biggest enterprises in China, have a monopoly in critical areas such as natural resources (in particular petroleum), steel, telecom and transportation. Usually unknown in the west, they are investing abroad and some are becoming major multinational companies in sectors ranging from oil to banking. Two thirds of Chinese enterprises which appear in the Global Fortune 500 are SOEs. They are managed by a central holding company known as the State-Owned Assets Supervision and Administration Commission (SASAC) and are listed on stock exchanges in Shanghai, Hong Kong or other world financial capitals (Lin and Milhaupt 2011). In a nutshell, they are the core and the engine of growth of China's bureaucratic capitalism. If China becomes the biggest economy in the world, one key issue is the control of world affairs it will give to the Chinese state. But can we seriously expect China to become the biggest economy in a foreseeable future? The answer is yes, although this is controversial.

In terms of absolute size of its Gross Domestic Product (GDP), China has become the second most important economy of the world in 2010 in current US dollars, overtaking Japan and catching up to the USA. The more optimistic commentators expect China to equal the USA before 2020. These estimates are based on various assumptions involving the respective growth rate of the US and Chinese economies, the inflation gap between the two countries and the evolution of the exchange rate of the yuan relative to the US dollar. For instance, the influential review, *The Economist* thinks the convergence at current exchange rates will probably happen in 2019[1].

The IMF estimates that China will overtake the USA in 2017, when the GDP is measured in purchasing power parity[2] (see Figure 1).

Figure 1: China is catching up

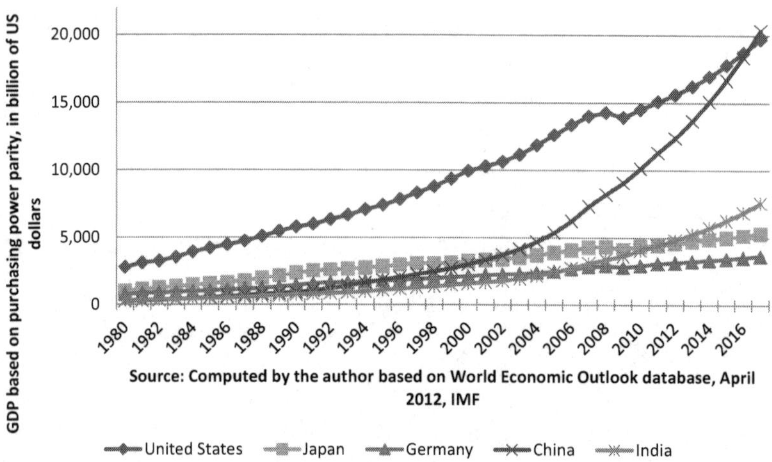

Yet, according to the same IMF data, but measured with the current exchange rate, the GDP of China in 2017 would still be below the US by 35 per cent but about twice the size of the Japanese economy and three times the size of the German economy (see figure 2).

Even if these predictions are in part overestimated and only proven correct with a delay, of say ten years, the fact remains that China is closing the gap with the USA in terms of economic might and is widening the gap with the other biggest capitalist economies. It will be the first time in modern history that a non-western country is not only able to enter the small club of countries that rule global affairs but also a country which, unlike Japan, is not under the political and military domination of the USA. In other terms, fast economic development gives China the necessary power to challenge US hegemony which no other country has been able to do since the collapse

Figure 2: GDP per capita of major countries, 1980-2017

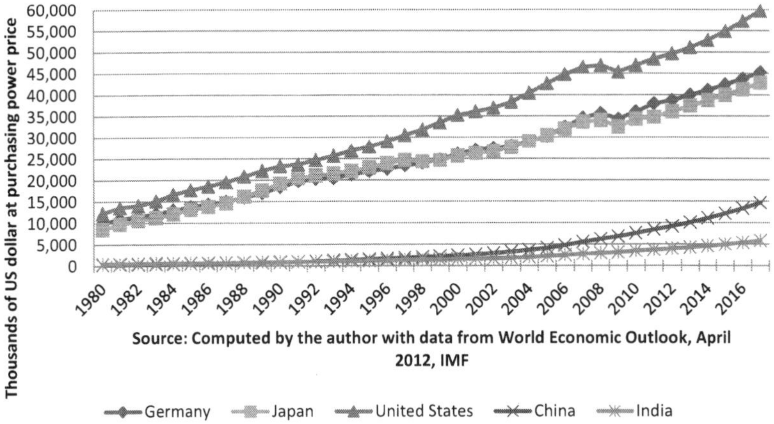

of the Soviet Union. The threat posed by China to the US is even more serious than the Soviet Union used to be since it rests on economic and not primarily military grounds.

One drawback of the comparison between the US and Chinese economies is that in terms of GDP per capita, which is a crude way to measure the average income of inhabitants, China is still lagging very far behind the average income of a US citizen. As figure 2 shows, in 2011 the GDP per capita in purchasing power terms (PPP) was 46,900 dollars in the USA and 8,382 dollars in China, i.e. an almost 6 to 1 difference. Still, in 2017 according to the IMF, the difference would narrow to about 4 to 1. This is still huge. In this sense, in 2011, China still looks like a developing country with a GDP per capita below Brazil (US$ PPP 11,769) and Russia (US$PPP 16,736). But these crude comparisons do not tell the full story for at least two reasons.

First, around this average, inequality of income has increased dramatically in China. This is true of every capitalist country when in the early stages of economic take-off even if the specificity of national political context makes future evolution different. In China, the number of absolute poor has diminished dramatically from 84 per cent of the population in 1981 to 8 per cent in 2008[3] but the income gap between the poor and the rich has widened. The Gini coefficient, which takes a value of zero when income equality is perfect and one when income inequality is extreme, has increased sharply to 0.47 in 2008, up from 0.25 in 1985 (Huang and Wang 2010).[4] This places China among the most unequal countries on a par with the USA and some Latin American countries. The widening gap between urban and rural household income, between coastal and interior provinces, between real income and labour productivity accounts for this growing inequality (Zhu and Wan 2012).

Second, the tremendous size of the Chinese population gives a different dimension to the problem. In 2011, China has a population 4.3 times the size of the USA, 6.9 times the size of Brazil and 9.5 times the size of Russia. For all Chinese citizens to have the same income as the average American citizen, the Chinese GDP would have to be 4.3 times bigger than the US. This is clearly neither likely nor desirable for the conservation of the planet.

But this is not necessary for China to have a strong impact on the world economy. The high concentration of revenues and the huge size of the population combined will contribute to the formation in coastal China of a population exceeding the US but with the same average per capita revenue. According to Holz (2008 p 1688) 'one to two decades from now, coastal dwellers accounting for 42 per cent of China's population in 2005 and exceeding the US population by 87 per cent, may well be as rich, per capita, as the average US citizen. Focusing only on the five fastest-growing provinces in coastal China, with a joint population in 2000 that is 11 per cent larger than the US, moves the cross-over year a few years further to the present'. This historical event, which is probable unless the Chinese economy collapse in between, which is not plausible, will lead to a shift of the centre of gravity of global capitalist accumulation from West to East. To be more precise, if we define like Kharas (2010) the controversial notion of middle-income class[5] as the share of the population which earns from US$10 to US$100 a day, the Chinese middle-income class accounted for 157 million people in 2009 i.e. 12 per cent of the population. According to Kharas's scenario,[6] the Chinese middle-income class, so-defined, would be about 45 per cent of the total Chinese population in 2020 and 75 per cent in 2030: i.e. the same proportion as in the USA today. This amounts to about 625 million and one billion of Chinese people or two and three times the US population in 2020 and 2030 respectively. Of course this rosy scenario which sees China turning mechanically into a developed country is a mere extrapolation of present tendencies and cannot be taken as granted for at least two reasons.

First, the present rate of growth cannot be maintained around 8 per cent in the coming decades. Many factors that have contributed to a high growth will weaken and come to an end: the shift from low-productivity agriculture to high productivity industries, the high rate of capital to labour ratio leading to a decreasing rate of profit, the shrinking labour force and the doubling of old-age dependency, the exhaustion of natural resources and unbearable levels of pollution are some among other factors that explain why the rate of growth will decrease.

Second, and most important, the level of income and social inequalities makes it difficult to imagine a linear development of present China for economic reasons. The past experience of Brazil is enlightening as Kharas (2010 p 31) recalls:

> Between 1965 and 1980, Brazil grew at an average of 5.6 per cent per capita per year, becoming a middle-income country with a per capita income level of US$ 7,600. Yet due to its high income inequality, Brazil's middle class made up only 29 per cent of the country's population in 1980. This made it impossible for the country to rely on middle-class consumption to drive the transformation into an innovation-based economy. Since 1980 the country has remained primarily a commodity exporter, and has struggled to sustain growth. Per capita incomes today are only slightly higher than they were thirty years ago (0.7 per cent annual growth), and the middle class never took off, currently accounting for just 38 per cent of the total population.

The lesson is clear: if China wants to maintain a high rate of growth by making household consumption the main source of demand instead of investment and exports then it has to reduce the high income inequality which means a radical political and social reform.

But what if the rate of growth slows down? The consequence will be a delay in the advent of China becoming the biggest economy in the world but not a reversal of the trend. The World Bank for instance expects Chinese GDP growth to decline gradually from an average near 8.5 per cent in 2011–15 to around 5 per cent in 2026–30 (World Bank and Development Research Center of the State Council, 2012). China's economy would then become the dominant one in 2030 instead of 2020.

China, the biggest shopping centre in the world

Another way to gauge China's tremendous impact on global capitalist accumulation is to observe what it has already achieved instead of looking far into the future. To name a few instances, China has overtaken the USA in iron ore consumption since 1999, for mobile phones since 2001, in beer and copper since 2002, in energy consumption and car sales since 2010[7]. In short, for many products, China is already the biggest world market and for the whole range of retail sales is predicted to overtake the USA in 2014. This gives China the potential to substitute for the USA as the engine of growth for the world economy: one clear piece of evidence is the weight of China in world imports relative to other main regions of the world. In 2010, China's imports amounted to 9.3 per cent of world imports, behind the USA (13.3 per cent) and Western Europe (19.3 per cent).[8] In 2014, it could overtake the USA and Western Europe around 2020. The effect of growing Chinese imports on the world economy is already visible in world commodity markets. Because China's growth relies very much on its industry (which accounts for 46 per cent of its GDP), it has contributed to a commodity boom and a surge in commodity prices with long-lasting consequences on the global economy[9]: it is deepening the over-specialisation of African countries in primary products and producing a deindustrialisation and a return to the specialisation in primary products for some Latin-American countries like Brazil, challenging decades of industrial development. To cope with the boom, countries like Canada, Australia, Brazil and Sub-Saharan countries have increased their production of commodities, investing in mega-projects to exploit hard-to-reach reserves like oil reserves beneath the layer of salt in deep water near the Brazilian coast or tar sands in Canada – with disastrous environmental consequences. This hunt for commodities has also contributed to food price hikes and inflation in many countries which have been an important factor in social unrest.

China, the factory of the world

Of course, China is not solely responsible for these events. But its unique role of 'factory' of the world, beyond being the main 'shopping centre' of the world, gives China a special responsibility. In effect, a big part of Chinese imports is used to produce goods which are then exported to the rest of the world, in particular North America and Europe. This phenomenon, known as global production chain (GPC), which has existed for many years, has acquired a special importance with the capitalist globalisation that started in the middle of the eighties. It means that the various operations, from the design of the product to the manufacture of the components, assembly and marketing, have spread across the world. This international fragmentation of the productive process is especially important in Asia where China is the hub of many GPCs spread across Northeast and Southeast Asia. At the core of the GPC one finds the biggest multinational firms from North America, Europe and Japan and increasingly from emergent countries. These firms many of which were present in Asia for decades, have found in China the best place to assemble parts and components produced elsewhere in Asia and to a lesser extent North America and Europe, to turn them into final products that can be exported anywhere. The reasons to locate final assembly in China were obvious: an unlimited supply of very cheap labour, disciplined by official trade unions and other repressive state institutions, and a vast and growing domestic market. By law, these multinationals had to make partnerships with Chinese firms which were then in a position to learn from the foreign partner, from technology to production and marketing. The huge foreign direct investment that has poured into China since 1978 combined with strong domestic investment from State-Owned Enterprises (SOEs) and new private industrial enterprises contributed to a spectacular industrial development (see figure 3).

Figure 3: Industry share in GDP, 1970-2010

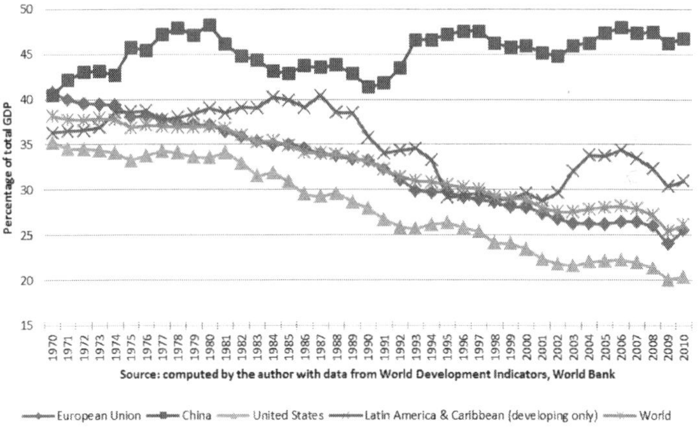

One can see that Chinese industry, measured as a share of GDP, experienced a period of decline between 1978 and 1991 due to the shock created by the reintroduction of market mechanisms but subsequently recovered and now represents 47 per cent of GDP. This appears in stark contrast with the decline of industry at the world level down to 26 per cent, in the US down to 20 per cent and even in Latin America down to 31 per cent in 2010. Even if it were too simplistic to attribute the full decline of the share of industry in the western world by the rise of industry in China, there is a link between the two which corresponds to transferring industrial production from the West to China. Nor can we explain the export boom of Chinese products by the sole role of the global production chain managed by multinational companies. Exports resulting from assembly by GPC are called 'processing exports' and in China represented over half of total Chinese exports in 2009, up from around 5 per cent in 1981 (Zhang, Tang and Zhan 2012). This is indeed a spectacular development which shows the importance of multinationals in Chinese trade. At the same time it shows that 'ordinary' exports realised by Chinese companies are responsible for the other half of Chinese exports which is an impressive result in itself. One important question is to determine the relative share of imported parts and components and domestically produced parts and components in total Chinese exports, in processing exports and ordinary exports. According to Zhang et al. (2012) the share of foreign parts and components in total Chinese exports is 32.2 per cent meaning that the share of Chinese parts and components in Chinese exports is 67.8 per cent, which places China in an intermediary position. It is less than in the USA and Japan, where it reaches about 75 per cent, but higher than in Taiwan (53 per cent), Korea (63 per cent) and Thailand (65 per cent). Of course, for processing exports, the share of domestic content is lower (44.4 per cent) than for 'ordinary' exports where it is very high (92 per cent). A closer look at processing exports reveals that the domestic content is significantly lower in capital-intensive and technologically sophisticated products like household video and audio equipment manufacturing, motor and generator manufacturing and electronic devices and communication equipment (Zhang et al. 2012 p 39:40). This shows that China's increasing export of these products linked to technological innovations such as the Iphone is largely due to its participation in GPC.

This raises the important question of the reality of China's progress in technological upgrading and its capacity to sustain its industrial development and because of the importance of industry in Chinese GDP, its capacity to develop as an independent country and not a country subordinated to foreign multinationals.

China joins the race for technological innovation

Assessing the capacity of China to catch up in the technological race is a difficult task. There are many questions for which there are no answers and no possibility to provide an answer. One can only rely on what is known and what the most relevant theory of technological progress, the theory of a national system of innovation (Freeman 1995), can help us to understand about Chinese transition from accumulation of production capacities to innovation capacities. This theory emphasises the role of the state in creating basic infrastructure, and in investing in education and scientific capabilities. It also underlines the importance of social institutions to facilitate the interactive process of development of technology between enterprises and support institutions and between enterprises themselves. Altenburg, Schmitz and Stamm (2007) have studied in details this transition in the case of China and India and their conclusion stresses how the sheer size of their economies and growth dynamics increases the possibility of leap-frogging certain developments and catch up with OECD countries. It is worth quoting them at length on this precise point:

> .... Fast growth and high savings rates enable China, and increasingly also India, to invest not only in huge infrastructure projects but also in major R&D programs, to set up first-class research and training institutions and technology parks, to acquire foreign licences and even entire firms, to provide competitive salaries and well-equipped research facilities to lure top researchers away from the United States and other industrialised countries, and so on' (Altenburg et al. 2007 p 338). They are helped in this task by the growing share of knowledge that can be transformed from tacit to explicit and thus traded and the participation of their firms in global value chains which gives access not only to markets but to international pools of knowledge, international professional networks. Most of all, because China is politically independent from the USA and European countries, it has been able to '... trade access to foreign technology for access to its national market' (p 337).

Thanks to the combination of these specific advantages, China has been able to climb up the technological ladder but has not been able to make any breakthrough so far in radical innovations. In terms of expenses in research and development, Chinese effort has increased a lot these last years in line with the programme announced in 2006[10] to make 'China an innovation-oriented society by 2020 and one of the world's leading innovators in the longer term' (Wu 2010). The key word is 'indigenous innovation' in 11 strategic areas such as energy, water resources and environmental protection. By 2020, 60 per cent or more of China's economic growth must derive from technological progress. According to Fabre and Grumbach (2012), this is a conscious decision of the Communist Party Political Bureau to base China's long-term growth on technological innovation to substitute a growth pattern based exclusively on capital accumulation and labour mobilisation. Fabre and Grunbach (op cit p 4-5) calls a 'real leap forward' the big push in education and science which started in the years 2000 as opposed to the 'Great Leap Forward' of 1958-59 which was based on the negation of science and technology and the expulsion of scientists and intellectuals in general from positions of power in the Chinese Communist Party and the State. The number of graduates has risen from 1.7 million to 7 million between 2000 and 2008, 39 per cent of them following a scientific curriculum compared to 5 per cent in the USA (Fabre and Grumbach 2012 p 4). To reach the objective '2020 programme', China is to spend by 2020 about 2.5 per cent of the country's gross domestic product in research and development. In effect, China's expenditure reached 1.70 per cent of GDP in 2009, up from 0.71 in 1990, which represents a major effort. Yet, China is still lagging behind Korea, Japan, the USA and Germany where R&D expenditure has also grown recently well beyond 2.5 per cent (see Figure 4).

Figure 4: Gross domestic expenditures in R&D, 2004-2009

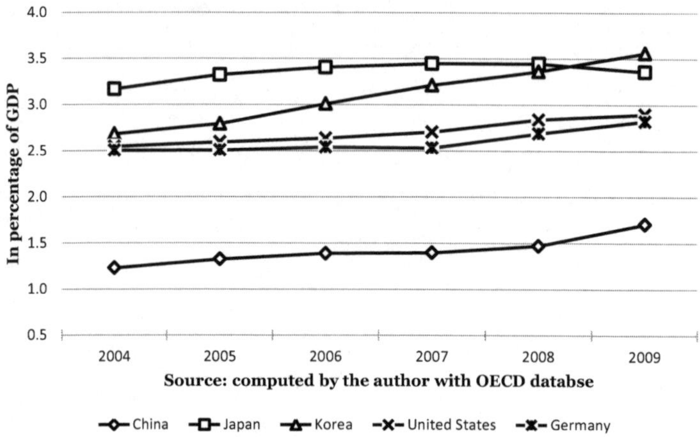

Source: computed by the author with OECD databse

Another limit of the Chinese effort is that in 2008 only 17.2 per cent of total expenditures on research and development were dedicated to research in itself[11] down from 30 per cent in 1995. In the USA, a stable average of 40 per cent is dedicated to research (Wu 2010 p 354). This is a matter of concern for the long term for it means that China is not really geared towards cutting-edge innovations but rather towards adaptation of innovations conceived in other countries. This assessment is confirmed by the small progress in terms of patents registered in the USA by Chinese firms belonging to the 'inventions' category (see Figure 5).

Although Chinese patents have grown in absolute numbers to 3,174 in 2011 up from 119 in 2000, it amounts to 2.7 per cent of total patents registered by foreign firms this year above India (1.1 per cent) but well below Japan (39.8 per cent), South Korea and Germany (about 10 per cent each).

These observations must not lead to dismissing China's push in technological progress. Scientific research takes time, patience and consistency. But it shows that money alone cannot bring short-term results and that leapfrogging is not always possible, especially if the social and political national context is not conducive to not only fast innovation but also mastering of technological progress. The example of the recent development of high-speed train is illustrative on this point.

Figure 5: Invention Patents granted by the US Patent and Trademark Office, 1985-2011

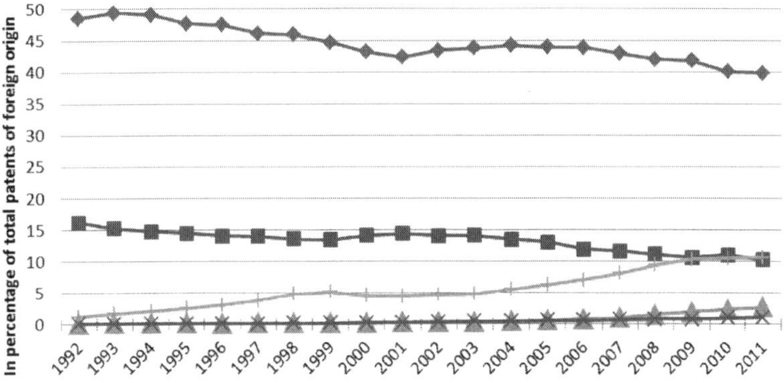

Source: computed by the author with data from the Office of Patents and Trademarks of the USA

JAPAN GERMANY SOUTH KOREA CHINA, PEOPLE'S REPUBLIC OF INDIA

China has embarked on a vast programme of railroad construction to become the biggest country equipped with high-speed train connections. The government and the leadership of the Communist Party have pinned their own and the country's prestige on the programme. It plans to have 19,000 km of high-speed railway in 2014, up from 649km in 2008. But on 23 July 2011, a collision between two high-speed trains which killed 40 and injured 191 people, shed a crude light on the limits of leap-frogging in the Chinese context. Officials attempted a cover-up, prompting public outrage, but this time to no avail. For the first time in years, public outrage turned against the president and the premier Wen Jiabao, who took a long time to pay his respects to victims. Usually, top leaders play the good guys who have to struggle against and punish the bad guys at local levels. This was the case for instance when the Sichuan earthquake killed 69 thousand people, among them many children in faulty-built schools. This time anger flowed on the Internet, Twitter and even the media: officials were at pains to censure it. This dramatic accident is the result of vast corruption from the Minister of Transport and other top rank officials[12], of corruption in enterprises which constructed the railways which preferred to use sand and stones instead of concrete to make more profit, and poor management of a complex rail network. It reveals the difficulty or impossibility to build at breakneck pace huge infrastructure that has taken decades to be constructed in other countries[13]. But more fundamentally, it reveals the difficulty in mastering complex technology in a country where there are no counter-powers to limit corruption, to correct bad decisions, to improve quality, and to challenge the legitimacy of decisions taken by bureaucrats. High-speed trains are too expensive for the majority of Chinese people, they serve primarily businessmen not the hundreds of millions of daily commuters who still suffer from the lack of efficient and secure public transport and often have to use motor vehicles.

Conclusion

This example, which in addition to the many food scams that create anguish and suspicion among the population, shows that it will be increasingly difficult for the Chinese Communist Party to pursue its development strategy to transform China into a developed country, even the biggest one, while maintaining a tight grip on a society that is getting more educated and more informed of the reality outside China. The Tienanmen Square massacre in 1989 happened before 500 million Chinese became Internet users. China's economic development may hit soon the limits of what a dictatorship can control and forbid while still trying to unleash innovation and development. I am not pretending that there exists a technological determinism which would favour the democratisation of a society once a certain level of development of productive forces is achieved. Many hopes have been dashed in Southeast Asia in this regard. On the other hand, it is hard to imagine, for many reasons, that the future biggest capitalist economy, China, could be a dictatorship like it is today. The growing number of protests by workers and farmers in China since 2008 in a context marked by a change in regime in the labour market with the end of surplus labour (Fang and Meiyan 2012) and the emergence of a second generation of migrant workers who do not accept the sufferings endured by the previous generation (Ngai and Lu Huilin 2010), not to mention the thousands of protests in the countryside against land grabbing, confirm the hypothesis that China is entering a new phase of growing social conflicts which will not be resolved by mere repression. Whether economic structural change will be combined with political change is an open question. But, as we have seen previously, China will not become a high per capita income country without a strong reduction in inequalities and this will not occur without a profound democratisation of Chinese society.

July 2012

References

Altenburg, T., H. Schmitz & A. Stamm. 2007. Breakthrough? China's and India's Transition from Production to Innovation. *World Development,* vol. 36, no. 2, 325-344.

Brandt, L. & X. Zhu. 2010. Accounting for China's Growth. In *IZA DP,* 59. Bonn: The Institute for the Study of Labor (IZA)

Chun, N. 2010. Middle Class Size in the Past, Present and Future: A Description of Trends in Asia. In *ADB Economics Working Paper Series No. 217.* Manila, Philippines: Asian Development Bank.

Fabre, G. & S. Grumbach. 2012. *The World upside down, China's R&D and innovation strategy.*

Fang, C. & W. Meiyan. 2012. Labour Markets changes, Labour disputes and Social Cohesion in China. In *Perspectives on Global Development: Social Cohesion,* ed. O.D. Center, 43. Paris: OECD.

Freeman, C. 1995. The 'National System of Innovation' in Historical Perspective. *Cambridge Journal Economics,* vol. 19, no. 1, 5-24.

Holz, C.A. 2008. China's Economic Growth 1978-2025: What We Know Today About China's Economic Growth Tomorrow. *World Development,* vol. 36, no. 10, 1665-1691.

Huang, Y. & B. Wang. 2010. Rebalancing China's economic structure. In *China: The Next Twenty Years of Reform and Development,* eds. R. Garnaut, J. Golley & L. Song, 422. Canberra, ANU E Press, The Australian National University and Social Sciences Academic Press (China).

Kharas, H. 2010. The Emerging Middle Class in Developing Countries. In *Development Centre Working Papers,* 61. Paris: OECD.

Lin, L.-W. & C.J. Milhaupt. 2011. We are the (National) Champions: Understanding the Mechanisms of State Capitalism in China. In *Columbia Law and Economics Working Paper,* 67. Columbia University.

Ngai, P. & Lu Huilin. 2010. Unfinished Proletarianization: Self, Anger, and Class Action among the Second Generation of Peasant-Workers in Present-Day China. *Modern China,* vol. 36, no. 5, 493-519.

Wu, Y. 2010. Indigenous innovation for sustainable growth. In *China: the next twenty years of reform and developpement,* eds. R. Garnaut, J. Golley & L. Song, 341. Canberra, ANU E Press, Social Sciences Academic Press (China).

Xiaolu, W. 2010. *Analysing Chinese Grey Income: 2nd Survey Study on China's Grey Income and Income Distribution.* Crédit Suisse Expert Insights, Asia Pacific/China Equity Research.

Zhang, J., D. Tang & Y. Zhan. 2012. Foreign Value-added in China's Manufactured Exports: Implications for China's Trade Imbalance. *China & World Economy,* vol. 20, no. 1, 27-48.

Zhu, C. & G. Wan. 2012. Rising Inequality in China and the Move to a Balanced Economy. *China & World Economy,* vol. 20, no. 1, 83-104.

Notes

1 This is based on the assumption of an average rate of growth of 7.75 per cent in China and 2.5 per cent in the USA, a 4 per cent inflation rate in China compared to 1.5 per cent in the USA and a 3 per cent appreciation of the yuan relative to the dollar on top of the inflation gap of 2.5 per cent. See *The Economist*, 'Becoming number one, 24 September 2011 and more recently http://www.economist.com/blogs/freeexchange/2012/03/china-will-overtake-america-within-decade-want-bet.
2 The purchasing power parity takes into account the fact that prices are usually lower in developing countries than in developed countries. For instance, if prices in China are three times lower than in the USA, then the Chinese GDP has to be multiplied by three to be compared with the US one.
3 These figures are provided by the World Bank and refer to its definition of absolute poverty as earning less than US 1.25 per day in purchasing power parity which is the minimum income to meet basic needs such as eating. In absolute numbers it means that the number of poor in China has decreased from 835 million in 1981 to 106 million in 2008, which is the biggest reduction registered to date.
4 Inequality is certainly underestimated because rich people hide part of their revenues or refuse to answer, especially in China where the 'grey economy' nurtured by corruption amounts to 15 per cent of the Chinese GDP. 51.9 per cent of disposable income is in the hands of the top 10 per cent of Chinese earners compared to 47.2 per cent in the US. 7.8 per cent of income is in the hands of the bottom 40 per cent of Chinese earners compared to 9.6 per cent in the US. The Gini coefficient would in fact be 0.5.See Xiaolu, W. 2010.
5 The notion of a middle class is much debated in economics, sociology and political science where it does not have the same meaning. One obvious error is to think that being part of the middle class in the economic sense entails mechanically adhering to an identical sociological identity with the same political ideas and behaviour. In economics only, there are various definitions, absolute and relative leading to different measures of the middle class. For an introductory survey and alternative measure in the Asian case, see for instance Chun, N. 2010..
6 This scenario rests on several hypotheses such as a technological progress of 1.3 per cent, per year which corresponds to the average long-run rate of the past 125 years observed in the USA; a typology of four group of countries (advanced economies, converging developing countries, stalled-middle income countries and poor countries with no convergence trends); capital accumulation consistent with the past historical average; country specific demographic changes of the 15-64 age group assuming constant labour force participation rates. Advance countries would grow at 2.3 per cent per annum in the next 30 years and convergent countries like China at 8.2 per cent. For more details, see Kharas (2010).
7 Source: 'The dating game', *The Economist*, 27 December 2011.
8 Source: United States Statistical Division.

9 China imports around 50 per cent of world production of iron ore and coal, 45 per cent of lead and zinc, 40 per cent of aluminium, copper and nickel and 10 per cent of oil.

10 The 'National Medium and Long-term Program for Science and Technology Development (2006–2020)'.

11 The rest, 82.8 per cent, is dedicated to development.

12 The Minister of Transport was sacked in February 2011 before the accident after he was accused of having skimmed off as much as 1 billion yuan ($152m) in bribes and of keeping as many as 18 mistresses.

13 Japan's bullet train has had just one fatality in 47 years, a passenger caught in a door. See, *The Economist*, 6 August 2011.

CHINA: GLOBALIZATION AND NATIONALIST RESPONSES[1]

Au Loong Yu

The anti-globalization movement again captured world attention in December 2005, when Korean farmers stormed the Hong Kong Police barricades to protest against the 6th Ministerial Meeting of the World Trade Organization (WTO). At the peak of the week of action there were 7,000 protesters. Local participation from Hong Kong was weak; 2,000 at most. It is striking is that mainland Chinese participation was even weaker. This was the first time that a global justice campaign took place at the door of mainland China. South Korea, with a population of 50 million, sent 1,600 protestors to Hong Kong. Meanwhile, only a handful of Chinese activists were present, and probably none from rural areas, despite China's population having reached 1.3 billion.

Was this because China plays an insignificant role in the era of globalization? Obviously not. Today it is common knowledge that China has emerged as a major global importer and exporter and is the top FDI (Foreign Direct Investment) recipient country. It is a big player in pushing for free trade as well. But contrary to what many Asian non-governmental organizations (NGOs) hoped or expected, at the last Ministerial Meeting of the WTO, China joined hands with India and Brazil to make a deal with the US and the EU, successfully concluding the negotiation and thus saving the Doha Round from a second failure.

The People's Republic of China, while pushing for a fiercely pro-free trade and pro-business agenda on the one hand, maintains an iron fist to crush any form of autonomous organization and social resistance against neoliberalism on the other, which explains why there were not so many mainland Chinese participants in the protest against the WTO in Hong Kong. The repressive regime in general and the ban on independent trade unions, strikes and demonstrations has helped China evolve into the sweatshop of the world – a great engine driving the global race to the bottom – and thus a great trading partner of the US. This has also, ironically, laid the ground for a rising nationalist response to globalization.

Although the global justice movement, defined as a mass campaign against neoliberalism from below, does not exist in mainland China at the moment, it will definitely develop in the medium term, for the simple reason that China's complete reintegration with global capitalism has resulted in ever-growing grievances. After more than 20 years of high growth at the expense of the toiling masses, we have recently witnessed a continuous development of spontaneous social resistance to the onslaught of privatization, exploitation and unemployment. In 2007, when the transition period for accession to the WTO is due to end, China will have to open up nearly all of its markets. Even if Chinese domestic industry and agriculture are able ultimately to survive or even enjoy more growth, this will be a period of even greater restructuring and crisis. China is now entering a new period of crisis; it is more a question of which direction the resistance will go, rather than whether it will die down on its own.

Though social movements have not been allowed to develop, for the past 10 years there has been a heated debate on globalization among Chinese intellectuals. In a broader sense there has already been an 'anti-globalization' movement for more than a decade, if we define the term to include theoretical debates. While the New Liberals embrace globalization, the so called New Left has been arguing against it. The outcome of the debate will have an important bearing on the future course of China and its social resistance to globalization. The purpose of this essay is to review this debate and, as well as identifying the rise of nationalism as the biggest challenge to the Left, to examine both the strengths and weaknesses of the New Left argument.

The nationalist version of anti-globalization

Corporate globalization has been remarkably successful in driving down wages and the welfare of working people across the world. Globalization as such must be and has been resisted, hence the birth of the global justice movement. The movement is vastly heterogeneous, but internationalist aspirations are strongly visible.

The foregoing statement should, however, be balanced by the fact that there exist nationalist sentiments and even far-right thinking in the discourses of anti-globalization as well.

Ray Kiely has observed that

> One of the most prominent populists in the United States, Pat Buchanan, has blamed globalization for the decline of manufacturing employment, the erosion of national sovereignty, increasing immigration, and the movement towards global socialism represented by institutions such as the IMF and World Bank ... This appeal to tradition is also a unifying theme among other right-wing challenges to globalization, including Hindu nationalism in India, Islamic nationalisms in the Middle East and Asia, and resurgent fascism in Europe. Right-wing nationalism therefore appeals to 'the people' and the nation as a defensive response to the uncertainties of globalization.[2]

Gerard Greenfield, in his essay *Bandung redux: Anti-Globalization Nationalisms in Southeast Asia* expresses deep concern over the rise of Asian nationalism:

> While the mass mobilizations that occurred in response to the Asian economic crisis of 1997-98 broadened the base of anti-globalization movements, the revolutionary potential of these protests and their limitations remain subjects of debate among activists. What these movements did show was the primacy of nationalism as the reference point for popular discontent with globalization.
>
> The desire for an independent strategy to emerge from a correct set of policy choices, unrelated to the structural power and interests of capital, is a recurring weakness in the (Thai) Visions Project. Insofar as capital is incorporated into the analysis at all, it is premised on a foreign-national dichotomy according to which national capital becomes virtually synonymous with the nation... These broad political alliances enabled Thai Rak Thai to channel nationalist sentiment into a comprehensive political project aimed at radically reorganizing the state to better serve the interests of 'progressive capitalists.[3]

In the globalized market today, large and even medium-sized domestic capital is integrated into global competition. It follows that the term 'national capital', understood as something separate from and opposed to foreign capital, is more misleading than ever. If the left and the labour movement align with national capital to oppose 'western imperialist'-led globalization, it might turn out that labour will merely be helping national capital to further reinforce the logic of globalization, albeit a version of globalization which is a bit more favourable to 'national capital's' needs. Thus the nationalist response to globalization necessarily subjects working people to the interests of ruling elites in the fight for the supreme cause of an often fictitious 'national' interest.[4]

A new banner for the CCP

The first well known Chinese Nationalist is He Xin, who was allowed to publish anti-Western books in the early nineties, against the background of the post-Tiananmen crackdown and the subsequent sanctions imposed by the west. What is worth noting is not He Xin's nationalist response to the hostility of the west at the time, but rather the fact that little debate was stimulated by his book. Even after the US stopped and searched the Chinese ship *The Milky Way* in international waters, little public protest could be heard. When in 1996 the nationalist Wang Xiaodong published the book *China Can Say No* targeting the US as the chief enemy, there was some sensation but this soon died down. It was not until May 1999 when the US bombed the Chinese Embassy in Yugoslavia, triggering off massive anti-US protests, that nationalism definitely made a comeback.

I define this as new Chinese nationalism. While old Chinese nationalism, from 1840-1949, was to a great extent a legitimate response to foreign aggression and popular aspirations for national independence, this new Chinese nationalism is entirely different. It is both a response by the ruling elite and some important intellectuals to internal and external problems, which have arisen during the course of re-integration with global capitalism, as well as a means of advocating the modernizing of China via the strengthening of the one-party state. The ultimate purpose of new Chinese nationalism is the re-building of the glory of the past great Chinese Empire, thus the propaganda on 'the rise of China'[5] does not contain anything progressive.

Zheng Yongnian of the National University of Singapore, in his book *Globalization and State Transformation in China*, argues that the revival of nationalism springs from the new needs of the CCP:

> In the post-Mao era, the search for political legitimacy has replaced the foreign threat and has become the primary factor underpinning the revival of Chinese nationalism. In other words, the main sources for nationalism in the post-Mao era are domestic rather than external.[6]

Elsewhere he elaborates what he means by 'the search for political legitimacy':

> Nationalism has been used by the Chinese Communist Party as a response to the decline in Maoist faith, and nationalism is ready to become another vision of the CCP ideology.[7]

Zheng's dichotomy of domestic/external is not entirely satisfactory. Yet his contention that the CCP needs nationalism for its new source of legitimacy is correct. In place of a vision of a world communism with China occupying the leading role (a vision which had become obsolete by the early 1980s), the project of building a great Chinese nation and recovering the leading position it enjoyed until 1840 seems more plausible. Moreover, it is in the interest of the one-party state to divert popular discontent, such as the 1989 democratic movement, to external enemies. Hence the CCP began to change course on the issue of nationalism and in practice encouraged its re-awakening. The CCP's previous position on nationalism was to condemn it as the 'bourgeoisie's viewpoint on nations'.[8] As a matter of fact, there has always been an element of nationalism in its policies on ethnic minorities, public education and cultural programs throughout its rule: however this has been packaged as patriotism. Yet it had never explicitly endorsed nationalism, let alone allowed openly nationalist writings to be published. The policy began to change in the 1980s, when the CCP gradually opted for a full-scale embrace of global capitalism.

The CCP may loosen control over part of the economy, perhaps even the financial sector, to private business and foreign capital, but it is not going to loosen control over production and distribution of information, because it does not want to concede power over what and how people think. When virtually all publishing houses, media and film companies etc. are still in state hands and have not been affected by the great wave of privatization, what the CCP allows or forbids to appear in public is paramount in the shaping of 'public opinion' and debate. No book is ever published, no film is ever made, without some form of censorship. It is here that the state's position or 'taste' becomes crucial. All dissident voices have been severely censored; democratic appeals, labour advocacy and even mild criticism of environmental policy. Conversely, the party allows the production and wide distribution of nationalist works in all areas.

For the past ten years we have seen book after book and TV programme after programme glorifying past great emperors, advocating Chinese chauvinism and anti-western thinking, or even outright social Darwinism and fascism. Between 2004 and 2006, a state publisher printed 900,000 copies of the novel *Wolf Totem*. The story tells of the fierce and vigorous Mongolian wolves. Fearing that readers might not understand him, the author wrote a long postscript to tell them his motive. According to him, the Chinese must learn from the Mongolian wolves in order to survive in the jungle of globalization; that Chinese civilization was once so great only because it had, for thousands of years, absorbed the culture of the wolves' worship of northern nomads, helping the elites to maintain a great empire. This is outright social Darwinism and Chinese messianism.

In the 1980s, the themes of TV programmes and books were often dominated by a deep sense of national inferiority, fear of being marginalized in global competition[9] and a yearning for social reform. The mood has radically changed since the middle of 1990s, when the CCP became confident that the west could not resist the temptation of the huge Chinese market, and that western governments and capitalists were ready to forgive the 1989 crackdown in order to have a share of the market. The fact that China has been able to avoid the miserable fate of the Soviet Union and in contrast has been experiencing high growth has further boosted the self-confidence of the CCP.

It is against this background that, since the middle of 1990s, there has been a change of tone in 'public opinion', TV programmes journals and books, etc. In place of national inferiority has come a sense of national self-assurance and an eagerness to recover the past glory of the Middle Kingdom. The 1999 bombing of the Chinese embassy by the US further reminded the CCP and common Chinese that the US is not a reliable partner after all, and the sense of an external threat further provided fuel for nationalist feelings. This also coincided with a period of intense negotiation with the US over China's accession to WTO, in which the US was forcing China into more concessions than most developing countries need to make. Furthermore, foreign capital has been fast in buying up Chinese firms, which many have regarded as a threat to the economic security of China.

New Liberals, nationalists, and the New Left

We have seen that Zheng thinks that 'the main sources for nationalism in the post-Mao era are domestic rather than external'. This is a hotly-debated issue between the New Liberals and the 'New Left'. By the term New Liberal we refer to Chinese liberals and neoliberals. Mixing the two together in the same category reflects the fact that it is difficult to distinguish the two in the Chinese context. Although in the west the dividing line between the two has been blurred, in China we can witness liberals like Yu Jie overflowing with such enthusiasm towards privatization, the WTO, the sacking of SOE workers, the US attack on Iraq and so on and so forth, that they carry few liberal values that are progressive. The New Liberals think that the greatest enemy of China is its own obsolete state institutions, while globalization is the incarnation of the main current of modernization and civilization. Accordingly, the greatest horror for China is to stop half-way towards full integration. So, if there is a rise in nationalism, it is only the fault of domestic institutions. Zheng's comment echoes what the New Liberals have been arguing in their debate with the New Left.

The New Left, according to Dale Wen, a visiting scholar in the US and also one of the New Left, may include people from 'social democrat to economic nationalist to Maoist'.[10] Its leading spokespersons tend to argue in the opposite direction of the New Liberals. If anything goes wrong in China, the blame should lie with external enemies, namely globalization and imperialism. Whenever prominent New Leftists make charges against the CCP, most likely they say that the CCP is too soft in dealing with external challengers.[11] In the dichotomy of market / state, foreign / national, west / east, the Liberals tend to argue in favour of the former paradigm, while the New Left tends to favour the latter paradigm.

In 2004 the New Liberals put together their polemics against the nationalists and the New Left in a book *Qian Liu (Under Current) – Critique on and Rethinking of Narrow Nationalism*. One of the authors, Xiao Xuehui, attacked the nationalists for believing:

> that 'the law of might makes right still constitute the basic principle of this world' … The nationalist cannot see that many countries in the world, US included, is …. making the rules (governing the world) more just, more fair and reasonable in their handling of international affairs.'[12]

The more famous liberal, Qin Hui, argued that

> Liberalism, in the final analysis, implies Universalism. This is because economic liberalization and its impartiality demands that all factors of production move freely around the globe … Under the conditions of fair competition, the return of the factors of production tends to be equalized …. For poor countries, to fight for free movement of all factors of production is more advantageous than to fight against free trade. Universal Liberalism is necessarily more effective than nationalism in the defence of national interest.[13]

The New Liberals actively support China's accession to the WTO. Liu Junning, another well-known liberal professor, suggested that:

> China's accession to WTO will pressure the Chinese institutions of economic management to reform ... When Western companies come to China in large scale, they will demand a more open and fair market economy ... Accession to WTO requires the Chinese government to increase openness of its policy and action... This is determined by the principle of openness of market economy and the principle of accountability as well ... Accession to WTO implies a China now officially integrated into the world capitalist system and its entire economic and political institution, characterized by market economy and democracy.[14]

This is the crudest version of market determinism one can imagine. But let us proceed to read their writings on politics and war. The famous Yu Jie condemned the New Left for their denouncing of the US's attack on Iraq in 2003, identifying this as support for Saddam. He wrote:

> There is a kind of war, which is fought to defend the ultimate value of liberty and humanity. We regard the USA's war against the Saddam regime of Iraq as one of these ... Days ago, a group of Chinese intellectuals issued a so-called anti-war statement. We believe the statement represents an exacerbation of the degeneration of Chinese intellectuals. The authors of this statement disregard the universal moral value of humanity, and express deep rooted hatred against the US which represents civilization and the progress of humanity.[15]

One may wonder if a sincere liberal could have written that. In Yu Jie's case one may even suspect that he is simply an accomplice of the US Empire. The New Liberals' enthusiasm for privatization, which has resulted in 40 million workers being sacked, has led to the New Liberals being nick-named the 'Partitionists' (of state assets).

While the New Liberals tend to embrace everything arising from globalization, Nationalists like Wang Xiaodong are just the opposite. In the aftermath of the US bombing of the Chinese embassy, Wang published a book *The Chinese Road Under the Shadow of Globalization,*[16] which mocks the post-Cold War world as nothing but the same old story of 'might makes right', in contrast to the notion of the New World Order as promoted by the elder Bush. He regards the pro-US Liberals as nothing but people who deny their own cultural and traditional identity, which he labels as 'inverse racism'. He repeatedly argues that since the nation state is still paramount for security, it follows that nationalism is still an important value. Instead of uncritical integration with globalization, China should opt for 'splendid isolation', should place no hope on any alliance with any state, and rely only on her own defensive capacity. In 2000 he released *On Contemporary Nationalism* which refers positively to the Nazi theory of 'living space', and openly embraces social Darwinism.

However, the rise of the 'New Left' and some of its main spokespersons' subsequent embracing of nationalism since the turn of the century is of more importance than the works of old nationalists. For, unlike old nationalists, major figures of the New Left are drawing the attention of the leadership of CCP.

The term New Left may lead non-Chinese readers to evaluate them in the light of the 1960s new left in the west. However there is no ideological link between the two. The Chinese New Left is a term used to distinguish it from the old left, or conservatives, who are die-hard Stalinists. The New Left is by contrast very diverse. People considered to be New Left have huge differences among themselves. Their main common ground is a critique of globalization, the market, privatization, and liberal democracy. There is less agreement among them as to the alternatives to liberal or neoliberal discourses. A common point among leading New Leftists may be the emphasis on the role of the one-party state, the value of collectivism, the importance of holding the multi-ethnic Chinese state together, a more autonomous path of economic development, and reference to a Maoist legacy, although not every one of the New Leftists share all of the above.

Major spokespersons of the New Left display strong statist tendencies and support for the one-party state, going back as early as the post-Tiananmen crackdown, although at the time the term New Left had not yet appeared. While the New Liberals welcomed the collapse of Soviet Union, the New Left regards it as a disaster, a fate which China must try to avoid at all cost. In fact, their anxiety to keep the multi-ethnic Chinese state intact – with the Han being the dominant ethnicity – is so great that one may say that it is their primary concern, overriding all other values, be it democracy or equality. Their scepticism toward neoliberalism and liberal democracy is chiefly driven by their anxiety about 'stability', which they see as threatened by market reform, accession to the WTO, implementation of parliamentary elections, etc., which are not desirable because they may lead to the collapse of the Chinese state.

In fact, this train of thought echoes the Deng and Jiang administration's well known statement at that time: Stability overrides everything! The statement is a reply to any aspiration for the rehabilitation of the 1989 movement, or for democratic elections, or freedom of speech. It is obvious, then, that the first New Leftists are simply allying themselves with the authorities. The first well known New Leftists to write on this were Wang Shaoguang and Hu Angang. While the liberals believe the state must shrink in order to facilitate a growing market economy, Hu and Wang argue the opposite. In 1993 they published *A Study of China State Capacity*[17] in which they argue that a strong state is necessary for market reform. They argue that the revenue of the central government has been far too low, which makes China vulnerable to centrifugal forces that might lead to it ending up like Yugoslavia. While the particular issue of central revenue may be a case worth making, the authors in fact have a larger concern than this. Two years later Hu produced *Challenging China* expressing his worry about a possible collapse after Deng's death:

> Whether China can peacefully and stably make a transition to the post-Deng era is the core issue ... Mao Zedong knew that the Cultural Revolution which he had launched was very unpopular; in contrast Deng Xiaoping knows that the reform and openness which he launched is popular ... But he knows that a country's fate depending on the authority of one or two particular persons is unhealthy and dangerous ... which makes the present need to strengthen institutional reconstruction ever more important and urgent.[18]

The major advice he gives for 'institutional reconstruction' is not only the strengthening of central power through tax reform and the eradication of corruption, but the strengthening of the present one-party state. Another New Leftist, Cui Zhiyuan, refers to the Maoist legacy and calls for 'mass participation' and 'economic democracy'. He is deeply sceptical of liberal democracy and parliamentary elections, seeing them as vulnerable to manipulation by the wealthy. He praised Mao's idea of the Angang Charter as the best alternative. Angang is a steel mill that promoted the idea of workers participation in the mill's management in the sixties, while cadres took turns working in the workshops. The experiment received Mao's endorsement, for he saw it as an expression of economic democracy. Cui writes:

> The Angang Charter 'is the best part of Mao's Thought. Disregarding those mistakes made during the implementation of Angang Charter, its idea of economic democracy is still a treasure of spiritual resources for China in the coming of the 21st Century.'

The Angang Charter is largely forgotten in China now, but according to Cui it flourishes in Japan and has become the mode of operation of the Toyota Company, which due to its post-Fordist organization allows elements of economic democracy.[19]

Toyota as a model for economic democracy?

Cui favours elections as long as party politics is banned, because with the ban:

> It will avoid a scenario where opposition parties confront the ruling party … The Chinese Communist Party implemented the monistic leadership of the Party since 1943. This has two implications, firstly, it reinforces the control of the party (over the society), secondly, it makes the interests of the party and the interests of the country merge.'[20]

'Merge' by killing hundreds if not thousands of innocents in 1989?

But let us return to his model of Angang. It must be stressed that Angang never had workers' participation, through democratic election, in its top management, nor at the plant level, nor at the workshop level, but only at the level of the work team. It looks ineffectual when it is compared to the model of workers' self-management model in former Yugoslavia which granted workers power to choose the management. To make a big case of 'economic democracy' out of the Angang experiment is simply ridiculous. The experiment of requiring leading cadres to work on the frontline is just reviving the old vision of Xu You, who lived more than 2000 years ago. He advocated an equal society where kings worked side-by-side with farmers to till the land. This vision, however, has nothing to do with a contemporary view of socialism. The latter envisages an equal society, characterized not by coercing mental labourers to perform physical labour but rather the elimination of the social division of these two kinds of labour through technological innovation, the shortening of labour time and the elimination of exploitation. Mao's endorsement of the Angang experiment only betrayed the fact that his vision amounted to what Marx called 'crude communism'.

Unfortunately, such nostalgia for Mao's 'crude communism' is characteristic of today's New Left. They regard Mao's legacy as the only ideological alternative to neoliberal discourse, without noticing that it is Mao's overdoing of 'state socialism' in the first place, that made both Deng's 'socialist market economy' and the liberal discourse sound so convincing to a major section of the bureaucracy and the intellectuals. What is more problematic than the appropriate evaluation of the Angang model is Cui's attempt tocounterpose the Angang model to democratic reform. By making the Angang molehill into a mountain of 'economic democracy', he is rejecting political democratic aspiration and siding with the one-party dictatorship.

The merging of some New Leftists and Nationalists

By the late 1990s the New Left's appeal began to grow significantly, at the same time as great anxiety across a country in the midst of 'external' threats. China's opening to the world had entered into a new period. The fear that China's national industry would go under, in the face of direct competition in the domestic market, looked very real. In 2003, foreign firms accounted for 31 per cent of all manufacturing output in China, up from 9.5 per cent in 1992. The growth of the market share of foreign capital at the expense of state-owned enterprises (SOEs), and the immense pressure to restructure SOEs in order to maintain competitiveness after China's accession to the WTO, resulted in 40 million SOE workers being sacked. TNCs and the WTO, agents of globalization, were considered by some as an 'external threat' to China's economic security, and to a certain extent this observation has a grain of truth. Meanwhile, a new wave of nationalist feelings was triggered off by the 1999 US bombing of the Chinese embassy in Belgrade. Despite the fact that the US and China have been deeply dependent on each other economically, the US holds the view that China is one of her chief competitors and, as such, needs to be contained. In light of this, Zheng's argument that 'the main sources for nationalism in the post-Mao era are domestic rather than external', is problematic.

It is to the credit of the New Left that they were the first to criticize the New Liberals in this new period, for otherwise the dominance of the latter might have been even more pronounced. Two scholars, Han Deqiang and Yang Fan, became the most well-known spokespersons of the New Left at the turn of the century. They have written extensively against globalization and China's accession to WTO. In 2000 Han published *The Crash – The Global Trap and China's Realistic Choice.*[21] He describes the high hopes among Chinese on WTO accession and the supposed efficiency of the market as 'market romanticism'. Contrary to the neoliberals' claim, China's accession toward the WTO under the current terms would only jeopardize the infant national industry. He noted that:

> The effect of globalization is the rapid seizure of the high value-added branches of the Chinese economy by foreign capital and imported goods.

> Some of them have now been totally dominated by foreign capital. SOEs and other (domestic firms) have found their profit sources are drying up, losses are reported, bad debts are rising, firms are on the verge of bankruptcy, and real unemployment rises steeply. All of these seriously threaten the betterment of people's livelihood and social stability.[22]

In place of 'market romanticism' Han counter poses 'market realism', which sees protectionism, rather than free trade, as necessary for developing countries. In the book he does not oppose China's accession to the WTO in principle, but merely criticises the terms. He only argues for a better deal for China's accession, one that would better protect China's market and at the same time enable China to acquire a bigger share of the world market. The question is: how to achieve this? His answer is:

> Market realism demands that we take the state to be the embodiment of our highest interest, and to have a sober understanding of the market as a battlefield of competition. Under the guidance of market realism, all our infant industry will be combined and formed into a single unit under the auspices of the state, and then join competition in the world market, fight a pro-longed war of the weak against the strong, and eventually achieve the genuine rise of China.[23]
>
> When we ultimately win this economic war, China will not only develop fully within the WTO regime, but it will even become possible to dominate it.[24]

There was a story, often told in the media, about how a mother wrote a letter to her son, who was studying in the US and working part-time washing dishes. She told her son, 'Son, study hard. In the future, when our country grows strong and powerful, then we will make those Laowai (westerners) wash dishes for us.'

Han's critique of globalization and WTO is essentially what this mother advised her son. It is not really opposing corporate-led globalization as such, but essentially advocacy for Chinese version of globalization, one which may have a stronger element of protectionism, but which essentially is just a second route for China's integration with global capitalism, in contrast to the first route dictated by the US and EU. In place of the Americanization of the world, Han wants Sinolization. He is not very sure if China can attain this; nevertheless it is his objective. Hence there is always an element of Chinese messianism in Han's writings:

> If the Chinese path can solve what western civilization cannot not solve, the Chinese nation will be able to conquer the heart of the world, and China will stand in the East as a rich, democratic and civilized nation.[25]

Another well-known New Leftist, Yang Fan, lays out his programme in his recent article *2005-6: Ideological and Theoretical Struggle in Chinese Society*:

> On the question of development, (we need) to base our fundamental research on the theory of the Great Nation, with which we can find the path towards the rise of China as a special and great country.
>
> On the question of opening up to the world against the background of globalization, we need to explore the road to our national security and the rise of our nation. We need to break the logic of capital, to abandon the assumption of the absence of external enemies, and put national security as the core issue of our strategic adjustment.
>
> On the question of reform, we uphold the kind of reform which is fair, and to achieve theoretical transcendence over both right and left discourses and abolish the dogma and fundamentalism of both planned economy and the market. In place of those, we propose a new ideological guideline for reforms ... the concept of 'strategic national industry'. We must pay special attention to guide private entrepreneurs and private business into National Industry.
>
> On the question of theory, we uphold a kind of central left position which combines new socialism and patriotism. We are for an alliance with the centre right, the centre and the left liberals, even for a bloc with the planned-economy fundamentalists – the old left – in order to build a common front to oppose the Chinese neoliberals and the far right partitionists.[26]

This programme is nothing new. It is the same old story of state-led growth. Han and Yang embrace Great Han nationalism so completely that they have been urging the government to attack Taiwan and incorporate it as soon as possible. 'If we win this war,' Han wrote, 'the years of insult inflicted upon us by the US will be left behind, the Chinese people will once more unite around the CCP, and the development of the Chinese economy and society in the 21st Century will then be guaranteed.'[27]

Han and Yang, and many of the New Left as well as the CCP, have become so immersed in Great Han nationalism that they can never conceive that it is the democratic right of the Taiwanese people to decide for themselves if they want unification with mainland China and on what terms. It should come as no surprise that they are also blind to the fact that ethnic minorities in Tibet and Xinjiang have been denied basic democratic rights. If 'stability overrides everything', it must also, logically, override the rights of minorities and democratic rights.[28]

Domestic factors are also external

The essential argument of Han and Yang is neither market protectionism nor Keynesianism, but the strengthening of the one-party state as China's salvation from the external threat of globalization and as a tool for it to eventually out-compete rivals in the world market. Meanwhile the New Liberals argue the opposite. However, both commit the same fatal mistake of counter-posing 'internal' factors to 'external' factors, without taking note of the fact that they are complimentary to each other as well, and to a certain degree, one and the same thing. When Han and Yang argue that globalization is an external threat, they are blind to the fact that it has been their own one-party state that has not only opened up China to global capitalism, but also opted for a strategy that is fiercely dependent on foreign capital and the market, to a degree that surpasses many developing countries. It does all this consciously on its own. While it is not entirely free in the choice of policy (who is?), one can hardly argue that such policies have been forced upon China by the US empire or 'imperialism' in general.

Given the size of the country and the high degree of state control over all levels of society and the economy, China is in a much better position than many developing countries to compete with developed countries. The privileges of 'supra-national treatment' for foreign firms, means that they enjoy a level of tax on profits that is only half of China's SOEs, in addition to tax breaks and other privileges, demonstrating that there is a conscious decision taken by the top leadership to attract as much Foreign Direct Investment (FDI) as possible. The same goes for the humiliating concessions made during the negotiation of China's accession to the WTO. The choice of this path was not only dictated by economic rationality as understood by the ruling elites, but first and foremost motivated by their self-interest. The administrative bureaucracy of the Mao era has transformed itself into the kind of 'bureaucratic capitalists' that prevailed during the rule of the Guomindang before 1949. From Beijing to the county level, officials are often directly or indirectly (through family members and cronies) involved in business. It is in their interest to pursue a grand alliance with global capitalism and they profit from it immensely.

Peter Nolan provides a bigger picture as to the interdependence between China and US when he says that:

> China has become a 'supply engine' of the global economy, while the USA has become the world's 'demand engine'. Each is growing in a deeply unbalanced fashion (Roach, 2005) ...Today, the USA accounts for almost two-fifths of China's exports and China holds most of its foreign exchange reserves in dollars ... The Chinese and US economies have become deeply inter-twined.[29]

The grand economic alliance between the Chinese ruling elites and those of the west is of course not entirely stable, particularly in the context of the present apparent 'rise of China.' After twenty years of integration with global capitalism, Chinese firms have grown to a point that they are becoming confident enough to demand a larger share of the value added in the global supply chain: a development which is of course not welcomed by the west and Japan.

The race for oil between China and the rich countries has added fuel to the fear of the 'yellow peril'. However, these frictions do not and cannot make one deny that there is a basic common interest among them. This reflects a globalized world, where the dichotomy of domestic versus external becomes obsolete. This can be shown by one simple fact: today large Chinese firms, often SOEs, are more and more denationalized in their ownership, because either they are listed in Hong Kong or New York, or some of their shares have been directly sold to western or Japanese TNCs. This includes even state banks, which are considered to occupy the commanding heights of the economy.

Many more SOEs have already been involved in joint ventures with western, Japanese or Korean firms for the past 20 years. Leslie Sklair speaks of 'a transnational capitalist class based on the transnational corporations (which) is emerging that is more or less in control of the processes of globalization.'[30] While Sklair's formulation is still far from conclusive, one thing is sure: in the era of globalization terms such as 'national bourgeoisie', 'national industry', etc. have to be greatly qualified before they will have useful analytical value. The truth is that 'national' elements themselves often carry foreign elements as well, and vice versa. A more scientific approach is needed to move beyond the dichotomy of national versus foreign and to investigate the internal mechanisms of the global capitalist class and global capitalism at work.

Does the New Left represent working people?

This nationalist discourse is not merely the result of an incorrect theory. In fact, it *is* correct from the perspective of the Chinese elite, whose ambition now is to seize a larger share of the world market with the help of the state. From this position, the other nation states and TNCs all appear to be *external* contenders. Chinese workers and farmers appear to them as *domestic* only because they provide the sweatshop of the world – China – with cheap labour and cheap food, making Chinese firms more competitive on the world market. It is here that the dichotomy of national versus foreign makes sense. So, instead of advancing a common national interest, the nationalist discourse is in fact only defending the narrow interest of the ruling elites.

Zheng, however, has a different viewpoint: 'New Liberals represent the interest of the newly rising rich class, while the New Left represents the interest of workers and farmers.'[31]

While Zheng's view of the liberals is correct, he is fundamentally wrong about the New Left, as far as its major spokespersons are concerned. Han Deqiang in fact frankly admitted in an NGOs workshop held during the 6th Ministerial Meeting of the WTO that:

> The New Left does not have a workers' and farmers' position. Our main concern is how to avoid catastrophe. We hope to have adjustment (of government policy). We have widespread support among the middle and higher rank (of government officials). In the eyes of workers and farmers, we may be considered as running dogs of the capitalists. We do not want instability. We are reformists.[32]

Later Han wrote an article explaining further:

> The new leadership of the Central government has already noticed the problem (of the widening gap of rich and poor, unemployment etc). That is why they advocate sustainable development, harmonious society, autonomous innovation, etc. Their ideas are to a certain degree influenced by the New Left.
>
> As to the question of 'should we not do something for workers?' My reply is that I am more concerned about social crises and the outbreak of catastrophe. My position may be regarded by workers and farmers as a 'running dog of capitalists'. What I propose is to replace one-off exploitation with sustainable exploitation.[33]

This is not a slip of words but deliberate thinking. In another article he argues that

> The issue of today's Chinese economy is not whether we want exploitation or not, but whether we want a kind of exploitation which is one off, or the kind which is sustainable.[34]
>
> The casualties of mines accidents are called one off exploitation, because workers are killed. If workers (are treated as such that they) can survive, or even able to support their families, I think the miners should be thankful for having a kind of exploitation which is sustainable.[35]

Yang Fan also explicitly told his readers which class he favours:

> We are for upholding the banner of patriotism. Chinese national capital and state capital need the protection of the state. Without state protection, after we joined the WTO we would not be able to compete against TNCs.... I think most SOEs should be liquidated. We do not need so many SOEs. However, the state must play a role to support state capital and private capital, through making common rules to protect our intellectual property and brand names.[36]

The differences between the New Liberals and certain prominent scholars of the New Left (not all of them, of course) is not that they each represent diametrically opposed classes, but rather a different course for the one and the same class, namely the newly ascendant capitalist class. The greater influence of the New Liberals in the 1990s coincided with the tide of that time, when the government took a great leap forward to a policy of completely embracing foreign capital. At the end of the 20th century the tide has turned again, when after ten years of dependent growth, the danger of economic recolonization has become real. It is here that the New Left's discourse of national rebirth and self-strengthening becomes appealing to them.

Obviously, neither the bureaucratic capitalists nor the private capitalists are homogeneous in their direct interests. There is always a faction, because of its specific position in the economy, which sees closer partnership with foreign capital as a priority, or views more state intervention as a curse rather than blessing. They are therefore more receptive to the discourse of the New Liberals. Thus, instead of having the New Liberals and major figures of the New Left each representing the rich and the poor respectively, rather the truth is that each represents only a different course of capitalist development, namely one being more dependent on foreign capital and less dependent on the state and the other being the opposite.

This also explains why major spokespersons of the New Left have been excessively accommodating to state repression, even when the sword is directed at the Old Left or the Maoists. Han and Yang evade the question of state repression. Dale Wen answers the question as to why the Chinese resistance against neoliberalism is 'only rising now, later than in many other countries':

> It is because '1. the state's accumulation of considerable political assets during the pre-reform years; and 2. the successful disguise under which the reform was carried out.'[37]

What is so striking in her answers is that state repression of all kinds of social movements is not mentioned at all. In fact, it is completely absent in her 47 page report. The New Left see the state in general, but first and foremost the particular state of the CCP, as the sole salvation for China against foreign aggression and internal underdevelopment. While they exhibit deep hostility towards the New Liberals (and the New Liberals react similarly to the New Left)[38], they are exceedingly accommodating to state repression. Therefore, despite the fact that the new leadership under Hu Jintao has continued and even escalated repression to eliminate the possibility of a 'colour revolution' in China, Dale Wen (and Han and Yang), refuse to make any criticism of the one-party state. Towards the end of the Chinese version of her report she expresses these hopes for Hu:

> Fortunately, the government is responding to the people's appeal (on the social and environmental crises). Since 2003, the new leadership of the government has made many adjustments to solve the problems caused by the neoliberals' policies promoted during the past several years ... Will the Chinese government opt for a more thorough policy re-thinking and further break away from neoliberalism? We are optimistic about this.[39]

We are then told how the Hu leadership has adopted 'progressive measures': rural tax reduction, promises of additional funding for education and so on and so forth. At most they are economic improvements and very piecemeal at that. There is nothing in Hu's package which empowers the people with basic political rights like freedom of association and the press, etc. If the people had enjoyed these rights they would not have been totally defenceless in the face of expropriation by state officials in the first place! The CCP can always make episodic economic concessions from time to time, but it never allows political concessions, even if it is as basic as the right to demonstrate. It adheres to the political philosophy of all ruling elites and implements it to the last letter: 'one must work for the good of the people, but the people must do nothing for themselves.'[40]

Secondly, what matters is not really whether Hu will break away from neoliberalism, but rather what alternative the government may choose. There are many 'alternatives' other than neoliberalism. The problem is that they are not necessarily worth supporting from the perspective of working people. That perspective requires a particular kind of alternative which places democracy, equality and political liberty as its central concern. What is most troubling is precisely the fact that New Leftists like Han and Yang never include these values in their discourses. Rather, they advocate an 'alternative' of statism and nationalism, from which the new CCP leaders may happily take one or two doses in order to promote the 'rise of China'. Dale Wen is less nationalist in her report, but the absence of any democratic appeal and a necessary critique of the one-party regime, is pronounced. Such absence is by no means accidental. It is connected to the theme of most of the New Left; the reliance on the one-party state to build a modernized China. You don't criticize severely the one who will save you. However, they are hardly aware of the dilemma of their proposal. While the state appears to them as the solution, it is in fact also a very big problem. The degeneration and corruption of the one-party state has been so severe that Chen Yun, leader of the CCP, second only to Deng Xiaoping, remarked before his death in 1995 that it might end up with *wangdang wangguo* – the downfall of both the party and the state. More than ten years have passed and the corruption then pales in comparison with that of today. Widespread corruption and ruthless privatization contribute to growing centrifugal forces within the CCP. Corruption has become so rampant that a popular joke puts it this way: pick 100 medium-ranking officials at random and shoot them. Probably only 10 of them were innocent. Pick 100 big mandarins and do the same to them, maybe only one of them is innocent.

One need not take the figures in the joke seriously to recognize that it does reflect the degree of corruption today, and greatly weakens the administrative capacity of the state. Even when a policy is good in itself, its implementation is often obstructed or twisted by the profit-making incentives of the bureaucracy, resulting in chaos, mistakes and damage to people's lives. When problems arise and multiply, officials will only try to cover them up by all possible means.

It is common knowledge that all statistics in China are unreliable. For instance, trade balance figures for August 1998 recorded a US$ 20 billion surplus. Strangely, the foreign currency reserve recorded an increase of less than US$ 1 billion. This anomaly not only reflects the seriousness of unreliable statistics but also illegal capital flight (unreliable statistics masking theft). Hence, it is common for problems to accumulate to the point of crisis, only after which do they come to the attention of the central government – by which time it is often too late. Moreover, corruption is the most important issue that antagonizes common people. It has resulted in countless incidents of protests, strikes, and even riots. The Tiananmen crackdown is a message to all officials that even when these incidents happen, the Party will not yield to the pressure of the people. This is in practice a kind of *mianzui tiejuan*[41] or advance pardon for corrupt mandarins. No wonder that, since the early 1990s, the appetite of the bureaucracy has grown immensely and no wonder that a second wave of rebellion from below is brewing.

The crony capitalism of the CCP is also sowing the seeds for a financial and economic crisis for itself as well. For instance, no one knows the exact number of non-performing loans in the Chinese banking system, nor can they be sure that the books of publicly listed Chinese companies are accurate. One cannot manage something which one has no idea about. The reason why China escaped the 1997 Asian crisis was simply because the RMB was not convertible. Now, with its convertibility on the agenda of the government, there is great doubt as to China's ability to contain a second crisis. An economic crisis will further provoke a social upheaval, noted the China-friendly scholar Peter Nolan.[42] To sum up, in the course of robbing workers, farmers, and state properties, the bureaucracy also prepares for itself an outbreak of economic and social unrest.

What amazes us is that although Chen Yun made corruption his main concern, most prominent New Leftists tend to mention it only in passing. Even when they deal with it, they only repeat the truism of old party dogma that the top leaders should be determined in eradicating corruption; that corruption is the result of 'spiritual pollution from the west' or globalization – hence the necessity of party scrutiny and so on and so forth. Never do they turn to a much more simple solution: end the one-party regime and put the state bureaucracy under popular democratic control. Without this it is impossible to stop the bureaucracy from enriching itself through privatization and open or concealed corruption. The bureaucracy knows this very well, which is why they fiercely resist any moves toward democratization from above or below. It denies the people all their basic rights, so that the latter are absolutely defenceless. However, there is always a point beyond which no one will endure expropriation anymore, and this point is rapidly approaching today. The CCP is aware of this and its answer, apart from more repression, is to encourage the growth of nationalism to divert attention from domestic problems to external enemies. However, this is a recipe for international tension or even war. Going down along this path is no way out for the people.

Democracy is paramount

The Chinese party state is all-powerful. The social movement is close to nothing. The further strengthening of this state and the development of state capitalism under its auspices, only implies a further race to the bottom in the globalized market, or worse, war. Anti-globalization along Chinese nationalist lines only assists the CCP's effort in removing all obstacles to this road to hell. People who advocate such a course could hardly be described as New or Left. It is just the same old story of nationalism. Some of the New Left, in an attempt to differentiate themselves from Cui, Han and Yang, describe the latter as *qiangguo zuopai*, or left nationalists, rather than New Left.

We understand well that we must take into account that all the Chinese participants in the debate may not be able to speak freely under censorship. However, the truth is that even under the same censorship, there are some New Leftists, sincere Maoists or broad leftists who have not succumbed to nationalism and statism. Wang Hui, another prominent scholar of the New Left, exhibits little nationalism in his critique of globalization, and his emphasis on the active role of the workers movement in social changes is rare among the New Left. Kuang Xinnian, who is considered a Maoist, is in many respects remains faithful to the CPP's original critical position on nationalism and even in certain extent supersedes it:

> Nationalism is a kind of bourgeois ideology. Essentially it is a kind of thinking used to suppress the class consciousness of the proletariat and socialist ideology. One of the important causes for the collapse of Soviet Union is the limitation of 'socialism in one country', which resulted in ideological degeneration from a socialist vision to that of nationalism, and ultimately metamorphosis into social-imperialism ... If China simply endorses nationalism as an alternative ideology, it will not be able to solve domestic class antagonism and also the conflict between nation states: on the contrary, it only serves to reinforce these conflicts. This would be a tragedy not only for China, but also for the world.[43]

Unfortunately these voices are far too marginalized. Furthermore, the New Leftists seem to avoid direct debate with the Nationalists. This is by no means accidental, because these critical New Leftists are too heterogeneous to make effective responses to the Nationalists.

To conclude, there are good reasons to expect an ever stronger response to neoliberalism and corporate-led globalization in the years to come in China. About this we are optimistic. However, the one-party state, with the help of nationalists and the *qiangguo zuopai* like Han and Yang, has to a great degree shaped the response into a nationalist and statist discourse. If a movement from below is steered in that direction, it will add fuel to Chinese nationalism. It goes without saying that there is something the Left can do, other than just sit and wait to see what happens next. The urgent task of the Left is to make a thorough critique of the statist and nationalist tradition – which is deeply rooted in China – and the one party regime. Our vision for a just society cannot incorporate any nationalist or statist elements, or any accommodation to the one-party state. If another world is necessary, then it must make individual rights, pluralism in party politics, political and economic democracy, and last but not least, internationalism, its core values. This also implies a transcendence of the narrow discourses of both the New Liberals and the Nationalist Left.

3 August 2006

Notes

1 This essay was written in August 2006 and is slightly shortened for this book. The author wishes to thank Hidayat Greenfield and John Chan for their valuable comments, Tom Mertes and Saul Thomas for their patient proof reading.

2 *The Clash of Globalizations – Neo-liberalism, the Third Way and Anti-Globalization*, Historical Materialism Book Series, p.177.

3 'Bandung redux: Anti-Globalization Nationalisms in Southeast Asia', Gerard Greenfield, *Socialist Register 2005*, Merlin Press, p.170-1and 175.

4 We have to differentiate national identity and the attachment to national culture from nationalism, though. We have to be careful not to identify the Keynesian economic programme or of the welfare state with nationalism as well.

5 For more on this subject please refer to the author's *Post MFA era and the rise of China,* available on Globalization Monitor's website: http://globalmon.org.hk.

6 *Globalization and State Transformation in China,* Zheng Yongnian, Cambridge University Press, 2004, p.51

7 Ibid, p. 41

8 'Nationalism is the bourgeoisie's viewpoint on nations; its programme and principle in dealing with national issue..... In colonial, semi-colonial countries and independent nation, national struggles against imperialism, nationalism is to a certain extent progressive, but only to the extent that this is in accordance

to the interests of the bourgeoisie.....The world view of proletarian parties is internationalism, not nationalism.' *Ci Hai* (Dictionary), Shanghai Dictionary Press, 1980, p. 1805

9 There was then a common and deep anxiety across social classes about the danger of China losing *qiu-ji,* or global citizenship, because of the slowness of reform.

10 *China copes with globalization – a mixed review,* published by International Forum On Globalization, p.39

11 There are of course New Leftists who are less pro-government, but very often they are less well known. A major exception is Wang Hui.

12 *Qianliu – dui xiaai minzuzhuyi de pipan yu fansi, Under Current – Critique on and Rethinking of Narrow Nationalism,* edited by Le Shan, East China Normal University Press, 2004, p. 16

13 Le Shan, 2004, p.316-7

14 Beijing Spring, Jan 2000, Hong Kong.

15 *Zhongguo zhishifenzi guanyu shengyuan meiguo zhengfu cuihui sadamu ducai zhengquan de shengming, Chinese Intellectuals' Statement on Supporting the US Government Exterminating Saddam's Despotic Regime,* http://blog.boxun.com/hero/yujie/77_1.shtml

16 *Quanqiuhua yinyingxia de zhongguo zhilu, The Chinese Road Under the Shadow of Globalization,* Fang Ning, Wang Xiaodong and Song Qiang, Published by China Social Science Press, 1999.

17 *Zhongguo guojia nengli baogao, A Study of China State Capacity,* Wang Shaoguang and Hu Angang, Liaoning People's publisher, 1993.

18 *Tao Zhan Zhongguo, Challenging China,* Hu Angang, 1995, Xin Xinwen Cultural Ltd. Company, Taipei, Taiwan, p.248, 272-3

19 *Angang xianfa yu houfutezhuyi, The Angang Charter and Post-Fordism,* , Dushu, 3 (1996), 11-21.

20 *Mao Zedong wenge lilun de deshi yu xiandaixing de chongjian, The balance sheet of Mao Zedong's theory of cultural revolution and the reconstruction of modernity,* HuaXia Wenze, April 1997, http://www.cnd.org/CR/ZK97/zk117.hz8.html.

21 *Pengzhuang, The Crash – The Global Trap and China's Realistic Choice,* Han Deqiang, published by Economic Management Press, 2000.

22 Ibid, p. 5-6.

23 Ibid, p.160

24 Ibid, p.8

25 Ibid p. 264

26 *2005-6: Zhongguo de shehui sichao yu lilun douzheng, 2005-6: Ideological and Theoretical Struggle in Chinese Society,* 2005, http://www.tianya.cn/publicforum/content/develop/1/72060.shtml

27 meiguo zenyang zhizao he zhichi liangguolun (*How US manufactures and support Two States Theory*), 1999, http://www.edu.cn/20030127/3076681_4.shtml.

28 Tragically but not surprisingly, Great Han nationalism necessarily triggers the growth of Taiwanese nationalism.

29 *Peaceful Rise or Yellow Peril?* Peter Nolan, CITIC pacific research advance, 7 April 2006, p19-24.
30 *The Transnational Capitalist Class*, Blackwell Publishers Ltd, 2001, p. 5.
31 *Globalization and State Transformation in China,* Cambridge University Press, 2004, p. 186
32 *Shi gongnong de wuhui, haishi xinzuopai de wuhui? (Who have misunderstood things? The working people or the New Left?)*, a report on the workshop on China organized by Focus of the Global South, International Forum on Globalization, Globalization Monitor. See http://xinmiao.hk.st.
33 *Zai Tuopai yanzhong shui bushi zibenjia de zougou – huida yixie pengyou de yiwen,* In the Eyes of the Trotskyists, Who are not Running Dogs of Capitalists?, http://web.cenet.org.cn/web/shaocun/index.php3?file=detail.php3&nowdir=&id=83659&detail=2.
34 *lianhe qilai fandui xinziyouzhuyi,* Unite to oppose neo-liberalism, http://www.snzg.cn/article/2006/1111/article_1686.html.
35 *Ke chixu fazhan he shehui gongping,* Sustainable development and social justice, http://www.tt65.net/zonghe/luntan/wenxian/6/mydoc006.htm
36 *Zhongguo minying jingji yinggai shangshen wei minzu jingji,* Chinese Private Economy Should Advance into National Economy, http://yangfan.blogchina.com/62439.html
37 *China copes with globalization – a mixed review,* published by International Forum On Globalization, p.41.
38 Sometimes it goes so far as to applaud the suppression of the other side by the state.
39 *shi shaoshuren fuqilai de gaige – zhongguo yu tongwang jingji quanqiuhua zhi lu,* Reform which enriches a few – China and the road to economic globalization, p. 50. The quotation in the Chinese version is different from the English version, 'China copes with globalization – a mixed review'. Whereas the Chinese version is 'optimistic' about Hu's break with neoliberalism, in the English version this evaluation is absent.
40 A French conservative spoke these words against democracy during the French 1797 Revolution. Quoted from *Democracy and Revolution,* George Novack, Pathfinder Press, p.73
41 A kind of certificate, made of iron, was granted by the emperor to his favorite ministers, which pardoned in advance all the crimes they might be involved, except crimes like treason.
42 *Peaceful Rise or Yellow Peril?,* Peter Nolan, CITIC pacific research advance, 7 April 2006, p. 11
43 *minzuzhuyi yu zhongguo, Nationalism and China,* http://www.hexinbbs.com/article/Show Article.asp?Article1D=37

LABOUR RESISTANCE IN CHINA: 1989-2009[1]

Au Loong Yu and Bai Ruixue[2]

There has been no sustained labour movement in contemporary China in the strict sense of the word, i.e. an organised social movement initiated from below aimed at power-sharing or the redistribution of national income for the benefit of labour. The reasons for this are not entirely the same for different periods. The authoritarianism of the one party state remains the most important factor throughout all periods, but there were also significant differences between the Mao period (1949-1976) and the Deng/ post Deng period (1979-2009). In the former period, especially after 1956, workers were granted the title of *zhurenweng* (masters of the house) and as 'the leading class' in supposedly socialist China, they were seen by the party as the incarnation of 'socialist industrialization'. The working class was the class the party had to rely on in the fight against 'revisionism' or 'capitalist restoration'. These titles must be heavily qualified by the fact that the workers, like the peasants, did not enjoy basic political freedoms, let alone genuine democratic rights to elect their workplace managers, trade union leadership, or their national leaders. Although in their daily lives the honorary title of *zhurenweng* meant little to workers, who day in and day out had to take orders from their supposed 'public servants' i.e. the party cadres.

The official trade union the All China Federation of Trade Unions (ACFTU) was just part of the state machinery, neither elected freely by workers nor accountable to them. The Staff and Workers Representative Council (SWRC, *Zhigong daibiao dahui*), similar to the German works councils, was supposed to enjoy the power to examine the enterprises' strategic policies, to reject the appointment of new managers or dismissal of a current one, and share decision making about wages and workers' welfare. Yet, the arrangement of making the workplace trade union chairperson the executive of the SWRC guaranteed the party's grip over this organization, making it, like the ACFTU, more a window dressing than a real workers' organization. Both institutions were largely side-lined from 1957, and stopped functioning altogether during and after the Cultural Revolution. In political terms there was, and is, huge inequality. Nevertheless, in economic terms workers were more privileged than the peasants (while the landlord and business class was not even allowed to exist as a class at all). They were not as well off as the cadres in their workplace, but the inequality between the two social groups would be considered insignificant if compared to the post-Deng period. They were far worse off than top ranking provincial and central government officials, but this fact was not a direct reference point for these workers who stayed and worked in their workplace, often for life, and who were accustomed to being told to follow the party's line and ask no questions. Workers did enjoy the right to employment, social security and a higher living standard. The honorary title of 'leading class' also provided them a relatively privileged social status (for instance, in political movements they were the least vulnerable to repression; in marriage the identity of worker enjoyed obvious advantages), something which they could not even dream of before the overthrow of the Guomindang regime. Although not enjoying real power either at the workplace level or the national level, China's workers enjoyed job security, which meant that they could not be fired. This put a limit on the power of party cadres. Workers were fully aware that they were the only people who created, with sweat and tears, nearly all the industrial wealth of the country. Hence they were deeply attached to their plant, which they helped to create or to sustain, and took very seriously their entitlement to a fair share of the state owned collective property at the plant level. In a word, workers were the least discontented class in Mao's period, and this explains one of the main reasons for the absence of significant labour struggles. There were localized economic strikes during the first few years of the founding of the People's Republic of China, and also during the 'Cultural Revolution', but their scale was small and they rarely turned political or organized on a level higher than the workplace.

By contrast, in the post-Mao period, labour discontent began to rise since the capitalist market reform started because the workers felt they were being betrayed and their economic benefits were being eroded. This discontent turned into massive political struggle and independent organizing during the climax of the 1989 democracy movement. It was soon defeated by state repression, and in the subsequent 20 years China's workers have been kept in even heavier bondage. This has facilitated the CCP's privatization of the

SOEs (State Owned Enterprises). Despite the harsh repression, there were still numerous localized struggles against privatization among the state sector workers. They were followed by spontaneous strike waves among the emerging rural migrant workers.

The 1989 democracy movement

Deng Xiaoping's rise to power in 1979 was a turning point for the workers. Since then the market reforms have enriched the bureaucracy and private businesses at the expense of workers and common citizens. This was also the time when Deng started the first step of shifting the CCP's social base from workers to the newly born entrepreneurs. While the CCP began to attack workers' rights by abolishing the constitutional right to strike in 1982, it also began to introduce revisions of the constitution to support private enterprises and their private property. Since then Deng Xiaoping's agenda has been clear – to achieve harmonization with global capitalism. Deng was already preparing his way in 1984 when China signed the agreement with the UK to preserve laissez faire capitalism in Hong Kong for fifty years after the hand- over to China (in private talks Deng added that capitalism in Hong Kong could well be extended after that). He also strongly appealed for the nation 'to learn from Hong Kong', by which he only meant learning from its commercial skills, not its respect for civil liberties. In 1987 he told an African delegation 'do not follow socialism. Do whatever you can to make the economy grow.'[3] At the plant level, from the1980s, the enterprises reform began to empower the managers at the expense of the workers: work intensity increased, income inequality was greatly extended, contract labour was introduced, wages were tied to the performance of the enterprises etc. In the late 1980s, the rush to market reform accompanied by a steep rise in consumption among the bureaucracy, made the economy overheat thus creating inflation. As part of the market reform, price reform created two pricing systems, 'planned prices' and 'market prices', which gave the officials, known as *guandao* (literally meaning speculating officials), the opportunity to buy valuable products at the lower 'planned prices' and resell them at the higher 'market prices'. Meanwhile, nearly all levels of state departments set up different kinds of companies to make money. Bureaucrats were beginning to transform themselves into capitalists. This enraged the people who rose in protest against the government in 1989.[4]

Workers' participation in the 1989 democracy movement

> The Beijing Democracy Movement did not just shake the country; it shook the whole world. Apart from extreme frustration and great grief for those fighters and innocent ones who lost their lives, we did feel that this was yet another occasion when the Chinese people had risen up.[5]

This is how the 1989 democracy movement was described by an ACFTU trade unionist, who had been a supporter of the movement, after its suppression. The comment suggests the potential strength of the movement. At its height the democracy movement began to form a serious challenge to the legitimacy and authority of the CCP (Chinese Communist Party) as a regime able to act on and represent the interests of the working class. Such a challenge was only possible due to the participation of hundreds of thousands of workers.

Although generally known as a student movement, the significance of workers' participation in the later stage, leading to independent workers' organization, is often overlooked. This was a new development which alarmed the CCP, and was one of the reasons for its crackdown on the movement on 4 June 1989.

The democracy movement began after the death of Hu Yaobang on 15 April, when students in Beijing began protests against corruption, and official profiteering and for democracy. Many workers visited Tiananmen Square to listen to the students' speeches. At the beginning workers mostly visited the square spontaneously in a supporting capacity. Being able to identify with what the students were saying, they wanted to express their support for the students and their demands. In the words of one worker when asked why he became involved in the democracy movement, 'The students were criticizing the corrupt government and they voiced what we workers wanted to say.'[6] Many became especially outraged when some of the students who were staging a sit-in were beaten up by the police on 19 April.

Workers soon began to join in with the debate initiated by the students. With the help of their *Dazibao* (big character posters), leaflets and public speeches, they brought class insight to the movement. The students had largely confined themselves to demanding civil liberties. In particular they demanded freedom of speech, an end to corruption, dialogue with the authorities and, last but not least, a just appraisal of Hu Yaobang. As early as 18 April a worker wrote an open letter to the students:

> You must win over the support of the broadest mass of workers, peasants, soldiers and street vendors. How? First one must not only emphasize the salary of the intellectuals and the issue of increasing the education budget; one should also stay away from merely appealing for empty democratic slogans. This will affect the relationship between the students and workers/farmers, and will be harmful to their solidarity.
>
> We need to tell workers, farmers and soldiers that the 'ownership by the whole people' in practice means ownership by a minority of overlords. The wealth created by workers and peasants has been consumed by these people. They called us 'guojia zhurenweng' (masters of the country), yet the masters live in small apartments with their parents and children, while the 'public servants' build villas for themselves...Is there any difference between these people and feudal overlords?
>
> We need to build a sound democratic regime with freedom of speech, an independent judiciary, and free elections.[7]

On 17 April, a few workers including Liu Qiang (printer), Han Dongfang (railway worker), He Lili (lecturer at Beijing Workers University) had taken the initiative to begin to organize themselves and had formed the preparatory committee of the BWAF (Beijing Workers' Autonomous Federation). As well as wanting to organize to protect the students they felt that the workers should also raise their views. They made public speeches condemning the attack on the students and called on the workers to organize. They also made visits to factories and mines to publicize their policies and to encourage workers to join the Federation. The BWAF's demands included wage increases, price stabilization and the publication of the incomes and possessions of government officials and their families.[8]

The committee was determined that the organization was to be a workers' organization and only allowed workers to join. As Liang Hong, the captain of Supplies Division of the BWAF, explained, 'We decided that only workers might join and we checked their identity cards as well as their work cards. We issued our own BWAF identity papers to ensure the integrity of the Federation.'[9] Members also had to pay membership dues and pledge to observe the constitution and law of the state, abide by the organization's regulations and work for the interests of the entire working class.[10] Thus the organization was to be a law abiding organization with the aim of serving the working class. It drew up a set of regulations for its members to abide by and established committees to assist the carrying out of its operations.

On 26 April, in response to the students' demands for dialogue, the *People's Daily* released an editorial condemning the democracy movement for leading to riots. This triggered off outrage among the students and also Beijing citizens. The next day 200,000 students demonstrated, while a million Beijing residents stood on the side-lines to applaud them. It was not until 13 May when the students decided to stage a hunger strike that workers began to join in the struggle in any great numbers. On 15 May 600,000 took to the street. A further 200,000 students and workers demonstrated again the following day. Between 17-19 May, millions demonstrated in support of the students. Teams of workers carried banners which marked the names of their workplace. 200 workers from the Capital steel mill carried banners which read 'Support the students', 'Why is the Premier not responding to the students?'. The East Wind TV factory workers' banner read: 'we won't build any more TV sets until the *guandao* fall!'[11] One of the workers, when interviewed by the press, said that the TV sets they built had been taken by the princelings to resell and profit from this. Slogans also included Down with Li Peng, 'Down with Xiaoping, Our students are starving, what are you and your children eating?'

Many had realized that the official trade union the ACFTU was so tied to the CCP that it was powerless to represent them either. According to one former BWAF member, tickets for movies were the only activity organized by the ACFTU.[12] So the workers decided, for the first time since 1949, to set up their own independent workers' organizations to defend their interests and to fight for their rights. Under heavy pressure from their own members, the ACFTU donated 100,000 yuan to the students. Cadres from the official trade unions took part in demonstration to express solidarity with the students. A petition , signed by 'a section of the cadres of the ACFTU, a section of grass root cadres of the ACFTU and a section of teachers and students of the labour Movement College, had this to say:

> We demand that government:
> 1. Admit that the student movement is a democratic and patriot movement; Dialogue now.
> 2. Allow freedom of the press and association, guarantee the right to be informed, the right to monitor officials and the right to participate in political decision.
> 3. Punish the corrupt officials, promote political reform.
> 4. Reform the official trade union; realize self-management for the union. (slightly abridged) [13]

In the course of the radicalization among working people, the issue of the way in which they were exploited by the bureaucracy began to be discussed.

In a letter addressed to the whole nation on 17 May, the Beijing BWAF expressed their criticism and understanding of how the Chinese working class was being exploited by the Communist Party bureaucracy:

> We have carefully calculated the exploitation of the workers. Marx's *Capital* provided us with a method for understanding the character of our oppression. From the total value of output we deducted the workers' wages, welfare, medical welfare, the necessary social savings, equipment depreciation and reinvestment expenses. Surprisingly, we discover that 'civil servants' swallow all the remaining value produced by the people's blood and sweat![14]

In a further letter that was distributed by the Beijing BWAF in the middle of May they recognized that:

> The people constitute the majority. It is the autocrats who are a handful. If we, the workers, are bold enough to stand up and take a step forward, the dust we kick up can hurl the autocrats into hell.[15]

They called on compatriots to

> unite to build a system which is guided by an honest and incorruptible Chinese Communist Party, one which has the Chinese proletariat as its mainstay, one which is anchored by all patriots at home and overseas.[16]

Throughout May, the BWAF organized many meetings on relevant issues such as the productivity of the nation, the promotion of export earnings, workers' welfare, human rights, democracy and freedom. Over the course of the next few weeks the organization grew with 100 core activists and claimed to have 2000 members. Later it claimed a membership of 10,000. When the students began their hunger strike, the BWAF brought medicine, food and water for the Students Autonomous Federation. They also organized marches of workers in support of the students.

Many workers became increasingly involved as the movement developed. The story of a female worker, interviewed about her participation in the movement later in the year, provides one example. Inspired by what the students were saying as a result of having gone to listen to their speeches at Tiananmen Square on a number of occasions, she joined the march on 16 May. She tells how she followed the Capital Steel workers' banner at the demonstration because they were workers and so 'would voice the opinions of workers.' She then returned and joined in the processions on the following days. On the night of 19 May, hearing that martial law would be imposed, she and her friends stayed in the Square, along with many other people who had also heard the news, to lend their support to the students. She said: 'we all stayed there for mutual support, the power of the people would be greater than the students alone, and would be sufficient to defend Tiananmen Square.' On 26 May 26 she joined the BWAF, who she had first met when they supported the students on hunger strike. She then became involved with broadcasting their announcements at Tiananmen Square up until the suppression of the movement on 4 June.[17]

It was not only in Beijing that workers participated in the democracy movement. Huge demonstrations with workers participation soon erupted in most other big cities including Shanghai, Guangzhou, Hangzhou, Nanjing, Xian, and Changsha. Workers' Autonomous Federations were also established in several cities although this happened spontaneously but there was no major attempt to unite the organizations. One example comes from Guangzhou where, according to one former BWAF activist, people had heard about the student protests through the local media, Hong Kong radio stations and the Voice of America. They set up a Workers' Support Group to organize support for the Beijing students and to oppose the military curfew. It was the imposition of martial law that had made people become increasingly angry and to march spontaneously in the streets. It was also what prompted them to start thinking about the need to organize, leading them to take the decision to establish a Workers' Autonomous Federation. The activist recalls how:

> Our aim was to work for the interests of workers and the country, to promote democracy, etc. In society, there exists no organization that can engage in a dialogue with the Communist Party or even make suggestions to it, and so we wanted to set up such an organization to oppose dictatorship and to voice some alternative views on various aspects of our society.
>
> I felt that if similar autonomous unions were set up all over the place they would become a formidable political force if they could come together; a force which would destroy the dictatorial and autocratic system.[18]

On 19 May, the Beijing BWAF announced its official foundation and declared that if the students' demands were not accepted by the politburo within twenty-four hours then a one day general strike would begin. The politburo did not accept the students' demands. Instead the government declared martial law and announced the bringing in of troops and tanks to the city. This measure led to a quasi-revolutionary situation in Beijing. Over the next couple of days a million people took to the street again to defy the martial law. The BWAF set up Dare-to-Die Teams[19] and called on its members to block military trucks and armed forces from entering the city.

The sharpening of the conflict between the CCP and the demonstrators quickly politicized the workers and the BWAF. On 21 May the BWAF issued a 'Workers' Manifesto' which declared:

> The proletariat is the most progressive class in society. We have to display our strength as the central force within the Democracy Movement. The working class is the vanguard of the People's Republic of China. We have every right to expel dictators. Workers know full well the value of knowledge and skills in production. Thus we should allow no harm to come to any of the students nurtured by our society.[20]

While the workers were becoming more and more radical, the students remained suspicious of them, believing that the intervention of workers might damage the supposed purity of the students' action. On 17 April, when the preparatory committee of the BWAF had formed, their request to station themselves inside Tiananmen Square which the students had occupied was refused, and they were treated with suspicion. On 19 May, when the BWAF threatened to launch a strike, the Beijing College Students Autonomous Association released a statement appealing to the workers not to strike. It was only towards the end of May, when the violence of the government began to escalate, that the students allowed the BWAF to set up inside the Square. The fear of repression began to change many students' minds, and collaboration in resistance between student organizations and the Beijing BWAF began. Generally, however, the two social groups were unable to forge a firm alliance because of the reluctance of the students.

Meanwhile, although there were talks of preparation for strikes by the BWAF, they also had some disagreements amongst themselves. It was reported in the press that the Capital Steel Mill workers had founded their own WAF and were prepared to strike if the army opened fire on the students. Although there were lots of talks to prepare for strikes, a general strike never materialized. If there were strikes, they were not a result of coordinated action. Yet many factories had encountered the stoppage, or at least the significant decline, of production since so many workers had gone to demonstrate, and those who stayed at work became more interested in debating among themselves. The government tried hard to stop workers from taking part in demonstrations. Towards the end of May the Beijing municipal government instructed all the enterprises to make deductions from the wages of those who participated in demonstrations. This explains a temporary decline in the number of workers participating in the events.

Beginning with party secretary Zhao Ziyang's resignation (which was rejected by the party) on 19 May, the hardliners, with Deng Xiaoping and Li Peng at their head, began preparing for a crackdown towards the end of May. On 3 June, the Beijing ACFTU released a statement denouncing the WAF as counter-revolutionary and appealed to the government to ban it. On the same day, following the BWAF's call for all workers in the capital to go on strike the next day, troops began to advance into the city. Hundreds of thousands of workers and students responded by trying to use their bodies to block the 100,000 troops from entering Beijing. Thus when the workers rose up in support of the students, by threatening to withhold their labour en masse through a general strike, the state feared that it might lose control and responded with a massacre.

The crackdown on 4 June ended all resistance. Severe repression followed in which worker activists were generally much more severely repressed than the students. While students were sentenced to jail, at least 27 workers activists were executed in June alone, 14 of them were BWAF members. This was followed by a national purge led by the ruling party, targeting not only cadres in the political institutions but also covering those in the 'mass organizations', including the ACFTU.

The movement was ultimately defeated because it hadn't counted on and was not prepared for the government's violent response to its actions. Workers' participation in the democracy movement had only become prominent late in the day. It was still a young movement, largely spontaneous and lacking in experience. Nevertheless the social and political demands raised by the workers posed a serious threat to the legitimacy of a regime supposedly representative of the working class. Rather, the working class was coming to understand the CCP as being its oppressor. The workers' movement was never the pro-capitalist counter-revolutionary movement that the CCP presented it as. This movement, or at least its most advanced section, aimed at keeping the state owned property intact, while driving out the bureaucracy:

> This country was built by us workers, by the effort and labour of all mental and physical labourers. We are the master of the house and this is beyond question. What course this country should take must first consult

> us. We would never allow them to turn the dictatorship of the proletariat into dictatorship over the proletariat! We would never allow a handful of scum of our nation and scum of our class to suppress the students, killing off democracy and trespassing on human rights in our name! ... For the sake of the course of socialist reform, for the sake of our democratic patriotic movement, and for the sake of our next generation to be able to breathe freely after the wiping out of the despotism of Stalinism ... we appeal to our overseas country people to act immediately ... to support the democratic patriotic movement.[21]

No further such political actions have been taken by workers since 1989. It was only after the crackdown that individual members of the WAF (and the major student leaders) who fled from China became disillusioned with socialism and wished for a return to capitalism. It is ironical that after accusing the rebelling workers and the BWAF of being anti-socialist and counter-revolutionary, the CCP has orchestrated a harmonization with global capitalism and turned China into a mega sweat-shop. The brutal suppression of the crackdown itself has itself become a 'model' for repression of resistance in the ensuing period. It is not surprising to see how during the 2002 Daqing Oilfield workers' protest, the authorities sent in tanks to the outskirts of the city to make the workers cower into submission. Similarly during the Shanwei village protests, the authorities opened fire on the protestors, killing at least three and perhaps even more than 20 villagers.

The struggle against privatization

The CCP was particularly alarmed at the fact that huge numbers of workers came out to support the students' demand for basic democratic rights. After the crackdown, the CCP could no longer take workers' tacit consent to the CCP's leadership as granted. The social base of the CCP decisively shifted from workers to entrepreneurs. It decided to privatize considerable numbers of the SOEs, both to enrich the bureaucracy and the new class of entrepreneurs, and to inflict a second fatal blow to the workers in the state sector.

In 1992, the 14th Congress of the CCP inaugurated the construction of a 'socialist market economy', which amounted to giving the green light to privatization or the commercialization of SOEs. In 1996, the CCP launched the policy of 'retaining the large (SOEs), letting go the small'. In practice, even many medium SOEs have been 'let go' (i.e. privatized) as well. A great wave of dismissals began. For big SOEs, even when they remained in the state's hands, they have been restructured as commercial entities whose ultimate purpose was to make a profit. Hence they too have undergone huge downsizing. In many cases the SOEs were deliberately run badly and then made bankrupt so as to get rid of workers and allow the management to plunder their assets. Between 1996 and 2005, a great wave of privatization hit the workers hard in both state and urban collective enterprises (considered as quasi-state owned).

More than 60 million workers in the state and collective sectors were sacked, a scale never seen in history. In 2003, the active urban working population had grown to 200 million, and its composition had changed greatly. The number of workers in SOEs shrank from 112 million in 1995 to 69 million in 2003. In the same period the number of workers in urban collective enterprises declined from 35.5 million to 9.5 million.[22] At the same time, the flourishing private sector led 150 million poor rural residents to leave their land and roam the country as migrant workers in search of employment. The overwhelming number of them ended up working in private enterprises with wages so low that they were barely able to sustain themselves, and with little social security. The 'great social transformation' of destroying good jobs and creating bad jobs was a great social regression. Meanwhile, the old working class was 'restructured' so that today it has shrunk to a minority, alongside a new working class composed of rural migrants. The Chinese working class now consists of two major sectors: the state and the private sectors. Although the downward pressure on wages and working conditions are largely applicable to both sectors, private sector workers are even worse off than those in the state sector.

Gone is the honorary title of *zhurenweng* and 'leading class'. Workers have now become second-class citizens, and rural migrant workers are third-class citizens. In spite of this, there has been virtually no political opposition from the workers. The defeat in 1989 still weighs heavily around their neck. Even resistance to privatization which is confined to a single plant often draws harsh repression. At the height of the struggle against privatization in the Zhengzhou Paper Mill (see below), the police, using loud hailers, yelled at the protesting workers: 'We suppressed the movement in Beijing in June 4 1989! It was a big movement but we could still do it. You, you are just a handful of people!'

When there has been resistance against privatization, it has usually been too late. This is because workers had developed a mixture of trust and dependence on the party-state, a result of the development of a 'socialist' corporate state, which provided job security and welfare to them. Even when they became aware of the privatization of their plants, they were, in general, only able to oppose it at that level. Rarely were they able to oppose it on a national level – something that made the Zhengzhou Paper Mill case so special. The 1989 defeat had largely pushed the political imagination of workers to the background, and they had no idea of opposing the official line of 'market socialism' and 'reform' (which meant privatization or capitalism) with an alternative. Hence they were so confused that they lost the ability to think and act in time. In addition they were dominated by a mentality which believed that it was chiefly the fault of local cadres rather than the central government, and that if only the central government was alerted and intervened, things would be different. This kind of mentality was partly a result of demoralization, but also part of a legacy from Chinese culture where emperors were always seen as benevolent and it was bad ministers who stood in the way. Hence the first step of resistance that workers took was always petitioning Beijing, which for workers from outside Beijing was both time consuming and expensive. Moreover, even when workers acted, state repression made sure that resistance was confined to single plants. Generally, although it has not usually worked, workers have therefore pursued a strategy of limiting their actions in order to try to avoid such repression.

In the face of such a tremendous social regression, women workers are especially hard hit. As early as 1987, when the first wave of downsizing in the state sector began, women workers accounted for 64 per cent of those sacked. Accompanying the downsizing was a fierce propaganda campaign to tell women workers to go home, a place where they should stay. The elite claimed that the fact women can get pregnant made employing them economically unviable. Not only were women workers sacked, but young women, including recent college graduates, were repeatedly rejected for interviews simply because of their gender. Even if they were able to find employment, women's wages were lower than those of men. A national survey in 1988 showed that urban women wages was 84 per cent that of men; in 1990 it was 77.5 per cent, and in 2000 it had fallen even further to 70.1 per cent.[23] In the northeast, once a major industrial centre but then under depression because of the great restructuring, unemployed women workers often became sex workers in order to raise their families. For each transaction they may only receive 50 yuan because of fierce competition. In October 2002, 200 sacked women workers from a steel mill in the city of Long Yan, Fujian province, marched under a banner which read 'Too early to retire, too old to be a whore!'[24]

Workers did resist the privatization onslaught with protests of a significant scale in the latter half of the 1990s. In 1998 the then President of the National Political Consultative Conference was reported as saying that when he made tours of provinces he tried to avoid visiting government departments through the front doors, as they were blocked by workers protesters.[25] Although these kinds of protests were probably common, a greater number of sacked SOE workers did not put up any serious resistance. Due to censorship, no one knows the real situation across the nation. It was only possible for a small amount of news to leak out and be reported in Hong Kong or overseas. It was not until the turn of the century when access to internet became more affordable that the SOE workers' fight back became known to the public. Since then it is not uncommon to see protesting workers posting their cases on the internet. The turn of the century was also a period when the fight back began to escalate both in numbers and in organization, and sometimes even led to the occupation of workplaces and imposition of workers self-management, as the November 1998 Luoyang Cement factory case and the 2004 Chongqing 3403 Factory case show (see below). Since the beginning of the 21st century workers protests have tended to be more organized, but largely remain localized and confined to individual factories. Most of them are defeated, or at most have only won partial victories.

Zhengzhou paper mill struggle – transforming an official union into a real one [26]

There have been some successful cases of resistance against privatization. One example is the Zhengzhou Paper Mill workers' struggle in 2000. Furthermore, the workers also successfully transformed the official union into a genuine one. They did the same to the party-controlled SWRC (Staff and Workers Representative Council).

The national and provincial ACFTU has never played any role in resisting privatization. On the contrary, it has either helped the party secretary to carry through privatization, or has simply folded its arms and watched. At the workplace level, things are more complicated, but generally it does not perform much better. As for the SWRC its fate has been similar to that of the ACFTU; it has largely failed to function as a workers' institution at all. Yet things might turn out differently if workers fight hard and organize well. This has not been common, but neither has it been impossible at a workplace level. The ultimate outcome has been determined by the relationship of forces in the enterprises concerned, shaped by the concrete history of the enterprise and the development of a workers' tradition over decades.

The state-owned paper mill located in the city of Zhengzhou had around 2,000 workers in the year 2000. Up until 1988 when the old manager was sacked and replaced by corrupt people, it had been quite prosperous for many years. But then it was continuously plundered by the new managers so eventually it went into the red. In April 1995 the mill was ordered to stop production because of pollution by the municipal government, and workers were *xiagang*, meaning that they had no work to do but had not yet been made redundant from the mill. Workers received no wages from then on. In July 1996 the new manager Chen Wenhui, who had failed to sell the mill's warehouse due to workers' action, successfully sold the mill to Fenghua stock-holding company. In October 1997 the company, in its negotiation with the municipal government, promised the mill workers new investment and the resumption of production, payment of wages in arrears etc. In November the mill's SWRC was convened, and delegates happily endorsed the takeover plan. In August 1998, the municipal government endorsed the taking over of more than 100 million yuan of the mill's assets by Fenghua, and Chen became the general manager of that company. Between late 1998 and late 1999, Chen secretly mortgaged the mill's land to the bank and sold millions of yuan of its assets at rock bottom price. In August 1999, Chen revealed his plan to redevelop the mill into a residential area. Workers were now well aware that they were being cheated, hence they soon began to organize through the mill's trade union structure, conducted a serious investigation into the deal, and petitioned government departments and high officials more than 200 times. They demanded the cancellation of the deal.

In October a task force was established by the government which soon backed the deal officially, declaring that 'the country's reform shall not be backtracked'. In late October, Chen convened the SWRC and tried to manipulate it, but delegates responded with a vote of 50 to 5 to pass the resolution demanding immediate termination of the deal. Ten days later all workers returned to the mill and expelled the entire management of the Fenghua Company, though later the management was able to resume power. On 12 November, worker delegates of the SWRC found out about Fenghua's plan to sell the whole mill. The workers acted quickly. In the name of the SWRC, they took over the land certificate of the mill from the land registry. On 7 June 2000, the workers returned, expelled the management for a second time, took control of the mill and resumed production. They organized a new leadership which included the assistant chief engineer Li Jiaqing and the retired and popular woman worker Liu Yurui. Meanwhile the government was planning retaliation. On August 7, Li Jiaqing was arrested. The next morning the government's task force ordered 500 police to surround and then break into the mill. There were only 40 workers inside. They resisted the attack but in the end they failed and were heavily beaten up. One worker was arrested.

The factory was then occupied by police and the task force convened the SWRC in order to force the workers' delegates to endorse the deal. It failed. The municipal government then reorganized the task force and gave up any hope of reviving the deal. The workers retook the mill and on 16 September they formed a new leadership of the trade union branch of the mill with Liu Yurui as chairperson. In January 2001, the municipal government finally yielded to workers, cancelled the deal, and handed over management to the workplace union. On 9 January workers officially took over the mill. They demanded that the mill be returned into the hands of the state but the government refused and successfully persuaded the workers to set up their own company. In 2002 the SWRC was convened and founded a new company. The event had big repercussions. In the few years that followed the government's conceding to the workers' struggle, a dozen SOEs in Zhengzhou cancelled their privatization deals.

Meanwhile the municipal government refused to release the two arrested workers. The prosecutor still went ahead to charge them for 'disrupting social order' and on 13 February 2000, the court began to hear the case. The court was crowded with workers, and when Li Jiaqing appeared he was greeted by workers with the slogan 'long live Li Jiaqing!' He was in bad shape but his morale was still high. In his cell he wrote a letter to Liu Yurui, which showed his deep attachment to his factory:

> I heard that the collective property of us workers – that we bled and sweated for – has been returned to us. I heard that all the workers shed their tears upon hearing the news. I am being jailed in this cell with four high walls, but I am moved as well ... This property is created by hundreds of workers through more than 40 years of sweat. Five or even six workers have now passed away. Their souls are still watching us to see if we can save our property. We cannot let them down.
>
> I have been with the factory for 30 years. I hope I can do something to save the plant in the last stage of my life ... I am prepared to be sent to the jail vertically and sent out horizontally. When people no longer have regards of their lives, no evil can defeat them.
>
> I prophesized that those privileged swindlers, having failed to seize our factory, would take revenge on us by prosecuting me, in order to do away with the honour of the proletariat of this mill.

Subsequently the charges against Li were dropped and he was later released.

Cross factory solidarity: the Liaoyang metal factory struggle[27]

The Liaoyang case, from 2000-2, was the first reported effort to forge cross factory organization and joint struggles. This is rare because of the risk involved: the CCP hates any idea of cross factory solidarity. The city of Liaoyang, located in Liaoning province, is an important industrial base in north east China. Liaoyang Metal Factory had 8,300 workers. It had been doing fine until 1998. Workers believed that the management had deliberately run the factory in an inefficient way in order to bankrupt it. They petitioned Beijing in 2000 but got nothing. In November 2001 the factory was officially declared bankrupt. The workers responded with a demonstration in March 2002. On the morning of 11 March, 5,000 workers demonstrated in the open streets, carrying with them the portrait of Mao Zedong, and demanded payment of wages and an investigation into the factory's bankruptcy. The demonstration continued over the second and third day, and the number of participants rose to more than 10,000. This was because the factory workers were joined by workers from six other factories which had suffered more or less the same fate as the Liaoyang Metal Factory: a textile mill, a piston ring factory, an instrument and meter plant, a leather plant and a precision component factory.

The workers showed a high level of organization throughout the struggles. The petition to Beijing in 2000 was the first effort in organizing because it needed to raise a lot of money among workers. Activists visited fellow workers in the community to persuade them of the need to fight against the corrupt management and to get back their wages. In May the workers convened the SWRC to elect the delegation to take the petition to the capital. SWRC delegates were elected in seven different communities, with two delegates for each community. Eventually the SWRC elected a delegation of 32, and among them ten were to be sent to Beijing. The delegates knew very well that they were being closely monitored by police and spies. Hence they developed a way to get around the surveillance: there was division of labour between the two delegates for each community, namely one would be at the forefront and the other would be clandestine, doing dangerous work such as the printing of handbills. The latter would also act as an alternative delegate who would take up the first delegate's work when he/she was arrested. For each action they took, the delegates would first paste up handbills in the community to consult the workers, making amendments to their demands and action plan in accordance with opinion of the workers. Individual delegates might be bought over by the management, but the majority of them were able to stand firm.

This high level of self-organization and the workers' success in united action with six other factories greatly alarmed the authorities, who decided to crack down on the workers before it was too late. Between 17-20 March 2002, the authorities arrested four worker delegates: Yao Fuxin, Xiao Yunliang, Wang Jiaoming, Pang Qingxiang. A year later they were found guilty of 'subversion', and were sentenced to four to seven years in jail.

Although the workers were not able to achieve all their objectives, their action did allow them to force considerable concessions from the authorities. After the March 2002 action, the municipal government started to pay back the wages to workers in two instalments, and it also paid back 20 million yuan to cover workers' medical bills and other benefits. It also became more accommodating towards workers' grievances, as long as they did not challenge the bankruptcy of the plant. One of the workers drew the following conclusion from the struggle: 'Big struggle, big gains; small struggle, small gains; no struggle, no gain.'

In the aftermath of the struggle some workers summed up their experience as follows:

> It was a mistake for us not to organize fight back at the very beginning of privatization. Then the factory's assets were plundered step by step until nothing was left and bankruptcy fell upon all of us. It wasn't until that moment that we thought we had seized hold of enough evidence of corruption, but at the same time it was already too late to launch any effective fight back. The swindlers had already built up their supportive network or shifted to other cities to do their business. For the mass of workers they then knew very well that their struggle would not be very fruitful anyway, and we could only limit ourselves to getting back what the management owed us. This inevitably limited the dynamics of the struggle. Although workers were motivated by anger and the movement had been solemn and stirring, it had not changed the fact that workers had been thrown into passivity.

Independent organizing: the Daqing oilfield struggle[28]

The 2002 Daqing oilfield workers' struggle was important not only for its size and duration, but also for its organization. The Daqing oilfield is the largest in China. It is located in Heilongjiang province and is now the subsidiary of Sino Petroleum, which is itself a product of the great restructuring. Up until the late 1990s the oilfield had enabled China to be self-sufficient in its oil supply for decades. China's accession to the WTO in 2001 was conditional upon the opening of all important branches of its economic sector in 2007, including oil. Hence Beijing started a deep restructuring of the oil industry in order to make it competitive with foreign oil giants. Immense downsizing was on the agenda, which subsequently led to as many as 600,000 oil workers being sacked within a few years at the turn of the century.

On 1 March, 2002, 3,000 oil workers demonstrated in front of the managing bureau of the Daqing oilfield and at one point broke into it. Over the following days the workers actions continued to escalate and at a peak more than 50,000 demonstrated openly. The actions in Tieren Square lasted for more than four weeks. It is worth mentioning that the prolonged action and the massive mobilization were organized by the Provisional Committee of the Trade Union of Sacked Daqing Workers, even though it had not publicly appeared.

The workers demanded the repeal of the downsizing and re-employment. The climax of the one month long struggle was on 4 March when 20,000 workers first assembled in Tieren Square and then marched to the railway station to block the trains.

The organizers of the actions had not shown their faces but one could feel their presence when from time to time new handbills would appear and were distributed to protesting workers in the square. On 20 March a new handbill appeared raising new demands:

> We demand that:
> 1 It is our legitimate right to petition to higher authority. No police surveillance!
> 2 The managing bureau must begin dialogue with all sacked workers.
> 3 Fully protect the personal safety of our representatives and their legitimate rights.
> 4 Workers must be kept informed about the whole process of dialogue.
> 5 The managing bureau to bear all responsibility for anything that happens if they turn down our demands.

In response to the workers' petition to Beijing, an investigating team of the State Council arrived at Daqing and on 25 March expressed open support for the authorities. Meanwhile the provincial trade union also declared that the workers' initiative to organize an autonomous trade union was illegal:

> Trade union branches must be organized by upper level trade unions. We cannot accept any branch which is founded autonomously. Besides, these workers had already been dismissed. They do not have the right to organize a trade union branch.

On 26 March the organizers of the demonstration responded with a new handbill and had the following to say:

> The authorities claimed that downsizing will lead to increased efficiency. No more and no less, it only speaks for the fact that you people are simply incompetent! Only when you people can increase efficiency without downsizing workers, can you prove your ability ...
>
> Your superiors grant you people with a high position only because they want you to be competent. Now that you people are enjoying good houses with more than 200 square meters of space, dining in good restaurants and spending hundreds or even thousands of yuan per meal, travelling in nice cars which are worth hundreds of thousands of yuan, earning millions of yuan in bonuses, meanwhile thousands of sacked workers have to worry about their very existence and livelihood. How can you possibly remain entirely indifferent?

The success of the struggle very much depended on whether the dismissed workers could earn the active support of workers on the job. The latter, however, though very sympathetic to the struggle of the dismissed workers, did not act to support their dismissed colleagues for fear they themselves would be dismissed. Most jobs in Daqing were oil-related; therefore it was normal to have all adult family members working for Sino Petroleum. If those on the job also got sacked, the whole family would be at risk. For many families there was a kind of division of labour: those on the job should lie low, only those who lost their jobs went to demonstrate. This also explains why dismissed workers did not try harder to mobilize the workers on the job even though this strategy also limited the strength of the struggle. Having been kicked out of their workplace, the dismissed workers were robbed of their power to withhold their labour, and furthermore, demonstrating every day was too exhausting for many. Towards the end of March the size of the demonstrations began to dwindle. On 19 April 2002 the authorities sent in hundreds of police and began to arrest workers. Hundreds of them were put into 12 buses and taken to the police station until their respective workplace representatives came to take them home. On April 22, Tieren Square was declared a curfew zone. Soon all demonstrations died down.

The failure of the great Daqing oilfield workers' struggle – which had mobilized the greatest number of workers to fight downsizing in a key industry – seemed to signify that workers' resistance against privatization was a lost cause. White-collar workers entering into struggle has not reversed this trend. Accession to the WTO required China to open up its banking service in 2007. Thus, beginning in 2000, Chinese state banks began to cut their workforce. Within a few years, The Industrial and Commercial Bank of China shed 110,000 workers from a workforce of 400,000. The China Construction Bank sacked 150,000 workers. Dismissed workers began to link up among themselves and staged demonstrations in Beijing. Though the number was small, its significance was that it was the first time that white collar workers – who had always been considered relatively privileged, conservative, and separate from blue collar workers – entered into the resistance against jobs cuts. Unfortunately, their effort did not save their jobs. The authoritarian party-state proved too strong for state workers.

Socialist consciousness lives on: Chongqing 3403 struggle[29]

The People's Liberation Army Chongqing 3403 factory was founded by the military in 1958, with 3,000 workers. It is located in the city of Chongqing, Sichuan province. According to the workers, from 2000 the plant manager Zhang Chengyi began to plunder the plant. In 2002 he decided to enter into a joint venture with a private company (which originated from a privatized SOE) called Naide industrial stock holding company. The workers accused the boss of Naide, Lin Chaoyang, of being a swindler who had colluded with officials in the municipal government to privatize local SOEs at abnormally low prices, including Naide and the 3403 factory.

In August 2004 the workers heard news of the bankruptcy of the factory and then acted quickly. On 18 August, they locked up the factory, forbidding other people from Naide to enter, and demanded that the government provide an explanation of the deal and punish the factory manager, Zhang. The workers also proposed buying the factory, by pooling their resources together, and running it themselves. 'We want democratic management and produce for ourselves!' declared the workers.

On 20 August the municipal government began to press the workers to retreat but failed. In the afternoon Zhang mobilized more than 50 security guards and gangsters to force their way into the factory. After a small clash they retreated. On the second day, Zhang returned with a large crowd of workers from Naide Company to storm the factory. The 3403 factory workers shouted to the Naide workers: Brother workers! Don't let yourselves be made use of! Workers don't fight workers!

Some Naide workers retreated when they heard the 3403 factory workers' appeal. The attack became ineffective. For a week there was repeated harassment from local police, but no attack. However workers knew that the police were making preparation for a second attack. The workers' organizers kept disappearing. Plainclothes officers were everywhere. The workers called the Central Television but no reporters came. They sent petition letters to Beijing but received no response. The only way to alert the public was by posting information on the internet. They made appeals for public support for their cause. At the same time they knew it might not be effective and sooner or later they would be crushed. One worker wrote:

> The municipal government has fallen under the control of the dark force. To try to solve the case through legal means is more difficult than trying to fly through the sky with two arms. Several years back when the Chongqing machinery factory became bankrupt, the workers also fought against the management but failed. They were bloodily suppressed by police. Today, the same tragedy now befalls on us. Could we really hold the ground when the municipal government is so powerful?

On 30 August, the decisive night came. It was the 13th day since the workers occupied the factory. At 3.30am, when workers were asleep in the factory, more than 1,000 riot police along with 200 Naide workers who were forced to come, took 12 buses and at 5 am began to storm the factory gate. The police then beat the workers with batons. One of the workers, who was in his 40s, tried to escape but five policemen beat him with batons. When the policemen became tired another five took their place. A worker wrote in an article posted on the internet:

> The scream of the worker broke all our hearts. Everyone cried, some were so emotional that they were absolutely speechless. The police were so barbaric that they took his mother out, who is already 70, and beat her son in front of her. Eventually our comrade was lying in blood, and then taken away. We have not heard of him since then.

It is worth drawing attention to the fact that in this case the workers showed a type of radical social consciousness that is commonly lacking in SOE workers. Whereas few SOE workers' struggles have ever directly challenged the central government's 'ownership reform' policy – which was and is a taboo – the 3403 factory workers did. From September through to December 2004 they posted several articles on the internet making radical comments, expressing support to those economists who doubted the neo-liberals' programme of privatization. They criticized the CCP after the death of Chairman Mao for pushing for a kind of policy which overturned the leading role of the working class and turned it into an exploited class. In the article 'The privatization of SOEs will provoke a revolution', the workers had this to say:

> Our constitution stipulated that socialist public ownership is sacred and inviolable, and the ruling party is called the Communist Party. How is it possible, then, that the illegal privatization of public assets proceed so openly (and without prosecution)? Workers were sacked, why is this? For 20 years the reform has transformed from emphasizing both efficiency and equality to prioritizing the plundering (of public assets) over equality. The privatization policy has only resulted in workers becoming unemployed, with no clothing and nothing to eat. GDP is rising every year, but unemployment is rising as well, while the rich are getting richer. It has created a new class of capitalists and a 100 million strong new proletariat. Class contradiction is getting more and more serious. However the (official) propaganda still promotes the idea that all profits and public assets should be given to the capitalists, that the original sin of plundering state assets of this class should be pardoned. This was exactly what happened before 1949. If things should be kept this way, why then did we need a revolution in 1949 in the first place? ... If we cannot huoming (live) then we can only pinming (struggle to our death)!

After the authority crushed the workers' resistance, the latter declared that

> Even if the grassland is destroyed by fire in the autumn, it will be reborn again in spring. The same goes for our struggle. We, the workers of 3404 factory, will not bow before the evil power of these bandits; we will not kneel before the butcher's knife. We will fight prolonged guerrilla warfare.

No news has been heard of them since.

Downsized but still powerful

Between 2004 and 2008 the numbers of SOE workers further declined from 64.4 million to 61.3 million, and collectively owned enterprises from 8.5 million to 6.23 million.[30] The state workers were defeated, their numbers have greatly declined and most have become demoralized, but it looks like the great wave of SOE privatization has ended because the remaining SOEs are mostly too big and strategically too important for the government to give up control of them. Even if they have been privatized it has largely been partial, with the state retaining the controlling shares. Hence, if there is still pressure for downsizing or even privatization, it is now on a smaller scale if compared to the earlier period. Although there is now half the original number of SOE workers, they still occupy the most important branches of industry in China. Hence their potential power as the most important producing class is still intact. Secondly, they possess a strong class identity and maintain strong communal and workplace ties which give them strong potential for organizing, an advantage which the rural migrant workers largely lack. The ending of the first great wave of privatization, the fading of fear whipped up by the 1989 crackdown and the accumulation of experiences by workers in fighting back, have all contributed to a change in workers' morale. The more advanced sections of SOE workers are more determined to stand up for their rights. The 2009 Tonghua Steel Mill struggle might be a reference point here.[31]

The fight back of rural migrant workers

While the government destroyed more than 60 million good jobs in the state sector, it promoted the creation of new jobs in the private sector, the total of which was nearly double the jobs lost in the state sector. It did this by turning China into a sweat shop for the world's manufacturing industry.

Meanwhile, since the early 1990s rural regions have been bankrupted by taxes and levies, forcing 150 million migrant workers to leave their home villages and to search for jobs in urban areas. These migrant workers constitute a new working class that has been formed alongside the old one, and many of the new migrant workers are women. Migrant workers are doubly vulnerable, because they are considered less educated and less skilled than urban workers, thus the market value of their labour is substantially lower.

In the EPZs (Export Processing Zones), workers work from 12 to 14 hours a day. In times of rush orders, it is not unusual for workers to work from 8am to 10pm, and in some cases they may work until 2am. Many workers only have one or two days off per month, and some none at all. This greatly exceeds the maximum legal working hours. Workers find it hard to cope with such hard labour, but refusing to work overtime will result in being fired.

In the EPZs, the number of women far exceeds the number of men, making it difficult for women workers to find male companions. Moreover, some factories have rules that force women workers to resign if they marry. It is common for married couples who come to the same EPZ to live separately, each staying in their own factory's dormitory. Even when the couples work in the same factory, they still have to live in separate dormitories, making normal sexual relations. If women workers become pregnant, very often the only choice is resignation because they simply cannot continue to do such hard work, and management rarely transfers pregnant workers to easier jobs.

In spite of the repressive capacity of the government and factory owners, workers have begun to resist. In 2004 it was reported that in the Pearl River delta, there were more than 30 strikes that involved more than 1,000 workers (there are no official statistics on the number of strikes). Strikes that involved less than 1,000 workers were more numerous, and according to our interviews, unreported strikes are common. One Guangzhou worker told us: 'in our factory strikes are very useful and very effective. Whenever there are arrears of wages or the management introduces bad measures we will strike and it works.'

Women migrants are always considered to be more obedient, which is why EPZ employers like to hire them rather than men as the main source of labour. When women workers can no longer take being exploited, they too begin to resist and are sometimes even braver than men. In the 2004-5 Gold Peak case, it was women workers, not male workers, who formed the core of a network of activists in standing up against the employers.

More workers are now learning that the only way to improve their conditions is to resist, and partial victories are becoming more common. Most of these strikes however, have occurred spontaneously without prior planning. Even when workers have won concessions, there are few incentives for long term organizing. Most of the reported cases are leaderless strikes, and even if there was organization behind the scenes, its level is probably lower than that of state workers. The 2004-5 Uniden case[32] is one of the few exceptions where the workers struck five times and at the height of the struggle the leaders tried to organize a workplace union. They only failed because of heavy repression.

Well-planned strikes assume prior organization, but given the repressive regime from the central government down to the neighbourhood committees, from local police to community based 'public order teams' and factory security guards, workers' organizations are too difficult to sustain.

After more than thirty years of rapid growth, China may be entering a new period, simply because the growth has only been sustained at terrible human, social and environmental cost. The rising number of spontaneous strikes, road-blocks and occasional riots speak for the fact that conditions for the toiling masses have become increasingly intolerable. It was reported that in 1993, China experienced 8,709 cases of 'collective incidents' (this is to be understood as including public protests or strikes), 32,000 cases in 1999, 60,000 in 2003, 74,000 in 2004, and 87,000 in 2005. This is a growth of ten times within one decade. Among these cases 35 per cent

involved peasants, and 30 per cent involved workers.[33] Even the official media admitted that the tension between the have and the have-nots has reached new heights. The 2008 global financial crisis may bring China's continuous growth into question. The CCP will find it hard to manage all these problems. On the other hand, it requires a strong organisational drive and solidarity between the two sections of the working class to reverse their impoverishment. Although the struggles between 1989 and 2009 were not able to win substantial victories and were far from developing into political struggles, their partial successes have helped workers who are considering resisting to slowly regain their self-confidence in asserting their rights.
24 January 2010

Notes

1 This article was first written for the 2010 entry of the website of *the International Encyclopedia of Revolution and Protest 1500 to the present,* Edited by Immanuel Ness and hosted by Wiley Blackwell. It was then published in hard copy form in the Journal *Working USA*, volume 13, Issue 4, December 2010. It is slightly abridged for this book.
2 Au Long Yu and Bai Ruixue are on the editorial board of China Labor Net.
3 It was a supressed speech but it was reported in Hong Kong by the former chief of General Administration of Press and Publication, Dao Daozheng. See *Ming Pao*, October 14, 2008.
4 For a more detailed account on the background of the 1989 democracy movement, read part four of *The Deng Xiaopeng era: An Inquiry into the Fate of Chinese Socialism 1978-1994*, by Maurice Meisner, Hill and Wang, 1996.
5 *A Moment of Truth, Workers participation in China's 1989 Democracy Movement and the Emergence of Independent Unions*, Hong Kong Trade Union Education Centre, Hong Kong, 1990, p94.
6 *A Moment of Truth*, p25.
7 *Zhongguo minyun yuanziliao jingxuan* (Selected Original Documents of the China Democratic Movement), vol. 1, October Review, 25June , 1989, p. 33.
8 *A Moment of Truth*, p183.
9 *A Moment of Truth*, p2.
10 *A Moment of Truth*, pp 202-204
11 *Newspaper Front Pages on the Democratic Movement of China*, China Democratic Movement Resource Centre, June 1989, p. 209.
12 *A Moment of Truth*, p54
13 *Newspaper Front Pages on the Democratic Movement of China*, China Democratic Movement Resource Centre, June 1989, p. 192.
14 *A Moment of Truth*, 1990, p185.
15 *A Moment of Truth*, p191.
16 *A Moment of Truth*, p192.
17 *A Moment of Truth*, pp41-61.
18 *A Moment of Truth*, pp75-86

19 Dare to Die teams were groups of workers organised by the Beijing Workers Autonomous Federation to be the vanguard in the confrontation between the student demonstrators and the advancing army. This team of workers were prepared to die in this confrontation.

20 *A Moment of Truth*, p. 188.

21 *'Zhongguo minyun yuanziliao jingxuan'* (Selected Original Documents of the China Democratic Movement), vol. 2, *October Review*, November 1989, p. 44.

22 *China Statistical Abstract*, 2004, China Statistics Press, p. 41.

23 *Jingji zhuangui zhong de zhongguo nüxing jiuye yu shehui baozhang*, (China Womens' Employment and Social Security under Economic Transition), Pan Jintang, China People's University, Management World, Issue 7, 2002.

24 *Ming Pao*, Hong Kong, 25 October, 2002.

25 *Ming Pao*, Hong Kong, 29 April, 1998.

26 The sources of this case mainly came from reports by the workers or their supporters posted on the internet, which today has largely disappeared, though some still exists: http://www.maostudy.org/2000-10/henan1.txt, accessed 23 December 2009.

27 Human Rights Watch published a report on workers unrest in Northeast China in 2002, which carried a section on the Liaoyang case: http://www.hrw.org/en/reports/2002/08/02/paying-price. See also Workers Democracy website: http://www.xinmiao.com.hk/sim/index.html

28 Personal interviews and internet materials. *China Labour Bulletin* carries reports on the case: http://www.china-labour.org.hk/en/. See also Workers Democracy website: http://www.xinmiao.com.hk/sim/index.html.

29 The sources for this case mainly come from reports the workers or their supporters posted on the internet, and which today have largely disappeared. There is a collection of such reports on the Workers Democracy website: http://www.xinmiao.com.hk/sim/index.html.

30 *China Statistical Yearbook*, 2009, China Statistics Press, p. 111.

31 *Blood on the Hands at a Bleeding Steel Mill*, 21st August, 2008, Caijing, http://english.caijing.com.cn/templates/inc/webcontentens.jsp?id=110228012&time=2009-08-21&cl=104&page=all. For further reading, refer to the chapter in this book *New Signs of Hope: Resistance in China Today.*

32 http://bbs.chinaunix.net/viewthread.php?tid=468440

33 *'Zhongguo de saoluan shijian yu guanzhi weiji'* (China's riots and its Management Crisis), Yu Jianrong, *Method First Journal*, November 2007, Issue 7, http://www.chinaelections.org/newsinfo.asp?newsid=118361

FROM 'MASTER' TO 'MENIAL': STATE WORKERS IN CHINA TODAY[1]

Au Loong Yu

In July 2009 workers at the stated-owned enterprise (SOE) Tonghua Steel Mill in Jilin province violently resisted repeated attempts at privatizing their plant, to the point of beating the manager to death upon hearing his threat that he would sack all of them if he remained alive. Their struggle helped stall the privatization and encouraged similar struggles in other state-owned steel mills. This incident occurred against a background where the central government had previously issued instructions to local governments reminding them that local officials and SOE managers should respect the law, including the one concerning the consulting of Staff and Workers Representative Congresses (SWRC) before any change of ownership. After the incident the All China Federation of Trade Union (ACFTU) released a statement reminding its officials that they should uphold the rights of the union and the SWRCs.

Indeed it was not in the distant past when more than 100 million state owned enterprise (SOE) workers enjoyed job security and basic welfare, and the laws on industrial democracy granted them many rights which were even more far ranging than the German works council model. In addition to this, their 'leading role' in the running of the country and their political rights were (and still are) enshrined in the constitution. However, these legal rights neither enable most workers to protect their enterprises from being unlawfully privatized nor save them from being unlawfully sacked, because the laws are simply bypassed by the cadres. How this could have happened should be of interest to labour activists. This essay tries to look into the institution of industrial democracy in Chinese SOEs[2] and the political context which has hindered its proper functioning. This is then followed by an evaluation of the status of the working class in Mao's China. We hope that our narratives may help to shed light on how and why the alleged 'leading class' of China met its eventual downfall, and what lesson can be drawn from that page of contemporary history.

We believe our study is also relevant for making a more balanced evaluation of the more recent efforts by the ACFTU to promote a series of labour law legislation. While these efforts are welcome, we must not overlook the fact that these laws are often not implemented at a grassroots level. In a country which does not respect the rule of law and freedom of speech, it also means that wherever workers' legal rights are infringed, most of the workers concerned will find it hard simply to voice their grievances. This should not surprise us if we are aware of what has happened to SOE workers. No single labour law or single piece of social reform, or its effectiveness, can be correctly assessed without referring to broader societal factors and to lessons drawn from the recent past. It is with this in mind that we make the present investigation into SOE workers and China's model of 'industrial democracy'.

Privatization: 'Doing without saying'

Back in the late 1980s, there was already a popular saying about the course which the Chinese Communist Party (CCP) was actually taking: *Dazuodeng, xiangyouzhuan*. Using a driver in a car as a metaphor, it depicted the CCP as turning to the right while signalling to turn to the left. The people's intuition about what CCP was going to do was right: after the 1989 crackdown on the democracy movement, the CCP, while still talking about building 'socialism', made a great leap forward towards capitalism instead, and the first step was undeclared privatization.

China kick-started its wave of privatisation in 1996 when the CCP announced the 'Seize the big and let go of the small' policy under which it would simply sell off the small SOEs – in fact in the process many medium-sized enterprises were also privatized. It is true that big SOEs generally remained state owned, but their profitable subsidiaries were listed on the stock market so that they would be run on a commercial basis as private enterprises. Therefore today, even if they remain state owned, their nature is entirely different from the previous period when they were run for the public good. Now they are run to make money. As of 2001, 86 per cent of state industrial enterprises had been restructured and 70 per cent had either been partially or fully privatized.[3]

This overwhelming wave of privatisation directly led to the redundancy of tens of millions of state or collective enterprise workers. However, this process has differed from privatisation in the former Soviet Union, since the CCP has all along refused to admit that it is driving privatisation in China.

Instead, it claims that it is *gaizhi*: a reform of the system': i.e. renovating the old into a 'modern corporate system'. Even as late as March this year, the president of the Standing Committee of the National People's Congress (NPC), Wu Bangguo, still asserted in his report to the 4th Plenum of the 11th NPC the 'solemn declaration that we do not do privatisation'. The Chinese public have a very accurate saying to describe the CCP's entrenched hypocrisy: capitalism can be practised but not spoken, while socialism can be spoken but not practised.

The tragic defeat of the 1989 democratic movement made most workers demoralized and confused, largely disabling them from launching effective resistance to the privatisation offensive when it began. But since the late 1990s, sporadic protests against privatisation began to pop up all around the country. While there were numerous protests, they tended to arrive too late and in this rather limited struggle, the actions were mostly confined to single enterprises. The courageous 2002 initiative by the Liao Yang Alloy Enterprise workers to mobilise workers from other plants into the same struggle was an exception. Precisely because of this the local government quickly repressed their struggle and sentenced the leaders to prison. Given that the overall balance of forces has never been in the workers' favour, it is not all that surprising that most of the workers' anti-privatisation struggles have ended in defeat, or at most have led to improved redundancy packages (i.e. relinquishing their entitlements as state workers in an arrangement officially called *maiduan*).

'Public Servants' Turned into Masters

The flipside of workers being hit by redundancy was the rapid rise of the former SOE directors or chief executives, who became the new owners or senior management of the enterprises post-privatisation, undoubtedly also benefiting officials in the local governing authority in the process as well. The 'masters' were reduced to the unemployment scrap heap yet the public servants of the previous era turned into the masters virtually at the touch of a magic wand. Wang Lianli made this observation in his article 'Raise the reward of labour, press on with a preliminary (social) redistribution':

> The findings of the 'Report on the 2002 survey of private enterprises in China' reveal that among enterprises that had been transmuted into private entities following the 'system reform', in 95.6 per cent of cases their previous leadership during the SOE days became the enterprises' key investors-cum-chief executives following their privatisation. A similar party leaders-turn-investors/CEOs reincarnation happened also

> in 95.6 per cent of the cases of the previous municipal and town collective enterprises, and in 97 per cent of the previous rural village enterprises. By another measure, 60.6 per cent of those formerly in charge of a SOE bought up the enterprise during the 'system reform' transition.[4]

On the surface, workers were able to access shares of the privatised enterprises during the 'system reform' of SOEs into equitised entities. But in reality, the local authorities always favoured the enterprise directors, granting the biggest ownership slice to the operators to ensure that they held the controlling stakes. Workers' share of the ownership cake often ended up as little more than bait with which the enterprise director conned them out of the last bit of their savings. Starting as a compulsory exercise to coerce workers into taking part in raising an enterprise's capital, more often than not, it would not be long before the enterprise would enter bankruptcy, perhaps by design, thus looting workers of their hard-earned savings in the process. Alternatively, the operators might make up all sorts of excuses in order to get workers to forego or sell off their shareholdings. Or they might use a combination of these methods. This was the first act of appropriation of workers by the communist cadres. The second round of appropriation would take place soon after, either during or after privatization, when workers were dismissed en masse and lost their right to jobs altogether.

Staff and Workers' Representative Congress as an Institution of 'Enterprise Democracy'

The Staff and Workers' Representative Congress (SWRC) model was first introduced into China following the CCP's 1949 victory, and survived until the 1957 anti-'Rightist' purges at the latest, after which for twenty years it was little more than an empty shell. It was only after Mao died in 1976 that the issue of democratic management at the workplace was back on the agenda. At the time many people saw the autonomous workers' self-management regime in Yugoslavia as a model, and most were in favour of reviving the SWRCs as a means to keep the enterprise directors in check. While the State Council formally declared the reinstatement of SWRCs in 1980 and groomed them to be the means with which the working class was able to call the shots in their country under the CCP, the Solidarity strike movement in Poland made the CCP think again as it obviously did not want a similar thing happening on its own turf.[5] This partly explains why the establishment of SWRCs was designed in such a way as to weaken workers' control over the institution while empowering them in appearance (for more see below).

In 1991, SWRCs reportedly existed in 60.2 per cent of state enterprises.[6] According to a *Workers' Daily* report in 1998, the directors of 660 state enterprises in Tianjin had to leave their jobs after they failed to win more than 50 per cent support at their SWRCs.[7] Another *Workers' Daily* report in 2005 reported a successful case where a SWRC acted as an organ of workers' power at an enterprise called the Wuhan Iron and Steel (Group) Company:

> For us here, the SWRC is real.' Counting with his fingers, employee representative Nie Dehu from a coking division of the Jiao Hua Corporation, listed (the purported supremacy of workers) as he was attending the first meeting of Wuhan Iron and Steel (Group) Company's 11th plenum ... In recent years, more than 40 director-grade cadres were either cautioned or deposed after they failed to secure enough support from the democratic assessment process...[8]

An ACFTU study showed a different picture however. Kevin Jiang quoted an ACFTU 1987 survey indicating that only 29.26 per cent of respondents thought that SWRCs were very useful (6.25 per cent) or useful (23.01 per cent). But he also quoted the results of separate interviews with 10,000 workers from the same ACFTU report, which suggested that the percentage of interviewees who thought that SWRCs were either very useful or useful was considerably lower than 29.26 per cent. In the notes he further suggested the probability that the survey results were either a product of manipulation or the respondents were afraid of retaliation if they made undesirable responses.[9]

According to Zhu Xiaoyang and Anita Chan, the ACFTU conducted another survey concerning SWRCs in 1997 and found that in general 'only a third of the responses are positive evaluations of SWRCs, which is not enough to change the image of the SWRC system being largely window-dressing and the workplace union being nothing more than an arm of management.'[10]

Now even the official press carries de facto admission of the paralysis of the SWRCs because it is too obvious a case. Following the vigorous anti-privatisation struggle by the Tonghua Steel workers, a mainland China newspaper published an article in July 2009 that was entitled 'Why are SWRCs useless?' which went into detail about how and why the SWRCs fell short of their responsibility to protect workers' rights and interests.[11] (For more see below)

Legally SWRCs command sweeping power, and the CCP has seized on this all along to brag about how much it respects democracy at the workplace. According to article 52 of the 1998 'Law of the People's Republic of China on Industrial Enterprises Owned by the Whole People', the SWRCs general assembly has jurisdiction in five areas, summarised as follow:

1. to be consulted on major strategic policies of the enterprises;
2. to enjoy the right to co-determination over redistribution of income, including the share of wages/bonuses, and the right to make important regulations of the enterprises;
3. to decide, along with the management, on how to use the workers' welfare fund, the distribution of welfare houses among employees and all important issues concerning workers' welfare;
4. to monitor the performance of cadres at all levels and to make suggestion on rewarding or penalizing them;
5. in accordance with the arrangement of the supervisory government department, it has the right to appoint or dismiss the enterprise director, or at least to propose a candidate list.

The works councils in Germany are similar to SWRCs in China, except that the Chinese variety has more power than its German cousin. For instance, the German work councils do not have the right to be consulted or to decide on who shall be the enterprise director or personnel in the management. Zhu Xiaoyang and Anita Chan considered that 'if the SWRCs in China were indeed able to exercise their rights as defined by law, the rights enjoyed by Chinese workers of state and collective enterprises would far exceed those of workers under any capitalist system.'[12]

But the devil is in the detail. While the CCP deploys the most impressive-sounding punch lines on big issues such as 'enterprise democracy' and 'the labouring people take charge', in terms of the actual policies and legal fine print it is seeking to ensure that the party committee continues to monopolise all power, vaporising workers' statutory and political rights into thin air. Firstly, with regards to the qualifying conditions for SWRC candidacy, while enterprise management is barred from standing in elections in the German work councils, their Chinese counterparts – management staff members and leadership cadres – are not only eligible to stand for SWRC elections, it is in fact guaranteed that 'the leading management cadres of the enterprise generally, including those on the shop floor and various departments, shall comprise one-fifth of the SWRC delegates.' This stipulation was enshrined in article 12 of 'Staff and Workers' Representative Congress Bill for Industrial Enterprises Owned by the Whole People'.

The *Dong Fang Daily* points out another institutional defect as follows:

Under the existing legal framework, if the workers and their SWRC delegates were not happy with those decisions, there is no reasonable means of redress. What is more, article 54 of the 'Law of the People's Republic of China on Industrial Enterprises Owned by the Whole People' carries the special stipulation that SWRCs have the responsibility 'to support the enterprise directors in the lawful discharge of their official authority and to educate workers of their obligations to abide by the provisions of this law.'[13]

SWRCs and trade unions

Another difference between China's SWRCs and German practice is that in the latter's case, its works councils and trade unions constitute two independent systems. Neither is subordinated to the other, nor do they owe each other any rights or responsibilities. Works councils have the right to be consulted over enterprise management matters, but can't initiate a strike as a trade union can. While works council representatives are often also union members, they cannot put on their union hats while they exercise powers conferred to them by a works council. They have to keep the two identities strictly separate. It is quite the opposite in the case of China, where an enterprise union of the ACFTU is stipulated as the SWRCs' executive body and is also responsible for organising the election of SWRC delegates.[14] On the surface, a union is accountable to the SWRC. Yet since the SWRC does not have a standing executive body of its own or its own paid staff, and it can only meet at most once every six months, its real authority naturally falls into the hands of the union.

This arrangement thus ensures that CCP cadres can remove from the SWRCs even their nominal power and keep workers tightly in their grip more effectively. This is because the ACFTU has always been under the direct control of the party. Never has the ACFTU ever discharged its basic responsibility in defending the interests of workers independently of the party. Union leaders who have been sympathetic to workers have more often than not been demoted. This was what had happened to the first two prominent ACFTU leaders – Li Lisan and Lai Ruoyu – who were both criticised and lost their power based on the trumped-up charge that they sought independence for the trade union and 'opposed the party leadership'. Lai, during the Great Leap Forward was condemned for his policy of trying to accommodate simultaneously the 'leading role of the Party' and the union's role of defending the material interests of workers as 'economism' and 'syndicalism'. For the party, the union's central task was (and is) always to promote production [15] rather than defending the material interests of workers.

No wonder that soon after Lai was demoted, the Party, for a while at least, decided that in this climax of 'building communism' the ACFTU should simply 'wither away' and merge entirely into the newly built 'communes'. After the Party's retreat from this great adventure the union was allowed to recover some of its role. This was not to last for long though. During the Cultural Revolution, the ACFTU was completely closed for business for the same alleged mistakes of 'economism'.[16] Since Deng Xiaoping's return to power in the late 1970s, the party instructed the ACFTU to resume its role. The purges of more liberal minded cadres within the union did not end with the end of Mao's period. Due to the fact that a large number of workers and ACFTU rank-and-file cadres took part in the democracy movement of 1989, after it was suppressed the ACFTU engineered a new drive to purge from its ranks independent thinking cadres, including the head of the ACFTU Zhu Houze. After having purged its ranks repeatedly for sixty years, the ACFTU had long ago weeded out liberal minded cadres from its ranks. Little wonder that in this wave of privatisation at the dawn of the 21st century, all that the ACFTU could do was to bob along with it or even give it a gentle helping hand, at most offering some counselling for the redundant workers, urging them to retreat from their previous mindset of feeling superior to others.

In Tang Wenfang's book *Who is in charge: the contemporary enterprise policy in China*, the author conducted a survey in 1991-92 among SOE workers, i.e. in a pre-privatisation era. The survey reveals that whenever workers encountered problems with their job titles, housing, wages, dismissal and industrial injury issues, they would all, without exception, first approach the enterprise leadership or government authorities in looking for a solution.[17] The irrelevance of the union could not be clearer. With this in mind it should not surprise us that more often than not the workplace ACFTU, as the standing executive body of the SWRC, acted more as a brake on 'enterprise democracy' than a promoter of it.

While many commentators have praised the ACFTU's labour legislation drive, we will argue that the most important criteria for judging its success is looking at the results. Wages all round the country continued to slide: the labour share of China's gross national income fell from 52 per cent in 1997 to 40 per cent in 2007 (by contrast, the labour share of Thailand's gross national income stood at 65 per cent in 2007), or a 12 per cent drop in 10 years.[18] Meanwhile, the share of business profits surged. Given a mass ACFTU membership of more than 190 million members, with its chairperson being a Politburo member of the Communist Party and with the Chinese economy growing at nearly 10 per cent annually, this should put the union in a lot more favourable situation for collective bargaining, but allowing the workers' share of the national income to fall markedly is the best indicator of the failure of the ACFTU as a workers' institution.

The Law versus the Party

Since 1982 even watered-down 'enterprise democracy' has not been functioning at all in China. The law is often bypassed or ignored by leading cadres. For instance, the proportion of SWRC delegates with management background often exceeds the one-fifth limit, sometimes by more than half. The *Dong Fang Daily* report quoted earlier presents the following coverage:

> There just were not enough frontline workers involved in the actual running of the SWRCs. Those who stand a chance of being elected as SWRC delegates are mostly in middle management or even higher positions in the enterprise while the rank-and-file workers constitute only a tiny portion of the delegates. These middle management personnel did well from mergers and acquisition or other enterprise restructuring in an overwhelming majority of the cases...Therefore, it is not hard to understand the phenomenon where the interest of the average worker was far from adequately protected in the course of the 'system reform' of state enterprises.[19]

In addition to this is the fact that SWRC delegates rarely go through the proper procedure of a free election campaign where candidates contest for seats, hence more often than not the representatives are handpicked by the leading cadres, reducing the SWRCs into a rubber stamp, just like the trade unions are. Or if the management lacks confidence in manipulating the SWRCs then they are simply being bypassed altogether. In both cases they just ignore the laws.

There have been reports about workers successfully taking control of SWRCs to defend themselves. Zhu Xiaoyang and Anita Chan studied three SWRCs and found that two of them were 'successful SWRCs', with the first one acting as 'a consultation mechanism between workers and management', and the second one 'came closest to a democratically elected and functioning SWRC'.[20] The anti-privatisation struggle of workers at the Zheng Zhou Paper Manufacturing Enterprise in 2000 was also organized through the SWRC.[21]

These, nevertheless, were rare exceptions. In general most SWRCs have either long been paralyzed or have simply acted as rubber stamp for the party cadres before and during the privatization. In the aforementioned ACFTU's 1997 survey on SWRCs, only a third of interviewees gave a positive evaluation of SWRCs. Zhu Xiaoyang and Anita Chan admitted that even the minority opinion which gave a positive evaluation was 'likely to be overrepresented'. What is curious is that what follows is that, rather than seeing this as an indictment against this situation, they came to the defence of SWRCs as relatively effective workers' institution – relative to the Western practice of co-determination. They argue that since the European co-determination model does not really guarantee workers' participation, meaning that 'even under democratic systems, work councils and workplace unions do not get high evaluations from a majority of workers and employees', then 'we cannot expect the majority of SWRCs in China to operate close to the ideal'. This argument is a bit odd. If both the Western and Chinese models are equally bad, instead of using the failure in the West to justify the failure in China, the only possible and logical conclusion should be to criticize both of them.

In a country where basic civil liberties, especially freedom of speech, are absent and where by law even conducting a social survey requires permission from the authorities, some scepticism of all official surveys is required because we simply have no way to check their authenticity.[22] What is more is that when trying to make an evaluation of the effectiveness of SWRCs (or the trade union) it is always equally important, if not more so, to look at the end results. In just six years (1996-2001), as a result of privatization, 40.5 per cent of the entire manufacturing industry workforce was cut, equal to the elimination of 26.12 million jobs.[23] The total number of dismissals from all sectors of the economy was somewhere between 30 and 40 million. If most workers had real control over the SWRCs then the struggle between those supporting and those against privatization would have been a more long drawn out fight, or the struggles against privatization would have been more open and more widespread. This is based on the assumption that most workers did not support privatization, not on any independent and comprehensive survey which is quite improbable under the regime. This assumption of workers' attitude towards privatization is not unreasonable, however, given that SOE workers in general possessed some kind of class identity and collective consciousness. While evidence points to the fact that SOE workers were in general quite confused in their attitude towards the macro-economic decision of the Party to build a 'socialist market economy' – which in turn shows the limitation of their consciousness – they were sensitive to the looting of state property in their plants by the leading cadres because they knew only too well that it would be them who bore all the costs. In addition to this was that, under common ownership, they believed that it was their labour which had contributed to the industrialization of Communist China in general and to the development of their own plant in particular, hence they considered themselves having a rightful claim to defend their plants against theft. This is what Ching Kwan Lee described as 'workers' claim of collective ownership of their work units', or a 'social contract…between the paternalistic state and a politically acquiescent populace'.[24] Most SOE workers would oppose privatization if they were well informed beforehand and were given the chance to voice their opinion. The fact that despite repression, workers' anti-privatization struggles have still sprung up from time to time also acts as evidence for this.

If any SWRC, at some point in its existence, was to a certain extent a genuine representative of workers' interest but voted in the end to approve privatisation, it is most likely because either they saw no way out (mostly because of lack of capital to run the plant as collectively owned enterprises), or because the enterprise director succeeded in dragging the enterprise into bankruptcy, or the national policy had cornered state enterprises into a dead end (as banks stopped extending them credit lines), or a combination of all or most of these factors.

Whereas Ching Kwan Lee describes the struggles in SOEs as 'non-payment protests', 'neighbourhood protests' and 'bankruptcy protests' [25], I prefer to term these struggles as 'resistance to privatization' in general, despite the fact that only part of these struggles were explicitly opposing privatization. Lee's three categories may have the strength of referring to the direct nature of most of these struggles, but their weakness is also obvious: it leaves out struggles which *were* explicitly opposing privatization, from the 2002 Liao Yang Ferro-Alloy Factory struggle to the recent Tonggang Steel Mill workers' struggle. What is more is that it may lose sight of the fact that in most cases all three types of struggles targeted the one and same group of people – the leading cadres of SOEs and their supervising government departments. This applies to 'neighbourhood protests' too because in the old days SOEs also provided most of the social services in the neighbourhood, therefore privatization of the plants often also implies termination of free or accessible services in the neighbourhood. Hence what have appeared to be non-political and cellular struggles in fact carried the political potential of developing into struggles against privatization itself or even against local governments – after all, it does not require much hard thinking to figure out who the main enemy is. It is for the same reason, however, that the party-state must act swiftly to repress these struggles lest nationwide protests of the same kind of 1989 be triggered off once again. Similarly, this is also why when party cadres implemented privatization it has been conducted in a totally non-transparent manner, filled to the brim with intrigue, trickery and con jobs, including the ploy not to call privatisation by its real name, dressing it up as 'system reform' instead and pushing this agenda a step at a time. All this was geared to undermine workers' readiness to resist. Therefore what appears to be fragmented or what Ching Kwan Lee describes as 'cellular activism' among SOE workers is, after all, just an appearance. But beyond this appearance lies the deep contradiction between the cadres of the party-state and the working class and all the political dynamics which might follow. Refusing to describe the SOE workers' struggles, or at least an important number of them, as resistance to privatization or anti-privatization struggles might not only downplay their political potential but also might lead to the temptation of taking 'cellular activism' at face value, without probing into the inner contradictions of these struggles and their relation to the bureaucracy.

I also differ from Lee's optimism that 'we cannot underestimate the determination and effectiveness of the Chinese regime's self-reform to establish a law-based government, after its radical self-transformation from state socialism'[26].

Nor can I share the enthusiasm of Zhu and Chan's 2005 prediction that SWRCs 'may have room for development' in the coming few years because 'China is becoming more and more a legal society'. When I am writing this essay in August 2011 this bright prospect of SWRCs is still nowhere to be seen. Precisely because of this self transformation from state socialism to capitalism it is less, not more, possible for the bureaucracy to self reform itself into a rule of law regime, let alone implement democracy. The self interest of the Chinese bureaucracy simply goes against this. This bureaucracy simply refuses to be content with playing the role of compliant apparatus in the service of the bourgeoisie in return for a fixed amount of salary. On the contrary, it *is* the ruling class; it is simultaneously bureaucrats *and* capitalists, and therefore it wants a fixed salary and maximized profit at the same time. All levels of bureaucrats run or own companies directly or indirectly, and profit from these. This is a system of bureaucratic capitalism. Since its very survival rests on a fusion of political and economic power, it necessarily remains hostile to the rule of law and to a situation where the working class enjoys full political and labour rights. It is likely that the party will increasingly 'rule by law', but this is different from the rule of law and Lee makes the distinction between the two. However, whereas Lee suggests that there are two 'possible forces of change', namely one coming from the party's own initiative for self reform and the second one a workers movement from below, we think that the party in itself hardly constitutes a 'possible force of change' in favour of labour at all, and any serious reform has to come from the pressure from a movement from below.

'Socialism' from above: SOE workers in Mao's China

If it is the one party regime which has undermined the SWRCs or the trade unions as true workers' organs, we must add that it is really not something new, rather it has always been like this ever since 1949.

But until today a considerable number of people think otherwise. For them, SOE workers during Mao's period were genuinely the 'masters of the house' and therefore enjoyed real political power. This changed only when Deng Xiaoping came to power in 1979. This is what has been argued by Mingqi Li in his recent essay *The Rise of the Working Class and the Future of the Chinese Revolution.* 'In the Maoist socialist era, the Chinese workers enjoyed a level of class power and dignity unimaginable by an average worker in a capitalist state,' he said. He has not provided evidence for his statement though, other than to quote approvingly a worker saying 'the workers were masters of the factory'. [27]

Another academic, Cui Zhiyuan, in an earlier essay pointed to the 'Angang Constitution' to back up his case.[28] The Angang Constitution refers to Mao's call in 1960 during the Great Leap Forward for a new policy in the management of state enterprises, summed up by the slogan 'Participation on two fronts, one area of reform and the integration of three components'. 'Participation on two fronts' refers to the measure of making cadres participate in manual labour while encouraging workers' participation in enterprise management. The 'one area of reform' refers to doing away with unreasonable rules and regulations. The 'integration of three components' refers to the coming together of the working masses, leadership cadres and the technical personnel. Cui regards the measure of making cadres participate in manual labour while encouraging workers' participation in enterprise management as a kind of economic democracy.

It is difficult to comment on Cui's argument, because the article was too abstract and evasive. On the contrary, Xiao Duo, a follower of Mao, elaborated on the subject in greater detail in his web article '*Mao's socialism is not bureaucratism*'.[29] Xiao believes that the Angang Constitution allows 'the labouring masses to do away with the career officialdom and take part directly in the democratic management of society'.

The Angang Constitution has nothing to do with the 'democratic management of society', however, because it only applies at the enterprise level. In fact it was not even a case of enterprise democracy at all. It is merely a situation where workers took part in consultative meetings within the rank-and-file production teams to offer suggestions concerning how to raise productivity even further. These meetings rarely went beyond the workshop level and rarely enjoyed the power of decision making. On this point, China falls far short even of the Yugoslav's worker self management regime. While the Yugoslav Communist Party never had the guts to extend worker self management into state power, its workers did enjoy considerable power within the enterprise, which the Angang Constitution was far short of.

If the CCP was serious about implementing enterprise democracy, the most convenient way would be to revive its own institution of the SWRC (meanwhile getting rid of the crippling clauses in the relevant laws). Yet the CCP, during the Great Leap Forward, instead of choosing this option, promoted the so called Angang Constitution. This was because from the very beginning the intention of the Angang Constitution was less about empowering workers in controlling the management, even less about controlling the party, but more about how to motivate workers into contributing ideas in renovating and improving production technology so as to fulfil the dream of overtaking Britain and the US.[30] This is also why the promotion of the Angang Constitution was accompanied by coercing workers to receive lower wages by abolishing piece rate wages altogether, seeing this as a kind of 'economism'.[31] This practice repeated itself in the Cultural Revolution.

As for Mao's idea of 'cadres' participation in labour', this did not promote workers' participation in management. Since in practise it often meant making specialists and intellectuals do manual labour – during the Cultural Revolution it often became hard labour – it only resulted in a general waste of socially useful and highly skilled labour, hence a social regression rather than progress. In fact, Mao's idea is far from the vision of the contemporary idea of socialist equality. His approach was closer to the vision of Xu Xing in ancient China who advocated a kind of equal society where 'both the kings and their subjects (the peasants) till the land together'. The contemporary socialist movement aims to break down the social division of labour between the rulers and the ruled. This, however, is to be achieved not by making professionals and intellectuals do manual labour (voluntary work done by them is another matter). Rather, it shall be achieved firstly through the development of productive forces and then through the implementation of common ownership and a fully fledged democracy, and the shortening of the working week so as to allow workers the material conditions to participate in the running of society. By contrast, making professionals and intellectuals do manual labour is a kind of utopianism which echoes more what Marx criticised as 'vulgar communism' than a contemporary socialist idea. [32] This subsequent bankruptcy in fact helped lay the grounds for the eventual restoration of capitalism.

Xiao Duo mentioned how the working class enjoyed job security and was much better off during Mao's days than now. We are not prepared to dismiss out of hand the achievement in economic benefit for working people under Mao, as people who bitterly oppose the 1949 revolution did. But it is equally wrong to argue that Mao's period was a golden era where workers enjoyed real power. It is true that the workers could not be fired by the management and this placed considerable limits on the management's power, but neither did the workers have the freedom to make personal choices concerning their careers, let alone the freedom to speak or to organize. Without this one cannot simply speak of 'class power'. Under a 'planned economy', as the official theory at that time went, labour power was also supposed to be owned 'collectively'. This is the theoretical basis on which the practice of planned allocation of labour among production units began, under which workers were denied the freedom to choose their occupations or the freedom to choose the particular enterprises they worked in. In the same way, they were also denied the freedom to resign from their enterprises and shift to other plants of their free will. This is what they called *tongbao tongpei* ('guarantee full employment while allocating labour in a planned way'), or *rencai danwei suoyuzhi* ('the workforce within a production unit was thought to be owned by that unit'). What was more threatening for these 'masters' was that their personal files were held in the hands of the party committee and were kept secret from them. These included records of things which they might have said before, especially where they were critical of the party or cadres.[33] All this could be used to incriminate them in possible future political purges. All in all, workers had to behave under this system and became part of a system of personal dependence with a feudal flavour. Indeed, if workers had always been the genuine ruling class since Mao's era, how was it possible that they were defeated and appropriated without even an open and nationwide struggle?

US sociologist Andrew Walder called the enterprise management system in Mao's days 'Neo-Traditionalism'. While the appropriateness of this term is debatable, Walder is right in describing workers' class position as one of 'institutionalised dependence' – i.e. 'economic and social dependence on the enterprises; political dependence on the party and management; and personal dependence on (the) supervisors.'[34] It was less a kind of socialism but more a kind of paternalistic collectivism where, even if workers benefited in terms of economic welfare, supreme power first and foremost rested in the hands of party cadres, hence enabling them to control working people's lives to the extent that the latter were entirely dependent on them. It was (and is) also particularly hostile to any sign of autonomous thinking and organizations from below; in this sense the 'communist' bureaucracy echoed the motto of all elites: 'one must work for the good of the people, but the people must do nothing for themselves'.[35] Although during the Cultural Revolution Mao jumped to the other extreme by appealing for rebellion from below, this did not last long either. When Mao felt that the situation was beginning to run out of control he once again changed position and reached a compromise with the old guard and the army. The propaganda against bureaucratic privileges during the Cultural Revolution never came through as a policy for equality in any sustained sense. On the contrary. The top leaders regained all of their bureaucratic privileges in no time. In his 1996 book, *The Deng Xiaoping Era –An Inquiry into the Fate of Chinese Socialism 1978 –1994*, US academic Maurice Meisner wrote that:

> Mao Zedong was the creator of the Chinese Communist bureaucracy ... The Cultural Revolution, far from curing bureaucratic evils, only aggravated the arbitrary and corrupt bureaucratic practices from which the people suffered. Individual officials were attacked and purged, but the bureaucratic system survived. Even the hierarchical order of cadre ranks, which Mao had been criticizing since the mid-1950s, remained intact. In large measure, the failure was of Mao's own making, or, more precisely, the result of his ambivalent attitude toward the bureaucracy he had created and upon which his rule depended.[36]

A major blind spot in the notion that in Mao's China the working class were really the 'masters of the house' and that this only changed after Deng took power, lies in the fact that this notion only sees the rupture between the two periods (from anti-capitalism to pro-capitalism) and not their continuity. It is the continuity of the regime of the one party dictatorship and its repression of workers and farmers, whom the party claims to represent, which allows the cadres to rob the workers and farmers in Deng/post Deng period. But it is no accident that this side of the coin is often overlooked. This is because implicitly or explicitly the one party dictatorship is seen as more of an essential element of socialism rather than its crippling factor.[37] Therefore pro-Mao academics have had to look elsewhere to explain the reason for workers' inability to mount efficient struggles against privatization, and many think they have found it. Mingqi Li seeks the reason for the workers' defeat in the alleged 'politically inexperienced working class'[38]. This is also echoed by Cheng Guangsheng.[39] It seems the fact has never crossed their minds that when the party put the working class under its permanent tutelage and forbade it to be autonomous and to learn from its own errors, it necessarily remained politically inexperienced.

Democracy from below

Though the chapter of SOE workers in Mao's China is over, many are still trying to draw lessons from it. In his *The Plight of China's Working Class: Annals of Anyuan,* Yu Jianrong warned workers candidly that they should not fantasize about waging any struggles to become any sort of master as rhetoric like this only serves the interest of the populist parties:

> Workers are simply not a 'leading class' nor should they aspire to be one. What they should fight for is their rights as workers and shoulder their responsibility as workers. From my perspective, the real interests of the contemporary Chinese workers lie in the question of defending workers' rights. …if we steer away from this goal, it's possible that workers will be reduced to being a new breed of political tool.[40]

Although not explicitly, it is implicit in his argument that workers should accept the role as wage labourers and be content with undefined 'labour rights reform' within the system. The problem with this argument is that it forgets that wage labour is also a tool in itself, an economic tool in the hands of capitalists with the sole purpose of adding value to their capital stock; hence workers can be dumped as broken tools if their labour no longer serves that purpose. Surely Yu is concerned with 'workers' rights', but we are not sure what this means. The fact that liberal advocacy like Charter 08[41] leaves out the right to free trade unions and collective bargaining altogether should justify our suspicions. In the final analysis, there is no reason to assume that capitalists necessarily behave better than communist party cadres in their treatment of workers; rather, they can be equally, if not more, stubborn in repressing any demand for reform from the labour movement. This is especially so in China's case. Far from becoming the leader of a democratic movement, a once popular proposition in the late 1980s, this new entrepreneurial class is as fearful of democracy and the labour movement as its patron, the Communist Party.

If there is anything to learn from Mao's period, it is not that workers should be more practical and should be content with capitalism as the only viable system; rather, a correct understanding of the reason for the historic defeat of the working class needs to be made. The working class was defeated not because it was too high minded. On the contrary, workers were defeated precisely because most of them were too practical; as long as they could enjoy job security and a stable income they rarely challenged the one party regime, even if this regime denied them basic civil liberties in general and the right to free association in particular, hence all their legal rights, as enshrined in the constitution and in the law, were reduced to pure formalities. Rousseau once remarked that no one could be truly free who did not govern him/herself. Yet most SOE workers did not fully understand the primacy of democracy over economic benefit; rather they allowed their perpetual dependence on the party to do good for them. But no economic benefit is guaranteed as long as workers are denied the right to govern themselves. If workers rely on the bureaucracy to unilaterally hand down these benefits to them, this same bureaucracy could also take these benefits back when an unfavourable change in the class relationship of forces occurred. And when this happened, the 'masters of the house' simply had nothing in their hands to defend them from the attack.

With the full restoration of capitalism the Chinese working people will have to start all over again to build a democratic labour movement in the new century if they want to be free from exploitation and repression. This will not be accomplished unless they can keep the state under their democratic control.

The struggle of workers for democracy is the same thing as their striving to be the 'leading class'. Under rapid industrialization the worker population has been rising quickly at the expense of farmers to the extent that it will soon constitute half, or even more, of the population (if we define 'workers', correctly, as wage earners and those whose wages will not allow them to accumulate capital), hence they constitute the chief class in the alliance for democracy. Apart from the 'quantity' side one must also look at the 'quality' of the labour force: the youth exodus from rural areas means that the remaining residents are mainly children and the elderly. Therefore the working class is a growing class while the peasants are a declining class. The working class is increasingly the main class in democratic struggles in the future because it has a stake in winning democracy *and* the potential to win it. Surely nothing is determined in this. Either it eventually achieves democracy by taking the lead in the struggles, or it will continue to suffer under barbaric capitalism indefinitely. Suffice to say now that if the workers are, eventually, able to prove their ability to lead the democratic struggles and thus able to shape society according to their will, this is not something horrifying at all – at least not for working people. Indeed, the original meaning of democracy is nothing but the rule by the plebeian or the poor. Aristotle was very clear about this, although he, from an elitist position, was far from being sympathetic with the idea.[42] In this sense democracy is also synonymous with socialism. After all, one of the key features of socialism is precisely a complete democratization of society. Therefore, to strive to be the 'leading class' is really not a too high minded thing, it is just the same old goal of labour fighting for genuine democracy, or socialism if you like. Without this perspective, in the long run working people will not be able to keep their 'bread and butter' either. The imminent destruction of welfare states in the west should be another reason for making the link between a kind of democracy where working people play the dominant role and their economic betterment.

Sadly, most Chinese liberals continue to accommodate themselves to the ruling elites' hostility towards democracy and social movements. This negligence over workers' fundamental rights shows that they, like many elites, see the idea of a combination of radical democracy and an autonomous workers movement as too dangerous to the status quo.

If Yu's arguments sound convincing, it is not because his theory holds any real merit for working people. It is more because workers have already been defeated and the resurgence of a workers' movement looks very distant indeed. The disturbing news for the liberals however, is that the rise of labour struggles is inevitable in the long run. While the number of SOE workers in China fell substantially, the overall number of wage labourers has ballooned to nearly 400 million. China's working class population has never been as enormous as it is now. If this reversion to capitalism has anything positive about it, this is it. What is more is that the barbarian character and the barrack like factory regime are propelling workers to resist on a daily basis. So it is not at all surprising that when SOEs kept chucking workers out of their jobs en masse, a big number of migrant workers rose to strike spontaneously to resist against inhuman exploitation. To the surprise of the government, even the SOE workers' struggles against privatization have not died out. The July 2009 Tonghua Steel workers' violent occupation of their plant to resist privatization ended in a victory which proved that SOE workers' power, although weakened, can still be powerful enough to make the party-state afraid.

We have no idea how the combination of struggle for economic betterment and the struggle for democracy can be achieved, and we acknowledge that the outlook is not very optimistic for the moment. Instead of envisaging a saviour rising from nowhere and showing the road map to worker activists, we believe that eventually it will be decided by the workers themselves in struggle. After all, it is social movements which bring about democracy. And if the trade union movement has any merit, it is not just because it can win a rise in wages but also because it represents the aspiration of human beings to be free from exploitation and to take control, even in an elementary manner, of the conditions of their work.

For the moment, it is our duty to draw a balance sheet of the rise and fall of the older generation of SOE workers.

August 2011

Notes

1 The first draft of this essay was translated by Eva Tao from the original Chinese draft and the author wishes to thank her here. The present version is a heavily re-written version and was proofread by Bai Ruixue, whom the author would like to thank as well.

2 There is no space to discuss Collectively Owned Enterprise (COE) workers here. Their working conditions and mentality are be different from SOE workers, so it is difficult to say to what degree the explanation here might act as a reference point for analysing their situation.

3 *Exit the Dragon? Privatization and State Control in China*, Edited by Stephen Green and Guy S. Liu, Blackwell, 2005, p. 18.

4 *Tigao laodong baochou, zhuoli chuci fenpei* (Raise the reward of labour, work hard on the preliminary (social) redistribution), Wang Lianli, Hong Kong Faxes, Political and Economic Research Department of the CITIC group, December 12, 2007.

5 'In the June of this year the Vice Chairman of the CCP Li Xiannian said that if Beijing did not reform the economy, they too would face a Polish style crisis.' Ming Pao, December 11, 1981, Hong Kong. Translation by author. For the link between the Polish event and the Party's position on SWRCs, see footnote 14 of *Gonghui yu dang-guo de chongtu* (The Conflict between Trade Unions and the Party State), Kevin Jiang, Hong Kong Journal of Social Sciences, No. 8, Autumn 1996.

6 *Gonghui yu dang-guo de chongtu* (The Conflict between Trade Unions and the Party State), Kevin Jiang, Hong Kong Journal of Social Sciences, No. 8, Autumn 1996.

7 *Whither China's Industrial System and with What Implications for Labour? Labour History*, October 2006.

8 '*Qiye yingdui tiaozhan de liqi – wugang qianghua zhidaihui zhidu tuijin changwu gongkai jishi*' (The weapon with which enterprises face their challenges – Report on how Wuhan Iron and Steel strengthen its Workers' Representative Congress mechanism so as to promote transparency of the running of the enterprise), *Worker Daily*, June 10, 2005, http://www.sasac.gov.cn/n1180/n1271/n3420181/n3420283/3445501.html

9 '*Gonghui yu dang-guo de chongtu*' (The Conflict between Trade Unions and the Party State), Kevin Jiang, *Hong Kong Journal of Social Sciences*, No. 8, Autumn

1996.

10 *Staff and Workers' Representative Congress, An Institutionalized Channel for Expression of Employees' Interests?*, Zhu Xiaoyang and Anita Chan, Chinese Sociology and Anthropology, vol. 37 no. 4, Summer 2005, p. 6-33.

11 '*Zhidaihui weishenme meiyong*', (Why are SWRCs useless?) *Dong Fang Daily*, August 17, 2009. http://news.ifeng.com/opinion/political/detail_2009_08/17/1346610_0.shtml.

12 'Staff and Workers' Representative Congress, An Institutionalized Channel for Expression of Employees' Interests?', Zhu Xiaoyang and Anita Chan, *Chinese Sociology and Anthropology*, vol. 37 no. 4, Summer 2005, p. 6-33.

13 '*Zhidaihui weishenme meiyong*', (Why are SWRCs useless?) *Dong Fang Daily*, August 17, 2009. http://news.ifeng.com/opinion/political/detail_2009_08/17/1346610_0.shtml.

14 *Zhonghua quanguo zonggonghui qishinian*, (The Seventy Years of ACFTU), edited by the ACFTU, Chinese Workers Press, Beijing, 1995, p. 404-5.

15 This supposed central task of the ACFTU is still explicitly stipulated in the currently effective 1992 Trade Union Law, article four.

16 *Zhonghua quanguo zonggonghui qishinian*, (The Seventy Years of ACFTU), edited by ACFTU, Chinese Workers Press, Beijing, 1995, chapter eight.

17 *Shui lai zuozhu – dangdai zhongguo de qiye juece* (Who is in charge: the contemporary enterprise policy in China), Tang Wenfang, Oxford University Press, 1996, p. 88-89.

18 *The Crisis in Asia: Over-Dependence on International Trade or Reflection of 'A Labour Repression-Led Growth Regime'?* Bruno Jetin, October 2009, paper presented to the International Seminar on the Economic Crisis, Amsterdam.

19 '*Zhidaihui weishenme meiyong*', (Why are SWRCs useless?) *Dong Fang Daily*, August 17, 2009. http://news.ifeng.com/opinion/political/detail_2009_08/17/1346610_0.shtml.

20 'Staff and Workers' Representative Congress, An Institutionalized Channel for Expression of Employees' Interests?', Zhu Xiaoyang and Anita Chan, *Chinese Sociology and Anthropology*, vol. 37 no. 4, Summer 2005, p. 6-33.

21 The workers at the Zheng Zhou Paper Manufacturing Enterprise had for a while succeeded in holding back the privatisation of their plant by organising through the SWRC. But overwhelmed by debt, the enterprise was propped up in the end by the injection of private capital. Stephen Philion has discussed this case in an article, in which he holds the view that the SWRC leadership's acceptance of private capital means it turned its back on the original aspiration in banking on workers' democracy, and believes this change of tack could have led to the struggle's demise. See 'Democracy vs. Privatization in China', *Socialism and Democracy*, Vol. 21, No. 2, July 2007.

22 Although China is now securely on the track of capitalist accumulation, the practice of fabricating news reports for the sake of propaganda has never ceased despite the media nowadays being a bit more open in reporting bad news. Even in Guangdong where the media is considered less obedient to the Party's propaganda department in Beijing, and therefore much hated by the nationalists like the *Utopia* Website, the media still fabricates news reports

in order to provide propaganda for the Party. For instance the Hong Kong Ming Pao reported on how the Shen Zhen Commerce Daily created fake news concerning how a policeman remained on duty to guard the 26th Universiade games despite his son's death. See *Ming Pao* 15 August, 2011.

23 *Woguo zhongchangqi shiye wenti yanjiu* (Study on China's Unemployment in the Long and Medium Term), Jiangxuan, China People's University Press, Beijing, 2004, p. 181.

24 *Against the Law – Labor Protests in China's Rustbelt and Sunbelt*, University of California Press, 2007, p. 26 and 22.

25 Ibid, p. 71.

26 Ibid, p.242.

27 *Monthly Review*, June 2011.

28 *Angang xianfa yu houfutezhuyi* (Angang Constitution and Fordism), collected in *Di Er Ci Si Xiang Jie Feng Yu Zhi Du Chuang Xin* (The second round of thoughts liberation and system renewal), Cui Zhiyuan, published by Oxford University Press, 1997. (Translator's note: The Angang Constitution refers to a 1960 policy decree by Mao where he called for various reforms for democratise enterprise management. Two such measures were cadres' participation in labour and workers' participation in enterprise management.)

29 It was first published in www.gongnongbbs.net.tf but has since been taken down. It is now available on the 'Pioneer' webpage at www.xinmiao.com.hk/0000/6609T.htm.

30 In fact, the very title of the document written by the Anshan city party committee reporting to Beijing on the Anshan steel mill's reform plan during the Great Leap Forward – and on which Mao wrote his famous remark – was about how to promote a technological innovation there.

31 According to Maoist doctrine, workers' enthusiasm for increasing production should flow from political consciousness rather than from economic incentives, such as the raising of wages. The reliance on material incentives was considered 'economism'. In 1957 42 per cent of workers in SOEs were paid on piece rates. In 1960 this dropped to less than 5 per cent. It rose back to 19.9 per cent in 1963, but in 1966 piece rates were banned altogether. *Zhongguo jingji nianjian 1981* (Annual Economic Report of China 1981), Beijing Economic Management Journal Press, 1981, Overseas edition, Hong Kong, p. IV-180-1.

32 It is for this reason that Marx never envisaged that socialism could be realised in a backward country.

33 The cadres were also subject to the regime of personal files, but the fact that it was the cadres who kept and recorded these confidential files of workers once again shows who the real masters in Mao's period were. See *Zhongguo dangdai shehui ge jieceng fenxi* (An Analysis on China Contemporary Social Stratification), Yang Jisheng, Gansu People's Press, 2006, Gansu, p. 21.

34 *Communist Neo-Traditionalism*, Andrew Walder, Oxford University Press, 1996, p. 12-13.

35 *Democracy and Revolution*, by George Novack, Pathfinder Press, New York, 1971, p. 73.

36 *The Deng Xiaoping Era—An Inquiry into the Fate of Chinese Socialism 1978-*

1994, Maurice Meisner, 1996, Hill and Wang, p. 176.

37 Xiao Duo is explicit on this point.

38 *Monthly Review,* June 2011.

39 *Zhongguo gongren jieji de xingqi yu zhongguo geming de qiantu* (The Rise of Working Class and the Future of Chinese Revolution), Cheng Guangsheng, Spring 2011, second section. Pamphlet published by associates of the China Labor Research Web, although the pamphlet does not carry the name of the publisher.

40 *Zhongguo gongren jieji zhuangkuang– Anyuan shilu* (The Plight of China's Working Class: Annals of Anyuan), Mirror Books, Hong Kong, 2006, p. 471.

41 Charter 08 was a manifesto initially signed by over 350 Chinese human rights activists and others published on 10 December 2008. See Chapter 12 for more.

42 'Whenever men rule by virtue of their wealth, be they few or many, there you have oligarchy; and where the poor rule, there you have democracy,' he said. Quoted in *Democracy*, by Anthony Arblaster, University of Minnesota Press, Minneapolis, 1994, p 14-5.

DISPOSABLE LABOUR UNDER SOCIAL APARTHEID[1]

Au Loong Yu

The global financial crisis has begun to take its toll on China. China's exports have been declining rapidly, and in the south and the coastal regions where the export processing zones house millions of workers, nine million rural migrant workers have been sacked and returned to their home villages. Millions more will return for the Chinese New Year holidays towards the end of January 2010, and many of them will have to stay home after the holidays since the wave of plant closures will worsen by then.[2]

Rescue package for the rich, more unemployment for the people

Thousands of migrant workers have seen their wages disappear along with their employers, and they have to fight to get at least a portion of it back. Road blockages and demonstrations are not rare scenes. When the actions are large enough, they are often able to force local authorities to fund workers to go back to their home villages. In doing so, the local authorities are not only meeting the workers' demand, but also pursuing their own benefit: sending the migrant workers back home is much safer than keeping a large reserve army of jobless poor in the cities. After the onset of the economic downturn, both the central and provincial governments hastily announced plans of economic incentives to encourage migrant workers who had been dismissed to return to their home villages to farm small plots of land or establish small businesses. Although there is the rhetoric of protecting jobs for migrant workers, it is either merely advice to companies to be 'prudent' in sacking their workforce, or it is active support for these companies by providing credit to help them maintain liquidity. In a nutshell, the substance of the present rescue plan is for the benefit of the employers rather than for the employees.

On top of this, both central and local governments are, in practice, helping employers to shift the burden of the economic crisis on to workers.

The Ministry of Human Resources and Social Security declared a wage freeze on minimum wages on 17 November 2008 'in order to help the firms to withstand the economic downturn'.[3] Soon after, the Guangdong Provincial ACFTU (All China Federation of Trade Unions) advised workers that they must stick together with their bosses to overcome the crisis and therefore collective consultation over wages in those enterprises which face difficulties would be suspended.

The government declared a stimulus package of four trillion yuan to achieve its target of *baoba*, or keeping the economic growth rate at 8 per cent. The government controlled media reassured ordinary people that achieving the target is paramount because it would help save jobs.

However, even if the stimulus package eventually means that the growth rate stays at 8 per cent in the coming year, it has little bearing on job creation. This is because China's growth has been, to a great extent, a jobless growth. The International Labour Organisation (ILO) carried out a study in 2005 on the relationship between economic growth and job creation, and found that in the period of 1990-2002, an average 9.3 per cent growth only brings about 0.8 per cent of employment growth, while for manufacturing jobs it is actually negative.[4] No wonder the high growth rate of 8 per cent is accompanied by a high unemployment rate. The current official unemployment rate of 4 per cent is generally considered unreliable. According to the Chinese Academy of Social Science the actual rate for 2008 is as high as 9.4 per cent.[5] Again, this is an underestimation, because it does not take into account those migrant workers who have returned to their home villages.

Not only does economic growth have little to do with job creation, it also has little to do with wage growth. According to a World Bank report, wages in China as a share of GDP declined from 53 per cent in 1998 to 41.4 per cent in 2005, as opposed to 57 per cent in the US.[6] The law on the minimum wage has done little to stop the decline, simply because it is so low that it only equates to little more than 30 per cent of average wages, whereas in Thailand and US it is 50 per cent.

The implication of the discussion on jobs and wages is that, even if the 8 per cent growth rate is maintained during this downturn, thanks to the rescue plan, it probably will continue to have difficulties in generating enough jobs. This is especially so when we look at the main content of the package itself. Despite the rhetoric of creating jobs and promoting people's livelihood, the package delivers little resources to directly raise the share of wages (including social wages) to a reasonable level. It ignores calls for reform of social security to include, for example, free medical care and education from high school upward, a more effective unemployment benefit system and a pension fund with a greater contribution from the government. Introducing a more comprehensive social security may, it is argued, provide a sense of security to people and act as an incentive for them to spend money rather than saving it. According to *Newsweek*, only one percent of the total stimulus spending is pegged for health care, culture and education. Huang Ming, a Cornell professor who teaches at Beijing's Cheung Kong Graduate School of Business, says, 'It's in the interest of the government to develop the social safety net fast. It will stimulate consumption. [Chinese] save because they are frightened of getting sick.'[7] China's saving rate is as high as 46 per cent, as opposed to zero in US, and it becomes counter-productive in an economic downturn: less money goes to consumption. However there is little indication that the government is going to adhere to the welfare state discourse. Much of the 4 trillion yuan is spent on infrastructure. Although this creates jobs, its capital-intensive nature means that it is not going to create as many jobs as those lost in the export-oriented manufacturing industry.

With neither transparency nor democratic control, it is obvious that when the government hands out the rescue money it is not going to do it in an impartial way. Even the censored press finds it necessary to warn against corruption. The Legal Daily writes that the package is going to 'bring about a fierce competition between provincial governments for projects', and 'behind these big projects there are always big corruption.'[8] A part of the package is for reconstruction for the Sichuan region where an earthquake devastated one of its counties, Wenchuan. Since May there has been 40 billion yuan of donations but now as winter has already arrived there are still 100,000 victims, among them many children, who do not even have a pair of winter shoes.[9] It reminds us of one thing again: that the package will first and foremost benefit the power elite.

The government has been aware of the weakness of its growth model since before the US crisis set in. In April 2008 President Hu Jintao spoke of the need to change the model of development from export-led growth to more emphasis on domestic-led growth by expanding domestic demand. However, no growth model can change without some restructuring, and restructuring itself is not going to be painless. The only question is who is going to bear the pain? In a country where basic civil and labour rights are absent, the relationship of forces necessarily favours the strong (the bureaucracy and the entrepreneurs) in the most extreme way, and it is inevitable that working people, especially migrant workers, are going to bear the main burden of economic restructuring. The 200 million rural migrants are just disposable labour. When business is good they are called in to work in sweatshops 12 hours a day, and even denied the right to resign when they prefer to go back to their home villages, rather than to endure slave-like working conditions.[10] When business turns bad, they are told to go home and till their miserable piece of land. To some extent the migrant workers, as second class citizens, are quite similar to women as a second sex under capitalism: the last hired and first fired in an economic crisis. In the light of these fresh experiences during the crisis, it is doubly unconvincing to argue that China provides an alternative model for working people.

The regime of spatial and social apartheid

The reason that migrant workers have to return to their home village is, firstly, because they are guest workers who do not have a place to call home in the cities. When they have a job, most of them stay in dormitories because their wages are simply too low to afford renting a flat outside of the factories.[11] When they lose their job they lose their accommodation as well. Without income and a place to live they have to return to their home village. Their low wages, however, are not entirely the result of market forces. On the contrary, it is first and foremost the state which contributes to the miserable working conditions of rural migrant workers. What we are talking about is not just the harsh repression against freedom of association and the constitutional right to strike, but also the system of household registration, which institutionalizes rural migrant workers as second class citizens and disposable labour. In practice, this plays the same role as apartheid, but in China's case it targets a particular social class, namely the peasants, rather than a particular race.[12]

The birth of capitalism was associated not just with freedom of occupation but also, ironically, with restriction of workers' freedom of movement. Thus Marx found it necessary to attack the French system of a workers' pass, which gave the police the right to decide whether workers could stay and work or whether they should return to their place of birth, and depicted the regulation as an 'excess of despotism'.[13] What is more ironic is that it was the so-called socialist Soviet Union under Stalin which re-introduced the pass system in 1930s, while in western Europe the practice had long receded into history. Mao's China imposed the same system, yet even if the Communist Party drew a lot on the Soviet experience; it could also turn to China's own history of a similar system as a reference point in imposing restrictions on workers' freedom. Indeed one of the reasons that the state did not encounter much opposition from the peasants was that the latter had been accustomed to this kind of social control imposed by the absolutist state for two millennia.

The *hukou* system, or household registration, has a history of over two thousand years in China, and was established during the imperial era as a means of social control. The *hukou* system allowed the state to collect, on a regular basis, statistics concerning the number of labourers among the households, and the area of land they owned, so that it could draft the exact number of soldiers or collect the exact amount of taxes and levies. The *hukou* system thus constituted one of the important pillars of China's absolutist and centralized state.[14] When China entered the modern period in 1911, first the 'warlord' governments and then the Guomindang(KMT or Kuomintang – because transliteration norms have changed) government maintained the *hukou* system. However, it was under the CCP government that the *hukou* system's functions of political and social control grew to unprecedented levels. Whereas all previous practices had not nullified the peasants' right to move around the country, it was the CCP which did that. The 1954 constitution still recognized the right to move freely. However, with the onset of the 'socialist transformation' in 1956, the party began to restrict the peasants' right to move as part of its plan to put in place the command economy. In 1958, the state passed laws to prevent the peasants from entering the city altogether. In 1975 the nominal right to movement was simply deleted from the constitution altogether, and remains so until today.

The *hukou* regime divided citizens into urban and rural households, and it systematically discriminated against rural residents as second class citizens.[15] Until early 1990s, the *hukou* system was characterized by the following features:

1. It tied the residents to the city or the village of residence. Changing the place of residence required prior permission from local authorities. Mobility between villages and between cities was highly controlled. But the main purpose of the system was to forbid peasants from entering the cities. Peasants in cities could be arrested for failing to produce proper documents.
2. After the inauguration of the 'planned economy', only urban households could enjoy subsidized provisions from staple grains, education, housing to medical care, as well as job security and retirement benefits. One of the chief roles of the *hukou* was to segregate the rural population from the cities so as to keep them away from these social provisions and benefits. This basically barred rural residents from enjoying upward mobility. For instance, the lack of secondary

schools in rural areas practically barred the majority of rural children from getting a secondary education.

3. *Hukou* is hereditary. Rural citizens and their children remain as rural *hukou* in almost all circumstances, except if they join the army or enrol in college. Furthermore, until 1998, the system would further discriminate against rural women. Children would inherit their rural identity from their mother rather than from their father. This regime was particularly designed to exclude rural women and their children from becoming permanent urban residents, thus relegating rural women to the status of third class citizens. The serious consequence was that Chinese rural women were being robbed of any chance of upward social mobility by marrying an urban man. While a rural male migrant might be able to get an urban residence permit through marrying an urban woman, a rural woman migrant could not. This was why urban men would resist marriage to rural women; otherwise their children would inherit their mother's rural *hukou*, a severe decline in status that few would accept.
4. Until 2003, there were serious penalties for migrants who violated the *hukou* system, including being fined, jailed or being sent back home (at their own expense – those having no money were required to perform forced labour to pay for their travelling expenses). As was shown in the case of Sun Zhigang[16], sometimes failing to produce the proper documents could lead to physical assault and even the death of the migrant.
5. People do not have the right to vote for local deputies to the People's National Congress if they do not have a local *hukou*, regardless of the fact that they may have been working or living in a given area for many years.
6. Heads of household are responsible for keeping the 'household registration book' (*hukou bu*). This in practice gives the parents power to interfere in their children's affairs. For instance, when their sons or daughters marry they have to produce their *hukou bu* for inspection by officials. If the parents do not approve of their son's or daughter's marriage, they can prevent it by refusing to produce the *hukou bu*. Given the tradition of patriarchy in China, daughters are more vulnerable in this situation.

Since the middle of the 1990s, the *hukou* system has been gradually relaxed. First, rural residents were permitted to buy a temporary (usually one year) urban residential card, which allowed them to work legally. The fees for such permits gradually decreased to a fairly affordable level. From early 1998, parents have been able to pass down their *hukou* either through the father's or the mother's line, hence the triple discrimination against rural women has been alleviated. In 2003, after the uproar surrounding the death of Sun Zhigang which alarmed the authorities, the laws on jailing and repatriating 'undocumented' people (those failing to produce proper papers) were abolished. Thus the spatial aspect of the apartheid has now largely been eliminated. However, the substance of the social apartheid in general remains intact. The permanent mark of being an outsider and second class citizen remains, and this prevents migrant workers from achieving significant upward mobility in cities. Most decent jobs are still reserved for people who possess local *hukou.* Migrants can only get badly paid jobs. This segregation of jobs was institutionalized in the regulations issued by the Labour Department in 1994, according to which only when municipal governments find that the local labour force is unable to satisfy growing demand in particular sectors can they import labour from rural areas.[17] This regulation practically limited job seekers from rural regions to 3D (dirty, dangerous, demeaning) jobs. Hence it was common practice for cities to reserve certain jobs for local residents, particularly jobs in the financial sector, postal and communications sector, drivers and accountants etc.[18]

Before 1998, no rural children or youngsters could be educated in urban areas. Since then the ban has been relaxed. In many cities today, rural migrant workers can send their children to urban public schools as long as they can pay the extra money. The fact is, however, that most of them are unable to pay at all. This gives rise to a phenomenon of *liushou ertong*, or rural children left behind by their working parents. Some estimate that the number of children left behind in rural areas number 50 million. Very often these children are looked after by their grandparents, and are only able to see their parents once a year when they return home during the Lunar New Year holidays. Those who bring children along with them to the cities have to look for schools which educate exclusively children of rural migrant workers. Very often these schools are not subsidized at all because they operate illegally – local education authorities are more likely to make things difficult for them when they apply for a licence, as the authorities see them as competing with government run schools. It is not unusual to see local authorities demolish this kind of school without any regard for the students . The city government refused to grant any school educating migrant children an official school permit, therefore leaving them at the mercy of officials. In this environment Xingzhi School in Beijing was forced to relocate five times in seven years.[19] The case was widely reported, and in 2004 it was eventually able to get an official permit to run classes. Others are less lucky. In June 2011, thirty rural migrant schools were closed by the authorities in Beijing, leaving many students with nowhere to be educated.[20] The flip side to this coin is that entrepreneurs and high-ranking officials are able to send their children to elite private schools or to send them abroad. The difficulty for migrant workers in finding proper education for their children in urban areas continues to discourage many of them from bringing their children along. Under such a regime rural migrant workers are viewed as nothing but labourers, not humans who need a family.

This social apartheid is hugely profitable for the capitalists. The government has driven down rural migrant's wages by fixing minimum wages at a terribly low level. It has justified this practice by referring to the fact that rural migrant workers own plots of land which provide them a safety net and a subsistence income for their family, which urban dwellers do not enjoy. The government is allying itself with the employers in justifying that wages paid to rural migrants need not cover all the cost of the reproduction of the labour force.

There is much rhetoric about household registration reform but all these measures have not got rid of the essence of class discrimination in the system. Many cities have amended the law to allow rural migrant workers to change their *hukou* into an urban one as long as the latter can produce proof that they have 'fixed residence' and 'stable income'. The problem is that by 'fixed residence' they mean owning a flat and 'stable income' also means income which rural migrant workers are not likely to be able to earn. Furthermore, it is municipal governments today which allow rural migrants to change their household registration from rural to the cities, but the precondition always being that the rural migrants have to give up their plots of land.

Although the *hukou* can now pass down to children either through the father or the mother, it is still very far from gender equality. The elimination of legal inequality between the genders within the *hukou* system after 1998 does not imply the elimination of actually existing inequality. Rural women in general still receive less education, and women's 'proper' role is still considered to be looking after the family. Hence many women migrant workers, after working some years in the cities, have to go back to their home villages, after getting married, to look after their husband and children. It follows that these women must see their residence in the cities as something temporary, even more temporary than what male migrant workers envisage.

While workers in SOEs (State-Owned Enterprises) have some kind of collective identity due to their common experience built up over years, migrant workers generally have no prior collective experience whatsoever. They very much inherited the individualistic character of farming households, particularly because most migrant workers were born during the 1980s after the last trace of communal life was dismantled. When this generation of young rural residents come to the cities, they are totally atomized.

The *hukou* system reinforces the atomization of rural migrant workers because it makes their identity as workers temporary, even though many of them have worked in cities for years. It not only acts as a powerful force for depressing the wages of rural migrants and preventing them from getting better education and jobs in the cities, it also prevents them from organizing. Coming as they do from diverse provinces, being discriminated against, having a low self-esteem, being acutely aware of being alien and aware of the fact that they will sooner or later return home, the workers who make up this great army of migrant labour find it exceedingly difficult to involve themselves in any long term organizing effort, let alone develop a class identity. Even if there are individuals who are ready to fight for their legitimate rights, the penalty faced by those attempting to independently organize workers is severe enough to deter most of them.

Local Government and public order teams

At the factory level, a barrack-like regime is imposed to restrict the personal freedom of workers. Until recently, these measures included:

- Requiring a deposit from workers who were being hired;
- Requiring workers to hand over their identity cards to management when they were hired;
- Refusing to give workers a copy of their employment contract as required in law;
- Forbidding workers from resigning from the company at their free will (and in accordance with labour law), requiring them to seek approval from management;
- Management implementing strict discipline, the breaching of which resulted in workers being fined;
- Dormitories being guarded by security guards, with various restrictions governing these areas such as refusing friends from outside entering the dormitories;
- Security guards within factories usually having direct contact with local public order team, and who are in practice accountable to the

latter. Since workers' wages are generally too low to enable them to rent houses outside, many of them have to live in the dormitories, rendering them subject to constant monitoring.

- Factory management collaborating closely with local government to enforce those laws which aim at strengthening political and social control.

Following the decline in labour supply and workers' increasing resentment against the factory regime, in recent years employers have found it necessary to relax some of the restrictions or requirements. Compelling workers to pay a deposit or to hand over the ID card is now much less common. While it is true that the most excessive despotism is relaxed, the essence of a barracks-like factory regime, with workers under quasi-military discipline, is still largely in place. Although the management of the Taiwanese, Korean and Japanese firms are especially famous for this, it is not difficult to find the same kind of regime in European-owned companies. The case of Maersk in China is but one well-known example.[21]

Local government has a direct interest in enforcing such a factory regime. Since the reforms began, local governments have been encouraged by the central government to lure as much foreign direct investment (FDI) into their areas as possible. Both the regime and the reform policy are designed to ensure that local governments and their officials have a vested interest in attracting FDI. In the first instance, local governments increasingly rely on the income from taxes paid by foreign investors. Secondly, the careers of local officials very much depend on the amount of FDI they are able to attract. The Huizhou government information website has posted a document entitled 'Rules on encouraging foreign businessmen to invest in enterprises in Huizhou' which states:

> In our plan to attract inward investment, work units and individuals making positive and successful contributions will be directly recognised for their advanced work and receive due merit as well as cash rewards. Recorded merits shall become important criteria for promotion of cadres.[22]

Thirdly, SOEs that belong to municipal governments often closely collaborate with foreign investors, from close business partnerships to joint ventures. For instance, the Hong Kong based Gold Peak company, which is a major battery producer and which had poisoned hundreds of women workers, yet enjoyed local government support, has a very complicated shareholding relationship with various Huizhou City SOEs.

To sum up, it is in local officials' own interest to attract the maximum FDI possible to their own areas. The most effective way to achieve this is to bring down the cost of labour. When it comes to social and political control, local governments tend to enthusiastically implement all the repressive laws available to them to keep workers powerless, from laws that ban freedom of association to the *hukou* system. However, when it comes to those laws which protect workers, from the labour code to occupational safety and health (OSH) laws, local governments have little incentive to enforce them, and simply close their eyes to the violation of these laws by employers.

It is impossible to sustain such a repressive regime, both at the factory level and in society at large, without the boots of the state stamping down on all potential opponents at grassroots level. The lowest level of local government in cities is the neighbourhood committee, or in areas which once were rural, the village committee. Within the local police at this level are *hujijing*, literally household registration police, who specialise in managing household registration affairs. With the huge influx of rural migrants, local governments have found it necessary to run special task forces to deal with migrants; hence they run their own *zhiandui*, or public order teams.

They are not civil servants and have no legitimate power to enforce laws, but in practice they perform the function of the police. It is these people who implement the regime of political and social control over local residents, especially migrant workers. Their wages are in general low, and given the nature of their work as irregular police, it is more likely that recruits come from the mafia who extort money from the rural migrants to compensate for their low wages. Local officials also have the incentive to take on recruits from the mafia as public order team members to make sure they keep rural migrants under control. Although they are not technically allowed to carry arms, in fact they are generally armed with truncheons, handcuffs, and even electric batons, and never hesitate to use them against migrants. The size of these local public order teams are very often much larger than the regular police. For instance, the city of Foshan in Guangdong province has 11,000 police, yet the local public order team has 38,000 members, i.e., three times the regular police.[23] The combined strength of these two forces numbers 49,000 police officers for a population of 6.14 million (2006 figure)[24], or 0.8 police for every ten Foshan residents. In contrast, Hong Kong only has 0.04 police for every ten residents.

The continuous growth of their numbers is a response by the local governments to the huge influx of migrant workers. They target migrant workers because they are considered *wailai renkou* (literally outsiders) and people who are prone to engage in criminal activity. Thus a growing public order team is needed to enforce social apartheid against migrants. It is these local public order teams who make regular checks on migrant workers' papers and seize any opportunity to fine and harass them – anyone failing to produce the temporary *hukou* card will be fined. As a result, riots against public order teams by rural migrant workers occur from time to time.

Whenever there are workers' protests, local public order teams will act as informers, provocateurs, and informal police. In 2004, 3000 workers from the Juxi shoe factory went on strike to protest against forced overtime. The public order team of the industrial area where the factory is located arrested a dozen workers and jailed them for half a day in order to break the strike. Public order teams will also ensure that factory security guards work closely with them in monitoring workers. In the case of the Computime factory, the public order team took pictures of the protesting workers which resulted in two of them subsequently being arrested. In many cases, both factory security guards and local public order teams come from the same local security company run by local officials.[25]

The Beginnings of Resistance

Since public order teams are not civil servants, their wages are not covered by the government's budget, but by levies collected from local residents, including those considered 'temporary', i.e. the migrant workers. This system has become a burden for rural migrant workers and is, indeed, much resented by them. Unsurprisingly, the public order teams are hated by migrant workers, and it is not uncommon for confrontations between the two sides to develop into riots. This kind of spontaneous resistance has been successful, leading to local authorities cutting fees for passes and permits drastically, and checking papers in a less brutal manner. Despite this, occasional riots still occur, and even official research institutions admit that as long as rural migrant workers are treated as aliens without equal rights these kinds of riots are not going to disappear.[26]

Organizing is still very difficult due to restrictions on the freedom of association. Establishing independent NGOs is also not at all easy. After the crackdown in 1989, the state council approved a new regulation on the registration and management of social organizations which required every social organization to affiliate with a supervisory unit. This means that every NGO has to be monitored by the Communist Party as all supervisory organizations are Party-controlled. In 1998, a new more restrictive regulation was implemented. For example, only one organization in any particular sphere of activity may register at each administrative level.

Moreover, initial capital of 100,000 yuan for national organizations and 30,000 yuan for local organizations is required. This makes it very difficult for grass root organizations to emerge. One way to set up an NGO is to create a local organization which becomes part of a registered social organization or university. Another way is to register it as a business organization. These methods are, of course, not always accessible to most people, so a third method has developed: people establish informal groups like salons and clubs which have no legal status. These legal or semi-legal methods to form NGOs have many drawbacks, and in no way do they substitute for the need to enjoy full rights of freedom of association.

In Guangdong province, there are now quite a number of workers' legal aid centres, some from Hong Kong and some initiated locally. They are often registered commercially to a sole proprietor because they cannot obtain the licence for running a worker NGO. They are so vulnerable that many of them prefer to avoid operating in industrial areas because local authorities hate the idea of allowing these centres to have close relations with workers. Dagongzhe, or Workers, was a workers centre in the Shenzhen industrial area. The person in charge, Huang Qingnan, was seriously injured in 2008 when attacked by gangsters with knives after the centre had been repeatedly harassed.

In addition to workers' centres there are *heilüshi*, or 'bare-foot lawyers', who are often self-taught with no legal right to practice law. Some of them are workers who have become familiar with labour legislation after being engaged in year-long legal actions against their employer. In general both workers' centres and 'bare-foot lawyers' are met with hostility from the provincial All China Federation of Trade Unions (ACFTU) which views them as potential troublemakers and contenders. At one point, in a Guangdong city, the ACFTU opened an official workers' centre with the same name as another workers' centre, established much earlier by ordinary citizens, so as to put it out of action. In 2007 it was reported that the Shenzhen ACFTU had joined hands with the local government to crack down on the bare-foot lawyers and workers' centre. After the sticks came the carrots: the Shenzen ACFTU co-opted sixty bare-foot lawyers who agreed not to contact foreign reporters and not to seek funding from foreign agencies.[27] Since then the ACFTU has made 'procuring social services from NGOs' its official policy in order to win them over or at least to monitor them closely, especially over aspects such as overseas funding as the NGOs concerned have to open their books to the ACFTU for inspection.

We can expect further relaxation of the *hukou* system in the direction of narrowing the social division of rural *hukou* and urban *hukou* in the medium term. For instance, since 2008 many cities have begun to delete the word 'temporary' from the residential cards as a result of the growing resentment against the social apartheid. In some of the smaller cities, they have made it easier for rural migrants to apply for urban household registration. But if the government is going in this direction, it is because it is now finding that the system is less useful than in the past, or it is even gradually coming into conflict with a new capitalism which demands more and more the free flow of human resources rather than its restriction.

It should also be noted that there is a limit to how far the party-state can reform the *hukou* system. Abolishing it entirely is highly improbable, at least in the medium term, simply because the predatory nature of the bureaucracy determines that it will not allow millions of peasants to enjoy the same rights to welfare as urban dwellers without first being challenged by struggles from below. The municipal governments in the big cities are the most stubborn opponents of abolishing the social apartheid. The police and the national security department also find the system very useful for monitoring the population. It must be noted that although the *hukou* system first and foremost discriminates against peasants, it also enables the state to closely monitor urban dwellers and to maintain certain controls over them. For instance, only with the *hukou* system can the state implement effectively the one child policy. It also makes underground opposition extremely difficult. In a word, one should not expect that the social apartheid will disappear gradually and automatically as capitalism develops further. In the end, the realization of equal rights for all citizens will not be achieved without a political upsurge from below.

Notes

1 Note: This essay mainly draws from three previous articles: 1 'Women Migrant Workers under the Chinese Social Apartheid', Au LoongYu, Nan Shan, Zhang Ping, Committee for Asian Women, 2007; . 'Disposable Labour—Chinese Labour under Economic Downturn', *Asian Labour Update*, issue 69, Oct – Dec 2008; 3. 'China: End of a Model, Or the Birth of a New One?', *New Politics*, summer issue, 2009. This new version of the essay was proof read by Geoff Ryan.

2 Eventually it was reported that a total of 20 million migrant workers returned to their home village.

3 It was presented in a more ambiguous way as 'temporary suspension of readjustment of minimum wages', and 'suspending readjustment' can either means suspension of adjusting up or adjusting down, but judging from the main content of the article it must have meant the former. *Renbaobu: Zanyuan tiaozheng qiyezuidi gongzi biaozhun* (The Ministry of Human Resources

and Social Security says Adjusting Enterprises Minimum Wages should be Suspended), http://www.chinareviewnews.com/doc/1008/0/3/7/100803716.html?coluid=7&kindid=0&docid=100803716&mdate=1118095144.

4 'Employment in China : recent trends and future challenges' http://www.ilo.org/wcmsp5/groups/public/---ed_emp/---emp_elm/documents/publication/wcms_114032.pdf.

5 *Zhongguo gaijin tongji fangfa tisheng shuzi gongxinli* (China Needs to Improve Statistics Method to Raise Credibility), http://www.21cbh.com/HTML/2010-3-9/0MMDAwMDE2Nzg0MA.html.

6 *China Economy Quarterly Update*, Feb 2007, World Bank Beijing Office, p.6.

7 'Why China is so scared to spend', http://www.newsweek.com/id/174524.

8 Quoted from *Zhongguo siwanyi jiushi jihua guonei shoudao zhiyi* (China 4 Trillion Yuan Bailout Questioned), http://www.stnn.cc/ed_china/200811/t20081117_905748.html.

9 *Ming Pao Daily*, 12 December 2008.

10 Those who are more outspoken and who can afford to consult 'bare-foot' lawyers (who are self taught people with no legal rights to practice law) ask them to write letters of complaint on their behalf to force the employers to let them go and pay them their wages. Those less outspoken will be forced to stay. The laws do not allow the employers to do this, but when workers do not enjoy basic civil liberties it is common that labour laws are not enforced. On the other hand, in the current economic downturn, workers are dismissed before their contracts expire, again in violation of the labour laws.

11 It is also common that migrants coming from the same home villages may share a flat outside the factories.

12 For some scholars, the regime is similar to a caste society. See Kate Zhou, How Farmers Changed China, *Westview Press*, 2000.

13 'The Constitution of the French Republic Adopted November 4, 1848,' http://www.marxists.org/archive/marx/works/1851/06/14.htm.

14 In contrast, according to Victoria Tin-bor Hui, Europe did not have a comprehensive system of this kind of statistical collection until the Prussians introduced it in the 17th century. *War and State Formation in Ancient China and Early Modern Europe,* Chinese edition, Shanghai People's Publishing House, 2009, p. 136. See also footnote 83 of chapter two.

15 For English material concerning the *hukou* system, see Amnesty International 2007 report *People's Republic of China, Internal migrants: Discrimination and abuse, the human cost of an economic 'miracle'*. http://www.amnesty.org/en/library/info/ASA17/008/2007

16 Sun Zhigang was a college graduate from Hubei province. He was in Guangzhou in 2003. He was arrested for failing to produce his temporary residential card and then beaten to death by a local public order team.

17 *Nongcun laodongli kuasheng liudong jiuye guanli zanxing guiding* (Provincial Regulation on Rural Labour Force's Intra-provincial Movement), http://www.gdmz.lm.gov.cn/zcfg/7.htm

18 *Zhongguo de xianjing* (The Primary Capital Accumulation in Contemporary China), He Qinglian, Chinese edition, Mirror Books, Hong Kong, p. 282.

19 *Doors closing at school for migrant children* http://www.chinadaily.com.cn/opinion/2007-01/11/content_780626.htm

20 *Yaoyuan de shangxue meng: Beijing dagong zidi xuexiao bei guanting* (The Unfulfilled Dream of Getting Educated: Beijing Rural Migrant Schools were Closed), http://www.infzm.com/content/62287.

21 See the report by Globalization Monitor, http://www.globalmon.org.hk/en/01news/04report-on-maersk/the-background-to-two-violent-strikes-in-maersk-dongguan-china/

22 http://www.huizhou.gov.cn/tzhzviewArticle.shtml?method=viewArticle&id=2AA9A5E8F1404F8ABA172D158346A1D2.

23 *Foshan liangdui heyi qunfang qunzhi* (Foshan Uniting Two Security Forces into One to Attain Mass Participation in Maintaining Public Order), 24 August 2006. http://news.dayoo.com/guangzhou/gb/content/2006-08/24/content_2615060.htm

24 Among the population, 58 per cent were residents with local households, 42 per cent with either rural households or from other cities. *Foshanshi 2006 nian shangbannian renkou zhuangkuang* (Population of Foshan in the First Half of 2006), http://www.fsgp.cn/Article.do?req=showArticle&articleId=1594.

25 These cases were reported in the essay *Women Migrant Workers under the Chinese Social Apartheid,* Au Loong Yu, Nan Shan, Zhang Ping, Committee for Asian Women, 2007.

26 Development Research Centre of the State Council released a report in June 2011 on rural migrant workers, and according to the Chinese edition of BBC, the report put the blame for continuous riots on the system which marginalizes the migrant workers. http://www.bbc.co.uk/zhongwen/trad/chinese_news/2011/06/110620_press_china_migrant.shtml

27 *Shenzhen laogong weiquan zuzhi fuzeren beikan, zuotui jihu kanduan* (Shenzhen Labour Rights Defense Organization responsible person had his left leg nearly chopped off), 16 December, 2007, Xinhua Net, http://big5.xinhuanet.com/gate/big5/news.xinhuanet.com/local/2007-12/16/content_7258499.htm

THE ROLE OF THE ALL CHINA FEDERATION OF TRADE UNIONS: IMPLICATIONS FOR WORKERS TODAY[1]

Bai Ruixue

In the context of China's economic reforms and realignment with global capitalism, this article examines the role of the All China Federation of Trade Unions (ACFTU) and its failure to act as a genuine trade union organisation. Rather than putting workers' interests and the protection of their rights first, the ACFTU, as an organ of the Chinese Communist Party (CCP) has largely shifted its agenda in line with that of the party. The article looks at how this has often meant prioritizing the interests of business over those of labour and how subsequently the ACFTU faces a crisis of legitimacy in the eyes of many workers, who increasingly turn to alternative methods of struggle outside of the officially sanctioned union. While such struggle has alarmed the CCP and has led to apparent attempts at trade union reform, often this has meant little in reality. The article also addresses the changing relations of international trade unions with the ACFTU and challenges unions who are prepared to work more closely with it for giving the ACFTU a false credibility.

The ACFTU is China's sole union federation. Under China's trade union law, workers have no freedom of association and cannot simply join a trade union of their choice. To be a legally recognized union, all trade unions must be affiliated to the ACFTU; all independent trade unions and other such workers' organisations are prohibited. The ACFTU was originally founded in 1925 but was then soon severely repressed, under Guomindang nationalist rule. Following the 1949 revolution, it was re-established and became China's sole trade union organisation, which it has been ever since, bar a period when it was temporarily dissolved during the Cultural Revolution. By the end of 2009, total ACFTU membership had reached 226 million, which included 79.8 million rural migrant workers.[2] The situation in China has changed dramatically for workers as China has moved to reintegrate itself into global capitalism. The introduction of reform and open policy in the late 1970s indicated the start of this transformation and led to a huge influx of foreign capital being poured into the Pearl River delta region. To encourage further capital and investment, China has had to adapt itself to become more competitive to the market. In 2001, China joined the World Trade Organisation, marking a further step in its integration with the global market economy.

China's transformation has taken place at the expense of the working class. The restructuring and reorganization of its state-owned enterprises (SOEs) in the 1990s to make them more profitable, led to more than 30 million workers being laid off without full compensation. Eighty-six per cent of all SOEs had become fully or partially privatized by 2001.[3]

The process of restructuring resulted in numerous strikes and protest actions as workers were angry at the attacks. While workers were previously guaranteed a job for life this was abruptly brought to an end. The ACFTU did little to defend or protect workers during this period.

Furthermore, although the ACFTU supported the Chinese People's Congress and endorsed China's first Labour Code in 1995 – the implementation of which has been hailed an important step in providing legal protection to Chinese labour – it is necessary to understand the Labour Code in the context of the on-going restructuring process. While legal protection was given to rural migrant workers working in private enterprises for the first time (they had previously been denied the job security and high level of labour welfare of SOE and collective enterprise workers), from the perspective of SOE and collective enterprise workers, the 1995 Labour Code represented a regression rather than progress. This is because the guiding principle of the 1995 code was the implementation of a kind of 'socialist market economy' that saw labour as a commodity that should be regulated by the market. Hence, the 1995 code codified this philosophy (in clause 27), by legalizing the employers' practice of laying off workers when they faced bankruptcy or other serious conditions. This has provided a legal basis for the authorities to lay off state sector workers in tens of millions since then. The ACFTU's complicity in this thus made them an accomplice in the redundancy of millions of workers and the privatization that was part of the restructuring process.

It was not until much later that the central government began to acknowledge the cost of the restructuring process to workers. In March 2007, ACFTU Vice-Chair Xu Deming stated that as of June 2006, 2.05

billion yuan (US$150 million) of unpaid wages along with 700 million yuan of compensation were owed to workers from SOEs that were undergoing restructuring or bankruptcy procedures in 11 of China's cities and provinces. Twenty-five per cent of workers were also reported to have had their social security terminated, and in addition, he described the pay scale of workers as being far too unequal in the post-reform period.[4]

The layoffs also impacted on ACFTU membership as many members, union officials, and safety officers were amongst those laid off. Through the 1990s and the early 2000s, however, the key priority of the ACFTU was to encourage former SOE workers to adjust to the new mentality in which they could no longer consider themselves to be *zhuren* ('masters') and lost their 'iron rice bowl.' As a result, the ACFTU did little regarding working conditions and wages because they were afraid of weakening incentives for investment and reducing economic growth.[5] The failure to defend jobs and labour rights, which were increasingly eroded as workers were made to work faster and longer under stricter control in order to increase production output for the profit of capitalists during this period, brought into question the union's legitimacy. Even in the early 1990s when Chinese scholar Tang Wenfang conducted a survey of SOE workers' impressions of the union, he found that when workers had problems concerning housing, wages, dismissal, and work injuries, the majority were more likely to seek help from the workplace management and/or government department rather than the trade union.[6]

With many workers once again suffering increased hardship following the onset of the global economic crisis from 2008, the ACFTU has continued to fail in the eyes of workers. According to a recent report by the Hong Kong Liaison Office of International Trade Union Organisation (IHLO) the ACFTU's pro-business response to the crisis only furthers its poor reputation and weak relations with workers: 'The ACFTU's rather passive and establishment focused responses to the crisis as well as their focus on the survival of enterprises at the expense of worker benefits has done little to change the already poor image of them as a union in the eyes of workers.'[7] Indeed, when the central government demanded that the minimum wage be frozen in November 2008, the ACFTU simply towed the government's line.

The ACFTU and the Chinese Communist Party

The ACFTU's strong relationship with the CCP and the pursuit of its agenda is a key factor in explaining why the ACFTU has not and will not act in the interests of workers. Indeed, the ACFTU has been an organ of the

CCP ever since its establishment. The issue of greater union independence has surfaced in a significant way in the past though. In fact, following the commencement of economic reform, the 1980s saw great discontent and unrest amongst workers who responded to the resulting falling living standards with wildcat strikes. On top of this was the fact that, along with the reforms, factory directors and managers were given increasing power within the workplace while nothing was accomplished to strengthen unions and workers' congresses. The introduction of fixed term contract employment in 1986, for example, meant that it was theoretically easier for directors to dismiss workers as it meant that workers were now no longer permanently employed and could be dismissed if the management found it necessary.[8]

An ACFTU survey from spring 1988 revealed that less than 10 per cent of those surveyed believed that the trade unions could 'speak for workers and solve their problems.'[9] Fear of independent union organisation at this time therefore led the 11th ACFTU Congress in October 1988 to call for greater independence in order to head off this threat.[10] The party's fears were to be realized in 1989 as the increasing anger and frustration of workers led to the establishment of independent workers' organisations, most notably the Workers' Autonomous Federation during the Democracy Movement. With the Tiananmen crackdown, however, any possibility of independent trade unions was severely repressed and the official trade unions, some of which had initially supported the democracy movement, were brought firmly back into line. According to Chinese labour historian Jackie Sheehan, internal communications from the ACFTU in 1990 reveal complaints that they were being treated as a work department of the party and were unable to do little more for workers than to make sympathetic noises when presented with their problems.[11]

Even shortly after the Tiananmen massacre, ACFTU President Ni Zhifu warned that 'The trade unions must avoid simply acting as agents of the government and work independently so as to increase the attraction to workers and enjoy more confidence of the workers, leaving no opportunity to those who attempt to organise "independent trade unions." '[12]

Today, however, the ACFTU remains very much subordinate to the CCP, whose bureaucracy has increasingly assumed responsibility for roles usually associated with trade unions. In 2006, ACFTU Chair Wang Zhaoguo said, 'All trade union organisations must consciously accept the leadership of the Party, resolutely implement the Party's line and directives and also comply with all decisions and plans adopted by the Party Central Committee.'[13] The ACFTU's 'five faceted and unified' (*wuwei yiti*) model of rights' protection, adopted in 2007, shows its top-down approach. Listing the five facets in order of importance, it places the leadership of the party as the most important, while participation by the workers comes at the very bottom of the list. Support of the government, cooperation of society, and operation by the unions were listed second, third, and fourth, respectively.[14]

Placing workers as the least important facet in their own rights' protection is clearly very problematic. What this seems to amount to saying is that structurally, the priority in defence of workers' rights is compliance with the line of the party. Such an approach would provide little room for genuine involvement and initiative by workers.

Reform of the ACFTU

> We must give China's unions a backbone. We must understand how to organize the working masses in unions within China's socialist market economy, and particular attention should be given to private sector workers and migrant workers. We must learn how to truly represent the working class masses, and staunchly uphold the legal rights of workers ... We must transform the Party's leadership of unions, and allow for union workers to reflect their true conditions and engage in legal and proper struggle. Liu Shi (Former Vice Chairperson ACFTU, November 2003)[15]

Given its crisis of legitimacy and growing labour unrest as workers look to other more militant means of struggle, the ACFTU has been trying to transform its image over recent years. One way in which the ACFTU has sought to make itself appear more legitimate is through direct elections at enterprise level. The first experiments with direct elections actually took place in 1986 in the Shekou industrial zone of Guangdong province but plans to implement them further were abolished following the Tiananmen crackdown.[16] They have been taken up and promoted in some regions again since then by advocates in the ACFTU who argue that they will help to address the perceived failure of grassroots unions to protect workers' rights and help raise migrant workers' awareness about the function that the union plays in the workplace and in the process help them to develop working class consciousness.[17]

Jude Howell, a political scientist who examined trade unions in Guangdong, has identified four situations where provincial trade unions have been less keen to hold direct elections. These are when the trade union has only just been established, where industrial relations are tense or mass action has recently taken place and so workers may elect someone who might be prepared to fight the enterprise boss, where migrant workers have strong ties to a clan or their place of origin and so the provincial union fears it will be more difficult to control the union chair, and in an enterprise where production is unstable.[18] If this list is accurate, then it would suggest that the ACFTU is only happy for direct elections to take place if it is not likely to lead to conflict between workers and the interests of the enterprise; in other words, in unions that are likely to be more passive and the workers less prepared to fight for their rights.

Even where direct elections have been implemented, however, it has not always prevented managers from standing and being elected as trade union chairs. In a large number of cases, trade union officials will simply be appointed and no genuine election will take place. Furthermore, even though trade union law states that officers at each level of the union should be elected, candidates are still subject to approval by provincial level ACFTU committees.[19] Howell points out that elections are not seen by senior cadres as a right of workers but more a 'gift' from enterprise owners and the higher level trade union.[20] She cites a senior cadre from the Bureau for Construction of Grassroots Organisations in Guangdong provincial trade union as saying that the bureau will respond to requests from the enterprises themselves for a change to the trade union leadership but will then leave it to the enterprise to decide whether it will be a direct election or not.[21] This is just another example of the ACFTU placing the interests of enterprises above the interests of workers.

Despite apparent reforms, many unions at the level of the enterprise remain heavily dominated or controlled by management. An additional potential problem is that even where the direct election of a worker to the position of union chair has taken place, the worker then becomes a cadre, removed from the position of an ordinary worker, and begins to enjoy benefits, for instance a flat and a car, and same status of a deputy director.[22] There is thus still a distance between the elected chair and the workers.

Lack of membership has also been another key concern of the ACFTU. With the restructuring of SOEs and increasing privatization, the CCP's control and influence over the workplace was significantly reduced. The party has therefore been especially keen to establish unions in the private sector and particularly foreign-owned enterprises so that through them it can reassert some degree of its control and authority. In March 2006, President Hu Jintao reportedly ordered the ACFTU to do a better job at building trade unions and party organisations in foreign-invested enterprises, and subsequently, targets have been set regarding the percentage of foreign-invested enterprises to be unionised.[23]

The way that it has carried out its unionisation drive only goes to further confirm what the ACFTU's priorities are and moreover illustrates how the party's use of the union acts at the expense of the workers. Rather than seeking to organize the workers to form a union, the ACFTU's policy has been to visit private companies where they want to establish a union in order to persuade the companies to consent to the establishment of a union. Often, as a consequence, this has meant that where new unions have been set up they have still been controlled by the company's management.[24]

The ACFTU's success in establishing unions in Wal-Mart stores is one example that has been widely reported in the media, particularly as Wal-Mart was at first very keen to resist unionisation. China Labour News Translations, in fact, identify two stages in the ACFTU's union building at Wal-Mart. In the first stage Wal-Mart was still hostile to the establishment of union branches and so the ACFTU actually contacted the workers themselves and mobilized them to set up unions.

At this stage, where unions were established, workers were involved in the democratic elections of trade union committees and trade union chairs. In the second stage, after Wal-Mart had changed its position and approached the ACFTU, agreeing to allow the open establishment of unions in the remainder of its stores, the ACFTU went back to its old ways of establishing unions through the seeking of management approval.[25] In other words, once it had achieved its goal of being able to establish itself in Wal-Mart stores, it stopped directly mobilizing workers. Again, this only acts as evidence that the ACFTU is not primarily concerned with the interests of workers themselves but is more concerned with establishing itself and thus, also the CCP within the workplace. Indeed, when Wal-Mart was asked why it agreed to allow unions, a Wal-Mart spokesperson is reported to have said, 'The union in China is fundamentally different from unions in the West ... The union has made it clear that its goal is to work with employers, not promote confrontation.'[26] The effect of such a policy by the ACFTU is that it means it can therefore present itself and claim itself to be a defender of the workers while, in practice, its presence has more meaning for CCP control than for workers.

While there has been an increase in the number of official new unions established, even where enterprise-based unions do exist, many are little more than 'paper' unions with workers remaining unaware of their existence. A 2008 report from the *Nanfang Daily* describes how in Shenzhen workers have little opportunity to play an activist role in the grass roots trade unions that do exist.[27]

Again, lack of any real union activity has been recognized by some pro-business analysts. An article entitled 'The Effects of China's Growing Labour Unions on Your Company' for example, advises companies that allowing official unions to form may not be such a bad thing as it ends government pressure, and since the ACFTU does not authorize strikes and rarely passes on workers' demands to management, 'unionisation with the ACFTU does not necessarily mean increased worker activism.'[28]

A key piece of legislation that is often given as evidence of progress and reform is the Labour Contract Law that came into effect from 1 January, 2008, which the ACFTU played a significant role in helping to draft. This law has been interpreted as a significant step forward for labour rights in China. The law set out to clarify the laws and regulations relating to the content of labour contracts and to impose penalties for companies failing to provide proper written contracts to workers. The new law also should mean that employees who have worked for a company for ten years or more cannot be dismissed without good cause. As a result, one problem in the run up to the implementation of the law was that workers were fired so that they would not be covered by this condition.

Where the ACFTU is concerned, the law should technically strengthen the union's role in discussion of redundancies and other changes.[29] The problem with this is that while the law itself may have become strengthened, in practice, because the ACFTU is more committed to creating an environment that is attractive to investment and creating good business relations, it means very little in real terms for workers. The way that some local ACFTU branches responded to the economic crisis is a good illustration of this. There are cases where local branches either urged the government to allow or simply overlook enterprises that took a more flexible approach in enforcing the Labour Contract Law.

Measures taken by the Jiangsu Provincial Labour Protection Office with the pretext of relieving the burden on enterprises and stabilizing employment included cutting the rate enterprises paid toward unemployment benefit contributions, medical contributions, and work injury insurance, allowing enterprises facing difficulties to defer social insurance payments, using unemployment benefit to subsidize enterprises with economic difficulties, delaying payment of overtime and introducing flexible working time.[30] Many of these measures show complete disregard for the new Labour Contract Law.

Moreover, it is also important to consider how in a political and social context where there is a police state, where there is an absence of civil society/ social movements, where all media is state-owned and censored, where basic freedom of association and expression is denied (including the right to strike) and where the local officials and employers are allied to each other in pursuit of their common interests, no matter how many good labour laws are passed, these new laws will only do very little to benefit workers. The unholy alliance of local officials and employers ensures that even when they deny workers their legitimate rights, the workers will have no legal channel through which to voice their grievances to a higher level of government or to the public. If they strike or block the road to protest, they may be arrested for their actions. Because of its complicity and role in creating such a situation, this means that in the current context, it is not possible simply to think that the ACFTU can be reformed or changed into an organisation that is truly capable of representing Chinese workers.

Alternative methods of struggle

Without a union that prioritizes fighting for the interests of their rights, the majority of workers has either bypassed or simply not considered the ACFTU when involved in labour disputes with employers. Instead, they have either gone straight to petitioning the government or have taken further action and engaged in alternative methods of labour struggle such as going on strike, holding demonstrations, and blocking roads. Major causes of such action have included privatization, layoffs, and wage disputes. Recent years have seen a steady increase in the number of what are mostly spontaneous strikes, which are officially referred to as 'mass incidents', occurring with the union playing very little or no role in them at all.

According to the authorities, between 1993 and 2003, the number of 'collective incidents' grew from around 10,000 to 60,000—with the number of participants involved growing from 730,000 to 3,070,000.[31] In 2005, when the Public Security Ministry stopped publishing figures, the number for the year had grown to 87,000.[32] With the beginning of the economic crisis in 2008, the number of labour disputes has grown even further as factories closed and large numbers of workers were laid off. While it might be expected that workers would turn to a labour union to help them fight for their jobs, the ACFTU has been criticized by the IHLO for its 'slow off the mark and passive' reaction to the crisis, acting instead more as an official mouthpiece for the government and continuing to pursue their 100 per cent unionisation campaign.[33]

The right to strike is not protected under Chinese law, and violence and mass deployment of riot police have often been used to disperse strikes and protests, with criminal charges being brought against strikers.[34] The Liaoyang protest movement of 2002 provides a good example. The protests began as a result of workers being laid off when a large number of SOEs were declared bankrupt or insolvent. Despite the fact that the protests, involving up to 20,000 workers, were peaceful, police used repressive measures against the workers, monitored them closely using under cover surveillance, and arrested leading worker representatives.[35] Two of the workers' leaders were later found guilty of subverting state power. Yao Fuxin, one of the workers' leaders, however, explained the motives for organising the demonstration as follows:

> For more than 20 months, the Ferro-Alloy Factory workers had not received their wages, the older ones were unable to pay their medical bills, and some couldn't even afford to eat. I couldn't bear seeing the workers suffer similar to that, so I stood up to help them put food on the table.[36]

In addition to strikes and protest action, there have also been cases where workers have called for or attempted to form a union themselves. The most notable example to date probably comes from workers at the Ole Wolff (Yantai) electronics company in Shandong.

In 2006, workers established the Ole Wolff Yantai trade union (OWYTU) after the management had violated a number of labour rights (including failing to issue labour contracts, not paying labour insurance, excessive overtime work, refusing leave requests, and not providing treatment for victims of occupational hearing damage) and fired workers without giving any reasons.[37] In their application letter to form a union, the workers wrote:

> Workers are determined to get organised to keep their legal rights from being violated considering the fact it has become a common phenomena for workers' legitimate rights to be violated by the employers and our labour laws turned into a meaningless "scrap of paper" because of local protectionism. The situation described earlier highlights the reason and purpose of labour union.[38]

The establishment of the enterprise union at Ole Wolff represents a rare case, but it shows the possibility for workers themselves to establish fighting independent enterprise level unions inside the ACFTU.

On the other hand, although the local trade union acknowledged the legal status of the union the workers had established, and at first supported it, probably because of the support from higher levels of the ACFTU, it later increasingly sided with and defended the company management as the struggle with management developed. For example, it defended the company by claiming that the company had begun to comply with the labour law even though it was still acting in violation of the law.[39] It did not even do anything when Ole Wolff Yantai sacked nearly all the members of the workplace union leadership, instead turning away the latter when they sought help from the local union.

What is also significant about this union is that in its dispute with the company, the OWYTU became the first local enterprise union in China to actively seek international solidarity and receive assistance from unions overseas. It sought assistance from the Danish Trade Union Confederation, LO, and the Union Federation of Danish Workers, 3F (which corresponded with the ACFTU and tried to talk to Ole Wolff and Danfoss, the owner of the Ole Wolff company in Denmark on the workers' behalf.)

What is outrageous is that the head office of the ACFTU in Beijing came to the defence of the employer saying that 'the company was requested to take correction measures and now it has met the requirement of the Labour Law in the area of pay, working conditions and safety and health', when in fact it did not.[40]

Despite this example of workers organising and establishing a union themselves inside the ACFTU structure, in general the rise in number of strikes and other independent actions by workers has been seen as worrying by the ACFTU and CCP. Any attempts by workers to establish their own organisations are likewise seen as a threat to social stability. Independent actions have therefore been one of the chief motivating factors in driving forward reforms and changes to the ACFTU as the CCP hopes to avert or limit unrest and thus help it to maintain social stability and political order.

The so-called new wave of strikes and actions that were widely reported by the media in 2010 may be an early indication of some type of shift forward not only with regard to workers' struggle but also in terms of how the CCP is forced to position itself in relation to such action. The actions have seen workers win important wage increases, and perhaps just as, if not more, significantly where the demand for change or reorganisation of the workplace-based unions, or according to some reports, demands for independent trade unions, have surfaced they have not been met with such brutal repression as in the past.

In the Honda worker dispute, which lasted for almost three weeks from May to June 2010, for instance, one of the key demands made by workers was for the re-election of their enterprise union representatives. Indeed, the workers were very critical of the way that the union failed to do anything to help them in the dispute. In the words of one of the Honda workers:

> At this critical moment our great trade union did nothing for us. Instead they just wanted us to go back to the production line! Is this what a union should be doing? You take from our monthly wages five Yuan for union dues but look what you have done for us.[41]

In fact, during the course of the strike, some workers were physically attacked by men wearing trade union badges. The local ACFTU then retreated slightly, perhaps fearing the reaction by workers and later issued a vague letter of apology for the attacks. It nevertheless maintained its position as a mediator aimed at ensuring the workers returned to the production line as quickly as possible.[42]

When the strike came to an end, with the workers having won a pay rise, the demand for the reorganisation of the union had not been dropped. This therefore not only illustrates the ineffectiveness of the trade union in workers' rights negotiations in the way that it is keener for production to continue but may also show how workers may not always be prepared to go on tolerating the ACFTU's adoption of this role.

It was reported that since then, the local union is making plans to conduct re-elections of the workplace union in Honda Foshan. The official press reported on this positively. Yet, with the absence of freedom of the press, and with the workers banned from talking to foreign reporters, there is no way whatsoever to verify if the official press is telling the truth.

Migrant workers

China's economic growth has relied on the many millions of internal migrant workers who, attracted by the promise of jobs and better wages, have migrated from rural areas to sell their labour in the huge factories and construction sites of the cities. These workers, a large number of whom are female, are among the most exploited in China today. Working long hours for low wages, often in very poor or hazardous working conditions so that large corporations can make huge profits, migrant workers are also deprived of the same legal rights as workers born in the cities. The Hukou household registration system, which was introduced in the late 1950s, means that migrant workers are not allowed to permanently settle in the cities and so the authorities can choose to send them back to their villages if they are thought to be causing trouble.

The ACFTU for a long time has accomplished very little, if anything at all, to protect migrant workers. Its approach has also only partially begun to change recently because of the party's fear of lack of social stability and the alternative means of struggle adopted by the workers. With no proper form of representation, migrant workers have often resorted to either appealing to independent lawyers or the law directly, and perhaps more significantly, they have increasingly taken part in spontaneous collective action at their workplace. A number of scholars have argued that the formation of a new working class of internal rural migrant workers has been taking shape among these peasant workers, who are different from previous generations in that they have different life expectations and that one of the characteristics of this is that they are more likely to become involved in collective action.[43]

In addition, the lack of representation for migrant workers has also led to the formation of non-governmental organisations (NGOs) aiming to provide legal advice to workers who often have little knowledge of their legal rights. The CCP has presented this as a threat, and in February 2009, ACFTU Vice-Chair Sun Chunlan warned of the need to look out for 'hostile forces inside and outside enterprises using some of the difficulties of the rural migrant workers for infiltration and sabotage.'[44]

Because of these perceived threats of strike action and intervention by external organisations, the state, and subsequently the ACFTU, has been forced to take a seemingly more active role where migrant workers are concerned. As a result, for instance, in 2003 the ACFTU finally recognized migrant workers as members of the proletariat and issued a directive allowing and encouraging the recruitment of migrant workers to join the trade unions. Xinhua reported that 'to safeguard the legitimate rights and interests of the 210 million farmers-turned-migrant workers has become a new mission of trade unions nationwide.'[45]

In 2008, a new law on employment promotion also came into force, which for the first time states that migrant workers should have the same rights to employment as workers from urban areas and that if they have been a resident in a city for a period of more than six months, then they should be entitled to local government service and unemployment benefits.[46] Despite this apparent change in attitude toward migrant workers, it seems that it has meant little in reality. While the Hukou household registration system remains in place acting as social apartheid, migrant workers are still being fiercely discriminated against as they are denied the right to settle permanently in urban areas and restrictions remain on their access to education and social services. It is not surprising that the number of spontaneous collective actions looks set to continue to grow significantly.

Where the union is concerned, by 2008, a national survey found that only 23.5 per cent of the migrant workers interviewed knew of the existence of a trade union at their enterprise and that only 4.2 per cent would seek assistance from the trade union if they thought that their rights were being infringed.[47] This suggests that even where a trade union does exist, migrant workers still have little faith in its ability to help them.

Problems for grassroots organisation

As part of its attempt to maintain a harmonious society *(hexie shehui)*, which thus means limiting social and political unrest, the CCP has been keen that the ACFTU is seen as a means to reach grassroots workers. This has had some interesting implications for grassroots unions, and explains their insistence on a unionisation drive in an attempt to establish an ACFTU branch in as many enterprises as possible. A more positive example, which as outlined earlier is still extremely limited, is the growth in experimentation with elections on an enterprise based level.

At the same time, however, the organisation remains very top-down and there is almost no contact between the upper levels of the union organisation and ordinary workers. In addition, despite its eagerness to establish more unions, where an official existing union already exists, the ACFTU remains very reluctant to adhere to any demands by workers for unions, which might operate to better serve their interests. In Chongqing, for example, requests by taxi drivers who have tried to organise their own union, have been turned down by the ACFTU on the grounds that they 'should go through the [taxi company] to set up a union'[48] or that the official union (which would have been controlled by management) already existed.

It is local unions that have primarily been made responsible for protecting workers' rights. Changes to the ACFTU's organisational structure at this level have further eroded the ability of, the already very weak, grassroots unions to represent workers. In 2005, the ACFTU adopted rural township and urban district unions as a new level of union administration. This new level of union bureaucracy comes between grassroots enterprise-based unions and higher levels of the ACFTU. They are not formed in the workplace but function purely at a bureaucratic level with closer ties to the party and local government than workers. They are often based in party or government offices and it is usually a local government functionary, wh0 has little interest in union matters, who acts as the union chair.[49]

Furthermore, with local government being keen to present attractive investment environments, protecting workers' rights is more likely to be a secondary consideration. In a majority of cases, they are more likely to take the side of management rather than that of the workers.[50]

Despite many problems for grassroots unions, a few cases have been reported where unions have been active in trying to defend the rights of workers. In Wal-Mart's Nanchang Bayi store union, for example, the union chair, who was originally one of the store's workers, was successful in defending an employee from dismissal. This resulted in the union's reputation being dramatically boosted and led to the majority of the store's employees joining the union. The same chair then on another occasion actively tried to negotiate with the store's management over collective contracts in order to ensure a better deal for workers over overtime and wages. In this instance, Wal-Mart was only successful in getting their version of the contract signed by getting a union chair from a different Wal-Mart union branch to sign it.[51]

What is important in the case of this grassroots union, however, is that the union chair, Gao Haitao, having previously taught himself law and had passed a lawyer's qualification exam, was in full knowledge of trade union law.[52] He would therefore have been more confident of the rights workers were entitled to within the law. In another dispute where Wal-Mart management was claiming that bonuses should be paid out of union dues, he informed the workers of their rights with regard to union membership, 'As members you have the right to know. You have the right to decide the way in which union funds are used and to supervise that usage.'[53]

Nevertheless, partial success in this union did not last long. Two years after the Wal-Mart organising drive, Gao Haitao was forced to resign from both the union and the company because both had made things very difficult for him.

International perceptions of the ACFTU

There have been mixed reactions toward the ACFTU from the international trade union movement. Although critical to varying degrees, there has been a tendency to show some degree of cooperation with the Chinese union. In more recent years, some international unions have begun to consider that some sort of positive change is possible from the ACFTU and so have begun to work more closely with the latter. In general, the international trade union community has been critical of the lack of freedom of association in China and will often cite lack of key labour and human rights among its concerns. An International Confederation of Free Trade Unions (ICFTU) report, for instance, concluded that in China:

> Workers are deprived the rights to organise freely, to form independent trade unions, and to engage in collective bargaining. The right to strike is not recognised. The state and government use a variety of anti-union tactics to control workers, including crack downs on industrial actions and imprisonment of those fighting for workers' rights.[54]

The report is also critical both of the ACFTU's monopoly and the way that repression means that any attempt to form an independent union is very short-lived. It highlights how the ACFTU plays a role to assist the government with its task of encouraging social stability and so is likely to want to avoid shop floor and large-scale collective action.[55]

The ICFTU has also stated that the ACFTU is not a free and independent union organisation. Nevertheless, within the ICFTU, an approach of engaging in critical dialogue with the ACFTU has been agreed, although different interpretations of what this means has led to some unions to engage in 'constructive dialogue' with the ACFTU, while others have virtually 'no contacts' at all.[56] As a result, the Federation of Dutch Trade Unions (FNV) has raised the concern that such different approaches open the way for the ACFTU to play ICFTU affiliates and global unions federations off against each other.[57] The ICFTU has, in fact, also been criticized for its downplaying of the Tiananmen Square massacre in order to allow further cooperation with the ACFTU.[58]

The FNV is an example of one of the union confederations to be more critical of the ACFTU. In a 2002 report it states:

> The FNV not only takes the view that the ACFTU is not an independent trade union, but concludes from its mission to China (November 2001) that the ACFTU is not an engine for change ... The ACFTU will only change when changes take place at a political level. For this reason, the FNV attaches little importance to contacts with the ACFTU, except for the purpose of raising the matter of violation of trade union rights, pressing for compliance with ILO conventions and drawing the ACFTU's attention to the necessity of representing the interests of workers.[59]

Such an approach is realistic in that it does not have any illusions about top-down change within the ACFTU itself and so does not give the ACFTU the legitimacy and credibility that it is keen to achieve.

Another example of a more critical attitude toward the ACFTU comes from the American Federation of Labour and Congress of Industrial Organisations (AFL-CIO). One of its main concerns has been the way in which the US has lost hundreds of thousands of manufacturing jobs to China because of the suppression of labour rights and low wages. Its responses to this concern have included the initiation of petitions to the US government recommending the imposition of 'trade remedies' against China, arguing that a trading partner's denial of workers' rights constitutes unreasonable trade practice.[60] It has argued that if 'the workers' rights of one-quarter of the world's workforce are radically suppressed – as they in fact are in China – then labour conditions for the world's skilled and semi-skilled workers are worsened; domestic and global demand is depressed; excess production capacity is created; and a path of inequitable unsustainable development is promoted.'[61]

At the same time, however, there is a problem with the position taken by the AFL-CIO's petition as it sees the root of the problem coming from the lack of a free labour market: 'China will continue to serve as the world's sweatshop, producing low-technology goods alongside high technology goods for decades to come—unless the Chinese government radically reverses course and dismantles its control over factory workers.'[62]

Thus, for the AFL-CIO, it is the Chinese government alone which is seen as responsible for the sweatshop conditions. This does not of course take into account the complicity of US companies, which have chosen to relocate to China specifically to lower their production costs by taking advantage of such conditions. Therefore, while the AFL-CIO's critical stance and boycott of the ACFTU is welcome, such an overall position is something that should be challenged. As previously noted, a significant number of unions, while critical of China's labour rights record and the ACFTU, have been more willing to engage to some extent with the ACFTU because they have taken the view that the ACFTU can be reformed. Svenska Metall, the Swedish metal workers' union, is one such union. While criticizing China's rights record and recognizing that the ACFTU operates more as a third party between the employee and employers and so does not negotiate on behalf of the workers, it states 'The ACFTU regards itself as an organisation which protects the best interests of the workers, and it does so in many ways. Ordinary trade union activities in China include organising leisure activities, accommodation and to some extent education of the workers.'[63]

Svenska Metall goes on in its 2005 report 'The Challenge of China' to explain how it believes it is adopting a pragmatic approach to its relations with the ACFTU. It has taken part in information exchanges with the ACFTU since the early 1990s and claims it hopes, 'that these contacts will prove one of a number of ways which can contribute to influencing the system from within, in a democratic direction.'[64]

Its reasons for adopting such a position are explained in connection to Sweden's investments in China, which also accelerated from the early 1990s. With Swedish companies relocating to China, Svenska Metall argues that it was necessary for it to learn about the way in which conditions were developing in Swedish companies.[65] While it is true that knowledge of the conditions for workers in companies that have relocated to China is important, the idea that the Swedish union might be able to influence the ACFTU by engaging in relations with it is very naïve.

It is almost as though Svenska Metall, in its justification for its willingness to work with the ACFTU, is claiming that it can teach what has been won with regard to trade union rights through workers' struggle elsewhere to the ACFTU, but also because of the ACFTU's strong ties to the authoritarian state, along with the fact that more often than not it is the enterprise management that has a hold over union positions at the workplace, it is very unlikely that an international union organisation can make any significant difference to the way that the ACFTU operates. Moreover, such relationships with the ACFTU should also be challenged as they give false credibility to the ACFTU. Rather, it can only be through workers' struggle for representative organisations that such a degree of positive change has a chance to occur.

An even more worrying recent development is the way that some union organisations have gone further still in their keenness to develop stronger ties to the ACFTU. The new US trade union Change to Win, for instance, has been very keen to break the so-called boycott of the ACFTU by the larger AFL-CIO and has sought to actively foster good relations with the ACFTU. In summer 2009, Change to Win and the ACFTU signed an agreement reaffirming the commitment of both parties to further cooperation. In a Change to Win report on the event, it emphasizes only what it views as positive aspects of the ACFTU.

As though to place it on an equal footing with trade union organisations in countries where there is freedom of association and the right to strike, Change to Win Chair Anna Burger proclaims that they were bringing together 'two great union federations that share a common vision of advancing workers' interests in China and around the world.'[66] This, then, is to ignore or forget the fact that the ACFTU is tied to the CCP and that its first priority has been to try to pursue party policy regardless of whether this conflicts with that of workers.

This has meant, as this report has tried to show, that the ACFTU will more often favour a good business investment environment and so side with management rather than the interests of workers. Change to Win, however, seems not to recognize this. Rather, they go on to report on how the ACFTU 'represents':

> 219 million workers in China and has collective bargaining agreements that cover 80 per cent of Fortune 500 companies, of which, 'Those collective bargaining agreements include all Wal-Mart workers, thus

recognising their right to union representation in China—a right that is denied to Wal-Mart workers in the United States.'[67]

Thus, they are falsely presenting the ACFTU as progressive by claiming that it has achieved things that have not yet been achieved in the US. Not only did Change to Win not mention the lack of quality of this so called 'representation,' moreover, its position acts to deny that in a country where workers are not free to form or join a trade union of their choice and workers are frequently banned by local authorities from speaking to the press (especially the foreign press), making it very hard for any third party to verify the real situation at a grassroots level, there is a problem with the form that any trade union representation takes. Such an approach to legitimize and give an even higher level of credibility to the ACFTU is clearly a very dangerous development.

Conclusions: proposals for workers' responses?

It has been argued that one of the problems with the ACFTU is that workers do not understand what a trade union should be. In SOEs, workers do not make a conscious choice about joining a union as they automatically become members of one. In addition, there is the argument that migrant workers have little understanding of a trade union's role as they come from rural backgrounds and so have little consciousness of being part of the working class.[68]

While it is true that many workers in China do lack understanding of the significance and role a genuine fighting union could play, a key part of the explanation for this also comes from the ACFTU's failure to act as a genuine trade union organisation. When the ACFTU has sought to establish new unions, it would rather approach the workplace management rather than the workers themselves. As an organ of the CCP, it has been complicit in China's realignment with global capitalism and the sacking of millions of workers as part of the restructuring process. Since then, where the trade union has existed, it has continued to repeatedly fail workers by siding with the enterprise management and favouring business so as to encourage a good business investment environment.

Thus, this explains why when workers have had grievances and decided to fight, they have often looked elsewhere to alternative forms of struggle. Indeed, there is an ever growing number of examples of how workers have actively got involved in collective workplace struggles. This sort of action is something that is greatly feared by the CCP and so in its efforts to create a 'harmonious society,' it has made some very limited reforms on the surface.

Nevertheless, as it is clear that the CCP has completely committed China to capitalism and the global market economy, while at the same time, such a high degree of strict control is retained over society, it is very difficult to see how any serious and meaningful reform of the ACFTU will take place. This means that while organisations such as the ICFTU are right to criticize the ACFTU for not being a free and independent union organisation, moves by parts of the international labour movement to view the ACFTU more positively and to work more closely with it are unhelpful.

Instead, it is worth looking more at the cases where workers have advocated for the union to carry out a more active role in fighting for and protecting workers' rights at an enterprise-based level. The OWYTU and Wal-Mart Nanchang union both provide a good example. The more recent call by Honda workers, during their strike in May–June 2010, for the reorganisation of their trade union in order to elect their own representatives further provides a positive example of how workers may begin to demand more from the union at a grassroots level.

While we should not place hope in reform of the ACFTU, if workers are able to gain more understanding of the role a union could play at a grassroots level and fight for their ability to utilize it, then there is room for some hope. The continuous rise in the number of strikes, road blocks, and other forms of collective action in recent years, although at the moment mostly spontaneous and isolated, has proved workers' willingness to fight and has deeply unsettled the CCP.

Additionally, with the onslaught of market reforms, the ACFTU itself has become more heterogeneous. While the central leadership has recently pushed for certain labour law reforms and has even become less explicit in supporting business interests, it has never ceased to act as the 'transmission belt' of the party. At the local level, the ACFTU is still as fiercely pro-business as before, and at the workplace level, the unions are mostly controlled by employers. Even where more progressive people may exist inside the ACFTU, their numbers are few and they have little room to achieve much, while those who have spoken up in favour of more independent unions in the past have been purged.

Nevertheless, because of the fact that in the workplace, the employer controlled unions can be directly challenged by a discontented and angry rank-and-file and the possibility of changing the union's leadership, although difficult, does exist, it still makes sense to support a re-election of the union when it is called for or echoed by the rank-and-file. This should not, however, be confused with the illusion that a thorough reform of the ACFTU as a whole is possible without first shaking off the 'leadership role of the party.'

References

Change to Win. 2009. *China trade unions sign first formal agreement.* http://www.changetowin.org/no_cache/ for-the-media/press-releases-and-statements/change-to-win-china-trade-unions-sign-first-formal- agreement.html?sword_list[]=china (accessed December 18, 2010).

China Labour Bulletin. 2008. 'Chongqing taxi strike just the latest in a long line of driver protests'. November. http://www.clb.org.hk/en/node/100335 (accessed December 18, 2010).

China Labour Bulletin. 2009. 'Protecting workers' rights or serving the party: The way forward for China's trade unions', *March.* China Labour News Translations. 2008. The emergence of real trade unionism in Wal-Mart stores. http://www.clntranslations.org/article/30/draft (accessed December 18, 2010).

Clarke, S, and T. Pringle. 2007. *Labour activism and the reform of trade unions in Russia, China and Vietnam.* NGPA Labour Workshop.

Greenfield, G. 1997. *Bill Jordan's ICFTU: British unions' 'new realism' goes global.* http://www.hartford- hwp.com/archives/26/031.html (accessed December 18, 2010).

Gross, A. 2009. *The effects of China's growing labour unions on your company, venture outsources.* http:// www.ventureoutsource.com/contract-manufacturing/outsourcing-offshoring/china-manufacturing/the- effects-of-china-s-growing-labour-unions-on-your-company (accessed December 17, 2010)

Howell, J. 2006. *New democratic trends in China? Reforming the all-China federation of trade unions.* Institute of Development Studies, March.

ICFTU. 2002. *China policy.* http://www.icftu.org/displaydocument.asp?Index=991217172&Language=EN (accessed December 18, 2010).

Ifeng.com. 2010. *Zhongguo Gonghui Huihui Dadao 2.26 yiren.* [China union members reach 226 million]. February 25. http://news.ifeng.com/mainland/201002/0225_17_1555055.shtml (accessed December 18, 2010).

IHLO. 2004. *Trade union elections in mainland China.* http://www.ihlo.org/LRC/ACFTU/000504.html (accessed December 18, 2010).

IHLO. 2009. *ACFTU in a time of crisis: Back to the old ways?* April. http://www.ihlo.org/LRC/ACFTU/070509A.html (accessed December 18, 2010).

ITUC. 2009. *Annual survey of violations of trade union rights.* http://survey09.ituc-csi.org/survey. php?IDContinent=3&IDCountry=CHN&Lang=EN (accessed June 7, 2010).

Jian, W. 2008. *The struggle of a self-organized workplace union in China: Report on the labour dispute between Ole Wolff Yantai and the Labour Union.* Wang Jian, Globalization Monitor, September 10.

Jiangsu province. 2008. *Sheng Laodong Baozhang Ting Sheng Caizhengting Sheng Dishuiju guanyu Caiqu Jiji Cuoshi Jianqing Qiye Fudan Wengding Jiuye Jushi de Shishi Yijian.* [Joint instruction from the provincial labour protection department, provincial financial department and provincial land rent bureau to alleviate enterprises' burden and to stabilize employment]. December 27. http://www.jiangsu.gov.cn/shouye/ zwgk/jszb/2009/1/sjbmwj/200901/t20090123_301587.html (accessed December 18, 2010).

News.163.com. 2006. *Quanzong Yanfang Didui Shili dui Nongmingong Qunti Jinxing Shentou Pohuai.* [ACFTU sound the alarm of hostile forces' infiltration and sabotages among rural migrant workers]. February 18, 2009. http://news.163.com/09/0218/06/52DPRDBH0001124J.html (accessed December 18, 2010).

NFDaily 2008. *Quanxin Xiuding de 'Shenzhen Shishi Gonghuifa Banfa, 8yue 1ri qi Zhengshi Shixing.* [The wholly revised 'Shenzhen ways of implementing the trade union law' will be implemented from August 1]. July 31. http://epaper.nfdaily.cn/html/2008-07/31/content_6676018.htm (accessed December 18, 2010).

No Way Out: Worker Activism in China's State-Owned Enterprise, Reforms Rights & Democracy, *China Labour Bulletin* (2008).

Pun, N., C. King, C. Chan, and J. Chan. 2010. The role of the state, labour policy and migrant workers' struggles in globalised China'. *Global Labour Journal* 1 (1):132–51.

Sheehan, J. 1998. *Chinese workers: A new history.* London and New York: Routledge.

Svenska Metall. 2005. *The challenge of China: Trade union and industrial perspectives.* Svenska Metall.

Wenfang, T. 1996. *Who should be the master: Enterprise decision in contemporary China.* Oxford: Oxford University Press.

WTO. 2006. *Internationally recognised core labour standards in the People's Republic of China.* Report for the WTO General Council Review of the Trade Policies of the People's Republic of China, April.

Xinhua. 2008. *ACFTU down path of building trade unions with Chinese characteristics.* October 19. http://en.chinagate.cn/news/2008-10/19/content_16633507.htm (accessed June 7, 2010).

Xinhuanet.com. 2005. *Zhongguo Quntixing Shijian Shinian Zeng Liubei.* [China's 'collective incidents' increase six times in ten years]. July 31. http://news.xinhuanet.com/mrdx/2005-07/31/content_3290161. htm (accessed December 18, 2010).

Zhaoguo, W. 2005. *Zai Qingzhu Zhonghua Quanguo Zonggonghui Chengli 80 Zhounian Dahuishang de Jianghua.* [Speech to the eightieth anniversary ceremony of the founding of the ACFTU], Wang Zhaoguo, April 25. http://www.lucheng.org.cn/p/a/ArticleShow.asp?ArticleID=57 (accessed November 3, 2010).

Notes

1 Originally published in *WorkingUSA: The Journal of Labour and Society* – 1089-7011 · Volume 14 – March 2011.

2 *Zhongguo Gonghui Huihui Dadao 2.26 yiren* (China Union Members Reach 226 million), (25 February , 2010), http://news.ifeng.com/mainland/201002/0225-17-1555055.shtml.

3 No Way Out: Worker Activism in China's State-Owned Enterprise, Reforms Rights & Democracy, *China Labour Bulletin* (2008).

4 *Gonghui Jiebie Weiyuan Pilu 11 Shengshi Tuoqian Guoqi Zhigong Gongzi 20 duoyi* (Trade Union Committee Member Reported that Eleven Provinces and Cities Have Wage Arrears Reaching More than Two Billion Yuan), (March 13, 2007), http://www.clssn.com/html/report/1981-0.htm.

5 *Labour Activism and the reform of trade unions in Russia, China and Vietnam*, by Simon Clarke and Tim Pringle (2007), NGPA Labour Workshop 2007, 23.

6 *Shuilai zuozhu: dangdai zhongguo de qiye juece* (Who should be the master: enterprise decision in contemporary China), Tang Wenfang (1996), Oxford University Press, 1996, 88–9.

7 *ACFTU in a time of crisis: back to the old ways?* ILO, April 2009, http://www.ihlo.org/LRC/ACFTU/070509A.html.

8 *Chinese Workers: A New History*, Jackie Sheehan (1998), London and New York, 1998, 200–1.

9 *Chinese Workers: A New History*, Jackie Sheehan (1998), London and New York, 1998, 202.

10 *Labour Activism and the Reform of Trade Unions in Russia, China and Vietnam*, by Simon Clarke and Tim Pringle (2007), NGPA Labour Workshop 2007, 3.

11 *Chinese Workers: A New History*, Jackie Sheehan (1998), London and New York, 1998, 223.

12 Cited in Labour Activism and *the Reform of Trade Unions in Russia, China and Vietnam*, by Simon Clarke and Tim Pringle (2007), NGPA Labour Workshop 2007, 5.

13 *Zai Qingzhu Zhonghua Quanguo Zonggonghui Chengli 80 Zhounian Dahuishang de Jianghua* (Speech to the Eightieth Anniversary Ceremony of the Founding of the ACFTU), Wang Zhaoguo, (April 25, 2005), http://www.lucheng.org.cn/p/a/ArticleShow.asp?ArticleID=57.

14 Protecting Workers' Rights or Serving the Party: The Way Forward for China's Trade Unions, *China Labour Bulletin* (March 2009).

15 *Trade Union elections in Mainland China,* IHLO (2004), http://www.ihlo.org/LRC/ACFTU/000504.html.

16 '*New Democratic Trends in China? Reforming the All-China Federation of Trade Unions,*' by Jude Howell (2006), Institute of Development Studies, March 2006.

17 Howell (2006).

18 Howell (2006).

19 *2009 Annual Survey of Violations of Trade Union Rights*, ITUC (2009), http://survey09.ituc-csi.org/ survey.php?IDContinent=3&IDCountry=CHN&Lang=EN.

20 '*New Democratic Trends in China? Reforming the All-China Federation of Trade Unions*', by Jude Howell (2006), Institute of Development Studies, March 2006.

21 Howell (2006).

22 Howell (2006).

23 *2009 Annual Survey of Violations of Trade Union Rights*, ITUC (2009), http://survey09.ituc-csi.org/survey.php?IDContinent=3&IDCountry=CHN&Lang=EN.

24 Protecting Workers' Rights or Serving the Party: The Way Forward for China's Trade Unions, *China Labour Bulletin* (March 2009).

25 *The Emergence of Real Trade Unionism in Wal-Mart Stores,* China Labor News Translations, 2008, http://www.clntranslations.org/article/30/draft.

26 Cited in *Labour Activism and the Reform of Trade Unions in Russia, China and Vietnam*, by Simon Clarke and Tim Pringle (2007), NGPA Labour Workshop 2007, 20.

27 *Jiti tanpan shouci rufa daiti pingdeng xieshang* (Collective Bargaining was enshrined in the law for the first time, replacing the original notion of equal consultation) (July 31, 2008), http://epaper.nfdaily.cn/html/2008-07/31/content_6676018.htm.

28 *The Effects of China's Growing Labour Unions on Your Company*, by Ames Gross (2009), Venture Outsource, http://www.ventureoutsource.com/contract-manufacturing/outsourcing-offshoring/china-manufacturing/ the-effects-of-china-s-growing-labour-unions-on-your-company.

29 *2009 Annual Survey of Violations of Trade Union Rights*, ITUC (2009), http://survey09.ituc-csi.org/survey.php?IDContinent=3&IDCountry=CHN&Lang=EN.

30 *Sheng Laodong Baozhang Ting Sheng Caizhengting Sheng Dishuiju guanyu Caiqu Jiji Cuoshi Jianqing Qiye Fudan Wengding Jiuye Jushi de Shishi Yijian* (Joint Instruction from the Provincial Labour Protection Department, Provincial Financial Department and Provincial Land Rent Bureau to Alleviate Enterprises' Burden and to Stabilize Employment), (December 27, 2008), http://www.jiangsu.gov.cn/shouye/zwgk/ jszb/2009/1/sjbmwj/200901/t20090123-301587.html.

31 *Zhongguo Quntixing Shijian Shinian Zeng Liubei* (China's 'Collective Incidents' Increase Six Times In Ten Years) (July 31, 2005), http://news.xinhuanet.com/mrdx/2005-07/31/content_3290161.htm.

32 Protecting Workers' Rights or Serving the Party: The Way Forward for China's Trade Unions, *China Labour Bulletin* (March 2009).

33 *ACFTU in a time of crisis: Back to the old ways?* ILO, April 2009, http://www.ihlo.org/LRC/ACFTU/070509A.html.

34 *2009 Annual Survey of Violations of Trade Union Rights*, ITUC (2009), http://survey09.ituc-csi.org/survey.php?IDContinent=3&IDCountry=CHN&Lang=EN.

35 See http://www.xinmiao.com.hk/0000/6300T.htm and http://www.xinmiao.com.hk/0000/6400T.htm for more details of the protest movement.

36 No Way Out: Worker Activism in China's State-Owned Enterprise Reforms, Rights & Democracy and *China Labour Bulletin* (2008).

37 The Struggle of a Self-Organized Workplace Union in China: Report on the Labour Dispute between Ole Wolff Yantai and the Labour Union, Wang Jian (2008), *Globalization Monitor*, September 10, 2008.

38 Cited in *The Struggle of a Self-Organized Workplace Union in China.*

39 http://blog.sina.com.cn/youyudzhongguoren.

40 *The Struggle of a Self-Organized Workplace Union in China.*

41 Cited in *Honda Workers Strike for Labour Rights and Trade Union Representation*, by Bai Ruixue, June 2010, http://www.worldlabour.org/eng/node/363.

42 Ibid.

43 See for instance 'The Role of the State, Labour Policy and Migrant Workers' Struggles in Globalised China', by Pun Ngai, Chris King Chi Chan, and Jenny

Chan (2010) in *Global Labour Journal*, Volume 1 Issue 1 2010, 135–6.

44 *Quanzong Yanfang Didui Shili dui Nongmingong Qunti Jinxing Shentou Pohuai* (ACFTU Sound the Alarm of Hostile Forces' Infiltration and Sabotages among Rural Migrant Workers), (February 18, 2009), http://news.163.com/09/0218/06/52DPRDBH0001124J.html.

45 *ACFTU down path of building trade unions with Chinese characteristics*, Xinhua (2008), October 19, 2008, http://en.chinagate.cn/news/2008-10/19/content_16633507.htm.

46 *2009 Annual Survey of Violations of Trade Union Rights*, ITUC (2009), http://survey09.ituc-csi.org/survey.php?IDContinent=3&IDCountry=CHN&Lang=EN.

47 ITUC (2009).

48 Chongqing taxi strike just the latest in a long line of driver protests, *China Labour Bulletin* (November 2008), http://www.clb.org.hk/en/node/100335.

49 Protecting workers' rights or serving the party: the way forward for China's trade unions, *China Labour Bulletin* (March 2009).

50 *China Labour Bulletin* (March 2009).

51 'A Grassroots Union's Struggle with Wal-Mart,' Southern Weekend (Nanfang Zhoumo), September 17, 2008, translated by China Labour News Translations (2008).

52 China Labour News Translations (2008).

53 Letter from Nanchang Bayi Wal-Mart Branch Union Committee to all Employees, January 13, 2007, translated by China Labour News Translations (2008).

54 Internationally Recognised Core Labour Standards in the People's Republic of China: Report for the WTO General Council Review of the Trade Policies of the People's Republic of China, April 2006.

55 WTO (2006).

56 ICFTU (2002) China Policy, 2002 http://www.icftu.org/displaydocument.asp?Index=991217172& Language=EN.

57 China, FNV, 2002.

58 *Bill Jordan's ICFTU: British Unions' 'new realism' Goes Global*, by Gerard Greenfield (November 1997), http://www.hartford-hwp.com/archives/26/031.html.

59 China, FNV, 2002.

60 Section 301 Petition of American Federation of Labour and Congress of Industrial Organisations, 2004.

61 Section 301, 2004.

62 Section 301, 2004.

63 *The Challenge of China: trade union and industrial perspectives*, Svenska Metall (2005).

64 Svenska Metall (2005).

65 Svenska Metall (2005).

66 Change to Win (2009), *China Trade Unions Sign First Formal Agreement*, August 2009, http:// www.changetowin.org/no_cache/for-the-media/press-releases-and-statements/change-to-win-china- trade-unions-sign-first-

formal-agreement.html?sword_listt[]=china.

67 Change to Win (2009).

68 See for instance, *New Democratic Trends in China? Reforming the All-China Federation of Trade Unions*, by Jude Howell (2006), Institute of Development Studies, March 2006.

NEW SIGNS OF HOPE: RESISTANCE IN CHINA TODAY

Au Loong Yu and Bai Ruixue

The number of cases of resistance in China continues to grow. Protests both large and small are an extremely frequent occurrence in China. They range in scale and nature from workers' protests against unpaid wages and demands for increasing labour rights, to protests against corrupt officials and environmental protests. While protests have often been brought to a swift end by repressive means, struggles have also frequently led to concessions being granted to the protesters, as the party-state will adopt different means by which to limit social unrest and restore 'social harmony'. The fact that the overwhelming majority of protests are spontaneous or limited to one locality or to a single issue, and furthermore due to fact that information and reports concerning struggles are frequently censored; makes it very difficult to view or comment conclusively regarding an in depth overall picture of resistance in China.

However, some struggles that have emerged more recently stand out for their significant new features, and which are worth commenting on as they seem to mark unprecedented steps forward or at least a change from the past. For twenty years, since the crack-down on the democracy movement in 1989, deep demoralization has persisted among workers in the declining state sector, whilst among the booming private sector the low expectation of rural migrant workers has meant they have been unaware of many of their rights. Thus workers' economic struggles in both sectors have been highly atomised and spontaneous. Recent cases show that things may begin to change, as they reflect higher awareness of the need for the coordination of struggles and even an aspiration for grass-roots democracy. Although the party-state apparently remains very strong, there are signs at the provincial level that it has to come to terms with this growing aspiration of the grass-roots, hence these struggles subsequently offer us some new signs of hope.

We would like to attempt here to provide an assessment of some of the more significant struggles of the last three years, to try to illustrate why they are significant in the context of China and why such forms of resistance could potentially be of importance for the future of wider resistance in China.

Labour struggles

The Tonghua anti-privatisation struggle.[1]

The Tonghua anti-privatisation struggle of July 2009 is the first of such struggles that we would like to look at. The struggle by steel workers at the Tonghua Steel Mill in Jilin province, which led to the death of a factory boss, resulted in a victory for the workers and led to the plans to buy out and privatize the steel mill being dropped. The protest had begun when workers found out about the plans for Jianlong steel to take over and control the company. The workers already had cause to resent this. Jianlong had already bought a 36 per cent share in Tonghua in September 2005 and this had resulted in a wave of layoffs. In addition Jianlong had previously temporarily controlled the company in 2008 and had fared badly financially when steel prices fell. Afraid of further job losses, in a city where the steel mill was the only major employer, when they found out about the planned takeover the workers decided to take action to protest against it. On 24 July a worker who had previously been laid off hung a banner outside the Tonghua main office building saying, 'Jianlong, Get out of Tonghua' and workers started to blockade a railway in order to stop supplies reaching the mill so as to cause the company to suspend production. Approximately 30,000 present and former workers and their families were involved in the protest.

The action ended after 10pm that night following factory boss Chen Guojun being beaten to death during the protest. Jianlong withdrew their offer to buy out the mill just hours after Chen was killed. Much of the workers anger had been specifically directed at Chen, who had first come to Tonghua in 2006 not long after Jianlong had first purchased a stake in the company. He was resented because he was seen as the representative of Jianlong and in addition was known for his tough disciplinarian management style, but also because of workers' recognition of the increased inequality and injustice in the pay differential between management and themselves that had occurred since Chen arrived. One report claimed, for instance, that while Chen was paid 3 million Yuan in 2008, some of the company retirees were receiving as little as 200 Yuan per month.[2]

The struggle successfully stopped Jianlong's privatization of Tonghua. The following year China's Shougang Steel Group, a giant SOE, acquired a majority share in the company. Although this was a victory, it remains to be seen how long the workers can keep their jobs, since after restructuring SOEs are run as any other commercial entities with pressures to cut labour costs.

The Tonghua struggle is significant for a number of reasons. Firstly, it not only illustrates yet another case of resistance where Chinese workers are not prepared to passively sit back in the face of privatisation, the fact that in this struggle a manager was killed only goes to reflect the growing depth of anger and desperation of workers whose livelihoods and means of survival are at stake; while management reap in the rewards and grant themselves even higher salaries.

During the enterprise reforms of the late 1980s, it was not uncommon to read in the news that individual workers killed the managers for sacking them or for cutting their wages, but this was never a collective action. Where there were collective actions – mostly demonstrations, camping in front of factories etc. – they were moderate and very self-disciplined due to fear of retaliation. The Tonghua incident is the first case where a manager was killed by a large group of workers and was supported by most other fellow workers. The workers' violence was also widely supported by netizens[3]. Such a massive outbreak of anger by workers frightened the local government and forced the latter to make significant concessions to the workers. Whether it represents an individual case or is a sign that the demoralizing effect of the 1989 defeat on workers is now receding, still remains to be seen, but future SOE workers' struggles may refer to this example and continue draw inspiration from it.

Secondly, at more or less the same time as the Tonghua struggle, workers at the Linzhou Steel Company in Puyang city were also fighting against privatization and the victory at Tonghua greatly encouraged their struggle. At the height of the incident the workers locked up an official from the municipal government for 90 hours. They also ended their fight with a victory.

Thirdly, the Chinese steel industry, which is the world's largest, is an example of one of the industries in which many workers have lost their jobs as they have become victims of the large scale lay-offs resulting from the central government policy of pushing industry into privatization or a series of mergers aimed at making them globally competitive. In the ferrous metal industry from 1996-2001, the workforce declined from 3.37 million to 2.04 million, a 40 per cent fall.[4] The Tonghua struggle proves that SOE and collective enterprises workers can still be a formidable force although they now make up just one fifth of the working class. In addition , although the weight of both SOEs and their workforce has declined, even post-restructuring the most important industries are still SOEs, and this gives more power to these workers than numbers alone might suggest.

Finally, in the Tonghua and Linzhou cases all the supposedly pro-labour institutions within the plants – the trade union, the staff and workers representative congress etc. – proved ineffective at representing workers' interests. This was why workers at both plants took actions independently of the official trade union, despite many of the workers being members of it. One Tonghua employee speaking to China Daily commented that, 'I can't remember the last time we had a conference with our union representative. The union certainly didn't do any good the day Chen was killed'.[5]

The Honda workers' strike

In May 2010, probably the most high profile incident of strike action in China's recent history began when Honda workers in Foshan, Guangdong province, took action calling for higher wages and, perhaps even more significantly, for the reorganization of their workplace trade union, triggering off a wave of strike action by workers in foreign-owned car plants that summer. Unlike in the case of the Tonghua struggle, these workers did not take action in the face of an imminent attack on them caused by potential job losses due to privatization, but already working at a privately owned enterprise, took action in order to actively improve their current situation.

The strike action, which first began on 17 May with around 100 workers coming out, was followed by two further strikes on 21 May. This led to retaliation by Honda management who dismissed two of the workers' leaders. However, the workers did not give in, and the following day the whole factory went on strike bringing production to a complete halt. The strike lasted for more than two weeks and only ended after regular workers at the plant had been offered a 35 per cent pay increase and those working as interns at the factory had received a raise of more than 70 per cent. Previously the Honda workers had been receiving wages which were well below the industry standards. Honda had also been particularly quick to exploit those on internship programmes, as they were not protected by Chinese Labour Law and so paid wages that were far below the minimum wage.

Despite the different circumstances in the action taken, as that of the Tonghua struggle, the ACFTU at the Honda plant was failing to protect the interests of the workers. Indeed, in the course of the strike the local level trade union showed that its interests did not really lie with the workers at all. On May 31 some of the striking workers reported that they had been physically attacked by men wearing union badges. Even after it issued a vague apology letter it was still clear that the union was keener to encourage them to go back to work as quickly as possible, than to ensure a positive outcome for the workers. At an enterprise based level, however, the Honda workers recognized that their union was failing them and thus had made the reorganisation of the workplace based union a key demand of the strike. In an open letter by worker representatives they condemned the branch trade union saying, 'We are outraged by the trade union's appropriation of the fruits of the workers' struggles. We insist that the branch trade union of the factory shall be elected by the production line workers'.[6]

In the end, the workers were not able to realize this demand in their settlement with the management. Although the local trade union was soon to announce an election of the workplace union at the factory in late August 2010, it turned out that this was only a by-election, where only part of the workplace union leadership was open to election and the original chairperson, who was very much resented by the striking workers, kept his seat. According to a study by Globalization Monitor in May 2012, the election of a new leadership of the workplace union in November 2011 was not genuinely democratic either, as the outgoing leadership monopolized the nomination of candidates of the incoming leadership, and the elections of delegates of the congress and of shop stewards were deliberately arranged in a highly complicated and undemocratic way such that members of the management were elected as members of the leadership, while the activists who led the strike in 2010 were pushed out altogether. Nevertheless, one positive development reported to have taken place is that the workplace union was able to negotiate a further wage increase in March 2011 as a result of collective bargaining with the management.[7]

The fact that many of the workers were so young – more than 50 per cent of those who took part in the first strike in Foshan were high school students on internship programmes – is in itself significant. This is because it means that the strike represents the actions of a new generation of Chinese workers, who have no memory of the defeat of the 1989 democracy movement – in fact most of them probably do not know of the event at all because of censorship – and are prepared to fight to improve conditions at their own workplace. Whereas SOE workers generally were not prepared to call for the re-election of workplace unions due to fear of being accused of 'trying to get rid of the leadership of the party', these young workers in the private sector, mostly rural householders or those coming from small cities, dared to break the taboo and call for the re-election of the workplace union.

Secondly, the Honda workers showed that they have a much broader vision than their parents. At the height of their struggle they made it clear that they saw their actions as being in the interests of the whole Chinese working class. In the words of the striking workers, 'Our struggle to defend our rights is not just about fighting for ourselves, the 1800 workers of Honda. We are concerned about the rights of all the workers in the whole country. We want to set a good example of workers struggling for all their rights.'[8]

We are not sure how many workers may share this kind of vision, but one thing is certain, they are quite unlike their parents, who may say *'ershi ding chushan, sishi ding shoushan'* (when we are at twenty we all go to cities to work, and when we turn forty we all go back to our home village). Instead this new young generation of rural migrant workers generally have a strong desire to establish roots in the cities, and are more likely to view themselves as part of the urban working people rather than as *nongmingong – migrant workers.* In fact, they rarely till the land at all and have little intention of living as peasants. Those who receive secondary education or vocational training are more likely to have a broader vision than their parents too. Even if the Honda case remains an individual case, like the Tonghua case, it will nevertheless be referred to as an important signpost for the development of resistance among young rural migrant workers. What they can accomplish is still largely unknown but these young workers may surprise us in many ways in the near future.

The Pepsi workers' struggle

Another significant recent example of action by workers was the protest by thousands of workers from Pepsi bottling plants, on 14 November 2011, against an agreement between PepsiCo. Inc and Taiwanese Tingyi Holding Corporation (also known as 'Master Kong'). As a result of the agreement, which involves PepsiCo giving up its bottling operations in China and transferring its equity interests to Tingyi-Asahi Beverages Holding Co. (TAB), a joint-venture between Tingyi and Japanese company Asahi Group Holdings Ltd, in exchange for a stake in this joint-venture company, workers were to have their existing contracts with PepsiCo terminated and would be forced to renegotiate them with TAB. On hearing the news, the workers, who claimed that they had previously known nothing about the deal between the companies, took the day off work[9] and protested to demand either the takeover be halted or that if their contracts were to be terminated then they had a right to compensation from PepsiCo for its violation of the original contract.

The protest by the workers is significant because, unlike most workers' protests in China, the workers took the unprecedented step of coordinating their action. Protests took place at bottling plants in more than five different cities at the same time, including Chongqing, Chengdu, Fuzhou, Changsha and Nanchang. Moreover, following the protest action, an online campaign was organised to try and involve workers at all of PepsiCo's bottling plants across China.

Subsequently on 30 November, Pepsi did announce some compensation packages for the workers, who were given the option of either staying on and working for one more year and then receiving a higher level of compensation pay, immediate compensation of a smaller amount, or keeping their current labour contracts without making any changes. Nevertheless posts on workers blogs, which were quickly deleted soon after they appeared, have indicated that at least among some workers there was still dissatisfaction with the situation. On 1 December for instance, a Lanzhou Pepsi workers' microblog stated that the workers did not agree with the terms offered by their employers and that workers were still demanding that their employers respond to the demands of their working party. If the management did not respond in time the workers threatened to do whatever they could within the law to express their grievances.

The alliance between PepsiCo and Tingyi was finally approved by the Chinese Ministry of Commerce at the end of March 2012. While there are reports that the workers remain dissatisfied with the proposed compensation package, it remains to be seen whether any further action will be taken.

The Wukan protests

Probably the most remarkable case of resistance of the last year was the 2011 struggle by villagers in Wukan, a fishing village with a population of approximately 13,000, in Guangdong province. This struggle saw the ruling Communist Party temporarily losing complete control of the village to the villagers, and then even when this came to an end it was with a partial victory for the villagers, who were able to set about preparing to organise new independent elections to their village committee for the first time.

The Wukan incident began due to action taken by villagers' due to their opposition to illegal land seizures by corrupt government officials. 'Land grabbing' is a common problem in China, and indeed it has been officially acknowledged that more than 43 per cent of Chinese farmers have been victims of this and that local governments have made huge profits as a result.[10] Nevertheless, protests in opposition to this corruption have also been extremely frequent, something which has become of growing concern to China's leadership who are keen to maintain social stability; leading them to state at least in rhetoric that there is a need to protect peasants' rights. In

Wukan, according to villagers, the problem of their land being taken from them and sold off to property developers was something that had actually been going on since the mid-1990s. It was not until a few years ago, however, that a group of villagers had first begun submitting legal complaints about corrupt officials misappropriating village land. It was then, in September 2011 that the villagers finally decided that they had had enough and came out onto the streets, this led to mass protests, the storming of local government offices and the driving out of the party secretary.

In this instance, riot police were soon sent in to attack the villagers and the villagers were driven back. Although shortly afterwards, the local government asked the villagers to choose 13 representatives to represent them in mediation, as soon as the villagers' anger had died down, the government tried to get the village back under their control and in early December the representatives were arrested at a restaurant in Wukan; they were interrogated and then thrown into jail. Two days later, when riot police were again sent into the village, they were met by more mass protests from the villagers and despite attempts to regain control with use of tear gas and water cannons, police were pushed out of the village. They retreated to a road block a few miles away, from where they tried to prevent food and water from entering the village as the protests continued. When it was heard that, Xue Jinbo, one of the thirteen village representatives had subsequently died in custody, anger at the news of this death only fuelled the determination to protest.

The Wukan protests were significant for a number of reasons. In the end, despite the initial brutality and the horrendous death of Xue Jinbo, the protests were not fiercely suppressed, as they had been in the past, but rather they resulted in the release of those detained and the promise that the villagers' complaints would be addressed. What is more, for the first time in decades, the municipal and provincial governments officially recognised a provisional committee, founded by the villagers,[11] hence allowing the villagers a vehicle to make preparations for elections for a new village committee to be held, in which they could themselves actively participate. This shows that struggle from below has the potential to change the party's practical ban on any form of autonomous organisation.

In February 2012 this then led to genuine elections being held in Wukan for the first time, to create an 11 member elections committee which would organise the election of a new village committee the following month. The old officials who had overseen the illegal selling off of the land had already been driven out. Much was done to ensure that these elections were open and democratic. Prior to these elections a census of the village population was conducted with the aim of aiding transparency and, according to a Xinhua report, more than 70 per cent of those eligible took part in the ballot. Furthermore, all candidates were required to make a public statement announcing that they would not run in the forthcoming election to the village committee and were required to collect 50 signatures from their fellow villagers to support their running in the election so as to make sure that they at least had minimum support. According to the report many of the villagers, who were participating in an election for the first time, were very enthusiastic about it.[12] Following the February election of the election committee, in March the election to the new village committee was held. One of the representatives hoped that this election might inspire the nation and that all levels of the government, from the villages to the central government would be democratically elected in the future.[13]

The fact that the villagers won the right to these elections no doubt represents a remarkable and previously unprecedented step forward for the villagers in Wukan. Recent online comparisons have been made between the Wukan elections and the election for the Hong Kong Chief Executive have shown how Wukan is now more democratic than Hong Kong, both a reflection on the achievement of the villagers in Wukan as well as the lack of democracy in Hong Kong. What this new democracy will actually mean for the villagers of Wukan, however, is yet to be seen. Indeed, the problem of the illegal land seizures initially raised by the villagers, and which was the cause of the protests, has not yet been resolved and it is uncertain as to whether it really adequately will be.

It is also worth commenting on how despite the protesters denouncing the corruption of officials, the protest was not a protest against the Communist Party. There were in fact many banners and statements throughout the incident which actually expressed support for the party, something commonly expressed at all varieties of different protests in China, and often reflecting the feeling that it is corrupt local officials rather than the central government who are to blame. Indeed among the protest leaders were Communist Party members, one of whom, Lin Zuluan has since been promoted to the position of party secretary of Wukan. The villagers' trust in him is reflected in how he was then later also elected by villagers to head the village committee in the March election, meaning that he now holds both the position of party secretary and head of the village committee.

The Wukan protests are also significant because they have the potential to act as inspiration to other struggles in China. One question which has frequently surfaced in the discussion over the implications of Wukan is how far the event or the subsequently much more democratic model that has emerged as a result of the protests has the potential to be replicated elsewhere in China. However, talk of a 'Wukan model' is overly optimistic if not misleading. The events at Wukan can be seen as a victory brought about by determined grassroots resistance on such a scale that it led to a situation in which, in order for the authorities to peacefully regain control of the village, they had no option but to grant major concessions. Furthermore it was also dependent on specific conditions, namely that one of the leaders of the struggle was a popular and skilful Communist party member, and that it had the support of a fully developed network of young villagers who made all efforts, through electronic devices and the internet, to break news censorship. An additional factor is probably the fact that the Guangdong provincial government has, in recent years, been seen as being a bit more tolerant of economic protests, as it realizes that these are not necessarily threatening to the party-state. If such reforms were to be introduced elsewhere from above, however, they would most likely only be on a limited scale and could be easily reversible at any time, for instance if candidates who lack party approval or are seen as a threat are elected. It would only be through more widespread struggle that saw beyond the immediate issue, that a more genuinely democratic and accountable model could emerge in China.

Environmental protests

Environmental issues are also a major cause of protests in China. Despite government claims about aims to reduce environmental pollution and to create a cleaner environment, such claims usually have little meaning or are put aside where they conflict with the desire to attract investment. Nevertheless, due to feared social instability, environmental protests have been known to have at least some successes.

Dalian

One recent example of a widely reported environmental protest comes from the Dalian struggle of August 2011, in which protests in the city of Dalian, Liaoniang province, northeast China, led to authorities ordering a petrochemical plant to be shut down immediately and pledges were made to relocate it elsewhere. The protest began after Dalian residents became concerned about the potential spill of toxic chemical paraxylene (PX) from the Fujia chemical plant following a heavy storm which had caused high waves to burst through the dyke protecting the plant. Despite the authorities insisting that there had been no spills, thousands of residents nonetheless took to the streets in anger about the spill and the safety risks they were being exposed to by the plant. Many claimed that toxins had in fact leaked from the plant and used slogans demanding 'PX out of Dalian' and 'Refuse PX'. It was furthermore said that Chinese reporters who had tried to investigate at the plant had been beaten up by security guards.[14]

Authorities were keen to limit the scale of social unrest and early into the protests the mayor of Dalian, Li Wancai, tried to appease protesters by offering to relocate the plant, however many of the protesters demanded that a clear timetable should first be established before they would stop. Indeed one of the key issues, which this protest highlighted, was the clear mistrust of the authorities by the residents. In the words of one demonstrator, 'Even if there was contamination, the government would restrict the news.'[15]

This was not the first protest to lead to the scrapping of a project involving the chemical PX. Following protests in Xiamen in 2007, for instance, the authorities there were also pushed into halting a similar project and moving it out of the city's jurisdiction.

Despite the Dalian protest ending with what seemed like a victory for the protesters with the plant being shut down and the promise that the authorities would relocate it to Xizhong island, reports have since suggested that the Dalian factory may have been reopened, although much of the news reporting on the plant's resumption on mainland websites has since been removed.[16] If the plant has indeed reopened then it reflects just how little the word of the authorities' means and how easy it is for them to backtrack on their promises at any time.

Haimen

In December 2011 thousands of villagers protested for four days in Haimen, a town in Guangdong province not far from Wukan, by blocking a road and surrounding government offices, to express their opposition towards the planned expansion of a coal-fired power station owned by state-run Huaneng Power. The residents were prompted to protest due to concerns about the high levels of pollution, which they said was already leading to health problems including a rise in the number of cancer cases, just from the existing power station.

In this case riot police who fired tear gas at the crowd were sent in to try to break up the protest, which resulted in injuries and two reported deaths. The incident also resulted in a few of the protesters being detained, allegedly for vandalism. Due to fear that the protests might grow, and probably with Wukan in mind, many efforts were made to deter protesters. Students, for instance, were reported to have been prevented from leaving school until late in the day for fear they might join in with the protest. [17] Meanwhile, local television broadcasts had clips showing legal experts warning that those who joined the protests could face up to five years in prison.[18]

Reports have indeed suggested that many of the residents in Haimen had been following the situation in Wukan and were influenced by it. The fact that these two events were taking place at the same time would doubtless have added to the pressure put on the provincial government and may also have contributed to the quick decision being made as to the suspension of the power station project, once the immediate response of trying to deter protesters had failed. Authorities would certainly not want there to be any chance of events at Haimen spiralling out into another Wukan, potentially involving even larger numbers. The protest therefore resulted in the Shantou city government, under whose jurisdiction Haimen falls, announcing that the project was to be temporarily suspended and the detained protesters released. However, no promises were made to put a stop to the plan altogether.

Conclusion

As the cases here have shown, resistance in China can bring about limited positive change. This is important not only in terms of the benefits of the immediate victory, such as to halt privatisation, or to win better working conditions or to limit harm to the environment, but more importantly such victories can act to inspire the future action of others and help to impact on the potential for their positive outcome, as is illustrated by the influence that the struggles of the Tonghua steel workers, the Honda workers and the villagers of Wukan had on other similar struggles at the same time. The forms that resistance have taken also reflect how the current generation are becoming increasingly bold. Although still on a small scale, the attempt by Pepsi workers to coordinate their action is of particular note in this respect. Even if such coordination was contemplated in the past, fear of the consequences would only have acted as a deterrent. The fact that the young Honda workers made the claim that they were acting in the interests of the whole Chinese working class again shows how there are signs that this new generation, free from the memory of the terrible defeat of 1989, has the potential to see beyond their immediate concerns and to identify with wider issues. Although at present these remain only small signs, they give us reason not to give up hope.

Notes

1 The following sections on the Tonghua anti-privatisation struggle and on the Honda Workers' Strike are adapted from our article 'The Case for an Autonomous Labour Movement in China,' by Au Loong Yu and Bai Ruixue.
2 '30,000 China steel workers in deadly clash', http://www.google.com/hostednews/ap/article/ALeqM5jioPQNV87uBjYSGuPr-LgcBJNdiAD99LC8900.
3 People who communicate through the internet – a portmanteau word of internet and citizen
4 *Woguo zhongchangqi shiye wenti yanjiu* (Research on China Medium and Long Term Unemployment), Jiang Xuan, China People's University Press, Beijing, 2004, p.181.
5 Cited in 'China debates the lessons of Tonghua tragedy', *China Labour Bulletin*, http://www.clb.org.hk/en.
6 'Open Letter to the Public and All the Workers in Honda Auto Parts Manufacturing Co. Ltd.', 3 June 2010, http://worldlabour.org/eng/node/361.
7 *'Nanhai bentian laozi tanpan, jinnian gongzi zaizhang 600 yuan'*, (Honda Nanhai Wage Negotiation Resulted in Raising 611 Yuan wages for This Year), http://gcontent.oeeee.com/7/1b/71bfbe458113bbc3/Blog/b4f/433268.html.
8 *Nanhai bentian gongren daibiao fachu gongkaixin* (Honda Nanhai Workers Representatives' Open Letter), June 3, 2010, http://www.sina.com.cn.
9 Workers are reported to have claimed that they were not on strike but simply protesting to demand their rights.
10 Nearly half China farmers suffer land grabs, AFP, 7 February 2012. http://www.google.com/hostednews/afp/article/ALeqM5h-rLJET4ZgujQMlrTl_iSjaErNLQ?docId=CNG.9a22c95cb0e7b0a49350a92381891d4c.221.
11 Although, it is also significant that the Honda Foshan workers representatives won official recognition as elected as grassroots representatives, which is rare, in their negotiating with the management.
12 *Guangdong Wukan cunmin yiren yi piao tuixuan cunmin xuanju weiyuanhui*, Xinhua Guangdong, 2 February 2012.
13 *Ming Pao*, 18 December , 2011.
14 Cited in 'Tens of thousands protests against chemical plant in Northern China', *The Guardian*, 14August 2011, http://www.guardian.co.uk/environment/2011/aug/14/china-protest-against-px-chemical-plant
15 Ibid.
16 'Dalian Plant Re-opens after protests dissipate', http://rightsite.asia/en/article/dalian-chemical-plant-re-opens-after-protests-dissipate.
17 'Chinese official denies reports of deaths at Haimen Protest', *Reuters*, 2 December 2011, http://www.reuters.com/article/2011/12/21/china-protest-plant-idUSL3E7NL0KR20111221
18 'Police fire tear gas at protesters in Chinese city', *New York Times*, 23 December 2011, http://www.nytimes.com/2011/12/24/world/asia/china-jails-rights-activist-chen-wei-for-9-years.html.

MAOISM: CONTRIBUTIONS AND LIMITATIONS[1]

Pierre Rousset[2]

This book deals essentially with China at the end of the 20th and the beginning of the 21st century, which is a very different China from what it was during the 1950s and 1960s. The rupture with the past is very deep. It is quite difficult to know how much the memory of the Maoist past will influence tomorrow's popular resistance against the demands of Chinese capitalism and whether this history will be a reference point for new left political currents. The factional violence of the Cultural Revolution (1965-1968) provoked a real trauma. The hyper-bureaucratic rule of the Gang of Four which followed, discredited so-called 'revolutionary' rhetoric through its record of deceit.

This is also true at the international level. Yesterday Mao Zedong was admired by many, but today he is vilified. Maoism has created its own caricature; a frenzied cult of personality and the universal virtues (later) granted to 'Mao Zedong thought'. More generally, there is a tendency for the whole experience of the revolutions of the 20th century to be ignored by the new generation of militants, as if an entire chapter of history, weighed down with many deceptions, is definitively closed.

It is impossible to understand the current century by forgetting the shattering impact on the previous century of world wars, revolutions and counter-revolutions. This past should not be eradicated from our knowledge. It is rich in lessons, some negative and others positive.

The Chinese revolution is one of the major events that have shaped the contemporary world; a revolution personified by the Maoist leadership, and which remains, in spite of all its shortcomings, a reference point for many contemporary radical movements. We will try in this chapter to look again at the Maoism of the Chinese revolution, its contribution and limitations, going beyond the clichés in order to help a critical understanding of the lessons of this page of history.

The unexpected as context

We witnessed a number of unexpected events in the 20th century: inter-imperialist wars (1914...); victorious revolutions on the eastern periphery of Europe (Russia), and then in the third world (China...), and not as expected in the industrial centres of the west; Nazism and Stalinism; geopolitical blocks born out of the Second World War; the complexity of the 1965-1975 period; the implosion of the USSR and the development of neoliberal globalization.

Each time, revolutionaries have been confronted with the need to develop new responses; a difficult exercise, with uncertain results and debatable conclusions, but nevertheless an enriching process. It is from this viewpoint (questioning what is new...), that we try to carry out a retrospective examination of Maoism and the Chinese revolution.

The entry of Marxism across the world

It is difficult today to realise how iconoclastic the idea of the possibility of a socialist revolution in China was. Of course, there was the precedent of October 1917, which had already overturned the assumptions of the Second International. This precedent offered tools for understanding the dialectic of the national and social struggles in a third world country: the analysis of combined and uneven development, the theory of permanent revolution. Nevertheless, Russia was a European power, albeit in decline. Under the devastating shock of the First World War, a pan-European revolution was on the agenda: Germany was one of the major challenges between 1917 and 1923.

There was certainly a debate on Marxism's relationship with the 'east' and the 'west', but the East was then Tsarist Russia! What was in question were the 'Asiatic' influences in the East of Europe and the Russian empire rather than Asia's own relation with modern revolutions; backwardness versus modernity. On the whole, the geo-political horizon of the socialist movement was still rather narrow. It suddenly broadened out because of the consequences of the First World War, the impact of the 1917 October Revolution, the new wave of anti-colonial struggles in the third world, and the defeat of the German revolution in 1923 which led Moscow and the Third International to turn itself to the East beyond Europe to avoid the isolation of the USSR.

The Chinese question became a central issue in the geopolitics of the 1920s. On the Siberian borders of the USSR, the Middle Kingdom was in open crisis. The Qing dynasty had been brought down by the first Chinese revolution of 1911. The May 4th 1919 Movement was an encouraging renewal of progressive anti-imperialist resistance. But the 'republican' revolution of 1911 had posed more questions about the new 'possibilities' than it offered answers. It was only a warning shot, fired a bit too early and too limited in range, to be able to clarify the possible role of the various classes that were still off-stage. The character of a new party such as the Guomindang, which at the time of Sun Yat-sen embodied national consciousness, was still largely undefined. To what extent were the lessons of the Russian revolution valid for China in the 1920s? It was only the dramatic experience of the Second Revolution of 1925-1927 that clarified strategic issues, at the cost of a bloody counter-revolution.

China is at the same time another social formation, another path of civilisation, part of another geopolitical entity – in short, the outcome of another history. At the same time, the Comintern[3] was confronted by the 'Muslim question' with the presence within the Soviet system of the republics of central Asia. This was at the centre of the debates of the 1920 Baku congress, known as the 'Congress of the Peoples of the East'.

The birth of communist movements, and more broadly, the development of anti-imperialist struggles in the East from central Asia to China, opened a door to the world for Marxist thought. Previously, western Marxists educated within the framework of the Second International had looked at the world in a manner which could be described as 'from afar'. From now on, communists had to look at their societies and the world from a non-European point of view. The task was not that obvious as the notes of Marx on the plurality of historical developments, which can be found in the *Grundisse*, in the preparatory work for *Capital*, and in correspondence, were unknown to most – and ignored by those who knew of their existence.

This 'entry into the world' opened a particularly interesting chapter of the history of Marxism; a chapter which is not yet closed.

Maoism: 'Chinese' Marxism?

Born in Europe and inheriting a specific history, Marxism could not be exported as it was without remaining in other ways the privileged asset of a westernised intellectual elite. It was not a given that it could root itself in every society, but where it could do so it needed to find fertile native ground, integrate the originality of social structures, speak a language that was understandable to the mass of people and therefore link itself to other cultural legacies, find other 'sources' than German philosophy, English political economy, French historiography or the traditions of the European workers movement.

The Maoism of Mao is often presented as 'the' Chinese version of

Marxism. He can certainly legitimately claim to have worked upon a Chinese Marxism. This theme was explicitly developed from the late 1930s on, and is repeated in the official history of the CCP. Mao insisted on the need to give a 'national form' to Marxism to be able to 'apply it', to make Marxism 'concrete'. He often made references in his speeches to the history of China, its cultural traditions, its wars and military theory, and its peasant uprisings rather than to European theoreticians or to the USSR. He more closely resembles a philosopher in a society inspired by Confucius than a Western one. It is nevertheless important not to confuse the 'Chinesification' of Marxism, its 'nationalization' (what is usually called the 'sinification of Marxism') and 'Maoization'.

Maoism is one of the components of 'Chinese' Marxism, but it has no monopoly. There is not 'one' Chinese Marxism, just like there is not 'one' Western Marxism, which could be incarnated by a particular political current. The 'sinification' of Marxism has been a collective effort, carried out more or less consciously, because the Chinese revolutionary left was pluralist at its birth. In the 19th and at the beginning of the 20th century, anarchism was influential in Eastern Asia. The relationship between tradition and modernity was passionately debated in the May 4th Movement, which was a place of intense intellectual debates. The Communist Party, founded in 1921 by strong personalities, was far from a monolith. People like Li Dazao, Chen Duxiu and many others, had each in their own manner carried out the twin exercise of opening up China to Western thought and re-transcribing Marxism for that country, well before the formation of Maoism.

In the light of the role played by the envoys of Moscow in determining the political orientation of the young CCP, the need to break free from Soviet supervision was felt particularly strongly by the cadres who survived the defeat of 1927. Some, like Chen Duxiu, identified with the anti-Stalinist theses of the Left Opposition inside the Communist International. Others, like Mao, were trying to work out how to save the revolutionary military forces that had regrouped after the defeat into a few 'red bases'.

How to start again? It was by trying to answer this question that Maoism emerged between the end of the 1920s and the middle of the 1930s. It did so as the new Stalinist orthodoxy was smothering theoretical debates within the Comintern. The thesis that the whole of humanity could only experience a single form of historical development, a single succession of different modes of production, was being imposed as an unchallengeable dogma. Even in the West, it was only in the 1950s, and even more in the 1960s with the circulation of hitherto largely unknown works of Marx, that a process of reflection on the complexity of history was begun again. It was impossible in these circumstances to open a genuine discussion on the uniqueness of Chinese society in contrast to that in Europe.

The process of 'nationalization' of Marxism by the CCP remained doubly dependent: first on the recent legacy of the Second International and then on the triumph of Stalinism in the USSR. The specificity of social formations in China was not clarified theoretically. European concepts, such as feudalism, were simply translated in existing terms onto imperial China. The differences between these terms and the historical realities they referred to, were not clarified with grave consequences, which are still being felt today. Rather than analyse the originality of their societies, most Maoist currents in the third world were satisfied with uniformly describing them as 'semi-feudal, semi-colonial'. The 'semi' at best only identified a question without providing an answer, and minimised the implications of capitalist domination.

The official CCP policy of the 'sinification' of Marxism was implemented while the pluralism of the Chinese left was reduced to shadow of its former self under the impact of the counter-revolutionary repression of the Guomindang, then that of the Japanese occupation and finally the Stalinization of the Comintern. It was also combined with the initial formulation by Mao of the personality cult of Mao. The abstract universalism of Stalinist dogma in the USSR was intended to reinforce the cult of Stalin and the authority of Moscow internationally. The 'sinification' of Marxism legitimized a rival cult and allowed the Maoist leadership to more easily marginalize rival factions inside the CCP, including that of Wang Ming who supported Stalin.

Thirty years later, during the Sino-Soviet conflict, the cult of Mao took on an international dimension. Official Maoism became a dogma and an ideological commodity suitable for export, emptying from the theme of 'nationalisation' of Marxism its content. But the substantial question is still nevertheless relevant. By internationalizing itself, Marxism takes on regional and national aspects in order to better root itself in different societies.

Creative strategic thinking

The Second Chinese Revolution (1925-1927) was brought about by vast social movements: strikes by workers, the struggle of the poor urban masses, uprisings of peasants, and the organisation of self-defence through militias. But it was also characterised by confrontation between regular armies: that of the Guomindang or warlords. After the Guomindang of Chiang Kai-shek (Jiang Jieshi in today's pinyin transcription) turned against his communist allies and the popular movement, sections of the army rebelled and joined the 'red bases', the last territorial bastions of the CCP.

The 'armed struggle' appeared in China in very different forms than often evoked by this formula. There was no gradual development of small guerrilla units. There were millions of soldiers in China, and the Red Army, created in response to the 1927 counter-revolution, initially had 300,000 privates led by political commissars, but also by officers who had graduated from military academies.

How would it be possible to start again following the succession of defeats between 1927 and 1935? The answer had to include a military dimension: how to save the forces of the revolution that were surrounded and threatened with annihilation by an army ten times greater in number and with superior weapons? This situation contributed to a complex debate on the military question inside the leadership of the CCP in the middle of the 1930s and this led to the development of Maoism. Mao was not content to find an answer to a conjunctural situation. He drew lessons from the experience of the Second Revolution to think through a new strategy.

A political approach to military questions

The Maoist leadership did not invent the idea of guerrilla warfare. It referred to previous debates between Marxists and to the experience of the Russian Revolution. It particularly benefited from a long national history of peasant wars and a rich thinking on military matters. But it brought all this up to date and integrated it into an overall perspective: closely linking the basis for a popular armed struggle, the social context such as the aspirations of peasants, and the political stakes such as the national question arising out of the Japanese invasion

The Red Army was almost annihilated, but during the Long March, Mao was able to create a leadership team which included extremely talented cadres coming from various factions of the CCP. This team gradually gave birth to the concept of the protracted revolutionary war, or protracted people's war, a new understanding when a civil war, whether it is combined or not with a war of national defence, starts a long time before it concludes with the conquest of power. It cannot be reduced to methods of operation such as mobility and flexibility, concentration and dispersion of forces, or guerrilla techniques, however important this military knowledge is. It order to be able to develop over a long period of time, it should indeed be conceived as a 'popular war'. In the context of the time, the notion of popular war immediately posed the question of the peasantry[4].

The question of the peasantry

The originality of Maoism is not that it recognised the importance of the agrarian questions and of the peasantry: this had already been the case in Russia. It was that it had been able to organise the peasantry directly and root itself in rural society, not to ally itself to peasant movements but to lead them. This was not the last time that a communist movement had been able to achieve this successfully, but it was the first, and a spectacular first at that!

One of the most interesting aspects of the Chinese experience was that it was carried out from the North to the South of the country, in regions with very different agrarian structures and where, for example, the meaning of 'rich peasant' varies considerably. It showed how traditions of collective solidarity of the village, against external enemies such as military forces, tax collectors and bandits, can slow down the class struggle within the village community and feed mistrust towards 'strangers', even if they are members of the Communist Party. The Chinese experience demonstrates how the elaboration and implementation of a programme of agrarian reform is an essential, but not a simple matter. This is probably just as true today as it was in the past.

The Maoist revolution was also able to think about the role of the peasantry over a long period of time, no longer just as a temporary ally mobilised against the old order. The world has changed considerably since then as the demographic weight of peasants, the landless and small farmers, is considerably reduced. Nevertheless, at a time of a food and ecological crisis, the political importance of the peasantry for any project of social transformation is considerable. Small scale agriculture appears as an alternative to that of capitalist agro-industry which imposes its domination on consumers and producers, expropriates entire populations and destroys social networks and the environment. The struggle today for food sovereignty is an integral part of the global defence of fundamental democratic, social and environmental rights.

The Protracted People's War

With the concept of protracted revolutionary war, the Maoist leadership opened a new chapter in strategic Marxist thinking. This is not the least of its merits. At the beginning, nevertheless, the characteristics of China seemed so particular that it did not envisage that this 'road' could be taken in other countries. It played on the fact that the huge size of the country enabled it to have a vast field of manoeuvre, that the size of the population enabled it to bring together a huge number of fighters in any region, on the existence of 'red bases' which constituted an original and long-lasting form of territorial dual power, on the inter-imperialist rivalries in a country which had not yet been colonised and on the fragmentation of the state following the fall of the Qing dynasty, which prevented the enemy from being a coherent force.

After the Second World War, the Protracted People's War was carried out in many different forms across Asia and Latin America, as well as in the Arab world and Africa. It contributed to strategic thinking which went through further developments, in particular that of the Vietnamese experience. Today, there is still an armed struggle being carried out in countries such as India, Nepal (recently), the Philippines and Colombia which provokes many debates within the revolutionary movement. The political-military thinking which arose out of the Maoist experience does not belong to the past.

The national question, alliances and the united front

The national question was at the heart of the Chinese crisis. The imperialist powers were consolidating their grip on the country, which was threatened with fragmentation into different zones of Japanese and Western influence. The invasion by Japan in 1937 was intended to make China its exclusive colony.

In such conditions, which were the forces that could achieve independence and national unity? Was it the commercial and industrial bourgeoisie? This was stronger in China than in most third world countries of that time. The Chinese Revolution thereby became a great historical laboratory for study of the links between anti-imperialist struggle and social dynamics.

As early as 1926-1927, the priorities of the Chinese bourgeoisie were confirmed. It saw that the anti-imperialist uprising was opening the way for popular movements that it could not control. The counter-revolution became its priority, even if it meant giving up the struggle for national reunification for the time being.

A decade later, in the face of the Japanese invasion, the Chinese bourgeoisie was divided between resistance and collaboration. On the eve of the Second World War, the Guomindang of Chiang Kai-shek gambled on the defeat of Tokyo by the United States. By using the immensity of the Chinese territory, it tried to slow down the advance of the Japanese forces while conceding territory to gain time and wait for the victory of Washington in the Pacific theatre of operations. It was thereby preserving its forces in order to use them later against the Communist Party.

The strategy of Chiang Kai-shek could have been successful if it had not been rivalled by the Maoist leadership. The latter implemented the principles of the People's War, including by sending units of the Red Army operating in the occupied areas behind enemy lines. Instead of conceding territory, the CCP extended its field of action. This orientation was triply effective: militarily, socially as it became implanted in new regions and politically as it appeared to be the best defender of the nation under conditions of emergency.

The lessons to draw from the Chinese experience are not limited to these questions. Between the beginning of the Second Revolution and the victory of the Third, there were several historical turning points that required important reorientations. The policy of the united front between the Communist Party and the Guomindang is one example. The very young CCP grew rapidly when it joined the party of Sun Yat-sen, carrying out the tactic known as the 'united front from within'. But under pressure from Moscow, it did not regain its organisational independence when, after Sun Yat-sen's death, Chiang Kai-shek was preparing to crush the workers movement, and when the war for national reunification of the country turned into a full-blown civil war. From being an ally, the Guomindang suddenly became the main enemy and remained so for a decade.

The invasion by Japan again posed the question of a united front of the CCP and the Guomindang as there was an extremely strong desire amongst the population for unity to defend the nation. But both of the protagonists knew that despite national unity, the civil war was smouldering and occasionally erupting into bloody battles between the armies of Chiang Kai-shek and the Reds. The defeat of Tokyo in 1945 opened the way for the civil war to be resumed and the Communist Party was victorious in 1949.

The Maoist legacy regarding alliances might appear to be very ambiguous if there is no concrete analysis of the sequence of events during the Chinese Revolution. The leadership of the CCP often formulated its orientation in a 'tactical' manner and sometimes even in a deceptive one. For example, under the label of the anti-Japanese united front, it praised Chiang Kai-shek, the butcher of the working class, without blinking. It announced the integration of its military units into the army of the Guomindang, without of course doing so.

Some Maoist organisations use such declarations to justify opportunist policies of subordinate alliances with 'national bourgeoisies'. But the conception of the united front by the leadership of the CCP was at the same time more interesting and more sectarian.

It was more interesting because it linked the construction of a block of social forces able to carry out a revolutionary struggle (the popular classes) over a period of time and the widening of this block to intermediary forces (e.g. students, intellectuals, the impoverished petty-bourgeoisie), with a tactic aimed at dividing the ranks of the enemy (which is where it is original compared to other political traditions).

It was more sectarian, because at the heart of this policy of alliance was the CCP and it alone. In the conception of the united front as a series of concentric circles, there is only a single centre. This does not allow the idea of cooperation between several revolutionary and progressive political organisations. But pluralism, including within the revolutionary movement, has again become what it was before Stalinism; the rule and not the exception.

As a result, the majority of Maoist movements engaged in armed struggle have been more sectarian than opportunist. The truth of the matter is that the Maoists have not been the only ones to find it difficult to recognise that, due to the complexity of historical experience, the existence of a plurality of revolutionary movements is normal, and that the question of their relationship and their unity is posed.

The model and its betrayal

The irony is that having insisted on the national specificities of the Chinese road, the Maoist leadership then erected the 'people's war' as a new orthodoxy. But every major new experience is necessarily original and therefore heterodox. And every attempt to create a new orthodoxy on the basis of such an experience will lead to misrepresenting the historical truth and hiding its real lessons.

Of course, behind the proclamation of orthodoxy, Maoist movements have been able to 'adapt' the orientation to better respond to the conditions of their country or of their period. But that so-called orientation became a strategic straitjacket. The Protracted People's War had to be carried out in all 'semi-feudal, semi-colonial' countries, which is roughly the whole third world. The question of revolutionary crisis, as a 'favourable moment' (a Vietnamese expression), was not to be posed in societies which are supposed to live permanently in such a state. The armed struggle was presented as the main form of struggle at all times; one to which other fields of mobilisations such as for democratic and social rights had to be subordinated. The countryside was to be the privileged location for the progressive accumulation of military forces which would encircle the towns. The struggle had to go through three stages: defensive, equilibrium of forces, strategic counter-offensive.

It is impossible with this rigid conception of the Protracted People's War, leading to military gradualism, to understand the history of the Chinese

Revolution and of the Red Army created with hundreds of thousands during a revolutionary crisis and in response to a counter-revolution. It is also impossible to grasp the implications of a sudden turn in the situation which dramatically changed the strategic framework, such as the Japanese invasion in 1937 which led for example to the reactivation of the united front policy towards the Guomindang. It is impossible to discern the importance of a 'favourable moment' which required the sudden acceleration of the rhythm of struggle, such as in 1945 at the end of the Second World War when there was a race between the CCP and the Guomindang to make the most of the defeat of the Japanese occupier. Finally, it is impossible to assimilate the lessons of other great revolutionary experiences such as Vietnam, Cuba, Algeria or Nicaragua, which all bear a hallmark of originality.

The Chinese Revolution and the Maoist leadership have contributed a great deal to the development of Marxist strategic thinking. Nevertheless, by retrospectively setting the 'principles' of the Protracted People's War in stone, the CCP made it very hard to pass on the lessons of its own experience.

The Chinese Communist Party

Which type of party conquered power in 1949? The analysis of the CCP has fed many debates within, in particular, the international Trotskyist movement. The debate was often unclear because the protagonists did not have the same definition of 'Stalinism'. For some, it meant the submission to the requirements of the Soviet bureaucracy, but for others it took on a mainly ideological meaning.

More generally, the Chinese experience demonstrates that the analysis of a party is not a simple matter, in particular during moments of transition and revolution. The trajectory of the Communist Party has frustrated many prognoses and contradicted many peremptory conclusions.

The CCP was supposed to become an obedient tool of Moscow after the social upheavals of the disaster of 1927. However, the Maoist leadership was able through intense internal factional struggles to maintain its capacity for making autonomous decisions, though without breaking with Stalin. The process of Stalinization of the Comintern, i.e. the subordination of its national sections, was faced with strong resistance in certain countries with including China but also Yugoslavia and Vietnam.

Defeated in the urban centres, deeply immersed in the vast rural areas the CCP had to become a peasant party. But immediately following its victory in 1949, it relocated its centre of gravity to the cities. Similarly, the CCP could have fallen into the hands of the military because of the framework of the armed struggle. However, right up to the end, as Mao said, politics leads the gun and the Political Bureau led the general staff, despite the weight of the commanders of the Red Army.

Analysing a party such as the CCP is never going to be a simple matter. It is one of the first of such parties to be born in the third world and steered its own course in the Third International before Stalin. Then it immediately threw itself into the revolutionary storm of the 1920s, experienced the rise of Stalinism in the USSR with all its implications, came under fire during the counter-revolution in China, radically changed its geographical and social implantation, moved from one type of war to another (civil, self-defence, national liberation, world-wide, and again civil) and found itself governing liberated areas of some hundred million inhabitants before conquering power in the largest country, demographically, in the world. It had about fifty members when it was created and 4.5 million when it celebrated its victory 30 years later!

No single label can do justice to the complexity of such a party. 'Stalinist' or 'anti-Stalinist', 'worker' or 'peasant', 'authoritarian' or 'liberating'..... what if all were correct at the same time? The important thing is to recognise the role played by the CCP in a very difficult revolutionary struggle, but also to locate its internal contradictions and their possible evolutions.

No abstract definition can replace concrete and dynamic historical analysis. Let's just say than in 1949, the CCP was both the party of a great victorious social and national revolution – hence the depth of its links with the population – and at the same time the new state-party within which the ruling elite would become autonomous and constitute itself as a bureaucracy. It went on to become the party of the bureaucratic counter-revolution, but not without suffering sharp convulsions and then became the party which would navigate the (re) formation of a Chinese capitalism.

A Maoist road to socialism?

When the People's Republic was born, the new regime had a tremendous amount of political prestige. The time should have been one of reconstruction, but the eruption of the Korean War in 1950, which lasted till 1953, meant this did not happen. China had not wanted this war, but it had nevertheless to send a considerable number of troops to the peninsular to stop the American forces and then push them back to the 38th parallel. It was another victory but one achieved at a high price: over 800,000 Chinese dead and wounded.

In China itself, the repression against 'counter-revolutionaries' hardened during the Korean War. The domination of the 'gentry', landowners and notables in the countryside had been broken, as well as that of the bourgeoisie in the cities. The state run by the Guomindang had disintegrated and its defeated armies retreated to Taiwan. Individual bourgeois and members of the gentry still remained on the mainland, some of whom had concluded more or less temporary deals with the CCP in various local arrangements. But the classes which had previously ruled over China had ceased to exist as a coherent social force.

The regime was not content to claim simply to represent the people. In 1950, the law on agrarian reform began to change relationships of power in the villages. The marriage law radically transformed women's legal status. With the development of a state industry, a new working class was born; one which had a frugal lifestyle but benefited from important social measures such as jobs for life, health services, housing, and the possibility of its children being recruited into that same class. Being an employee in a state enterprise was something to be envied. Access to university was opened up. Confucian, patriarchal and socially conservative ideology was pushed back.

The regime structured itself nationally around the three pillars – the army, which intervened in production, the administration and the Communist Party, not forgetting the security services. The CCP enjoyed a monopoly of political power at the heart of the state. In this vast country, the big picture remained complex nevertheless and the implementation of policies could vary significantly, depending on the relationship of forces at a regional and local level, including between different communist factions.

The Maoist leadership had not developed its own conception of social and economic transition. It based itself on the Stalinist model, which gave priority to heavy industry, although it also wanted to avoid the disaster of Stalin's agricultural policy. In its opposition to imperialism, it considered itself as an integral part of the 'socialist camp', but had not forgotten the orders, desertions and promises that Moscow had broken. The relationship between the USSR and China was marked by mutual suspicion: the seeds of the China-Soviet conflict of the 1960s had already been sown.

In the middle of the 1950s the leadership of the CCP was confronted by the question of what a 'Chinese road' to socialism could be. Stalin had died in 1953. Violent crises shook Eastern Europe – in East Germany, Hungary and Poland. The 'Secret Speech' of Nikita Khrushchev at the 20th Congress of the Soviet Communist Party in 1956, in which he denounced the crimes of Stalin, provoked a shock wave. In China itself, the limitations of the implementation of the first policies became evident and new social tensions arose.

Mao was a student of contradictions: if there is one thing which is eternal and universal, it is the existence of contradictions. His conception of history and his vision of transition were quite different to that of Stalinist ideology or the current Chinese leadership which sings the praises of the 'harmonious society'. For Mao, the fight for socialism was and remained the process of the class struggle. The internal contradictions of the People's Republic in his eyes constituted the main lever for social transformation.

This approach did not necessarily lead to a 'leftist' political line. In fact, in the middle of the 1950s, Mao believed that it was necessary to break with the period of the 'settling of accounts' with the counter-revolution which he had constructed following the conquest of power. He believed that there was a difference between the 'contradictions inside the people' which he considered to be 'non-antagonistic' and the 'antagonistic' contradictions with the counter-revolutionaries. As he was trying to liberate himself from the Stalinist model, he was trying to define a policy of balanced development which would not put undue pressure on the population. Some his most important writings deal with these preoccupations, such as the speech of 26 April 1956, delivered at a meeting of an enlarged Political Bureau of the CCP known as *On the Ten Great Relationships* or *The Correct Solution for the Contradictions amongst the People* (February 1957). He was relying on social mobilizations, controlled by but nevertheless outside of the party, to be a counterweight to the inflexibility of the regime – while at the same time reinforcing his own influence over the leadership.

But when the Chinese leadership attempted to implement this policy, nothing turned out as anticipated. The political and cultural freedom of the Hundred Flowers of 1957 opened the floodgates for a torrent of critiques against members of the party and the privileges of its cadres. Severe repression put an end to this outburst. In its wake, the CCP launched the Great Leap Forward which was designed to ensure the development of industry, infrastructure in the countryside and the establishment of social services within larger cooperatives. But the aims assigned to the Great Leap Forward became irrationally elevated, turning into a major economic crisis exacerbated by environmental problems, in addition to the breakdown of inter-regional communications, food shortages and famines which claimed millions of victims between 1959-61.

Mao's writing of the time indicates what he envisaged or was aiming at. But they also express the limits of his own historical experience, of his too marginal assimilation of international Marxist debates, of his empiricism and voluntarism. He had little to say about the working class, its organizations and labour relations (that was more Liu Shaoqi's field). He easily fell prey to the Stalinist dogma of the possibility of building socialism in one country.

At the same time, Chinese-Soviet tensions were becoming sharper:

Moscow was signing a treaty on nuclear testing with Washington and London from which China was excluded. Social tensions were again rising in China and the historical Maoist leadership was itself sharply divided. By 1965-1966, the factional struggles were no longer confined to the party apparatus. Mao called for the mobilization of the Red Guards while his rivals also called for street mobilizations. During this period, incorrectly called the 'Cultural Revolution', deep social, democratic and egalitarian aspirations were expressed. Whole sections of youth took the opportunity of an extraordinary freedom of action, criss-crossing the country. But chaos also swept the country. 'Revolutionary movements' fought each other. Red Guard units committed terrible crimes. The party and the administration were disintegrating and it required years for them to be rebuilt. Only the army maintained its unity. Mao turned to it to restore order, and repressed the youth and radical workers who had identified themselves with his call to 'fire on the general staff', that is the leadership of the CCP.

The development of a 'Chinese road' to socialism was cut short. Historical Maoism got lost in the convulsions of factional struggles. Thrown into confusion, the social and political movements didn't find a way forward. In these circumstances, the Cultural Revolution gave way to the particularly hard bureaucratic dictatorship of the Gang of Four with Jiang Qing, Mao's wife as its figurehead. At the international level, the normalisation of Chinese-American relationships led to the visit of US President Nixon to Beijing the in 1972. The arrival to power of the 'Shangai Group' certainly did not represent a 'left' turn.

Of the Revolution

Senile Maoism offers us only 'negative lessons'. Bureaucratic repression is equated to class struggle. The unilateral logic of the 'main enemy', in this case the USSR, is pushed in the most opportunistic manner, which is the alliance with American imperialism. This tragic ending should not overshadow the richness of the Chinese revolutionary experience. In addition to the themes touched upon previously, the following should also be examined.

The social components of the revolutionary process

In terms of the Second Chinese Revolution, attention is often paid to the large concentrations of workers, while for the Third Revolution the focus is on the peasantry (see above). Of course there were more components of the revolution than this; intellectuals, students, soldiers and impoverished groups such as homeless people or itinerant workers. In a remarkable manner, the diversity of these components was even reflected in the social origins of members of the Maoist leadership. Some were born within the elites and were 'traitors to their own class', as Zhou Enlai, who himself came from the milieu of mandarins, described them. Others came from different popular layers.

Chen Yi, the son of a magistrate, was a docker in France in 1919, then a dishwasher and then a worker at Michelin. Chen Yun came from a working class family. Deng Xiaoping came from a family of landowners. The father of Liu Shaoqi was a school teacher and that of Liu Bocheng (known as the 'One-eyed Dragon') was a travelling musician. Lin Biao came from the rural petty-bourgeoisie and Peng Dehuai from a rather poor peasant milieu from which he broke at the age of eleven, becoming homeless, 'uprooted' and living by doing odd jobs. Mao Zedong was born in a family of well-off peasants, while Zhu De came from impoverished peasants.

The 'semi-proletariat', 'lumpen' and impoverished masses played an important role all through the Chinese Revolution, including after 1949 when workers in unregulated jobs went into struggle during the Cultural Revolution. This struggle continues today with actions by 'internal migrants'; workers without official documents living illegally in the urban and industrial areas.

The struggle of women

Women cadres of the CCP also came from various social origins. Chen Shaomin, who came from a poor family, was a lace worker. Deng Yinchao was the daughter of a magistrate. Ding Ling came from a family of rich landowners. Kang Keqing came from an impoverished fishing family, who had to abandon her and she was then adopted by poor peasants and worked in the fields from a very early age. On the other hand, Xiang Jingyu was born to a well-off and modernist family. Yang Zhihua came from a family of silk merchants who owned land.

The Chinese leadership, particularly Mao, were initially heavily imbued with the movement of rebellion against Confucian ideology. This movement championed the emancipation of women and was very influential in progressive circles of the 1920s in the coastal regions. After the Long March, the CCP based itself in the rural areas of the interior which were much more conservative and its ideology suffered as a result. During the revolutionary struggle, village women were nevertheless organised as such not just to support the war effort but also against domestic violence.

It is particularly noteworthy that the first two great symbolic laws adopted by the new People's Republic were in the interests of women. This was the case of marriage law which gave equal rights to women, but also the law of agrarian reform, which allowed women to own land. When the 'spirit of the Paris Commune' was relaunched at the beginning of the Great Leap Forward, the development of collective services in village communes was aimed, amongst other things, at improving the condition of women. The Democratic Federation of Women had 20 million members in 1949 and 76 million in 1956.

However, despite important progress, women did not permanently and significantly break through the 'glass ceiling' of male domination. In 1957, despite being a rather young organisation with 25 per cent of its members under 25, there were only 10 per cent women. The higher up the structures of power, the fewer women there were. Of course, it is not just in China that this 'glass ceiling' exists, and in China like elsewhere the need for an autonomous women's movement is posed.

The limits of the Maoist conception of popular power

The question of autonomy of the mass organisations, in particular trade-unions, was raised during the 1950s right up to the highest levels of the party. The answer was negative. There is no autonomous movement of women (the League is run by the CCP) and no independent trade-unions.

Many writers considered that the social, economic and cultural conditions had not matured for popular socialist democracy in China. It is not possible to reject this argument straightaway. But the lessons of the Chinese experience is that the Maoist model did not work, even though Mao had declared his intention to fight the (re)appearance of a 'red bourgeoisie' feeding off 'bureaucratism', the conservative nature of the apparatus and privileges. More accurately, what worked in times of wars and revolutions no longer worked in times of peace.

In the Maoist model, the party cadre who 'listens to the masses' must gather their grievances and transmit them to the leadership. The 'transmission belt' of social organisations should work both ways: to implement the party's decisions but also to report back the state of mind of the population. In the end this 'transmission belt' worked only one way, leaving the leadership blind. The craze of the Great Leap Forward demonstrated the cost: many economic and social failures took place before the Political Bureau realised that the country was heading towards a catastrophe and rectified a policy which was far too 'maximalist'.

Mao was able to stress the legitimacy of disagreements, describing them as 'contradictions within the people'. But the recognition of liberties always remained a matter of political judgement and opportunity, and was therefore susceptible to suddenly being removed by the party, as happened during the Hundred Flowers. The special regime of the war period was carried over after the victory. Liberties were not a right, whatever was written in the Constitution. Politics continues to occupy the space of the law. One can understand that in these circumstances, the demands for socialist democracy and pluralism were central to the democracy movement of the early 1980s.

What the Chinese experience demonstrates is that 'socialist' or 'popular' democracy is a necessity and not a luxury. It is a practical necessity and not just an ideal. How is it possible to give it shape in a country such as China in the 1950s? The answer is not simple, but it is nevertheless necessary to pose the question, which means going beyond the limits Mao's legacy.

From one counter-revolution to another

Unlike the bourgeoisie, the bureaucracy does not exist as a ruling class at the moment of the revolution. It 'rises' progressively as a new ruling layer within the framework of the new state. A bureaucratic apparatus is 'crystallised' into a bureaucracy. This bureaucracy in formation codifies privileges and asserts its own collective interests. It ends up acting as a ruling class, even if it is not located within a mode of production which is distinctive to it, and in order to do that has to end the legacy of the revolution itself.

The process of bureaucratisation is insidious, but in the cases of the USSR and China, it is punctuated by revealing crises of the regime. The repression of the Hundred Flowers cut off the CCP from some progressive students and intellectuals. The failure of the Great Leap Forward provoked a loss of confidence between the party and whole sections of the peasantry while simultaneously undermining Mao's authority, which in turn provoked splits within the leadership. The massive repression during the Cultural Revolution led to a break between the Maoist faction and radical left-wing students and workers who, quite rightly, felt betrayed.

The historical Maoist team permanently broke up: eight of the eleven members of the Political Bureau were sent to prison or for re-education. Nine of the ten who were responsible for the main areas of work of the Central Committee were pushed aside. Of the 63 members of the Central Committee, 43 disappeared and 9 were severely criticized. This pattern was repeated from the top to the bottom. The CCP was in ruins in the aftermath of the Cultural Revolution, and the crisis of the leadership continued with the elimination of Lin Biao. The slow reconstruction of the party and the administration brought about the right conditions for the completion of the bureaucratic counter-revolution.

The bureaucratic order was first of all embodied by the Gang of Four which had only won a Pyrrhic victory. After Mao's death in 1976, the other factions of the apparatus took their revenge. It was the turn of Jiang Qing and her companions to be put in detention.

Following after the trauma of the Cultural Revolution, the rule of the Gang of Four, who discredited 'leftist' positions and 'revolutionary' language, created favourable conditions for the bourgeois counter-revolution. This was not obvious at the time. In a different national and international context, the reforms gradually introduced by Deng Xiaoping during the 1980s would not have necessarily led to the reconstitution of a Chinese capitalism. But at that time, it facilitated the convergence of sections of the bureaucracy with transnational Chinese capital established in Taiwan, North America and elsewhere. The CCP encouraged investments of expatriates and welcomed big capitalists into the party. In turn, the CCP appeared to be the only force able to maintain social order and guarantee the unity of the country, still threatened with fragmentation, in the eyes of transnational Chinese capitalists, who no longer had roots in the country. All this encouraged a gradual process of transformation of sections of the bureaucracy into a bourgeoisie – initially through the illegal privatisation of public assets and then legitimising the theft by changing the laws. The bourgeois counter-revolution took the form of a controlled transition to a semi-state and semi-private capitalism.

The reforms initiated by Deng Xiaoping opened the road for a regressive social upheaval, as radical as the one which followed the successful revolution of 1949. The economic assets of the state were partly dismantled and privatised. A new class of entrepreneurs was born. The old working class with protected status gave way on one hand to technicians and skilled workers, and on the other hand to a new proletariat born out of the rural exodus and often with no rights. After having first benefited from de-collectivisation, the Chinese peasantry found itself threatened with the same process of dispossession that fell upon peasants in the 'third world'. As a result, social inequalities exploded. The culture of the upstart triumphed and the rich are privileged while the poor are ignored once again. The counter-revolution has come full circle.

The bourgeoisie from one century to another

In the previous century, the development of the bourgeoisie was suffocated by the dictatorship of the Guomindang before being broken by the revolution. But today, Chinese capitalism benefits from the radical measures of the 1949 revolution. Without this, the country would have become a political and economic dependency of either Japan or more likely US imperialism. Furthermore like in other 'third world' countries, capital would have great trouble in freeing itself from traditional social relationships in the countryside and the weight of the 'gentry'.

Nationalism

The evolution of Chinese nationalism also illustrates the changes to the Communist Party. From the Opium Wars of 1839-1860 to the aftermath of the 1949 victory, nationalism has constituted an essential political and cultural framework for the resistance against Japanese and Western aggression, for the anti-imperialist struggle and for the desire for independence. At the same time it contained many variations and combinations such as between modernism and attachment to the past or internationalism and xenophobia.

In the 1920s to 1930s, the Communist Party included in its programme the right for self-determination for the peoples in the periphery of the Empire, such as in Tibet. Great Han chauvinism later strongly asserted itself as the new bureaucracy was strengthening its grip on the People's Republic, while Chinese-Soviet tensions degenerated into a major inter-bureaucratic conflict. The nationalism of an international power (small or great) is in some way consubstantial with the bureaucracy because the nation state is its framework of existence.

The current Chinese regime displays crude big power nationalism with its regional ambitions. The purpose of this nationalism is also to fill the ideological vacuum left by the discrediting of Maoism. It feeds off a deep 'Sino-centrism' inherited from a long history during which the ruling dynasties considered the countries on its periphery as vassal states: China must regain its glorious past.

'Study, study and study again'

Let us conclude on this famous saying of Lenin. We only learn from historical experience. Going from one unstable society in transition to another, 20th century China has gone from crisis to crisis. Its social structures have been thrown into chaos several times with the first wave of industrialisation, a very unequal 'development' from region to region, agrarian tensions, wars, revolution and counter-revolution.

Crises bring to light the underlying reality and contradictions working their way through a society. Modern China constitutes an extraordinary historical laboratory from which we can learn a lot, much more than I have briefly touched upon here. For example: the concrete manifestation of the dynamic of permanent revolution, the complexity of the relationship between parties and their social base, what allowed the CCP to function efficiently (including the role of experimentation, the conferences of cadres and the calibre of its militants), or what encouraged bureaucratism, privileges and the cult of personality.

The failure of the Great Leap Forward should not make us forget that the Maoist leadership was attempting to respond to real problems; such as how to develop the regions of the interior without creating a massive rural exodus towards the coastal metropolitan cities or how to envisage people's communes not just as production units but also the structure within which collective services can be delivered And even the Cultural Revolution, despite the tragic chaos into which it sank, cannot be reduced to a simple struggle between factions of the apparatus or a manipulation of the masses. It was not just a great play of lies in the theatre. If the chaos was so considerable and the mobilizations out of control, it is because there really were explosive social contradictions. There is always great benefit in studying the history of the 'revolutionary movements' of 1966-1968.

The manner in which the authorities were able to avoid social resistance in order to discard the entire revolutionary legacy is also very interesting. In Mao's time, peasants could not travel freely: they needed a permit to live in a city. This put a brake on rural exodus, which was the official intention of this policy. Nevertheless, later, when the rural exodus actually did begin, it created a mass of "internal migrants" without documents and therefore rights. This allowed the post-Mao regime to push the working class in the state enterprises – whose quiet resistance against the reforms had not been broken –out of the productive process. To this end, the regime used the Chinese 'migrant' workforce, particularly in the new industrial zones. This process of substitution is well known in Europe where public sector employees, with good terms and conditions of employment, are progressively replaced with private sector employees or temporary staff on worse terms. But in China, the substitution was carried out at the level of an entire section of the working class!

The emergence of China as a capitalist power owes a lot to the success of the previous Maoist revolution: liberating the country from imperialist domination, industrialisation, development of independent scientific knowledge and technologies, mass education and modernisation of society. Once Maoism was defeated, the new bourgeoisie stepped into its shoes. Having despised it, it could now be grateful for Maoism.

The big revolutions of the 20th century have lost their dynamism under the external pressure of imperialism, and because of the bureaucratic cancer destroying them from the inside. They nevertheless made a mark on the world. In particular, they have loosened the imperialist stranglehold, opened up breaches which now benefit some bourgeoisies of the 'third world'. But the game is not over. The memory of revolutions of yesterday can still contribute to the anti-capitalist uprisings of tomorrow, even in the heart of the new emerging powers, such as China.

July 2012

Bibliography

Belden, J. (1970) *China Shakes the World*. New York: Monthly Review Press.

Benton, G. (1982) *Wild Lilies, Poisonous Weeds: Dissident Voices from People's China*. London: Pluto Press.

Benton, G. (1996) *China's Urban Revolutionaries: Explorations in the History of Chinese Trotskyism, 1921–1952*. Atlantic Highlands, NJ: Humanities Press.

Bergere, M.-C. (1986) *Sun Yat-sen*. Stanford: Stanford University Press.

Bianco, L. (1971) *Origins of the Chinese Revolution, 1915–1949*. Stanford: Stanford University Press.

Carrere D'Encausse, H. & Schram, S. (1969) *Marxism and Asia*. London: Allen Lane.

Chan, A. (1985) *Children of Mao: Personality Development and Political Activism in the Red Guard Generation*. London: Macmillan

Chen, E. (1984) *China: Crossroads Socialism. An Unofficial Manifesto for Proletarian Democracy*. London: Verso.

Chesneaux, J. (1968) *The Chinese Labour Movement: 1919–27*. Stanford: Stanford University Press.

Croll, E. (1983) *Chinese Women since Mao*. London: Zed Books.

Hinton, W. (1966) *Fanshen: A Documentary of Revolution in a Chinese Village*. New York: Monthly Review Press.

Isaac, H. (1961) T*he Tragedy of the Chinese Revolution*. Stanford: Stanford University Press.

MacFarquhar, R. (1974, 1983, 1997) *The Origins of the Cultural Revolution*, Vol. 1: Contradictions among the People, 1956–1957; Vol. 2: The Great Leap Forward, 1958–1960; Vol. 3: The Coming of the Cataclysm, 1961–1966. Oxford: Oxford University Press.

Mao Zedong (1975) *Chairman Mao Talks to the People: Talks and Letters: 1956–1971*. Ed. S. Schram. New York: Pantheon.

Mao Tsetung (1992–9) *Mao's Road to Power: Revolutionary Writings 1912–1949*. (5 vols). Ed. S. Schram. Armonk, NY: M. E. Sharpe.

Rousset, P. *et al.* (2012), collection of studies and articles on the XXth Century China, Europe-solidaire (ESSF) website section 438: http://www.europe-solidaire.org/spip.php?rubrique438

Schram, S. (1969) *The Political Thought of Mao Tse-tung*. London: Pall Mall; New York: Praeger.

Snow, E. (1938) *Red Star Over China*. New York: Random House.

Wang, F.-H. (1991) *Memoirs of a Chinese Revolutionary*. New York: Columbia University Press.

Wolf, M. (1985) *Revolution Postponed: Women in Contemporary China*. Stanford: Stanford University Press.

Notes

1 This essay was translated by Fred Leplat and proof read by Geoff Ryan.

2 Pierre Rousset is member of the Board of Editors of *The International*

Encyclopedia of Revolution and Protest (2009) to which he also contributed on China, Philippines and Thailand. He is founding director (1982-1992), and presently fellow of the International Institute for Research and Education (Amsterdam).

3 The Comintern is an acronym for Communist International, also known as the Third International founded in 1917 and lasting until 1943.

4 The term peasantry is used here in the broad sense, including peasants as well as landless and small farmers.

HOW SOCIALIST IS THE CHINESE PARTY-STATE?[1]

Au Loong Yu reviews Wang Hui's *The End of Revolution: China and the Limits of Modernity*

The publisher of Wang Hui's book *The End of the Revolution: China and the Limits of Modernity*, Verso, described the book as follows: 'arguing that China's revolutionary history and its current liberalization are part of the same discourse of modernity, [2]Wang Hui calls for alternatives to both its capitalist trajectory and its authoritarian past.'

What follows is my review of the book in the light of this description: how far is this assessment correct and how relevant is it for those social activists who are pursuing just such an alternative in China?

Wang Hui is first and foremost a cultural and philosophy scholar who specializes in China's intellectual history. Therefore even though the book's name suggests a highly politicized debate, much of the content of the book is concerned with cultural and intellectual history of contemporary China, more so than its political aspects. For practical reasons I would like to focus my comments on Wang's political writings. This basically includes the first three chapters and accounts for half of the length of the book.

After defeating the 1989 democratic movement, the Chinese Communist Party under Deng Xiaoping pushed forward an agenda of full scale capitalist restoration combined with rapid industrialization, which was made possible only because of the opening up its market to foreign capital. The huge size of China and the gradual process of opening up gave enough space and time for domestic capital to grow fast enough to fend off foreign capital in becoming dominant in the commanding heights of the economy, which laid the base for the rise of China. This came at a price, though, and it was the workers in the state and collective sectors who paid for it with the loss of their jobs and the accompanying free medical care and accessible education for their children. Most intellectuals went along with this great tide of neoliberal attacks on the old welfare state. Most liberals enthusiastically embraced the downsizing of the workforce in the state sector, seeing it as part of the retreat of the all powerful state and the growth of an autonomous market which would lay the base for a democratic society in the future. The only complaint they had was that privatization was not accompanied by moderate constitutional reform.

The relevance of social movements

Wang Hui was among other leftists who argued against the liberal or neoliberal discourse. His earlier articles were published in English under the title *China's New Order* by Harvard in 2003. It contains a 1997 article *Contemporary Chinese Thought and the Question of Modernity* in which he mocks the liberal idea that the logic of the market is a free exchange of individual rights and therefore able 'to put certain restrictions on the excessive expansion of state power.' Echoing Karl Polanyi's[3] distinction of market and market society, he says:

> Within the dichotomy of planning/market, the notion of the 'market' has been assumed to be the source of 'freedom.' This notion, however, blurs the distinction between markets and a market society. If we can say that markets are transparent and function in accordance with the price mechanisms of the marketplace, then a market society would use market mechanism to govern the realms of politics, culture, and all other aspects of life – the working of market society cannot be distinguished from a monopolistic superstructure. It is in just this way that the notion of markets obscures the inequalities of modern society and its unequal structures of power.[4]

In this turn of the century debate, the liberals tried to defend market reform by disconnecting from it all the social ills which people commonly related to the reform: increasing social inequality, rampant corruption, open contempt for labour and environmental laws etc. They argued that neither the market, nor capitalism should be held responsible for these social ills; rather it was socialism and the party-state which should be held responsible. Wang Hui responded that they were:

> unable to come to an understanding of the fact that China's problems are also the problems of the world capitalist market and that any diagnosis of those problems must come to terms with the steadily increasing

> problems produced by the globalization of capitalism...Even the state behaviour that was the primary target of New Enlightenment thinking has been constrained by this huge market.'[5]

In China, where the memory of Mao still looms large, any attack on the capitalist reform from the left often results in references to Chairman Mao and his version of socialism to justify such an attack and looks to the party-state as the only salvation from the savageness of capitalist reform. They, like the neoliberals, rarely see movements from below as positive things. This was how a current of nationalist and statist discourses began to emerge among the so called New Left intellectuals – a label which Wang Hui himself finds problematic. Wang Hui may not be critical of the nationalist discourse, but he is one of the very few intellectuals who acknowledge the importance of social movements in the winning of social justice, be it under capitalism or socialism. Although he himself is not an activist he seems to pay attention to the birth of social movements in China. This is one of the threads running from *China's New Order* to *The End of the Revolution: China and the Limits of Modernity.* He reminds the liberals that when they hold western capitalism as a reference point for its respect for individual rights and its parliamentary democracy, they should not forget that these were the results of prolonged social movements. Not surprisingly, he is one of the few leftist intellectuals who value the 1989 democracy movement highly as well as direct participation in public affairs in general. Blinded by the false dichotomy of market/state and each seeking salvation from one end of the dichotomy, both neoliberals and nationalists are equally negative in their evaluation of the 1989 democratic movement and social movements in general, seeing the 1989 movement as either 'counter reform' or an 'anti socialist revolt incited by imperialism'. In the second chapter of the *The End of the Revolution: China and the Limits of Modernity* Wang Hui came to defend the movement by pointing out that there were socialist leanings deeply inherent in the movement[6]:

> Students, intellectuals, and other movement participants all supported reform (including political and economic reform) and demands for democracy ... What people were demanding was to proceed with economic reform, albeit upon the basis of democracy and justice; they were not demanding so-called absolute egalitarianism or moral idealism. These demands were in fundamental conflict with those put forward by the special interest groups demanding more radical privatization, even though the full extent of this conflict was not understood at the time.[7]

Having presented Wang Hui's ideas on market reform, social movements and democracy I think it is true to say that Wang Hui calls for alternatives to both a capitalist trajectory and authoritarian collectivism.

Socialist tradition: how much is left anyway?

One must also be aware of the limitations of such a call. Wang Hui's contribution lies in his attack on neoliberalism and the myth built around the market in the midst of a sharp turn to the right in government policy since the mid-1990s. However, he rarely carries his attack further to target the regime, which is precisely the force which has pushed through two waves of privatization; firstly of state and collectives enterprises, then, secondly, of urban land. Although Wang Hui is troubled by the rampant corruption of the party, he nevertheless only targets a force which he terms 'special interest groups':

> Among those strata participating in the 1989 social movement were those special interest groups that had massively benefited from the decentralization of power and benefits in the 1980s, and who were now dissatisfied with the impending adjustment policies.[8]
>
> The present issue of corruption not only involves individual corrupted officials but also the question of the relationship between social policy, economic policy and special interests. The development of the hydrocarbon industry and energy projects, for instance, are often impeded or led by individual special interest groups…Domestic and international special interest relations have now seeped into state mechanisms and even the process of legislation to an unprecedented degree. Under these conditions, the question of how the state can represent the so-called 'universal interest' has already become extremely tenuous.[9]

While the liberals put the blame for most social ills on the party-state alone, many left nationalists act in just the opposite way and blame the market economy alone so as to save the honour of the party. For the latter, if the party has a problem it is either from outside forces (the market or imperialism) or from some mysterious 'special interest group'. So logically it means that it is this 'special interest group', not the party, which is seen as responsible for the capitalist restoration and the imposition of an intensively anti-labour regime. It is problematic to make such an argument, however, because it is precisely the party which made the decision to crush the 1989 movement, to adopt full capitalist restoration from 1992 and to switch from being anti-bourgeois to deeply pro-bourgeois and anti-labour – to the extent that it sacked 60 million state-owned and collective enterprise workers. It is only in this context that this mysterious 'special interest group' can reap its own benefit at the expense of the people.

Wang Hui may not have gone as far as the left nationalists, but his uncritical usage of their discourse does not enable him to distance himself from them either.

May be it is because Wang Hui cannot speak freely. Anyone who is more or less informed about China knows about the heavy censorship there. Any writer who questions the official characterization of either the party, or the state, as bearers of 'socialism with Chinese characteristics', risks punishment from above. Indeed Wang Hui has already been punished by being sacked from the editorship of the well-known journal *Dushu*[10]. To avoid censorship it is common for Chinese writers to use all sorts of code to represent sensitive terms or critical ideas, and one of these terms is 'special interest group'. While this practice may enable writers to get around the censorship it also means sacrificing political clarity – people can have very different interpretations of what a 'special interest group' is. In fact, the rampant corruption in the party and the moral decay in society are increasingly compelling people to be more explicit in speaking out. Even the mainstream and well known economist Wu Jinglian now openly attacks the present system as 'crony capitalism' without fearing retaliation.

While I must take into account the factor of censorship, I suspect that the inner logic of Wang Hui's writings may carry enough weakness to obstruct him from further developing his call for a real alternative. The crux of the problem lies in the questions: What is the class role of the party-state since 1989? Which class interest has it served since then? If Wang Hui acknowledges the importance of providing his own answers to these questions but fears the consequences of speaking out he can choose silence. However, he, like many left nationalists, continues to give credit to the party-state which it does not deserve. He has done this by over-stressing the supposed living tradition of socialism within the party-state:

> The Chinese Communist Party, while thoroughly repudiating the Cultural Revolution, did not repudiate either the Chinese Revolution or socialist values ... This has created a twofold effect. First, the socialist tradition has functioned to a certain extent as an internal restraint on state reforms ... Secondly, the socialist tradition gave workers, peasants and other social collectivities some legitimate means to contest or negotiate the state's corrupt or inegalitarian marketization procedures.[11]

If there is a socialist tradition within the CCP the ensuing question will be: to what extent does it exist? Unfortunately, 'socialist tradition' theory proponents, including Wang Hui, never give us an answer. And with the two great waves of privatization and one great wave of dismissals of 60 million workers, should we not also ask the following questions as well: how capitalist is the CCP? Which tendency is more dominant within the party? I do not deny that occasionally common people may win partial victories when they invoke the socialist principle enshrined in the constitution, but one must not also lose sight of the other side of the story, namely that much much more has been lost, gone with the wind; that the party has undergone a qualitative change in its class role and now is at the service of capitalism, not socialism. No socialist tradition within the party-state has been able to stop this from taking place. No qualified accountant can draw up a balance sheet for a company just by entering a small sum of assets left without also entering the huge losses and mountains of debt it has incurred as well.

If Wang Hui has made that mistake, it also means that he is making a theoretical concession to the left nationalists, who have been trying to whitewash the Communist Party by arguing that although there was a break between Mao's China and Deng's China, fortunately it has only taken place in the economy, while at the political level there is more continuity because the Communist Party still rules and the 'socialist tradition' is still alive in the party-state, and what is left to do is to persuade this party-state to once again turn to the left. For instance, this is what Giovanni Arrighi argues in his book 'Adam Smith in Beijing'.[12] His idea was later echoed by a Taiwan scholar Huang Debei, who looks favourably at Mao's socialism and who argues that up until now the state of China is an autonomous Bonapartist state, which has not yet submitted to the class interest of the bourgeoisie, hence it can turn either to the right or to the left (how far?).[13] In contrast, I will argue that although in appearance the party-state stands above all classes, it does not imply that it is entirely 'neutral' or 'autonomous' from all classes. Rather, being autonomous in appearance does not contradict the fact that it is serving the narrow interest of the propertied class. Indeed a situation where the party-state maintains an iron grip over the country is precisely in the interest of the bourgeoisie because without this it is impossible to subject the more than 400 million strong working class – and the core of it bears the memory of a period where industrialization did not require the service of the bourgeoisie at all – to such miserable working conditions. The conclusion, therefore, is that since 1989 the party-state has betrayed its own founding principle to the full and has been transformed into a bourgeois party-state.

Sources of corruption: within or outside of the party?

This notion of 'socialist tradition' happily forgets that it is the party-state bureaucracy which constitutes the hard core of the newly born bourgeoisie at the expense of workers. In the course of making a U-turn in its class policy from anti-bourgeois to pro-bourgeois, the bureaucracy has first and foremost enriched itself. So when Wang Hui should look within the CCP for the source of capitalist restoration, he looks elsewhere. The truth, however, is that it does not require some exogenous 'special interests' to 'seep' into the state machinery to corrupt it; it *is* the source of its own degeneration.

For Marxists, the state is always an alienated force from society, and the bureaucracy always serves its own interest, and this is doubly the case when the state bureaucracy, the supposed 'public servants', have taken all political power from the hands of the 'masters of the house' very early on. They did this not just out of supposed necessity due to a state of siege during the cold war, but also because of their own need to monopolize the right to distribute social surplus and to benefit from it. Thus the degeneration of the party into a fully restoration party is more the result of endogenous than exogenous forces. Therefore leftists, including Wang Hui, erred in arguing that it was a wrong policy choice when the CCP embarked on the market reform; they forgot that what drove the CCP to take this decision was less to do with political correctness but more to do with the material interests of this hardened bureaucracy.

If there is any continuity between Mao's China and Deng's/post-Deng's China, it is less the continuity of a 'socialist tradition' but more the privileges of the bureaucracy as represented by the CCP: what 'ism' it follows is always of secondary importance; what is paramount is its monopoly of political power. As time went by the party became more and more conscious of the fact that without the introduction of the right to private property there was always the risk that its monopoly on political power, in order to distribute social surplus, would not pass down to its children. Therefore what characterizes the 60-year history of the People's Republic of China (PRC) is not just a break between an authoritarian collectivist past and an equally authoritarian capitalist present, but also the continuity incarnated in the monopoly of power by this party of the bureaucracy. The break occurs precisely because it was the only way to allow the party's rule to continue indefinitely. Therefore an alternative to both a capitalist trajectory and authoritarian collectivism can only be conceived by opposing the party, not giving it credit by saying that this party-state still carries certain aspects of 'socialist tradition', and is hence capable of self-reform, and what is left to do is to try persuading the CCP to make policy changes. To argue for the second option is bound to sow illusions among the rising new working class.

Where is the place of class struggle?

Wang Hui has not gone that far, but his characterization of the class nature of the party-state, or the lack of it, and his acceptance of the persistence of 'socialist tradition' theory, may act as a bridge to a position which simply accepts the role of lobbying the ruling party, while a revolt from below is both necessary and urgent. Indeed it is striking that in Wang Hui's writings the issues of classes, state and bureaucracy and their relation to contemporary China are always brief and abstract, if not largely missing. Nor is there any account of class struggle as one of the forces in moving contemporary Chinese history forward. In fact, Wang Hui treats the subject of the dramatic transformation of the role of the party-state so lightly that he just summarizes his observation in a few sentences in his first English book:

> The modern socialist movement was brought about by an analysis of the internal contradictions of capitalism and by the aspiration to overcome these contradictions, but the practice of socialism not only failed to complete the task of this aspiration, but it ended by being absorbed into global capitalism. At the same time, capitalism derived from socialism and from various movements for the protection of social rights opportunities for reform and self-critique, to the point where today, it is impossible to define socialism or capitalism in their original senses on the basis of the autonomous unit of the nation-state.[14]

It seems that there is a dose of fatalism in this description of the failure of socialism; that defeat is just a natural evolution of socialism. This kind of proposition makes too much of a concession to the neoliberal discourse of 'transitional economy', according to which the socialist movement in the 20th century was just a momentary departure from the market economy and its centrally planned economy was fated to abdicate its position to market economy once again as this is the only viable way of organizing an effective production and distribution system. Such a discourse is too a-historical, however, because it leaves out altogether the element of class struggle. Wang Hui's own account does not fare much better. Although Wang Hui highly values the 1989 democratic movement, he was not able to see this as a massive revolt against the CCP's agenda of capitalist restoration, that the aspiration of the majority of the participants was precisely an aspiration for 'alternatives to both its capitalist trajectory and its authoritarian past', that the intensity of the movement had for a time made the top leaders of the CCP so nervous that the latter feared that if they did not act fast to crush the movement the army might split. Although Deng Xiaoping eventually succeeded in his dirty work, after the crackdown most top leaders were probably still haunted by the scene of the biggest, boldest and most direct challenge to the CCP ever seen in the history of the PRC. It left such a deep mark in the memory of the bureaucracy that it became so paranoid about a movement from below that in the ensuing 20 years it turned China into a perfect police state by contributing a budget for internal security even larger than its budget for defence.[15] Therefore, neither was there anything natural about the metamorphosis of the class role of the CCP, nor was the capitalist restoration entirely fated by mysterious a-historical forces. Any suggestion of this sort is in fact depoliticizing a very political subject.

Yes, I am bringing back the old fashioned debate of capitalism and socialism, of classes, class struggles and the state. But this is not the same kind of squabbles as among little sects which are more interested in abstract political formula as they understand it, than real struggles in the real world. On the contrary, I bring it back precisely because many former state-owned or collective enterprise workers have asked these sorts of questions many many times over: why did the apparently most 'revolutionary' party end up becoming a party of restoration? Why was the CCP under Deng Xiaoping able to make this turn? Why was there no serious opposition to this turn? What is the nature of the CCP and the state it controls anyway? Isn't it true that it has now entirely become the protector of the exploiting classes?

What is most unfortunate is that few leftist intellectuals ask the same questions. Hence, even when some of them argue against the market and capitalism, either they do so in the most abstract and academic way (for instance reaffirming the priority of 'equality' over 'efficiency'), or if they ever argue in a more political way it is always trapped in the false dichotomy of state and market, and they end up supporting the party-state's continuous monopoly of power as a means to fight off capitalism. In this way they have written off the working class and socialism altogether.

Wang Hui is one of the few who performs better than most of the other leftists and part of his writing can act as a starting point to an alternative, but since he also makes so much of an intellectual concession to the official ideology his writings can also lead in the opposite direction.

While writing this comment I have tried my best not to misunderstand Wang Hui. It has proved to be a difficult task, however, because his writing, as usual, tends to be abstract and so densely loaded with so many references to schools of ideas in one single essay that it sometimes makes one doubtful of its usefulness. What is more, his Chinese essays can be very different from his English ones even if they bear the same title. For instance the essay *Depoliticized Politics: From East to West* is not a full translation of the Chinese original, rather, it is heavily abridged to just 15 per cent of the original. I am not sure of the reasons for making such a short summary of the original but, frankly, in my view the Chinese original is not quite so successful in bringing out clearly his train of thoughts. Another leftist writer Li Tuo complained, in a recent interview, about how he thought Wang Hui's style damaged the effective expression of his ideas.[16]

Wang Hui on national minorities

Western readers are warned that it is difficult to make full and fair comment on Wang Hui by reading English translations alone. For instance, the English translation of *The Year 1989 and the Historical Roots of Neo-Liberalism in China* deletes altogether from the Chinese original Wang Hui's wholly negative evaluation of the right to self-determination for national minorities.[17] His critique is merely based on associating the right to self-determination with the imperialist agenda in Yugoslavia, forgetting that it was Marxists, like Lenin, who were major proponents of the right to self-determination. By arguing in such a way, he is not doing enough justice both to the principle of self-determination and to all the oppressed minorities in the world, including China.

Indeed, Wang Hui, in another Chinese essay which was later published in book form along with other essays, denies the right to self-determination to Tibetan people by quoting approvingly Zhou Enlai, who rejected the right to self-determination. According to Zhou, in order for self-determination to work without creating conflicts among minorities, there must be a situation where these minorities each occupy a distinctive territory, as was allegedly the case in Tsarist Russia. That was why the Russian revolution could allow minorities the right to self-determination and secession and reunite them into a federation of soviets states. Since China, unlike the Soviet Union, – so the argument goes – had a Han majority and the minorities all mixed geographically, China should hence not adopt federalism; rather, there was no choice but to choose a unitary state. The second reason given by Zhou was that a federalist state solution (with the right to self-determination as its prerequisite) might invite intervention from imperialism.[18] Anyone with a fair amount of knowledge of the Russian revolution and its position on minorities knows very well that Zhou's remark was factually wrong and theoretically invalid. For Lenin, self-determination should never automatically imply secession or the founding of a new state or federalism.

It is disappointing to see that Wang Hui quotes Zhou approvingly.

But let me not be too harsh on Wang Hui. If I have to look somewhere else in search of an alternative it is less because of Wang Hui's personal failure, but more because of the general failure among the intellectuals to think independently in relation to both the official ideology and to western liberalism, or to the false dichotomy of state versus market. If the party-state, despite its betrayal of its founding principle, still maintains a spiritual hold on left intellectuals, this hold comes less from the party's supposed 'socialist tradition', but more from its stunning success in combining capitalist restoration with rapid industrialization, which in class terms means success in its apparent independence from all classes and its ability to make classes disappear and appear at will. It is the great success of this 21st century Leviathan which has stunned all classes and keeps them in submission. Anyone who seriously looks for a left alternative is, therefore, required to first look at the history of the PRC in terms of class, bureaucracy, and the state. It is precisely this aspect which few left intellectuals are able to provide in a satisfactory way.

10 April 2011

Notes

1 This is an edited version of an essay which was first published in *New Politics*, New York, Summer 2011, Vol:XIII-3
2 *The End of the Revolution: China and the Limits of Modernity*, by Wang Hui, Verso, 2011
3 Karl Polanyi, 1886-1964 a Hungarian economic historian whose most influential book was *The Great Transformation* but whose *Trade and Markets in the Early Empires* deals with China.
4 *China's New Order*, Wang Hui, Harvard 2003, 176
5 *China's New Order*, 180
6 *The End of the Revolution*, P. 22
7 *The End of the Revolution*, 32-33
8 *The End of the Revolution*,31
9 Preface of *The End of Revolution*, xxviii.
10 A Chinese literary journal published monthly since April 1979
11 *End of revolution*, 18
12 See p. 332 and 369.
13 *Dangdai zhoingguo guyong gongren zhi yanjiu* (Research on Contemporary Chinese Workers),Weber Publication International Ltd., 2008, Taipei, p. 18
14 *New Order* ,183
15 http://www.bbc.co.uk/zhongwen/trad/china/2011/03/110307_china_securityspending.shtml
16 *Jiushi niandai de fenqi daodi zai nail?* What was the differences of opinions

in the 1990s?, Interview with Li Tuo, 17 Aug, 2007, Southern Metropolitan Weekly, abridged version. The full version was published in the Utopia Electronic Monthly, Sept 2007.

17 *Qu zhengzhihua de zhengzhi,* (The Politics of De-Politicization), Joint Publishing Company, 2008, p. 150.

18 Quoted from Wang Hui's essay *Dongxi zhijian de 'xizang wenti'* (The Tibet Issue in the East and in the West), in *Yazhou Shiye: zhongguo lishi de xushu* (Asia Perspective: the Narrative on China's History), Oxford, Hong Kong, 2010, p. 140-141.

LIU XIAOBO AND THE CHINESE LIBERALS[1]

Au Loong Yu

In 2010 Liu Xiaobo was awarded the 2010 Nobel Peace Prize for 'his long and non-violent struggle for fundamental human rights in China'. He was sentenced to 11 years' imprisonment in 2009 on charges of 'inciting subversion of state power', after he and dozens of well-known Chinese intellectuals launched the Charter 08 to call on the Chinese government to respect basic civil and democratic rights. The Norwegian Nobel Committee's statement praises Liu as one who has been 'a strong spokesman for the application of fundamental human rights in China. He took part in the Tiananmen protests in 1989; he was a leading author behind Charter 08, the manifesto of such rights in China.'

Anybody who claims to be a defender of civil rights should protest against the prison term, since no one should be treated as a criminal simply for what they have spoken or written. This also led many people, within and without China, to applaud Liu being awarded the Nobel Peace Prize, seeing this as an acknowledgement of both his innocence and his contribution to human rights' advocacy in China.

On the other hand, on the Utopia (*Wuyouzhixiang*) website, which is well known for being associated with some of the 'new leftists', articles were posted echoing the authorities' attack on Liu. In one of these articles, the author Xibeifeng denies that Liu's sentence has anything to do with freedom of speech, arguing that Liu's advocacy for Charter 08 is as criminal as a drunk driver demanding freedom to violate the rules of traffic.[2]

After Liu was awarded the Nobel Peace Prize, two professors in Hong Kong, Barry Sautman and Yan Hairong, argued that:

> There was no need to imprison Liu ... Rather, there has only been a need to bring to light Liu's self-proclaimed goals. If most Chinese, especially

> the non-elite majority, knew about his prescribed path for China, they would turn away from him as from someone with ignoble things on offer. [3]

By this they mean that Liu's pro-US and pro-privatisation positions are not beneficial to the Chinese people.

The problem with this comment is that it ignores the fact that it is the authorities who ban Liu's 'prescribed path for China' from being known to the Chinese public in the first place.

A Human Rights Charter that excludes the working people

It was both sad and ironic to see that the website Utopia, after posting articles implicitly applauding Liu's imprisonment, was closed by the authority in 2012 after posting articles supporting the former Chongqing chief Bo Xilai.

It is equally true that the Charter's interpretation of the term human rights carries strong class bias, however. While it emphasises the protection of 'private property', in the midst of a great privatisation, it does not bother to mention basic labour rights like the right to independent trade unions and collective bargaining. It only mentions in passing the right to strike, along with many basic rights.

What is also lacking is a critique of the terrible polarisation of wealth in the course of the capitalist market reform. In rural areas, CCP officials have expropriated agricultural surplus through direct taxes or through market measures to the extent of bankrupting farmers, leaving them no choice but to migrate to cities for jobs. These peasants are then expropriated a second time by the bourgeoisie under the prison-like factory regime. It is very clear that both the ruling party and the private business class benefit from the denial of basic rights to working people and farmers. To address this it is necessary to redistribute social wealth and recover these basic rights of working people. The Charter's silence on the vast injustices of sweatshops and the enrichment of the new bourgeoisie once again exposes its commitment to the class interest of the new rich, even though it attempts to speak for all citizens, the toiling masses included.

On the other hand, point 14 of the Charter explicitly calls for the protection of private property:

> We should establish and protect the right to private property and promote an economic system of free and fair markets. We should do away with government monopolies in commerce and industry and guarantee the freedom to start new enterprises. We should establish a Committee on

> State-Owned Property, reporting to the national legislature, which will monitor the transfer of state-owned enterprises to private ownership in a fair, competitive, and orderly manner. We should institute a land reform that promotes private ownership of land, guarantees the right to buy and sell land, and allows the true value of private property to be adequately reflected in the market.

Any comparison between the old Czechoslovak Charter 77 and the Chinese Charter 08 is out of the question: Charter 77 never made such an appeal. With this call, Charter 08 has become a tool for privatisation and as such is in the service of the new rich and party officials. In place of the CCP's crony privatisation Charter 08 wants a 'fair and competitive' privatisation. It is not clear how it will be done. The Russian nomenclatura have already done this through voucher privatisation, whereby the vouchers owned by ordinary people have simply ended up in the pocket of the new rich, along with their savings and job security.

Even in the era of petty commodity production where one may talk about 'fair and competitive' market exchange, the competition it involves necessarily brings with it the polarisation of the rich and poor. In a capitalist market where there already exists a class which owns simultaneously the means of production (*and* political power, in the case of China), and where the labouring class has nothing but its labour power to sell, a 'fair and competitive' privatisation is nothing but nonsense.

It is really ironic that the authors of Charter 08 have drafted this document at a moment when the greatest market failure since 1929 is unfolding on a global scale. Since 2008, prices nosedived in the US stock and property markets, but the neoliberal government decided that these market prices were neither fair nor just; hence it wasted billions of dollars to stop their further decline. It was soon followed by China. Ironically, the liberals' only complaint about the Chinese government bailout is not about the latter's intervention on a self-regulatory market, rather it is about the latter only bailing out state owned enterprises but not private capitalists.

It also goes without saying that indiscriminately putting the ownership of consumer goods by working people and the ownership of means of production under the same category of 'private property' only serves the purpose of covering up the true nature of such property. On top of this is the fact that in China today much of the private property of the new rich comes from plundering state-owned enterprises in great waves of privatisation. To strengthen the legal protection on private property indiscriminately serves the purpose of legitimising theft of publicly owned properties.

Chinese liberals are not only unable to learn anything from the past and the present; they also exhibit a hugely undemocratic position when they call for the freedom of selling and buying of farmlands. It never occurs to them to ask whether this is also the wish of the 800 million peasants (of whom 200 million are 'floating population'). Various surveys show that most of them do not like the idea at all. Li Changping, a rural expert, has argued convincingly that most peasants do not want their collectively owned land to be turned into their private land. One of the main reasons is the fact that peasants today are most likely to be in debt to the rural cadres (who most often than not are rich), and if there is privatisation of farm land their creditors will be able to seize their collectively owned land.[4]

A rural migrant labour NGO has done a small survey showing that 64 per cent of interviewees disagree with the free sale of land, 42 per cent of those who disagree think 'free sale of land will result in social polarisation of wealth and the return to old pre-1949 China'.[5] The 1949 revolution, despite its shortcomings and the fact that many of its accomplishments have now been undone (notably job security), lifted Chinese society to a new historical plane by the elimination of pre-capitalist landlord ownership. In contrast, the Charter sees the 1949 revolution as entirely destructive and negative, a view which I cannot share.

As a matter of fact, the present arrangement of collective land ownership and the right of usage for individual households (the family contracting system) gives peasants both the guarantee that land would not be concentrated in the hands of the new rural rich through the free sale of land, and their right to their contracted plot of farmland and land for their house. The present laws also give the village committee an exclusive right to handle the collective farmland. Thus in many cases the peasants have succeeded in stopping land sales to the rich or to cronies of officials by exerting their rights through the committees. If the liberals succeed in persuading the CCP to adopt their call for free sale of farmland, then in practice this amounts to overthrowing the democratic rights of farmers, which is in opposition to what the Charter claims to want.

We are in favour of paying fair prices for agricultural products. Low prices have robbed peasants of the necessary surplus and cash to invest. To address this problem people need to look beyond the market, however, because the factors which contribute to the lack of market power for peasants really lie beyond the market and enter the realm of political power. The peasants, like any common citizen in China, are denied basic civil liberties, let alone democratic rights, which explains, partly, their vulnerability. An additional factor which worsens the situation of the peasants is that they are treated as second class citizens under the household registration system. Also they are robbed of any kind of official representation in the party-state altogether. While workers, youth and women each have their own 'mass organisation', and the official trade union head sits in the politbureau, the peasants, since 1949, have not had any kind of 'mass organisation' for them, although they comprised the overwhelming majority of the People's Liberation Army that brought the CCP to power. It is true that official representation for different social groups in the party-state lacks substance, but the fact that peasants do not even have a single representative shows how marginalised they have been in the political and social lives of the country. For the peasants to be empowered, they not only need basic civil liberties, but also to use these rights to organise themselves to defend their interests. In other words, we need a 21st century peasant movement, side by side with the workers' movement.

This, however, is exactly what the liberals and the new rich most fear – and ironically, is equally shared by certain of the new left who in fact are nationalists. Hence they try to shift the debate to the half-false issue of 'unfair market prices' or the entirely false issue of a 'lack of a free market in land'. I must, though, qualify our remarks by adding the comment that this is only false from the perspective of peasants; whereas it is entirely valid for both the local officials and private business. After privatising the state owned enterprises and urban land, they are now looking for a third wave of privatisation: the privatisation of rural land. Whereas the top leaders of the CCP have not dared to risk rebellion by doing this, the liberals, in the service of local officials and the business elites, have been tirelessly pushing the government on this matter.

Professors Sautman's and Yan's critique of Liu's neoliberal position is not incorrect in itself; the problem with their criticism, however, is that they are both inconsistent and have lost all sense of proportion. If Liu's advocacy for privatisation should be criticised, then by the same logic the CCP must also be criticised even more forcefully, because it is the latter, not Liu, who actually pushed through privatisation. Curiously, Sautman and Yan do not criticize the CCP except to remark that 'there was no need to imprison Liu', as if the CCP's only error was having taken a slightly superfluous step. One may wonder if there is more miserable misjudgement than this.

But when some new left writers condemned the authors of Charter 08 as serving US imperialism, this is a gross exaggeration. No part of the Charter can be interpreted as political support for the US. Yet it is equally true that Liu was among those liberals who enthusiastically campaigned to support Bush's war on Iraq, saying that Bush's war was 'promoting liberty and freedom' when it toppled the 'evil regime' of Saddam Hussein[6]. Liu's record on the Iraq war should make us sceptical about his status as a genuine defender of human rights. One must be able to differentiate between the Charter and Liu, however. If I am also sceptical about the Charter it is more because it bears the birth mark of business elitism with its clause on privatisation, and less because it, allegedly, directly supports US imperialism.

How liberal are the liberals?

Liberals like Liu are a bit different from the liberal right-wing, who are in fact the worst kind of neoliberals as they vigorously defend corruption. The well known economist Zhang Weiying argues that corruption is beneficial to economic development under the condition of government's monopoly of important branches of the economy.[7] Another well known economist says that economics study is amoral and value free, and that if economists consider that market economy is the optimal economy it is not because it is morally good but because it enables the free exchange of commodities between common people, including immoral people.[8] For them, the vision for justice should be subject to the priority of economic efficiency. Another well-known liberal Li Zehou argues in his book *Good Bye Revolution* for a theory of four rigid stages of social development: first people can only strive first for economic development, followed by the realisation of individual liberty, social justice and finally political democracy, and that the present period only allows the full play of the first stage.[9]

Although Liu may not defend corruption with such intensity, he or his co-thinkers in general agree with the neoliberals' thesis on the roots of corruption: it is the unlimited expansion of state power and its infringement on the natural equilibrium of a private property based market which gives rise to corruption. For them the state is the root of all evils while the private property based market is the source of all kinds of freedom, from economic to political. In the words of Liu, 'to sum up, the root of social injustice originates not from the injustice of private property but rather from the (state) power expropriating, intensively, private property.'[10] That is also why Liu, like the neoliberals, put fighting for the further strengthening of the legal right of private property as a priority. Back in 2003 there was a debate among liberals as to whether they should advocate an amendment of the constitution to strengthen the protection of private property (although article 11 of the constitution at that time already explicitly stated that the legitimate interest of sole proprietors and private enterprises will be protected by the state, and likewise, article 13 stipulates that legitimate property of citizens will also be protected, but the liberals consider these clauses as inadequate). Certain liberals opposed the move, as they saw this, within the context of one party dictatorship, would necessarily fail to protect the private property of common citizens which was the original purpose of the idea. Therefore they argued that the priority should rather be advocating for an amendment to abolish the one party dictatorship. Liu Xiaobo joined the debate with conciliatory rhetoric but his conclusion is clear:

> Firstly, the constitutional protection of private property is one of the basic institutions of constitutional democracy on which a whole series of economic, political, and legal system, along with the institutional arrangement of the relationship between individual and government and those between rights and power, depend ... To protect private property through the constitution enables the individual to pursue his or her happiness independently, and which empowers him or her with legal rights to defy the arbitrary coercion of the government.'
>
> If one does not enjoy the protection of private property, even if one owns a mountain of gold one will not feel secure. In contrast, if one enjoys this protection then even if he or she only owns a piece of bread he or she will feel his or her property secure.[11]

It seems it never occurred to him that precisely because the rich person owns a mountain of gold and the poor person owns a piece of bread it necessarily creates a situation where the latter must sell his or her labour power to the former in exchange for wages so that he or she can have a meal more than just a piece of bread. His failure to take note of the inequality between employers and employees can be explained by his method: Liu is satisfied with observing, with great admiration, the equal exchange between the rich and the poor in the labour market, but never bothers to follow the footstep of the rich leading the poor to his or her factory to observe how the former squeezes as much labour as possible out of this poor worker. His total neglect of the plight of the working people is, again, not accidental; rather it is the inherent element in his thinking. He consistently campaigns against the idea of direct democracy which for him simply means rule by the mob, and which must be avoided at all cost. When he and his co-thinkers argue for constitutional democracy his main purpose is precisely to make sure that the CCP will not be overthrown by a popular revolt, a gradual political reform under the CCP will be able to fend off any chance for a radical democracy.[12] Liu's soft stance on the CCP drew open fire from liberals who fled to the US. In a petition letter to the Norwegian Nobel Committee, a group of exiled dissidents wrote that they thought Liu was not the appropriate candidate for the prize because he had not been standing firm in upholding human rights, and had even practically cooperated with the authorities by inappropriately praising the CCP's human rights rhetoric.

Liu's idea of moderate political reform, however, is to be realised in rigid stages. That is why Liu and his co-thinkers considered pushing for strengthening private property rights through amending the constitution as a priority in 2003. They succeeded. In March 2004, after more than a year of a strong liberal campaign, the People's Congress passed the amendment to the constitution, making compensation to the owners necessary if their properties are requisitioned by the state.[13] They scored another victory when in 2007 the People's Congress passed the Property Law which further strengthens the protection of private property. Their biggest success is making it legal that the 70 years' limit of land use right will be extended indefinitely. With this law it practically provides solid legal protection for the privatisation of urban land by municipal government officials and their cronies. The liberals' success in this also signifies their terrible failure in bringing democratic reform. With the strengthening of private property of the new rich the Chinese people only got a simultaneous strengthening of the despotic state. It is not difficult to see with hindsight that objectively speaking, by prioritising the issue of private property over the struggle for democracy, Liu and his co-thinkers have advanced not the interest of the working people but only the interests of the bourgeoisified bureaucracy and the private bourgeoisie. In this instance Liu is not so different from the neoliberals.

The obsession with the supposed magical nature of private property is not confined to Liu. Indeed it is common among the liberals. Another well-known liberal He Qinglian tries to differentiate herself from the neoliberals' stance that the study of economics is value free, by reasserting the value of justice. The title of her book is self explanatory: *Economics and Human Solicitude.*[14] However, like many liberals she puts defending and strengthening private property rights as her most important concern. She quotes approvingly Locke's idea that a natural property right is established when a man 'mixed his labour' with nature. But she quotes without knowing that Locke does not necessarily mean his own labour but also his servants' labour when he wrote 'the Grass my Horse has bit; the Turfs my Servant has cut; and the Ore I have digg'd in any place where I have a right to them in common with others, become my *Property*'. For Locke, Ellen Wood wrote, his own digging is the same as his appropriating the fruits of his servants' cutting.[15] This isthe best illustration of how the peoples' labour ends up being appropriated by property owners which is being justified by He Qinglian.

Who is the bearer of democracy?

In the 1980s and early 1990s there was a popular belief that the entrepreneur class was going to be the bearer of the Chinese democratic movement. Immediately after the crackdown in Tiananmen, an entrepreneur who fled overseas wrote 'the fact that the Chinese middle class has not yet been formed meant that the 1989 democracy movement was doomed to failure. Without the middle class there could not be any real democracy.'[16] This proposition is now much less popular. This is simply because the new entrepreneur class never bothers about democracy. The new Chinese business elite, which owes their very own existence to the one-party state and which benefits from the state's denial of civil rights to farmers and workers, are simply not interested in supporting the Charter's call for the realisation of basic civil and democratic rights. On the contrary, they need the one-party state to help them to stamp out any possibility of a labour movement. This is the main reason why the circles of liberal intellectuals dedicated to liberal democracy remain so small and powerless in the face of repression. If the business elite wants to push forward their agenda of more privatisation, isn't lobbying the CCP mandarins or becoming the latter's cronies much easier and more practical than the risky act of endorsing the Charter? In her book *China's New Business Elite*, Margaret Pearson explains why the market reform and the birth of this class have not led to civil society or democratisation:

> Members of China's business elite have shown few signs of becoming an independent, activist political force. They desire to escape from politics, not to engage in it or to create a 'civil society'… Having gained structural independence, they try to rebuild informal ties to the state. Members of the business elite are characterised by neither strong horizontal ties to each other, nor strong links to other societal actors, both of which we expect in an emergent civil society. '[17]

It is to the credit of Liu that he continues to advocate for political reform, which has cost him his liberty. Yet his idea of seeing democracy necessarily originating from private property also deeply weakens his cause. This is economic determinism of the worst kind, and a greatly mistaken version at that. The truth is that in general there is no necessary link between private property and democracy – even if it is just a weak version of democracy, namely liberal democracy. This is especially the case in terms of the Chinese bourgeoisie.

If the Charter authors remain true to their call for civil and democratic rights, the only forces they can rely on are farmers and workers, who for an extended period have been fighting against exploitation and state repression. The liberals do not welcome their struggles, however, fearing that any such movement would necessarily go beyond formal political rights and demand the redistribution of wealth, in addition to promoting resistance to privatisation. This is also in line with their open hostility towards mass movements in general and the labour movement in particular. These are regarded as potentially hazardous elements which may lead to senseless killings or 'class struggle' as they perceive it. The Cultural Revolution is their most often-cited best example of rule by the mob. But the Cultural Revolution was nevertheless largely a movement and even a grand plot by Mao to topple his opponents, even if it exhibited elements of spontaneity when at a certain moment he could no longer entirely control it.

The events of the Cultural Revolution should not lead us into believing that a labour democratic movement equates to rule by the mob. When the liberals throw away the baby with the bath water they necessarily end up where they were 20 years ago: not only hated by the one-party state, but also isolated from all classes in society. The capitalists do not need their services, while farmers and workers are indifferent to them, if not altogether alienated by their neoliberal agenda.

In short, Liu's mission of simultaneously trying to lobby the CCP for gradual political reform and to rely on this same party-state to tame the increasingly discontented toiling masses is like squaring a circle. With the rise of local popular revolt some of the liberals may try to adjust their open hostility towards the labour movement, especially when a 'depoliticised' trade union movement is now on offer from Han Dongfang's China Labour Bulletin which promises employers that they are their real friends.[18] This kind of clever tactical manoeuvring will not make their grand strategy more progressive however.

We support those parts of Charter 08 which uphold basic civil rights and democratic rights, first and foremost because without them the toiling masses have no means whatsoever to defend their direct or historical interests. On the other hand, writers associated with the Utopia website continue to show hostility towards democratic aspirations of all sorts. It is because they continue to see the one-party state as a solution to social problems created by market reform. In opposition to the liberals' proposition that a free market based on private property is the source of freedom, they opine that salvation from the predatory market comes from the state and the state alone. But this is not just any state, no; this could only be the current CCP regime. Hence they tend to downplay the importance of the struggle for civil and democratic rights. In the worst case, implicitly if not explicitly, they support the one-party state in the name of maintaining social stability. Sautman and Yan condemned Liu 'who has long been financed by the U.S. government's National Endowment for Democracy, proposes an instant shift to electoral democracy as the solution to China's problems.' They see electoral democracy as bad for China because:

> States that have made the transition to electoral democracy at low levels of wealth (and China is still very much a developing country) have low levels of development and considerable instability... In many cases the transition to electoral democracy in developing countries worsens rights.

Sautman and Yan indeed went even further than the CCP. Whereas the latter justified its despotic rule by saying that Chinese people do enjoy all rights enshrined in the constitution –an absolutely stupid defence – Sautman and Yan provided the CCP with a more sophisticated argument by telling Chinese people that fighting for electoral democracy now jeopardises their own interests.

The dichotomy of market versus state is a false dichotomy in the first place. It only reflects the differences between two sections of the bourgeoisie, namely the private bourgeoisie and the bureaucratic bourgeoisie. However confrontational their fight between themselves, they share the same fears in relation to a rise of social movements from below, and therefore share the same interest in maintaining the rule of the economic and/or political elites over working people.

For working people, only when both the market and the state are put under their direct control can they make both institutions less alien and gradually make their elements of economic and political compulsion wither away. This is what I mean by direct democracy or socialism if you like. Hence real leftists should demand a kind of democracy which goes beyond liberal democracy; to empower working people to have direct access to the means of production, i.e., to put an end to capitalism. Yet free elections, even if not a sufficient condition for socialism, are nevertheless its necessary condition. Therefore working people should fight for free elections unreservedly. Any attempt to minimize the importance of advocating democratic rights, including free elections, is objectively justifying the absolutism of the one-party state.

Rosa Luxemburg once reminded us that

we have always distinguished the social kernel from the political form of bourgeois democracy; we have always revealed the hard kernel of social inequality and lack of freedom hidden under the sweet shell of formal equality and freedom – not in order to reject the latter but to spur the working class into not being satisfied with the shell, but rather, by conquering political power, to create a socialist democracy to replace bourgeois democracy – not to eliminate democracy altogether.[19]

Notes

1 This essay is a lengthened version of two articles in 2010 and 2009 respectively: 'Neither Washington nor the Party State', *Against the Current*, 'A Human Rights Charter that Excludes the Working People', *China Labour Net*. The current version was proof read by Geoff Ryan.
2 *Liu Xiaobo huojiang shi xinzhiminzhuyi zai zhongguo zouxiang zhibian de biaozhi* (Liu Xiaobo being Awarded with the Peace Prize Signifies Neo-Colonialism in China Now Reaches Qualitative Changes) , http://www.wyzxsx.com/Article/Class4/201010/190345.html
3 Liu Xiaobo Deserves an Ig Nobel Peace Prize *South China Morning Post*, Oct. 12, 2010
4 *Shenyan nongcun tudi siyouhua* (Be Prudent about Proposing Privatization of Farm Land), Li Changping, http://club.kdnet.net/dispbbs.asp?id=629177&boardid=52
5 *Rural Survey 2008-2010.*This is a survey conducted by the China Labour Study Group and published by Globalization Monitor. http://www.worldlabour.org/eng/node/484
6 *Yizhan yu meiguo daxuan* (The Iraq War and the US Election), 2004, http://www.observechina.net/info/artshow.asp?ID=33140
7 See his interview http://finance.sina.com.cn/review/zlhd/20060312/15162409879.shtml
8 *'Bu daode' jingjixue* (Amoral Economics), Fan Gang.
9 *Gaobie geming*, Li Zehou and Liu Zaifu, Cosmos Books Ltd, Hong Kong, 1995.
10 *Baohu sichan: xiuxian yu fan xiuxian zhizheng* (Protection of Private Property – the Debate Between those who are for Amendment on the Constitution and those who are Against), 2003, Liu Xiaobo, http://www.hkday.net/ytht/civic_life/4/36/2/11.html
11 Ibid.
12 *Bengkui yuqi qianghua ducai wending* (Expecting the CCP's Collapse Reinforce its Dictatorship and its Stability), http://www.epochtimes.com/gb/3/9/18/n378307.htm
13 Zhonghua renmin gongheguo xianfa xiuzhengan, 2004 (The 2004 Amendment on the Constitution of the People's Republic of China), http://news.xinhuanet.com/zhengfu/2004-03/16/content_1367942.htm
14 *Jingjixue yu renlei guanhuai*, Guangdong Education Press, 1998, p. 200.
15 The Origin of Capitalism, Ellen Meiksins Wood, *Monthly Review Press*, p. 86.

16 *Hong Kong Economic Journal*, 12 August, 1989. From the context of his opinion one can see that by middle class he chiefly means entrepreneurs.

17 *China's New Business Elite*, Margaret Pearson, p.4, University of California Press, 1997.

18 In its Chinese edition of a report it reassures employers that enterprise based collective bargaining does not necessarily result in a wage rise, it may also result in wages being frozen or even the lowering of wages because it respect the free market as a fair mechanism for deciding wages. "When the ACFTU depoliticizes its labour protection activities, and returns to the workers and to industrial relations within enterprises ... when its workplace union can really enter into collective bargaining with employers, this is the time when the ACFTU can really function in accordance with the market economy, and take a step forward in its self-reform." *Shuilai weiquan, weishui weiquan – Lun quanzong weiquan de zhengzhihua ji zhongguo gonghui yundong de chulu* (On ACFTU's Politicization of Workers' Rights Protection and the Way Forward for Chinese Trade Union Movement), CLB, Hong Kong, 2008, chapter four. Translation by the author.

19 The Russian Revolution, http://www.marxists.org/archive/luxemburg/1918/russian-revolution/ch08.htm

VOLUNTARY UNION OR FORCED ASSIMILATION – THE CCP'S POLICY ON TIBET[1]

Au Loong Yu

> In the first 10 years (1950–60) we lost our land [i.e., Chinese troops entered and took control of Tibet];
> In the second ten years (1960–70) we lost political power [i.e., the traditional government was replaced by a Han-dominated Communist government];
> In the third ten years (1970–80), we lost our culture [i.e., the Cultural Revolution destroyed religion and other old customs];
> In the fourth ten years (1980–90), we lost our economy [i.e., the open door economic policy allowed non-Tibetans to dominate the autonomous region's economy].[2]

After the 2008 riot in Lhasa, the spokesperson of the Chinese Foreign Ministry Qin Gang accused the Dalai Lama of being 'the chief representative of the theocratic regime and of serfdom'. The accusation is only half correct. Qin forgot that even if the Dalai Lama wants, he cannot be 'the chief representative of serfdom' because Qin's party state had already abolished serfdom there more than fifty years ago. The former serfs have long become individual farmers and herdsmen. Or does the Dalai Lama still seek to restore serfdom despite its improbability? To be fair, both the Charter of the Dalai Lama's government in exile and his own words do not suggest that it is on their agenda or their programme. The Dalai Lama has made a historic leap forward, although this was forced upon the Tibetan ruling class by the CCP. No one knows better than the CCP, therefore, if it continues with the old accusation that the Dalai Lama is the chief representative of serfdom, this is more of a slander than the truth.

It is true that the Dalai Lama is 'the chief representative of a theocratic regime', however, although one should add that it is a regime in exile. Article nineteen of the Charter of the Tibetan government in exile stipulates that the supreme power of the government in exile rests on the Dalai Lama, that before any laws are enacted his prior consent has to be sought, and that he can dissolve parliament at any time. Therefore, the Dalai Lama is not just a religious leader, he is also the head of a theocratic government in exile, and this government's mission, according to clause three of the same Charter, is to build a 'democratic' state which is also a Tibetan Buddhist state (literally 'a state which fuses religion and politics).[3] Therefore anyone who presents the Dalai Lama as solely a religious leader is misleading. And it is very doubtful that a theocracy is in the best interest of Tibetans even if I respect the democratic choice of the Tibetan people. Despite his ability to appease the western media, the fact that he remains committed to a theocratic Tibetan state nevertheless implies that he is not as progressive as he is portrayed. The Dalai Lama is aware of this inconvenience, therefore he keeps on repeating that if he returns to Tibet he will be only a religious leader and leave to others the role of political leader. However, if the Dalai Lama really believes in democracy, he could do it now by repealing the theocratic clause of the Charter.

It was ironic that in 1995 the CCP, an atheist party which should not believe in the Buddhist doctrine of reincarnation, not only imprisoned the reincarnated Panchen Lama, Gedhun Choekyi Nyima, chosen by the Dalai Lama, but even appointed Gyaincain Norbu as the 'reincarnated' Panchen Lama. This action is simultaneously a gross violation of religious freedom and a violation of the principle of a secular state. The Chinese government should not have intervened in the choosing of religious leaders, even if they are also political leaders. Pay unto Caesar what belongs to Caesar and to Buddha what belongs to Buddha. If the Chinese government does not abide by the secular principle or even exhibits religious intolerance, it is because the government, to a certain extent, also exhibits features of a theocratic state – it sees its own rule as one which has received Heaven's mandate, with its version of 'socialism' as state religion, and no subjects under its rule can disagree with this. That is why it remains hostile to any religion whose leaders do not endorse its ideology.

The Chinese government accused the Dalai Lama of seeking to separate Tibet from China. The Dalai Lama denied this, as usual, and stressed that he changed to the 'middle way policy' a long time ago. His present objective is the pursuit of 'one country, two systems', and it was the Chinese government who refused to negotiate with him over his proposal. Before I go on to explore this issue perhaps I should first answer the question "is the Chinese government practicing national repression towards Tibetans?" For many in the West this is obvious. But what is significant in China today is that not only the CCP denies this, many liberals and leftists concur. A discussion on this topic will not only help to clarify the real situation in Tibet but also reveal how the Han Chinese may think and act over the ethnic question, which has a serious bearing within and outside of China.

A fake autonomy

The CCP considers the Tibetan separatist movement as equivalent to a betrayal of the People's Republic of China. One must remind the CCP that it is it which first betrayed Lenin's doctrine of the right to self-determination for minorities, including the right to secession, despite adhering to Lenin's doctrine 80 years ago when it was founded. At the end of 1931, the Chinese Soviet of workers, peasants and soldiers held its National People's Congress and adopted the CCP's proposed 'outline of the Soviet Constitution'. The outline re-asserted the right to self-determination of minorities, including the right to secession. This position was gradually eroded when the CCP became a formidable force after the war of resistance to Japanese imperialism and was eventually replaced with a position advocating ethnic autonomous regions. At the same time, the federal state formula for a future Chinese republic was also abandoned in favour of a unitary state. From then on, whoever has talked about national self-determination and federalism has been condemned as a traitor.

This hostility towards the right to self-determination for ethnic minorities is shared by different, sometimes opposing, currents among Han Chinese. Xu Mingxu, a liberal opponent of the Beijing government, explains in his book why he opposes self -determination:

> In the world there are 3,000 ethnicities, but only 170 countries. If each and every one of the ethnicities seeks self-determination and builds one's independent country, it implies that most of these countries will sink into wars between ethnicities.[4]

It is not necessary to go into detail in refuting Xu's argument. Suffice to remind ourselves how Lenin rebutted this same old argument by pointing out that establishing the right to divorce does not equal encouraging divorce.

The problem is that even the autonomy promised by the Chinese government is fake. The Chinese government replies to its critics by stressing that Tibetan autonomy is real because it allows Tibetans to manage their own affairs, and the evidence is that the majority of party and government cadres are now Tibetan. This argument cannot withstand scrutiny. It can only be called localization of the civil service, just as Hong Kong's colonial government did in the latter part of the transition period. The secretary of the party in Tibet, and all posts which wield real power, remain in the hands of Han Chinese, and the predominant official language used is Chinese. If it is Tibetan police shooting at Tibetan demonstrators, the policemen are still seen as a repressive tool of the Han Chinese government.

When the CCP implemented its policy of ethnic autonomy after it came to power, it was clear that it only meant *administrative autonomy*, never *political autonomy*. Even after the Cultural Revolution, a period during which the CCP admits it adopted an ultra-leftist ethnic policy which did serious damage to ethnic minorities, the 1984 law on Regional National Autonomy does not confer any meaningful degree of autonomy to ethnic minorities. While article 4 of the Law prohibits ethnic separatism, the clauses on autonomy confine ethnic minority rights to their language and customs. The third chapter of the law defines autonomy in such a way that there is no real autonomy. Article 19 stipulates that the People's Congress of ethnic autonomous regions has the right to make laws in accordance with their special needs, but it is immediately followed by a clause stating that the bill has to seek the approval of the National People's Congress Standing Committee before enactment, which in practice nullifies the regions' autonomy. Article 20 is basically the same: 'If a situation arises that the resolutions, decisions, orders and instructions of higher levels of the state organs do not suit the actual situation of the ethnic autonomous regions, the organs of the autonomous regions can, upon consent from higher state organs, flexibly carry out these resolutions, decisions, orders and instructions, or stop their execution altogether.' If every decision has to seek approval from Beijing, then obviously there is no autonomy. Therefore the statement that the Tibet Autonomous Region government is a puppet of Beijing is not an exaggeration.

Two scholars from mainland China, Xu Xiaoping and Jinxin, admit in their book *Report on Chinese national problems* that the 1984 Law on Regional Autonomy only covers areas like 'marriage, inheritance, elections, family planning, compulsory education etc', and 'is completely silent on the regions' economic rights to control finance, taxation, foreign trade, development of their natural resources etc'. They said that the rights to autonomy for these regions as stipulated by law

> are also indisputably enjoyed by any other non-ethnic autonomous regions. In coastal areas their economic autonomy is much higher than what the ethnic autonomous regions enjoy, especially in terms of the rights of exploitation of resources. In contrast, the ethnic autonomous regions have little power over their own resources.[5]

Even in language rights Tibetan students are only allowed to use their mother tongue as the teaching medium during primary education. From secondary schools upwards Chinese is used much more regularly, even though students perform better when they use their mother tongue.[6] Xu Mingxu defends the Chinese government's practice on the ground that the Tibetan language is unable to express modern scientific concepts, although he himself admits he cannot speak the language.[7]

The Chinese government banned all religious freedom in Tibet during the Cultural Revolution, when nearly all monasteries were ransacked. Restricted freedom of religion has been restored since the 1980s. Initially the Chinese government pursued a conciliatory line in relation to the Dalai Lama. After a visit by the Dalai Lama's brother to Tibet in 1980, the government policy reverted to a hard-line again, when contrary to what the Chinese government expected (that the Tibetans, being grateful for the CCP's liberating them from selfdom and theocracy, would greet the delegation with hostility), the delegation was greeted with joy and emotion, which greatly annoyed the government.[8] The 1987 riot led the Chinese government to pursue even more restriction on the freedom of religion and eventually, in 1996, a total ban on the worship of the Dalai Lama. But a Tibetan Buddhism without the Dalai Lama is no longer Tibetan Buddhism, just as a Catholic Church without its Pope is no longer the Catholic Church as we know it.

Another defensive argument mounted by certain Han Chinese intellectuals, be they pro Beijing or not, is that Tibetans are privileged in government policies on economy, culture, education and family planning – for instance, the one child policy does not apply to minorities.[9] This line of argument is unconvincing because all these 'privileges' cannot be substitutes for political rights, which have been continuously denied to the Tibetans. As long as minorities do not enjoy political power in deciding their own fate they are in constant fear of being bullied.

What is even more ironic is that Hong Kong residents are not ethnically different from Han Chinese but they enjoy a relatively much higher degree of autonomy than the non-Chinese minorities. Hong Kong does enjoy political autonomy; we make our own laws without seeking consent from the central government and we even have our own currency. Hong Kong's autonomy is eroding, but for the moment it is still largely intact. This is also what led the Dalai Lama to abandon his previous position of fighting for independence and to propose one country two systems as a solution to the Tibet issue. The Dalai Lama's proposal is a moderate and logical one. It is the Chinese government which openly rejects negotiation with the Dalai Lama on this proposal, and which maintains the deadlock between the Tibetans and the Chinese government.

A mainland Chinese scholar Zheng Yongnian, currently professor and director of the East Asian Institute, National University of Singapore, argues that self-determination is no good as this is equal to pursuing independence. Maybe the Tibetans and the Uyghur should be content with something lesser than real autonomy? Zheng again says 'no', because "complete autonomy is not so much different from self-determination ... Experience proves that ethnic autonomy is still too idealistic. A too idealistic minorities' policy is not only detrimental to national and ethnic integration, it lays the ground for separatism."[10] Although it is not clear what he means by 'complete autonomy', his message is not ambiguous; it is nothing but a defence of the Chinese government's very incomplete autonomy policy for the minorities.

Quite a few liberals, although sympathetic to the Tibetans, do not admit that the Chinese government's policy towards Tibet is a kind of national oppression. They consider that it is just one manifestation of the nature of the CCP's despotism, which is equally oppressive to all citizens, be they Tibetans or Han Chinese. Hence the solution they offer is neither self-determination nor genuine autonomy, but democracy, as simple as that. Wang Lixiong is a well-known writer whose book *Sky Burial* expresses open sympathy for the Tibetans. He wrote that

> The oppression of the CCP targets people, not nationalities ... The oppression which the minorities face should not be defined as national oppression, rather it should be seen as oppression on the whole people exercised by the despotic regime.[11]

A Tibetan replies to this type of discourse with this: the suffering of Han Chinese has nothing to do with the Tibetans, but the suffering of the Tibetans is associated with the Han Chinese. When the Chinese government denies the Tibetans their language rights and the freedom to worship the Dalai Lama, or breaks its promises of autonomy for national minorities, it is obviously practicing national oppression, which the Han Chinese do not experience. And no representative democracy can right the wrongs here when the Tibetan population is no more than 6 million.[12]

Tibetan nationalism, old and new

The Tibetan independence movement as it is now is very different in its class base from what it was sixty years ago. Although under the leadership, directly or spiritually, of the same Dalai Lama, the old independence movement had a much narrower class base, chiefly composed of nobles and monks. If some of the serfs followed their masters it was more out of feudal allegiance than nationalist awareness. A second element to be taken into account is the alleged power the Dalai Lama and his monks possessed over their subjects' 'next lives'. In contrast, today's Tibetan nationalism is a cross-class response among Tibetans to more than six decades of national oppression by the CCP, as well as its enforced modernization project.

What marks the CCP's policy over Tibet is its jumping from one extreme to the other, as was similarly the case in the rest of China. When the Chinese government and the Dalai Lama's delegates signed the 1951 Seventeen Points Agreement the former agreed not to impose political and land reform in Tibet, though the Agreement also urged the latter to promote reform on its own accord. Its class policy was to rope in the Tibetan ruling class, to the extent, even, of banning party members from propagating the idea of democratic revolution or atheism, let alone socialism. A Maoist Yanfeng wrote approvingly in a 2010 pamphlet that

According to the instruction of the Central Committee of the Party and of Chairman Mao, not only reform of the Tibetan social system was not touched upon (in the Agreement), the army and cadres entering Tibet even refrained from conducting class education, to the extent that films like White Haired Lady were banned in Tibet.[13]

It is not convincing when the Dalai Lama defends Tibetan serfdom by saying that the Tibetan people were happy and the society was harmonious.[14] Being free from exploitation in general and from feudal obligation in particular is always much more desirable than otherwise. The problem with the CCP's 'democratic reform' after its suppression of the 1959 rebellion was not that it overthrew serfdom as such, but rather the way it was done: not only that it was imposed from outside and from the top, but also the fact that just some time ago it was still flirting with the upper classes in Tibet, which made its sudden about-turn look unconvincing and dishonest in the eyes of many serfs. The serfs did benefit from land distribution and the abolition of feudal obligations, but it was difficult for them to be enthusiastic in siding with party cadres in denouncing and attacking their former lords. According to Grunfeld, the Tibetan people, who never experienced or knew any other kind of lives except their own, feared the Han Chinese and were puzzled by these 'liberators' who had forged an alliance with their masters not long ago.[15]

The 'democratic reform' would have been received much better if it was initiated not by outside forces but by the Tibetan people. Back in 1939 Phuntso Wangye had already founded the Tibetan Communist Group, which joined the CCP ten years later. During the negotiation with the Dalai Lama he tried his best to mediate between the two parties. He was critical of the then Tibet party secretary Fan Ming for being disrespectful of the Tibetans, and this led to him being purged in 1957 and eventually thrown into jail for 18 years. Many of his Tibetan comrades met the same fate.[16] Their tragedy was a result of the Great Han chauvinism of the CCP, whose top leaders never trusted Tibetan communists, and never considered the option of supporting the Tibetan communists to gradually take root in Tibetan society and to make a democratic revolution from within. The CCP simply decided to export the revolution to Tibet, without any regard for Tibetans' national and religious rights.

The mistake of the CCP flowed partly from their erroneous theory on the national question at that time. Back in 1958 the Central Committee declared, in an internal report, that 'in class society, the national question is in essence a class issue, one cannot solve completely the national question without first grasping the essence of class.'[17] According to this proposition, national identity (and, in fact, also religion) was just the exploitative class's tool to fool the people, so annihilating this class, followed by the realization of communism, would automatically solve the national question. Or, in a slightly different version, the party would argue that Tibetans' national identity and its link to their religion was just a reflection of their low level of economic development, and modernization would cure all these diseases of backwardness. The two different versions were complementary to each other, as the party saw both the projects of communism and of modernization as pretty much the same thing, and both would succeed under the party's leadership. This led the party state to impose class struggle in Tibet from without during the 'democratic reform' in 1960. In 1962 Mao Zedong made his famous speech reminding his comrades not to forget 'class struggles'. This gave more impetus for party cadres in Tibet to pursue an even more ultra-left and repressive policy.

Even if the serfs did benefit from land reform, they were also dismayed to see the government expropriating the monasteries, which their entire culture depended on, and they resented it bitterly. Panchen Lama had been a loyal supporter of the CCP's policy in Tibet even after the 1959 rebellion. Only when he returned to Tibet and found that, in his absence, in his own monastery half of the population of monks were to be dismissed, and that everywhere there was brutal repression of monks, a great number of whom were innocent, did he make up his mind to write an internal report to the party's leadership.[18] In 1962 the CCP launched a fierce public attack on Panchen Lama for his '70,000 character report' and after his public condemnation in 1964 (prior to that he was already under house arrest) he was sent to prison for 12 years.

Even Ngapoi Ngawang Jigme, Commander-in-chief of the Tibetan armed forces at Chamdo in 1950, who signed the Seventeen Point Agreement and was one of the most prestigious Tibetan elites who cooperated with the CCP loyally through to the end, never enjoyed any real power when he became the first president of the newly established Tibet Autonomous Region in 1965.

This was also the time of a purge of those leading party cadres who had argued for a more moderate policy towards Tibet. The person then in charge of the United Front Work Department of the CCP (who also took charge of national minority affairs), Li Weihan, had repeatedly warned that 'no matter how great a help the Han Chinese can give to the Tibetans, it should not be imposed on them.'[19] This eventually led to his being purged in 1964 for committing the grave mistake of only being concerned about national rights and neglecting the class issue.

The former serfs also felt they had been fooled when in 1964, the Tibetan government collectivised their lands into communes, which very soon resulted in a serious decline in grain production. Many more brutal excesses soon followed during the Cultural Revolution when the *Gyenlok* (Tibetan red guards), with the encouragement of the Cultural Revolution Group in Beijing, began to implement their agenda of totally eradicating religion and the culture of all exploitative classes. What was more ironic was that the *Gyenlok* counterposed the cult of Buddha or the Dalai Lama with their cult of Chairman Mao, which had very much in common with religious worship and which was something that the Cultural Revolution Group under Mao wanted to eradicate in the first place. The aforementioned Yan Feng today still approvingly writes that during the 1960s the serfs were happy and, allegedly, had this song to sing

> The sun of Dalai only shines on the nobles, whereas the sun of Chairman Mao shines on us. Now is the time for the nobles' sun to go down the hill, and for our sun to rise up.[20]

The collectivisation of land and the ransacking of the monasteries as part of the campaign to eradicate religion finally drove ordinary Tibetans to widespread rebellion in 1969. The army was brought in to restore order, followed by even more rapid and forced collectivisation.

Hence in ten years the CCP's policy zigzag ultimately antagonized all classes and strata in Tibet. From those who first rebelled against the Chinese government like the Dalai Lama, to those Tibetans who once faithfully supported the CCP, from Panchen Lama to communist Phuntso Wangye, or those common peasants and herdsmen, without exceptions they were all expropriated or persecuted or both. This common experience of being maltreated by the Han Chinese government united them under the banner of modern Tibetan nationalism. With the coming to power of Deng Xiaoping in 1979, the party began to acknowledge its ultra-left mistake in general and in Tibet in particular, which was followed by the adoption of a resolution on the party's history which criticized Mao. This did not win back the hearts of the Tibetans, however.

If Mao was held responsible for the mistakes in the Cultural Revolution, wasn't it proof that he was not infallible after all? And if he was a false god then wasn't it logical for the Tibetans to draw the conclusion that they should return to their own religion and worship their true god, Buddha or the incarnation of Avalokite vara, the Dalai Lama? At least these gods had not inflicted so many wounds on their spiritual and secular lives in so short a time as the CCP did. However, one must take note of the fact that not all Tibetans shared the same kinds of experience or exactly the same interests. Nations are not homogeneous entities. After all, there were classes in Tibet before the CCP took over.

Yet, if the serfs had serious grievances against their masters, the social relationship between the two dated back thousands of years and had maintained, until the CCP took over, a certain balance within which the serfs had not yet embraced the idea of rebellion – there was no indication whatsoever of revolution brewing within Tibet in the 1950s. The feudal society of old Tibet only fell apart when the CCP broke its back from without, and rebuilt its social structure without any regard to the lower classes of Tibet, which the CCP claimed to represent, let alone the deposed upper classes. This common experience of being repressed by Han Chinese looms much larger than the conflict of class interest among Tibetans, and this has led many Tibetans to come to a common conclusion: get rid of the Han Chinese invaders, long live independent Tibet!

In the 1980s the CCP's Tibet policy went all the way back to its starting point, although within a social context in which the class composition was entirely transformed. It roped-in the old aristocracy and the monks for a second time, without, of course, giving them any power. Yet this could at most keep them from rebelling and was not able to attract their support, let alone convince them to give up worshipping the Dalai Lama in private. On the other hand, although absolute poverty among the Tibetan toiling masses had declined, the gap between the rich and poor was widening at full speed and what was a greater cause of resentment for common Tibetans was the fact that in Lhasa it was chiefly the Han Chinese and the Hui who benefited from the 'reform and opening up' policy. Meanwhile the old grass-roots Tibetan cadres who once were active supporters of the CCP now began to retire in poverty, complaining that:

> People now said that the CCP has changed. In the fifties they chose us. In the eighties they choose the aristocracy, again. There is a saying among the people, all the (favourable) policies for the upper class, including their stones and their dogs, have been fully implemented. But how about the common people? And the retired workers and cadres? They have no money, and no houses to live in.[21]

It is not clear how deeply Tibetan nationalism has taken hold among different classes in Tibet, or how strongly it is linked to Tibetan Buddhism or the Dalai Lama. Yet there is enough evidence showing that the CCP has lost its entire mass base in Tibet and is left only with the native Tibetan bureaucracy to sustain its direct rule. This native Tibetan bureaucracy was formed during the period of the CCP exporting revolution to Tibet. In the 1960s, among those Tibetans who joined the CCP's land reform, there were quite a few gangsters but there were also those who were committed to the liberation of the serfs. Yet with the successive purges within the regime it was more likely that the latter category of cadres vanished and only 'yes men' remained. The latter now constituted the backbone of a new born native bureaucracy who, although never able to rise to a position of real power, nevertheless did share some marginal power. It is aware of its unique role in the CCP's forced assimilation of Tibet, and uses it as leverage to advance its own interests, first and foremost by blackmailing the central government for more subsidies. Phuntso Wangye once remarked that the native Tibetan bureaucracy 'feed themselves from anti-separatism, promote their ranks through anti-separatism, and enrich themselves through the same anti-separatism.'

They have no difficulty in going one step further and drawing the conclusion that it is not in their interest to eliminate Tibetan separatism altogether – if they do then the game of balancing themselves between the two sides will come to an end. Therefore, it is commonly believed that they encourage small incidents of instability to prove to the central government their usefulness in putting down disturbances.[22]

Given their second class nature, it is not hard to imagine that certain sections of the native Tibetan bureaucracy have also developed resentment against the Han Chinese rulers. These rulers have to live with the fact that a significant number of native Tibetan cadres live double lives, attacking the Dalai Lama when on duty and secretly worshipping him when off duty, or sending their children or relatives to India to pay him tribute. The joke at the beginning of this essay in fact first became popular among native Tibetan cadres, reflecting this resentment.

Forced modernization

From 1979 onward, the CCP's policy somersaulted once again, abandoning its so-called 'class struggle' line for 'developing the productive forces'. It thought that by modernising Tibet through market (this should be read as 'capitalist') reform the Tibetans would be better off and hence more pro-China. They were wrong, again.

Tibet was so poor that the capital needed to modernize it came almost entirely from central government funding, which was more generous to Tibet than other ethnic minorities. It was thought that this might buy off the rebellious Tibetans. In the thirty years of Mao's rule, state subsidies to Tibet increased by 65 times.[23] Phuntso Wangye remarked ironically that 'the Central government gives money to Tibet even if the latter does not want it, while Xinjiang people only got money when they ask for it, and Inner Mongolia is not given any money even if it is asked for.'

The problem with this approach is that the modernization project, instead of being tailor-made under local initiative, was as top-down as everywhere else in China, and implemented through a corrupt and despotic bureaucracy. This is shown in the high inefficiency of investment. According to Dreyer, in the period between 1949 and 1979, although output increased fourfold, one yuan in output value required an increase of 1.21 yuan in state subsidies, that is, Tibet had a negative multiplier effect on investment. And then in the Seventh Five Year Plan (1986-1990) Tibet's total factory productivity was as low as 0.3, and it dropped further to -0.1 in the Eighth Five Year Plan (1991-1995).[24]

Despite this, the CCP's modernisation project did promote the development of Tibet. In the 1950s Tibet had almost no modern industry, whereas today it has four modern industries: electric power, textile and crafts, mining and tourism. This new economic structure has also created new classes and class relations.

The native Tibetan officials are undoubtedly the first social group to have benefited from modernisation projects subsidised by Beijing. Wang Lixiong remarked that the native Tibetan bureaucracy

> is entirely nurtured by outside force and is completely alienated (from Tibet). In the past half a century, it relied on the feeding from Beijing, sank its root there and grew into a monster.[25]

Apart from profiting from Beijing's subsidies, it also compels common traders and vendors to pay bribes or fines to them. One official journal admits that 'the phenomenon of certain law enforcing state organs abusing their power to impose fines on sole proprietors and small enterprises is common.'[26]

Today's Tibet has long ago embarked on the road to capitalism. Between 1980 and 2000, the number of Tibet's small private enterprises increased from 489 to 43,000, a growth of nearly 100 times. In Lhasa the proportion between the Han Chinese and Hui businesses and the Tibetans is 7:3, indicating that Tibetans do not have a share fair of the market in their holy city (Beijing exempted Tibet from the general rule that one must be a permanent resident of an area before one can open a business there, which is much resented by Tibetans). A great number of Tibetans are disgusted with the commercialisation of their holy city. It must be pointed out, however, that the proportion throughout Tibet is precisely the opposite than in Lhasa itself, where 70 per cent of small private business is in the hands of Tibetans.[27]

In Tibet in the 1950s, an industrial working class did not exist. It only started to grow when modernisation projects began. In 2005 farmers and herdsmen as a share of the labour force dropped to 60 per cent, and the remaining 40 per cent were either workers or small traders. In 1981 Tibet had 170,000 employees, mainly workers in state-owned or collective enterprises. In 1995 the figure declined to 160,000, and stayed at that level in 2005. At the same time, workers at small private enterprises rose from a negligible level to 63,198 in 2000, reflecting the growth of capitalism.[28]

With the emergence of capitalist wage labour, there are reports of more and more labour disputes in Tibet:

> Many private businesses ignore or even infringe on workers' basic legitimate rights, which have resulted in more conflicts in industrial relations, and industrial dispute cases have been increasing. This has become a more and more prominent social conflict which seriously affects the social stability.[29]

Reports indicate that youth and ordinary Tibetan workers were one of the chief components of the 2008 Tibet riot. It will be an interesting topic for future investigation as to how far this kind of industrial dispute helps to promote some kind of class consciousness and how it may interact with Tibetan identity.

Conclusion

In the 2007 white paper on Tibet the Chinese government dismissed the Dalai Lama's 1988 Strasbourg Proposal as nothing but a proposal for an independent Tibet. The accusation was repeated again and again, for instance in the aftermath of the March 2008 Tibet riot, the People's Daily accused the Dalai Lama of pursuing a future Tibet with its own foreign policy, which they see as equivalent to demanding independence. This is just slander. The Dalai Lama long ago abandoned his demand for independence and his 1988 Strasbourg Proposal explicitly said that the Chinese government 'could remain responsible for Tibet's foreign policy'. As for military presence, the Dalai Lama proposed that

> A regional peace conference should be called to ensure that Tibet becomes a genuine sanctuary of peace through demilitarization. Until such a peace conference can be convened and demilitarization and neutralization achieved, China could have the right to maintain a restricted number of military installations in Tibet. These must be solely for defence purposes.[30]

The Chinese government attacked this proposal as, again, amounting to demanding independence. But this contradicts its own proposal of one country two systems for Taiwan, which allows Taiwan to keep its own army and which Beijing considers to be highly consistent with its claim of sovereign right over Taiwan. At the end of the day, it is clear that the Chinese government's rejection of the Dalai Lama's proposal is less because it really amounts to pursuing Tibetan independence but more because Tibet is already within its grip and it would not loosen this grip whatsoever. The former president Jiang Zemin told the visiting president of Qinghua University in Taiwan in 1992 the reason why he would not consider applying 'one country two systems' to Tibet is because 'we have gone so far already, and cannot go back to apply one country two systems in Tibet.'[31]

The reason for the Dalai Lama's retreat from calling for independence is obvious: the Chinese government is too formidable a force. On top of this is the fact that the latter's Great Han chauvinism is still shared by a great number of Han Chinese, who account for 92 per cent of the Chinese population. This is not only the result of the CCP's decades-long brain washing but also a response to one hundred years of foreign aggression. In contrast, demanding a high level of autonomy along the one country two systems proposal is more likely to win sympathy among certain sections of Han Chinese, although even this is not easy as ordinary people do not have access to a free flow of information and therefore do not know what the Dalai Lama is proposing or the real situation in Tibet.

On the other hand the Dalai Lama's moderate policy is increasingly questioned, or even attacked, by more radical Tibetans. The CCP's continued refusal to negotiate with the Dalai Lama and its slander against him only serves to provide a rationale for the cause of radical Tibetans. Hence China-Tibet relations fall into a vicious cycle of rebellion and repression which may continue for decades, everything being equal. This is not only detrimental to the Tibetans but also harmful to ordinary Han Chinese as the CCP's repression in Tibet necessarily strengthens its despotic rule even further throughout the whole of China. A nation which represses another nation can never itself be free.

This is also why the party has been more and more interested in promoting nationalism or even xenophobia in recent years – the more the party bureaucracy finds itself the main target of all classes the more it finds it necessary to divert domestic problems into external ones. Yet there are signs showing that ordinary Chinese working people today are more concerned about their misery under the CCP's despotism, from lack of political rights to their job security, their pension and a future for their children, than fighting imaginary foreign invaders plotting to split up China. In September 2006 the Netease website conducted a survey on 'whether you wish to be Chinese again in your next life', and it found out that 64 per cent chose not to be and the most popular reason given was 'being Chinese lacks basic esteem as a human being'.[32] It proves again that 'nation' is not a homogeneous whole, and the Han Chinese are no exception. It is the duty of all progressive forces in China to win over all thinking people to the idea of real equality between all nations, and this should begin with respect for the right to self-determination for ethnic minorities.

In the same vein, I also hope that the Tibetan people can continue to reject the narrow idea of seeing all Han Chinese as equally responsible for the misery of the Tibetan people, especially when this idea has turned into undifferentiated attacks on and the killing of Han Chinese, such as in the 2008 riot.

Notes

1 This essay is a re-written and abridged version of the Chinese original, published under the penname Xu you in the Tatung Series no. 1, Sun Miu Press, Hong Kong, June 2008.
2 *The Snow Lion and the Dragon: China, Tibet, and the Dalai Lama*, by Melvyn C. Goldstein, Chinese edition, Mirror Book, 2005, Hong Kong, p. 160.
3 *Liuwangzhong de minzhu – Yindu liuwang zangren de zhengzhi yu shehui 1959-2004* (Democracy in Exile – The Politics and Society of the Exiled Tibetans in India), Su Jiahong, Buffalo Book, 2005, Taipei, Appendix three.
4 *Yinmou yu qiancheng – Xizang saoluan de laolongqumai,* (Intrigues and Devoutness – The Origin and Development of the Tibet Riots), Xu Mingxu, Mirror Books Ltd., 1999, p. 373.
5 *Zhongguo minzu wenti baogao* (Report on Chinese National Questions), Xu Xiaoping and Jin Xin, China Social Science Press, 2008, p.99.
6 Goldstein, 2005, p. 162.
7 Xu Mingxu, 1999.
8 Goldstein, 2005, p. 104-6.
9 Tibetan families are allowed to have no more than three children.
10 *Zhongguo shaoshu minzu zhengce de wenti daodi zai nail?* (What is the problem with China's policy on ethnics minorities?), Zheng Yongnian, Zao Bao Daily, July 21, 2009. http://www.zaobao.com/special/forum/pages7/forum_zp090721.shtml
11 *Tianzang – Xizang de mingyun* (Sky Burial: The Fate of Tibet), Wang Lixiong, Mirror Books, Sixth Edition, 2006, p. 241-2. I am not sure if his opinion has changed since he wrote the book.
12 In Tibet Autonomous Region alone the Tibetan population is around 3 million.
13 *Gaige kaifang niandai de ziben yundong* (The Movement of Capital in the Age of Reform and Opening Up), Yan Feng, China Cultural Communication Press, Hong Kong, p. 69. The White Haired Lady was an opera first performed in 1945, describing the misery suffered by peasants. For years the opera and then the ballet and the film became a favourite tool for promoting class education by the party.
14 Chinese edition of Tibet mort ou vif by Pierre-Antoine Donnet, p. 85, Reading Times, Taipei, 1994.
15 *The Making of Modern Tibet,* Tom Grunfeld, Quoted from Wang lixiong, 2006, p.170.
16 *A Tibetan Revolutionary – The Political Life and Times of Bapa Phuntso Wangye,* Goldstein, Sherap and Siebenschuh, University of California Press, 2004.
17 Xu Xiaoping and Jin Xin, 2008, p. 76.
18 Tibetan Nation – A History of Tibetan Nationalism and Sino-Tibetan Relations, Warren W. Smith, Jr., Westview Press, 1996, p. 521-525.
19 Wang Lixiong, p. 169.
20 Yan Feng, p. 73.
21 Wang Lixiong, p. 503.

22 *Economic Development in Tibet Under the People's Republic of China,* June Teufel Dreyer. Contemporary Tibet – Politics, Development and Society in a Disputed Region, Edited by Barry Sautman and June Teufel Dreyer, M.E. Sharpe, New York, 2006.

23 Dreyer, 2006.

24 Dreyer, 2006.

25 Wang Lixiong, p. 235.

26 *Xizang feigonghouzhi jingji fazhan cunzai de wenti yu duice yanjiu* (Research on the Problems with Tibet Non-Common Ownership Economics and its Counter Measures) Nima Lamu and Pan Mingqing, Jingjishi (Economists), Issue 9, 2006.

27 Dreyer, 2006.

28 China Statistical Yearbook 2006, http://www.stats.gov.cn/tjsj/ndsj/2006/html/E0503C.HTM

29 Nima Lamu and Pan Mingqing, 2006.

30 1988 Strasbourg Proposal, http://www.dalailama.com/messages/tibet/strasbourg-proposal-1988

31 *The Dalai Lama's Autonomy Proposal, A One-Sided Wish?* He Baogang, in *Contemporary Tibet – Politics, Development and Society in a Disputed Region,* Edited by Barry Sautman and June Teufel Dreyer, M.E. Sharpe, New York, 2006.

32 *Diaocha laisheng shifou yuanyi zuo zhongguoren rehuo, wangyi zhubian tuzao jiegu* (Survey on 'Whether You Wish to be Chinese Again in Your Next Life' Causes Troubles, Netease Editor Got Sacked), Apple Daily, September 17, 2006, http://hk.apple.nextmedia.com/international/art/20060917/6321968

ALTER-GLOBO IN HONG KONG

Au Loong Yu

An interview with *New Left Review*[1]

Can you tell us something about your background?

I was born in Hong Kong in 1956. My family had come from Guangdong in the early 1940s—my father was an artisan, making small ornaments and the like. He came from the city of Foshan, which was known over centuries for its porcelain. In Hong Kong, he did several brief spells in factories, but couldn't endure factory discipline; he loved his freedom as a craftsman. My mother worked alongside him in their workshop at our house. They didn't earn much: my three brothers and I sometimes had to walk the streets with my father selling souvenirs he had made. We lived in Kowloon, but I went to a Catholic secondary school – though I'm not a religious person – on Hong Kong Island.

How was the PRC[2] perceived while you were growing up in the 1960s?

People were divided in their attitudes towards China – though not the Hong Kong bourgeoisie, who of course loathed the CCP. But in the labour movement, there was a deep split between Communist-led unions and those run by the KMT, which lasted up until the early 70s. The hostility between the two peaked in 1956, when the KMT trade unions physically attacked CCP unionists. The CCP had extensive influence among workers: the 'Socialist Fatherland' was seen as a counterweight to colonial rule. But then in 1967 the Maoist pro-CCP union called a general strike that no workers supported, and then in the wake of its failure launched an 'urban warfare' campaign. This was a bitter disappointment to many workers who had been dedicated to the cause, and who paid a high price for the CCP-led unions' desire to emulate the Gang of Four. The popular saying at the time was that they wanted a big strike, Da Bagong, but instead it was Dahua Bagong, a big exaggeration.

I was a schoolboy during this period, but two things in particular made a strong impression on me. I remember seeing long queues at the post office in the early 1960s: people were sending rice, clothes, and daily necessities back to their relatives in China because of the famine. And in 1967 and 68 there were stories of people beaten to death during the Cultural Revolution, and their bodies floating into Hong Kong harbour from the Pearl River.

How was British rule viewed at this time?

British rule in the post-war era can be divided into two periods either side of 1971. In the earlier period, there was a form of spatial apartheid—the Tai Ping Shan area was restricted to Westerners.– and conditions were much more oppressive: working hours were long, wages low and strike activity ruthlessly suppressed by the colonial government. National oppression took a very visible form: nearly all high-ranking posts were occupied by Brits, and English was the only official language; at school, we would be refused permission to go to the bathroom if we didn't ask in English.

The British clamped down hard on the labour movement after the 1967 events – perhaps 4,000 or 5,000 trade unionists were sacked, and thousands put in prison. This took a toll from which the Maoist unions never recovered. Nevertheless, by the early 70s, pressure had begun to mount on the British, both from within and from without, to make some reforms in order to maintain any legitimacy. Hong Kong students and social activists were agitating for Chinese language rights, and against the possible transfer of Diao Yu Island to Japan. A key turning point came on 7 July 1971, when the colonial government harshly repressed a demonstration by radical nationalist youth movements. A wave of further protests ensued, and the government was forced for the first time to permit demonstrations. After that student groups mobilized with some success against official corruption, and in 1973 pressured the government into forming an Independent Commission, which continues to function. Externally, China's rising international status – its assumption of a UN Security Council seat in 1971, Nixon's visit and so on –.was an important factor pushing the British into granting limited political freedoms.

How and when were you radicalized?

By the 1971 mobilizations around the Diao Yu Island. They were organized by young students, many of whom were beaten and hospitalized by the colonial police. The worldwide radicalization of the 1960s was late in coming to Hong Kong – it wasn't till 1970 that young people began to respond to socialist or Marxist ideas, for instance. Though the CCP had lost much of its base among the Hong Kong workers after 1967, it benefited greatly from the upsurge in national sentiment among students and intellectuals. China, and its Maoist model, was seen as an alternative to British rule – though during the course of the 1970s the local CCP moved away from advocating the end of colonialism, in the name of stability. In student circles, the Maoists were constantly challenged by liberal currents and the radical left, notably Trotskyists and anarchists. The Chinese Trotskyists had had a presence in Hong Kong since the 1940s, while anarchism had become fashionable in the early 1970s. I followed lively debates in the papers between the two groupings, and read Marx and Trotsky as well as Marcuse and Fromm. I was attracted to Fromm's humanism, and found Trotsky's analysis of bureaucracy highly relevant to contemporary Chinese history. Many of my classmates became Maoists, but despite my youth I felt a strong aversion to the cult of personality. I joined the Young Socialist Group, which moved increasingly in a Trotskyist direction, but disintegrated in the early 1980s.

What did you do after graduating?

I finished high school in 1974, and worked in the offices of a British and then US trading firm until 1977. After that I spent two years working in factories, making garments and Japanese watches. I then enrolled at Hong Kong Baptist College to study Chinese, which I went on to teach in high schools until 1995.

What was the response in Hong Kong to Tiananmen Square and to the democracy movement more generally?

The initial reaction was both horror and anger – including among pro-Beijing groups, though these repented their criticisms of the CCP soon enough. Many dissidents fled China in the wake of the repression, but they mostly went to the US, and so had little impact on Hong Kong's political scene. The real effect of Tiananmen Square was to bolster the liberals in Hong Kong, who became dominant in the opposition camp – a position derived not from any innate strength, but from the degeneration of 'really existing socialism'. The 1989 crackdown made for a glaring contrast between colony and mainland, which increasingly came to be seen as a barbaric, absolutist regime.

Not that Hong Kong itself was an authentic liberal democracy, even by the time Britain's ninety-nine year lease expired. For all the rhetoric, Patten did little towards democratization: prior to the 1997 handover, only half the seats in the legislative council were directly elected under universal suffrage. It was only the fierce opposition of the Chinese government and its backers in Hong Kong to such a small step that enabled the UK to garner some credibility. This was nothing new: in the early 1980s, when the colonial government began to introduce direct elections, the heads of the pro-CCP unions opposed it, claiming that 'We workers only care for *fan piao* [rice voucher], not *xuan piao* [ballot]'. The CCP's rigidity made Patten's piecemeal democratic engineering appear more significant than it really was. In fact, London's reforms simply served to ensure that in 1997, power was peacefully retained by the same set of mandarins as before, the colony's Administrative Officers, only this time under the leadership of a governor appointed by Beijing, Tung Chi Wah.

Nevertheless, there has been significant progress for Hong Kong Chinese since the days of my youth. There is now a clear agenda for universal suffrage and parliamentary democracy, which was totally lacking in the 1970s. The democratic movement in Hong Kong is important, since freedom of the press and assembly are the only weapons we have to defend our autonomy, and resist the political convergence between the one-party regime on the mainland, and Hong Kong's mandarins and tycoons. Liberal democracy does provide working people with a space to resist, which is entirely lacking in mainland China. However, because of the dominance of liberal ideas, these democratic aspirations are never linked to social and economic rights. Even three or four years ago, the minimum wage was seen as a radical demand. Hong Kong society is very atomized: few people join political parties, social movements and trade unions are very weak, and it is difficult to mobilize rank and file members in any great numbers. Movements are often led by paid officials. Such a low organizational starting point makes it hard to wage a prolonged democratic struggle, and it seems likely that if full universal suffrage and parliamentary democracy arrived in Hong Kong, the same clique would be able to monopolize it.

Can you tell us about what has happened since 1997? What has the process of integration with the PRC involved?

The idea of 'one country, two systems' was essentially the invention of Deng Xiaoping. When the PRC's leaders spoke in the 1980s of learning from Hong Kong, they naturally did not mean freedom of the press or limited democratic rights, but the example of Hong Kong capitalism. After 1997 mainland corporations rapidly moved to strengthen control over Hong Kong's media –.TV, newspapers and so on –.resulting in growing self-censorship on the part of broadcasters and journalists. In economic terms, Hong Kong was already undergoing de-industrialization before the handover: whereas manufacturing accounted for a third of the labour force in 1986, by 1996 it had dropped to a tenth. The overwhelming bulk of jobs.–.over 90 per cent today—are in the service sector. A deep restructuring of the working class is under way, as hundreds of thousands of workers, especially women, have been forced into increasingly precarious employment. The main effect of the handover was to greatly accelerate this trend towards downward mobility. Even service jobs have shifted to southern China: banks, insurance companies, airlines and accounting firms and so on all have their logistics bases in Shenzhen or Guangzhou, where wages are a fraction of those in Hong Kong, and white-collar workers never strike. As a result, Hong Kong wages dropped by a third or more across the board after the Asian Crisis.

Many people left Hong Kong before the handover: there was an enormous middle-class migration to the West. The shortage of teachers, incidentally, made it easier for me to secure jobs in better schools. But Hong Kongese are still much more able to travel than mainlanders. Under the rules of 'one country, two systems', citizens of both Hong Kong and the mainland PRC need an internal passport to cross from one side to the other; but it is easy for Hong Kongese to get this passport, whereas mainlanders face a number of obstacles – notably the Hukou household registration system, which practically makes second-class citizens of the rural population. In effect, the richer you are, the easier it is to come to Hong Kong – making for a form of combined spatial and social apartheid.

Beijing mandarins from time to time warn Hong Kong residents not to turn the region into an 'anti-communist base'. But for all its distaste for Hong Kong's autonomy, 'socialist' Beijing has long depended on the capitalist colony: from 1949-79, one third of all foreign exchange earned by the PRC came through Hong Kong. For the moment, they cannot take any drastic measures to curtail that autonomy, which would greatly radicalize local opinion. Gradual erosion seems the most likely path in the long run, barring the advent of significant resistance on the mainland.

What sort of campaigns have you been able to mount?

In 2004, through our mainland contacts we heard about two battery factories in Huizhou owned by Gold Peak, where 177 workers were diagnosed with cadmium poisoning. The company has 12,000 employees worldwide and annual revenues of over $500m. We leaked the story to the press in Hong Kong, and it hit the headlines: the CEO of Gold Peak, Victor Lo, is a member of the Hong Kong Executive Council. The company also has factories in Shenzhen and one in Hong Kong, where we heard about more cases of cadmium poisoning, which we also publicized. The story was picked up by the mainland press, and in late 2004, Central China TV made a programme about it that was—by their standards—surprisingly critical.

This made a big contribution to raising public awareness about the costs of the 'Chinese miracle': a previously indifferent public now at least had some knowledge of what was happening. We've circulated the programme to workers on DVD as an educational tool, to show them that it is possible for the national media to pick up their stories. This hope is the real gain from our action; sadly, the report on national TV was not enough to pressure Gold Peak into meeting workers' claims for compensation. Three times in 2006 we arranged for Gold Peak workers to come to Hong Kong, where they tried to meet with senior executives of the company, and publicly picketed Victor Lo. In November 2006 we finally succeeded in setting up a meeting between Lo and the workers. But he rebuffed their claims—and is now suing Globalization Monitor and the CTU.

What has been the impact of WTO accession on China?

Overall, the impact has been to speed up capital-friendly restructuring. State-owned enterprises, initially the manufacturing and energy sectors, bore the brunt of this: a total of 26 million manufacturing jobs were lost between 1996 and 2001. The effect of the WTO on agriculture will destroy the basis of the small peasant economy. Agricultural tariffs have been slashed as per WTO requirements, and are now among the lowest in the world, while domestic farm subsidies were cut from 10 per cent of total agricultural production value to 8.5 per cent. China recently became a net importer of agricultural products, an alarming development for a country of its size and agrarian traditions. Government officials point to the abolition of agricultural taxes as a measure beneficial to farmers. But this tax only ever accounted for a fraction of the money peasants pay to officials, who impose all kinds of 'fees' for education, infrastructure or even local militia. Moreover, there are numerous cases of land being expropriated from farmers for commercial purposes.

In accordance with WTO rules, in 2007 China will have to open its service sector, including banking and finance. In the last few years the banking sector has shed 250,000 workers. There has already been a general commercialization of services, which has affected education in particular. It will also make China much more vulnerable to regional financial crisies than was the case in 1997. This is all the more pressing in view of the unreliability of official data: no one knows the real amount of non-performing loans, or of hidden foreign debt. There is a range of estimates for illegal capital flight—perhaps as high as $70bn, much of it laundered through Hong Kong or Macau.

The lack of transparency surrounding the true state of the Chinese economy is obviously connected to the issue of corruption. The reality is that elites are immune to prosecution despite the occasional trial of an official. In fact, very often these trials are more about faction fights than weeding out corruption. Tiananmen sent the message that the bureaucracy is entirely above the law. We are witnessing a revival of the ancient tradition according to which criminal charges applied only to commoners; perhaps an even better analogy would be *mianzui tiejuan*—a kind of certificate, made of iron, granted to the emperor's favourite ministers which pardoned them for all crimes in advance. In these conditions, there can be no rule of law. The same principle helps make sense of the post-Soviet experience. A European activist I met in 1990 argued that the Soviet bureaucracy could not go capitalist, because it lacked the money to buy the national assets; but since they were above the law, they could simply plunder them.

Has there been any opposition to the WTO within China?

Owing to severe censorship, most workers in the PRC don't really understand much about what impact the WTO will have on them. State-sector workers are more knowledgeable—those in auto factories will have heard, for example, of tariffs on cars being cut, and know that this will affect their jobs. But the general response from workers has been apathy. Some opposition has come from inside the party bureaucracy and academia, though before 2001 this was confined to a very small circle of New Left intellectuals. Since then, critics have become more outspoken, but often on purely nationalist grounds. They will attack a mode of accumulation that is too dependent on foreign capital, but they are not opposed to the WTO on principle; rather, they support entry on more favourable terms. Han Deqiang, for instance, has advocated pushing for better protections while China gains greater access to the world market, allowing it to increase its share of global trade.[3] From a nationalist perspective, China has every right to seek profits—hence the recent recurrence of arguments for a strong military to defend China's geopolitical interests; after all, there are oilfields in Indonesia, coal and iron ore mines in Peru to be protected.

Some have argued that the best way to mobilize workers in order to secure their rights is through using legal means. What is your view of such a strategy?

Han Dongfang, who founded the *China Labour Bulletin*, has been arguing on these lines for over a decade.[4] I think these tactics have been a failure. To begin with, workers always act according to the law in the first, second and third instance. In almost every case we have come across in the course of research for Globalization Monitor, before they had gone on strike or organized demonstrations and roadblocks, workers have been petitioning the government or private companies for years. And officials or managers have always turned them away. In the private sector, where the worst abuses and violations of labour rights take place, the situation is far worse: there are no genuine trade unions at all. Often the boss will simply assign union posts, and the personnel manager is usually chairman of the union. In the Gold Peak factories on the mainland, assembly line supervisors have been appointed union members.

In his two books on Chinese labour, Han has made clear the rationale behind his legalistic strategy: pointing to the terrible consequences of the Cultural Revolution, he says explicitly that a popular uprising is to be avoided at all costs. We understand his concern, but reject the idea that the legal path is the only avenue of attack. In fact, in the majority of cases, when workers go on strike or block the road, nothing terrible has happened, no one has been killed—and the workers at least manage to win back some of their wages, or score other partial successes. Moreover, Chinese peasants can endure a tremendous amount. If they do become violent and burn your property, it is nearly always your fault. In a Taiwanese-owned shoe factory at Xing Ang, the workers had become so downtrodden that they virtually destroyed the place; several of them were sent to jail, but we would see management as being responsible for their condition in the first place. On the whole, outcomes are more peaceful, and any violence tends to be in the private sector, where workers are more vulnerable. The predominance of rural migrant workers there, however, makes organizing more difficult—they are from a more individualistic farming culture, and are deeply divided among themselves. But spontaneous strikes are in our experience more effective than approaching personnel managers or government officials.

Overseas labour organizations have taken divergent stances on China's official unions—some pointing to limited achievements such as securing permission for union branches in Wal-Mart. What approach would you recommend?

In my view, supposed gains such as in the case of Wal-Mart are largely meaningless. The ACFTU (All-China Federation of Trade Unions) pockets union dues without providing the workforce with any bargaining power. It presents a very convincing façade to organizations such as the International Confederation of Free Trade Unions, but does not permit workers to speak freely to foreign delegates. The official unions are not run for the benefit of the workers. Their Western counterparts should really oppose recognition of the ACFTU, and refuse to talk to them unless they allow people independent trade union rights.

What role did China play in the WTO negotiations at the Hong Kong ministerial conference in 2005?

The most important factor allowing the Hong Kong meeting to advance beyond the Doha round was the betrayal of small developing countries by the G20 leaders, China, India and Brazil, who sacrificed the former's interests and made a compromise with the EU and US. Many Asian NGOs and delegates were reluctant to criticize China—as a 'socialist', anti-imperialist state—but the position of the Chinese government was completely clear: it would fully accept the Doha agenda, especially non-agricultural market access and the General Agreement on Tariffs and Trade (GATTS)[5], as long as a few token concessions were made to developing countries to sweeten the pill. The Trade Minister Bo Xilai said that 'China enjoys comparative advantages in low- to medium-end products. Therefore, China hopes to develop a new market for herself.' The Chinese delegation took part in all Green Room negotiations, from which all but a handful of developing countries were excluded. Those expecting China to defend their interests were sorely disappointed.

Can you tell us more about the Hong Kong People's Alliance (HKPA)?

The HKPA was set up in 2004, and its backbone really came from the CTU and its affiliates, the Asia Monitor Resource Centre, the migrant workers union, and Globalization Monitor. A range of other organizations also participated—independent trade unions, migrant workers, sex workers, student and community groups—but the Hong Kong branches of Greenpeace stayed away, perhaps with one eye on their operations in China. The migrant workers have been an especially strong component. Filipinos and Indonesians working in Hong Kong can mobilize in far greater numbers than local Chinese, which is rather shameful. It's a very diverse coalition, with around three dozen member organizations in total. In the run-up to the WTO Ministerial, the HKPA's dozen-strong coordinating committee linked together international and local mobilizations. The latter remained small compared to the international delegations, at least until the 18 December demonstration.

How did the protests against the 2005 WTO Ministerial unfold?

We spent a year preparing for the Ministerial. Campaigning against free trade in Hong Kong has been difficult—it has been a free port for 150 years, a status which has supposedly made it so prosperous. Thirty years ago activism on this front would have been easier. Working conditions were much harder, and people still remembered imperialist sponsorship of the opium trade. We expected a cool reception, but the response has been surprisingly positive, in part because of the educational work Globalization Monitor has done over the past few years. We are no longer so isolated.

But it was the international support that was the most significant element in the protests' success. The fact that 2,000 Koreans would be attending, including 150 delegates from the Korean Confederation of Trade Unions and ten times that number from the Korean Peasants League, was widely reported in the media. Attention was drawn to the plight of Korean farmers, whose livelihoods had been

destroyed by the WTO. They were fantastic, very organized and well drilled: the women beat their drums at the back, and the men advanced on the police barricades as one. The Koreans also won over local opinion by leafleting in Chinese, and had banners written in Chinese proclaiming 'Agriculture is the base of a nation'. On the very first day, 13 December, I was one of dozens of speakers at a rally organized by the HKPA, and had just handed over to the next speaker when the demonstration suddenly dispersed – everyone had rushed to the waterfront to watch over a hundred Koreans jumping into the sea. The police had no idea what to do. There were some skirmishes with the police on 14 December. Then, on 15 December the Korean farmers did a march involving one step forward and kneeling three times—a gesture to a shared Confucian heritage that resonated with many Hong Kongese. Local TV journalists interviewed members of the public, who generally expressed sympathy for the farmers—their livelihoods are under threat, they had to protest. Interestingly, the news coverage was rebroadcast in South China, something local Chinese governments don't generally do. However, some of the local groups, as well as fishermen's and farmers' organizations from other countries, were not happy about this: the Korean farmers deflected attention from demonstrations they had organized, which were scarcely reported.

The ante was really raised on 17 December, when protestors – Koreans at the forefront—broke through the police cordon and shut off the entire Wan Chai district, where the Ministerial was being held. In the evening, the police used tear gas on the crowds and made hundreds of arrests — including Kang Ki Kab, a Korean MP who had accompanied his countrymen; he was told by police to persuade them to retreat, but he refused. A demonstration had been planned to coincide with the closing ceremony the following day, but some of the HKPA's leadership wanted to cancel it, fearing police repression. Fortunately it went ahead, and over 1,000 locals spontaneously joined in; some even sent food and medicine to the Korean delegates. Altogether the demonstrations involved around 8,000 people. Hong Kong residents had never seen confrontations like this, which proved a great education for them.

Notes

1 Interview in *NLR* 42, Nov/Dec 2006, reprinted with the permission of *New Left Review*. It is slightly abridged for this book.
2 People's Republic of China
3 Han Deqiang, *The Crash – The Global Trap and China's Realistic Choice*, Pengzhuang 2000.
4 See Han Dongfang, 'Chinese Labour Struggles', *New Left Review* 34, Sept–Oct 2005.
5 The General Agreement on Tariffs and Trades was part of the mechanisms imposed by the US and the EU to force 'free' – actually very expensive – trade on the developing world.

GLOSSARY

This glossary contains all acronyms used in the text, with the acronym first followed by the spelling out the relevant words. It also contains all foreign words with the original language first followed by the English meaning. Non- English words are italicized. The list is in alphabetical order. *Eds*

ACFTU – All China Federation of Trade Unions

AFL-CIO – American Federation of Labour and Congress of Industrial Organisations

A & M – Acquisitions and Mergers

Baoba – keeping the economic growth rate at 8 per cent

BWAF – Beijing Workers' Autonomous Federation

CCP – Chinese Communist Party

CEOs – Chief Executive Officers

Chaoyingganmei – to overtake the UK and US in the Cold War

Choulaojiu – literally 'stinking number nine', implying the lowest social status for intellectuals. A term used in China under Mao

Comintern – an acronym for Communist International, also known as the Third International founded in 1917 and lasting until 1943

Dazibao – big character posters

Dazuodeng, xiangyouzhuan – indicating a left direction while actually going right

Ershi ding chushan, sishi ding shoushan – when we are twenty we all go to cities to work, and when we turn forty we all go back to our home village

Fan piao – rice voucher

FDI – Foreign direct investment

FNV – Federation of Dutch trade unions

FPI – Foreign portfolio investment

GATTS – general agreement on tariffs and trade

Gaizhi – a reform of the system

GITIC – Guangdong International Trust and Investment Corporation

GDP – gross domestic product

GNP – gross national product

GPC – global production chain

Guandao – speculating officials

Guanerdai – children of mandarins recruited to comfortable state posts

Guojinmintui – the advancement of the state sector at the expense of the private sector

Gyenlok – Tibetan red guards

Heilüshi –bare-foot lawyers

Hexie shehui – harmonious society

HKPA – Hong Kong People's Alliance

Hukou system – household registration system

Hukou bu – household registration book

Huoming – live

Houtai – the backing of a patron

Hujijing – literally household registration police

ILO – International Labour Organization

ICFTU – International Confederation of Free Trade Unions

KMT – Guomindang, previously Kuomintang – because transliteration norms have changed

Laowai – westerners

Laodage – Literally 'eldest brother', a complimentary title for the working class during Mao's era for their alleged 'leading class' status

liushou ertong – rural children left behind by their working parents.

Maiduan – relinquishing the entitlements of state workers

Mianzui tiejuan – A legendary kind of certificate, made of iron, was granted by the emperor to his favorite ministers, which pardoned in advance all the crimes they might be involved in, except crimes like treason

Nongmingong – migrant workers

NGOs – non-governmental organisations

OWYTU – Ole Wolff Yantai trade union

PRC – people's republic of China

Pinming – struggle until death

QDII – Qualified Domestic Institutional Investors

Qiangguo zuopai – leftists who called for the strengthening of China

Rencai danwei suoyuzhi – the workforce within a production unit was thought to be owned by that unit

Svenska Metall – the Swedish metal workers' union

SHEs – state holding enterprises

SOEs – state owned enterprises

SWRC – Staff and Workers' Representative Council – *Zhigong daibiao dahui*

Tongbao tongpei – guarantee full employment while allocating labour in a planned way

TNCs – Trans-national corporations

UNCTAD – UN Conference on Trade and Development

Wailai renkou – literally outsiders

Wangdang wangguo – the downfall of both the party and the state

WTO – World Trade Organisation

Wuwei yiti – five faceted and unified model of the protection of rights

Wuyouzhixiang –Utopia, here means the website run by people who claimed to be leftist/Maoist in China, and which was supportive of the former head of Chongqing Bo Xilai. In April 2012, the website was closed by the authorities after the downfall of Bo

Xiaojinku – literally 'little treasuries' – off-book accounts found in many government departments or SOEs in China for the purpose of rewarding the cadres there

Xiagang – workers who had no work to do but had not yet been made redundant

Xuan piao – ballot

Yinjinlai – literally meaning 'inviting in' (inflowing FDI)

Zhiandui – or public order teams

Zhigong daibiao dahui – SWRC – Staff and Workers' Representative Council

Zhongguancun – the so-called Chinese Silicon Valley

Zhurenweng – masters of the house, indicating the alleged "leading role" of the working class

Zouchuqu – 'going global' (out-flowing FDI)

About Resistance Books and the IIRE

Resistance Books

Resistance Books is the publishing arm of Socialist Resistance, a revolutionary Marxist organisation which is the British section of the Fourth International. Resistance Books publishes books jointly with the International Institute for Research and Education in Amsterdam and independently.

Further information about Resistance Books, including a full list of titles currently available and how to purchase them, can be obtained at http://www.resistancebooks.org, or by writing to Resistance Books, PO Box 62732, London, SW2 9GQ.

Socialist Resistance is an organisation active in the trade union movement and in many campaigns against imperialist intervention in places like Afghanistan or Iraq, in solidarity with Palestine and with anti-capitalist movements across the globe. We are eco-socialist – we argue that much of what is produced under capitalism is socially useless and either redundant or directly harmful. Capitalism's drive for profit is creating environmental disaster – and it is the poor, the working class and people in the global south who are paying the highest price for this.

We have been long-standing supporters of women's liberation and the struggles of lesbians, gay people, bisexuals and transgender people. We believe these struggles must be led by those directly affected – none so fit to break the chains as those who wear them. We work in anti-racist and anti-fascist networks, including campaigns for the rights of immigrants and asylum seekers.

Socialist Resistance believes that democracy is an essential component of any successful movement of resistance and struggle. With Britain and the western imperialist countries moving into a long period of capitalist austerity and crisis, deeper than any since the Second World War, Socialist Resistance stands together with all those who are organising to make another world possible.

Socialist Resistance is the bi-monthly magazine of the organisation, which can be read online at www.socialistresistance.org. Socialist Resistance can be contacted by email at contact@socialistresistance.org or by post at PO Box 62732, London, SW2 9GQ.

International Viewpoint is the English language online magazine of the Fourth International which can be read online at www.internationalviewpoint.org.

The International Institute for Research and Education

The International Institute for Research and Education (IIRE) is an international foundation, recognised in Belgium as an international scientific association by a Royal decree of 11th June 1981. The IIRE provides activists and scholars worldwide with opportunities for research and education in three locations: Amsterdam, Islamabad and Manila.

Since 1982, when the Institute opened in Amsterdam, its main activity has been the organisation of courses in the service of progressive forces around the world. Our seminars and study groups deal with all subjects related to the emancipation of the world's oppressed and exploited. It has welcomed hundreds of participants from every inhabited continent. Most participants have come from the Third World.

The IIRE has become a prominent centre for the development of critical thought and interaction, and the exchange of experiences, between people who are engaged in daily struggles on the ground. The Institute's sessions give participants a unique opportunity to step aside from the pressure of daily activism. The IIRE gives them time to study, reflect upon their involvement in a changing world and exchange ideas with people from other countries.

Our website is constantly being expanded and updated with freely downloadable publications, in several languages, and audio files. Recordings of several recent lectures given at the institute can be downloaded from www.iire.org - as can talks given by founding Fellows such as Ernest Mandel and Livio Maitan, dating back to the early 1980s.

The IIRE publishes *Notebooks for Study and Research* to focus on themes of contemporary debate or historical or theoretical importance. Lectures and study materials given in sessions in our Institute, located in Amsterdam, Manila and Islamabad, are made available to the public in large part through the Notebooks.

Different issues of the Notebooks have also appeared in languages besides English and French, including German, Dutch, Arabic, Spanish, Japanese, Korean, Portuguese, Turkish, Swedish, Danish and Russian.

For a full list of the *Notebooks for Study and Research,* visit http://bit.ly/IIRENSR or subscribe online at: http://bit.ly/NSRsub. To order the *Notebooks,* email iire@iire.org or write to International Institute for Research and Education, Lombokstraat 40, Amsterdam, NL-1094.